Cases on Managing E–Services

Ada Scupola
Roskilde University, Denmark

INFORMATION SCIENCE REFERENCE

Hershey · New York

Director of Editorial Content:	Kristin Klinger
Director of Production:	Jennifer Neidig
Managing Editor:	Jamie Snavely
Assistant Managing Editor:	Carole Coulson
Typesetter:	Cindy Consonery
Cover Design:	Lisa Tosheff
Printed at:	Yurchak Printing Inc.

Published in the United States of America by
Information Science Reference (an imprint of IGI Global)
701 E. Chocolate Avenue, Suite 200
Hershey PA 17033
Tel: 717-533-8845
Fax: 717-533-8661
E-mail: cust@igi-global.com
Web site: http://www.igi-global.com

and in the United Kingdom by
Information Science Reference (an imprint of IGI Global)
3 Henrietta Street
Covent Garden
London WC2E 8LU
Tel: 44 20 7240 0856
Fax: 44 20 7379 0609
Web site: http://www.eurospanbookstore.com

Library of Congress Cataloging-in-Publication Data

Cases on managing e-services / Ada Scupola, editor.

       p. cm.

 Summary: "This book lays the theoretical foundations for understanding e-services as well as provide real life cases of e-services"--Provided by publisher.

 Includes bibliographical references and index.

 ISBN 978-1-60566-064-6 (hbk.) -- ISBN 978-1-60566-065-3 (ebook)

 1. Electronic commerce. 2. Customer services--Technological innovations. 3. Service industries--Technological innovations. I. Scupola, Ada.

 HF5548.32.C3657 2009

 658.8'72--dc22

                            2008010312

British Cataloguing in Publication Data
A Cataloguing in Publication record for this book is available from the British Library.

All work contributed to this book set is original material. The views expressed in this book are those of the authors, but not necessarily of the publisher.

List of Reviewers

Anders Henten
Ioannis Chochliouros
Flavio Corradini
Alberto Pozzetti
Barbara Re
Raquel Gurrea Sarasa
Manel Khadraoui
Gille Pache'
Jari Salo
Mirjana Pejic-Bach
Benita Gullkvist
John Wang
Qiyang Chen
Ruben Xing
James Yao
Ahonen Aki
Huong Ha
Morten Falch
Hanne West Nicolajsen

Esko Penttinen
Alexander Yap
Dominique Drillon
Andrea Resca
Simon Heilesen
Dr. Gogia
Markus Hallgren
Robert Rubeck
Federici Tommaso
Calin Gurao
Carlo Medaglia
Ada Scupola
Maria Akesson
Ping Gao
Mauricio Featherman
Anssi Oorni
Sergio Viademonte
Stephen Burgess
Assion Lawson-Body

Table of Contents

Section I
Issues and Challenges of E-Services

Chapter I

Anders Henten, Center for Communication, Media and Information Technologies (CMI),
Aalborg University, Denmark

Chapter II

Ioannis P. Chochliouros, Hellenic Telecommunications Organization S.A. (OTE), Greece
Anastasia S. Spiliopoulou, Hellenic Telecommunications Organization S.A. (OTE), Greece
Tilemachos D. Doukoglou, Hellenic Telecommunications Organization S.A. (OTE), Greece
Elpida Chochliourou, General Prefectorial Hospital "Georgios Gennimatas", Greece

Chapter III

Flavio Corradini, University of Camerino, Italy
Alberto Polzonetti, University of Camerino, Italy
Barbara Re, University of Camerino, Italy

Chapter IV

Călin Gurău, GSCM – Montpellier Business School, France

Detailed Table of Contents

Section I
Issues and Challenges of E-Services

Chapter I

Anders Henten, Center for Communication, Media and Information Technologies (CMI),
Aalborg University, Denmark

This chapter examines the provision and co-development of electronic services, content, and applications at the conceptual level. There is focus on the provision of services electronically (e-services) and the development of user-produced electronic content and applications (nonservices). The chapter points at codifiability, digitization, and interpretation as three crucial conditions for the development of e-services and nonservices. Codifiability is the basic prerequisite, but even if knowledge is codifiable, it does not necessarily follow that it can be entirely digitized or that it will be interpreted in the same manner in different contexts. Regarding implications, an important issue is whether the development of e-services and nonservices leads to specialization and/or convergence in the production and marketing of informational services. Is there reason to anticipate that the production and marketing of informational services will develop differently from other production areas with respect to the implications of technology on the combination of specialization and convergence?

Chapter II

Ioannis P. Chochliouros, Hellenic Telecommunications Organization S.A. (OTE), Greece
Anastasia S. Spiliopoulou, Hellenic Telecommunications Organization S.A. (OTE), Greece
Tilemachos D. Doukoglou, Hellenic Telecommunications Organization S.A. (OTE), Greece
Elpida Chochliourou, General Prefectorial Hospital "Georgios Gennimatas", Greece

The chapter dentifies and evaluates at a primary level the basic components/modules of EESSI's specific results, already developed and offered in the market either as technical regulations and/or as recognized standards, with respect to essential requirements imposed by the European regulation. The chapter discusses relevant "feedback" already gained from various market areas and focuses on challenges for further implementation, progress, adoption, and development, especially in the framework for the promotion of converged broadband (Internet-based) communications facilities. It is important for the market that expected standardization work takes into account new technological developments as, in the future, users will move their e-signature key from device-to-device in a connected world. The added value of standards in the e-signatures sector, for both end users and assessing parties (judge, arbitrator, conformity assessment body, etc.) is of extreme importance for the future of the European electronic communications market.

Chapter III

Flavio Corradini, University of Camerino, Italy
Alberto Polzonetti, University of Camerino, Italy
Barbara Re, University of Camerino, Italy

The quality assessment of e-government services is more and more emerging as a key issue within public administrations. Ensuring a proper quality of digital services is mandatory to satisfy citizens and firms' needs and to accept the use of ICT in our lives. The chapter proposes a methodology for quality assessment that takes e-government quality features into account. The chapter also defines a reference model to provide a single quality value starting from a set of service parameters. To validate such approach, the chapter assesses the goodness of the 'TecUt' shared services management system.

Chapter IV

Călin Gurău, GSCM – Montpellier Business School, France

The evolution of information technology applications has changed the landscape of the service industry, offering the possibility of customer empowerment through self-service applications. Considering the main three streams of research already applied in the study of self-services, this chapter investigates customers' perceptions about eight dimensions that characterise the quality of the self-service experience. On the other hand, the study attempts to analyse the influence of the self-service users' profile (gender, Internet usage experience, and online self-service usage experience), and to provide specific insights about the needs and wants of various categories of customers.

Chapter V

Carlos Flavián Blanco, University of Zaragoza, Spain
Raquel Gurrea Sarasa, University of Zaragoza, Spain

The new online communication has had a considerable impact on the activities of the newspaper industry. As a result, analysis of the duality of journalism has aroused increasing interest. This chapter analyses the readers' behavior in relation to digital and traditional media. The chapter dentifies the main reading motivations and the behavior patterns in each medium. Besides, it examines the possible relationship between readers' objectives for reading and the choice of each channel. The results confirm that the electronic and traditional channels are compatible, but suggest that it is necessary to take the process of differentiation in order to enhance this complementarity, meeting readers' needs in different circumstances and combining effects to raise loyalty to a newspaper.

Section II
Cases on Business-to-Consumer E-Services

This chapter explores the possibilities for small and medium-sized enterprises (SMEs) to find their way to success in e-business. The basic assumption of this chapter is that the Internet allows SMEs to access the niche markets which have not previously been accessible to them. The chapter presents a case study of one Croatian online store developed as a portal which targets the niche market and the focus is on the following issues: subcultures as niche markets, criteria for selecting suppliers, developing a new brand, designing an online store as a portal in order to attract visitors, and opportunities for growth. The authors hope that presenting this particular case will help small companies to take into account niche markets when designing their online stores, but also it will help researchers to further explore niche markets as a possible business strategy for SMEs while entering the e-commerce arena.

This chapter analyses and provides an example of the introduction and first years of the management of accounting services and e-services in a professional accounting firm. It argues that e-services, as a result of adoption and use of Web-based digital technology, are slowly emerging within the accounting field. Further, the change to e-services implies a significant change in the business model for professional service providers as well as acceptance and adoption of the new services among customers. Furthermore, the author hopes that by identifying development and learning issues, the case cannot only be used for implementation of similar initiatives within other organizations but will also assist students in their understanding of the process of change and e-service management.

The chapter introduces an innovative organizational logic for developing and designing electronic services especially in the context of financial services, such as insurance. Furthermore, a novel electronic insurance service concept for consumers is introduced in the chapter. The authors argue that development of electronic service solutions for the use of financial sector formerly rather conducted in an organization may well be executed through a multi-organizational project-based working logic. In fact the chapter establishes that the multi-organizational project-based logic results in a more creative outcome. Hence, the authors hope that the chapter encourages both academics and especially practitioners within the insurance business sector to take steps towards more collaborative working practices in order to generate more creative electronic service solutions for customers.

eBay provides online marketplaces for the sale of goods and services, online payments, and online communication offerings. Their three primary business segments are: eBay Marketplaces, Payments, and Communications. The Marketplace platform has grown beyond the initial auction platform to include Rent.com, Shopping.com, Kijiji, Craigslist, mobile.de, and Marketplaats.nl. PayPal enables individuals and businesses to easily and securely transact payments. The overgrowth of eBay may have brought about the management problems in a young company that grows so fast. As the eighth largest global retailer, eBay's mission is to pioneer new communities around the world built on commerce, sustained by trust, and inspired by opportunity. Their ability to maintain or enhance this position will depend on their ability to adapt to new technologies while facing increased competition and anticipating customers' needs. This chapter will address management's philosophies, the corporate business model, its challenges, and network relationships, and examine corporate growth to date as well as future horizons.

Section III
Cases on Business-to-Business E-Services

Chapter X

 Hanne Westh Nicolajsen, CMI, Aalborg University, Denmark
 Morten Falch, CMI, Aalborg University, Denmark

This chapter analyses organizational challenges when an engineering consultancy in the building industry integrates information and communication technologies (ICT) in the production and delivery of their services, and discuss how the e-service concept can be applied in this context. The analysis is based on a field study on introduction of 3D-modeling tools within one of the leading engineering companies in Scandinavia (Ramboll). The analysis focuses on the changes in knowledge creation and transfer both within the company and in inter-organizational relations. The analysis points towards a need to change the business model as the projecting part of the technical engineering service becomes standardized.

Chapter XI

 Esko Penttinen, Helsinki School of Economics, Finland
 Timo Saarinen, Helsinki School of Economics, Finland
 Pekka Sinervo, Lexmark, Finland

Today, many manufacturing companies are focusing on their service operations, which are often seen as a better source of revenue than the traditional product business. E-services can accelerate this process by offering companies new ways to control products and monitor equipment from a distance. This chapter describes the changes which are taking place in the printing business. It tells the story of Lexmark, a printer manufacturer that has recently created differentiated offerings to its business customers. In the case of Lexmark, this repositioning of offerings has been enabled by e-services. Here, the e-services consist of the Lexmark Fleet Manager system which monitors the use and availability of the equipment and makes suggestions on how to improve the printing processes on the customer site. The case ends with a description of the actual challenges that Lexmark is currently facing.

Chapter XII

 Alexander Yap, Martha and Spencer Love School of Business, Elon University, USA
 Wonhi Synn, Martha and Spencer Love School of Business, Elon University, USA

This chapter focuses on the theme of e-service innovation in financial electronic markets. The discussion will cover the theories of "technology bundling" and how bundling creates value-added in servicing electronic markets. More specifically, this chapter looks at innovations created through e-service bundling for online brokers connected to various financial electronic markets. The proliferation of different e-trading systems raises the question of which systems provide better service to online stock traders. Many online brokers (e-brokers) now provide low-cost transactions and financial research capabilities, so where is the next level of innovation? The objective of this chapter is to show that several innovations in broker e-services are critical in the following areas: (a) how order processes are efficiently managed in financial e-markets; (b) how responsive e-trading systems are in handling trading rules and regulations; (c) how different systems address unique niches in financial e-markets; and (d) improving systems stability and reliability.

Section IV
Cases on E-Government

Examining electronic services both as products and as organization, this chapter discusses the development and management of e-services at Roskilde University, Denmark. The services in question can be distinguished according to purpose into products meant for administration, communication, education, and integration. The chapter discusses several examples of e-services from the point of view of adoption of technological innovation. Further, it is argued that participatory design and voluntary adoption are factors favourable to, but also challenging to the adoption of e-services. The technical and organizational integration of e-services are also touched upon, as is the importance of maintaining a creative environment for developing the services. The chapter concludes by outlining some challenges to the continued diffusion of e-services in the organization.

This chapter reports the findings of a case study of e-services adoption at research libraries. The case under consideration is Roskilde University Library (RUB), a research library supporting learning activities at Roskilde University. The research focuses on the main issues that RUB had to deal with in the process of adopting e-services and the future challenges that e-services provide for RUB. The chapter also presents the consequences of e-services adoption for Roskilde University library's organization, its business model and the relationships with customers, publishers (providers of knowledge), and other research libraries in Denmark. The main results can be summarized as follows: (1) adoption of e-services has forced RUB to innovate rapidly. Innovation is driven, among other factors, by ICT developments (technology push), but innovation is also user-driven and pervasive throughout the organization; (2) e-services have changed RUB's organizational structure and division of labour by moving more and more towards IT-based jobs and competences; (3) e-services have changed the relationships between users and publishers; (4) e-services have changed and continue to change the business model of the library; and (5) RUB is becoming a combination of a virtual and a physical library, moving more and more towards a virtual library with electronic resources and online communities, but still keeping the traditional function of a "knowledge space."

This chapter deals with the introduction of electronic procurement in the public healthcare domain. After a brief discussion on the healthcare spending characteristics and on the suitability of e-procurement tools in the public sector, the long-lasting experience of e-procurement implementation promoted by an Italian Local Healthcare Public Agency is described. This initiative included some pilot projects and applied many different solutions, always involving both a new ICT tool and a thorough process redesign. The development of the innovation introductions is discussed, together with their organizational and managerial background, the description of the new processes, and the analysis of the most relevant results. The chapter provides a fairly comprehensive illustration of available solutions, opportunities, and challenges in this still neglected topic.

The preparation and involvement of people is the key to success in most IT projects. In this case the problems faced were related to a general lack of awareness and non penetration of IT in the community assisted with the telemental health service. If people are using IT in their day to day work, adoption of telemedicine and other e-services will be far simpler after a disaster.

The need of rural and reservation residents to receive better government services has been long-standing. In spite of the best efforts of the Social Security Administration, a vast number of Native Americans living in rural and remote areas have had their access to program information and social benefits limited by distance, economic, and cultural challenges. A project at the University of North Dakota has found a way to transform the delivery of government services to these citizens. As an off-shoot of work in telemedicine and rural outreach, staff members of the Center for Rural Service Delivery collaborated with the Social Security Administration and the Indian Health Service to create the first video link connecting a hospital to a Social Security Office. The IHS hospital, in Belcourt, ND was connected to the SSA office in Minot, ND, some 120 miles away. The video link went live in October of 2003. The social benefits of remote video access to SSA services have been measured by the number of citizens who use video access to seek answers to questions and to make application for benefits each year. Since it went live, the link has resulted in more than 300 completed applications for disability benefits or income supplements. That total is more than 50 times the number produced through conventional service delivery. The economic impact to VSD has been measured as the cumulative value of monthly Supplemental Security Income and Disability payments to individual citizens and the total of annual Medicare and Medicaid reimbursement payments made to local healthcare facilities. The service impact includes increased application completion rates, accelerated claims processing, and increased third party assistance in the application process.

Foreword

It is increasingly all about services. Whether we talk about traditional manufacturing industries or Internet based social media services, and everything in between, there is a mental shift from focus on products to focus on services. Both the business managers as well as the academics have realized this, and lately a lot of attention has been devoted to issues such as services as an arrangement for coordinating production and consumption, effective service arrangements, and service delivery within ICT-enabled channels.

Services are, of course, not a new thing, as such, but now the service sector, including government, healthcare, education, retail, professional services, transportation, communication, and utilities, is increasingly starting to dominate the economies of the world. E-services, or services that are created, facilitated, or delivered through ICT-mediated networks, are in the heart of this whole new era of services. To this date, there has been a wealth of experiences as well as research around what might already be called "traditional" e-commerce or e-business, but the new technologies and the new business models together with the new consumers preferences and behavior make the area of e-services an important area to understand.

Services are not easy to configure and manage. In this highly timely book, services are looked from the perspective of how ICT can be used to facilitate, create, and deliver services, or more exactly, from the perspective of e-services. As e-services are proliferating, it is extremely important to understand the field also from theoretical perspective, as provided by this book. To fully understand the possibilities as well as the challenges involved, this book also provides a number of case examples, ranging from applications in the area of business-to-business and business-to-consumer, to different e-government services.

This book can sincerely be recommended to all those interested in e-services, in business and academia, alike.

Virpi Kristiina Tuunainen

Virpi Kristiina Tuunainen is a professor of information systems science at the Department of Business Technology and director of GEBSI (Graduate School for Electronic Business and Software Industry) of Helsinki School of Economics (HSE). Her research focuses on electronic and mobile business, software industry, and economics of IS. She has published articles in journals such as MIS Quarterly, Communications of the ACM, Journal of Management Information Systems, Journal of Strategic Information Systems, Information & Management, and Information Society.

Preface

BACKGROUND FOR THE BOOK

After the first wave of e-commerce and e-business, we are witnessing a paradigm shift in the way businesses, governments, and consumers are using Internet-based technologies and mobile communications to innovate and produce new products and services. This paradigm I call e-services. This trend is also affected and accelerated by a corporate shift from the provision of goods to the provision of services, with a parallel development of relevant new business models and marketing paradigms (Rust, 2001). The concept of e-services is relatively new. The purpose of this book is to lay some theoretical foundations for understanding e-services as well as provide real life cases of e-services. The cases have been chosen in different fields such as accounting, libraries, martial arts, and insurance to illustrate the complexity and the infancy of the e-service paradigm. This preface provides a definition of e-services, creates a typology of e-services, and presents the main characteristics of e-services. The challenges that e-services are posing for companies, businesses, and governments are also discussed.

E-Services: Definition, Characteristics, and Taxonomy

Networked information communication technologies (ICTs) such as the Internet or mobile communications are having a dramatic effect on how services and especially knowledge services are innovated, designed, produced, and distributed (Scupola, 2008). In addition, ICT networks such as the Internet have created the basis for the development of new types of services. These networks may also change the way customers or users experience service functions. For example, in the case of hospital services, "relational times" (person-to-person relations) are increasingly replaced by "technical times" where people are moved from one technical system to another. ICT networks seem to be a catalyst to a renewed use of services, here called e-services.

One feature characteristic of services is that customers are more involved in the service delivery process per se; therefore the service consumption is characterized by a high involvement of the customer or customer interaction. Concerning customer interaction, there are different types of services ranging from customer interaction with less standardized service components to customer interaction with highly standardized service components (self-service). To guarantee that customers' demands are best served by the provided services, the level of customer interaction has to be reflected in the innovation management process of the company. This development could lead to a self-service society. Innovative changes may come in customer relations (service encounters and quality), in organizational forms such as the introduction of virtual organizations (Travica, 2007), in competencies developments, and customer driven innovation (Scupola, 2008). As a result service firms, manufacturing firms and governmental organizations might face new challenges and may introduce new business models.

Even though the concept of e-services is relatively new, different authors have tried to define e-services. For example Rust (2001) defines e-services as the provision of services by electronic networks such as the Internet (Rust, 2001). According to WhatIs.com, e-services is a business concept developed by Hewlett Packard (HP) and it is based on the idea that the World Wide Web is moving beyond e-business and e-commerce (that is, completing sales on the Web) into a new phase where many business services can be provided for a business or consumer using the Web (Henten, in this book). Some e-services may be provided by the company Web site such as e-accounting; other e-services, such as news updates to subscribers, may be sent to your computer (Ihlstrom Eriksson, Kalling, Åkesson, & Fredberg, 2008). Other e-services such as those functioning as intermediary services and often orchestrating networks of companies will be carried out in the background without the customer's immediate knowledge.

There are many definitions and conceptions of e-services as it is showed by the chapters in this book. Therefore, here a broad definition is used according to which e-services are defined as services that are produced, provided, and/or consumed through the use of ICT networks such as Internet-based systems and mobile solutions. However, e-services also include, for example, the online selling of real estate property or the purchasing of physical goods that are then delivered by other means such as a book that is purchased online, but delivered by surface mail to the buyers. E-services can be produced by consumers, businesses, and governments and can be accessed via a wide range of information appliances (Hoffman, 2003, p. 53). In addition there are three main characteristics of e-services:

- The service is accessible via the Internet or other electronic networks
- The service is consumed either directly or indirectly via the Internet or other electronic networks
- There might be a fee that the consumer pays the provider for using the e-service, but that might not always be the case as is exemplified by some e-services offered by the government.

Normally the production, provision, or consumption of a service requires the interaction between the service provider and the user of the service. Traditionally, this has been based on personal interactions, most often face-to-face interactions. In e-services, the production, consumption, and/or provision of services takes place through the intermediation of an ICT network such as Internet-based systems or mobile solutions.

Familiar e-services are online banking or online retailing (e.g., www.Amazon.com). Other types of e-services are e-learning such as courses offered online, e-health such as remote or online medical advice (see the chapters by Gogia and Rubeck and Miller in this book), e-government (e.g., e-procurement as in the chapter by Federici), e-libraries providing electronic access to journal articles or book chapters (see the chapter by Scupola in this book), and information and location services (Yee, 2006). As a result, four types of e-services can be conceptualized:

- business-to-business
- business-to-consumer
- government-to-business or to-consumer
- consumer-to-consumer

The advent of e-services has raised a number of challenges for knowledge intensive service organizations such as consulting companies, accounting companies, libraries, and publishers as well as for companies selling physical goods, especially those in transition from being a manufacturing to becoming a service company. For example companies have to innovate, have to develop strategies and new business models for the production and provision of e-services, and acquire or develop new competencies (see for example the chapter by Gullvist and Nicolajsen and Falch in this book).

Structure of the Book

The book is organized into four sections, each one dealing with different aspects of e-services.

The first section is a theoretical section. It presents some different definitions of e-services and touches upon some theoretical issues such as e-services quality, the profile of users of self-services systems, electronic signatures as a necessity for the provision of secure electronic services, and the characteristics of online journalistic services.

The first chapter of this section examines the provision and co-development of electronic services, content, and applications at the conceptual level. It focuses on the provision of services electronically (e-services) and the development of user-produced electronic content and applications that the author defines as "nonservices." The chapter points to codifiability, digitization, and interpretation as three crucial conditions for the development of e-services and nonservices. Codifiability is the basic prerequisite, but even if knowledge is codifiable, it does not necessarily follow that it can be entirely digitized nor that it will be interpreted in the same manner in different contexts. An important issue pointed to by the chapter is that of whether the development of e-services and nonservices leads to specialization and/or convergence in the production and marketing of informational services. Is there reason to anticipate that the production and marketing of informational services will develop differently from other production areas with respect to the implications of technology on the combination of specialization and convergence?

The second chapter examines the role of standardization activities for the promotion of several needs of an "open" European market based on the effective usage of e-signatures. Two major streams of possible standards-setting work have been pointed to by the chapter: (1) qualitative and procedural standards for the provision of certification services; (2) technical standards for product interoperability. The chapter also discusses relevant "feedback" already gained from various market areas and focuses on challenges for further implementation, progress, adoption, and development, especially in the framework for the promotion of converged broadband (Internet-based) communications facilities. It is important for the market that expected standardization work takes into account new technological developments as, in the future, users will move their e-signature key from device-to-device in a connected world. The chapter also concludes that the added value of standards in the e-signatures sector, for both end users and assessing parties (judge, arbitrator, conformity assessment body, etc.), is of extreme importance for the future of the European electronic communications market.

The third chapter proposes a methodology for the quality assessment of e-services. This methodology takes e-government quality features into account. The chapter also defines a reference model with the aim of providing a single value starting from a set of service parameters. To validate the validity of such a methodology, the authors apply it to a case of a shared services management system called TecUt implemented in the Italian region called Marche.

The fourth chapter investigates customers' perceptions of eight dimensions that characterize the quality of the self-service experience. The study attempts to analyse the influence of the self-service users' profile such as gender, Internet usage experience, and online self-service usage experience on the use of self-services, and to provide specific insights about the needs and wants of various categories of customers.

The fifth chapter analyzes the readers' behavior in relation to e-newspapers and traditional newspapers. It identifies the main reading motivations and the behavior patterns in each medium. In addition it examines the possible relationship between readers' objectives for reading and the choice of each channel. The results confirm that the electronic and traditional channels are compatible, but suggest that it is necessary to take the process of differentiation in order to enhance this complementarity, meeting readers' needs in different circumstances and combining effects to raise loyalty to a newspaper.

Section two deals with business-to-consumer e-services and presents four cases.

The first chapter of this section explores the possibilities for small- and medium-sized enterprises (SMEs) to find their way to success in e-services. The basic assumption of this chapter is that the Internet allows SMEs to access niche markets which have not previously been accessible to them. The chapter presents a case study of a Croatian online store developed as a portal which targets the niche market of martial arts. The case focuses on criteria for selecting suppliers, developing a new brand, designing an online store to attract visitors, and opportunities for growth. The authors hope that this particular case will help small companies to take into account niche markets when designing their online stores but also it will help researchers to further explore niche markets as a possible business strategy for SMEs while entering the e-services arena.

The second chapter of this section provides a case about the management of accounting services and e-services in a professional accounting firm in order to identify development and learning issues, which can be used for implementation of similar initiatives within other organizations in the future. The focus is on the perceived problems and opportunities in transforming services into e-services as well as the operational and strategic solutions used to solve the emerging problems by the case company. The professional accounting firm in this study is a service provider of financial, accounting, and taxation related services for client companies, but not internal or external auditing services.

The third chapter of this section introduces an innovative organizational logic for developing and designing electronic services especially in the context of financial services, such as insurance. Furthermore, a novel electronic insurance service concept for consumers is introduced in the chapter. The authors argue that development of electronic service solutions for the use of financial sector formerly rather conducted in an organization may well be executed through a multi-organizational project-based working logic. In fact the chapter establishes that the multi-organizational project-based logic results in a more creative outcome. Hence, the authors hope that the chapter encourages both academics and especially practitioners within the insurance business sector to take steps towards more collaborative working practices in order to generate more creative electronic service solutions for customers.

The fourth chapter is the case of eBay. It addresses management's philosophies, the corporate business model, its challenges, network relationships, and examines corporate growth to date as well as future horizons. As the eighth largest global retailer, eBay's mission is to pioneer new communities around the world built on commerce, sustained by trust, and inspired by opportunity. The chapter concludes that eBay's ability to maintain or enhance this position will depend on their ability to adapt to new technologies while facing increased competition and anticipating customers' needs.

The third section focuses on business-to-business e-services and illustrates their complexity with three cases.

The first chapter of this section analyzes the organizational challenges that an engineering consultancy in the building industry has faced in integrating ICTs in the production and delivery of their services, and discusses how the e-service concept can be applied in this context. The analysis is based on a field study on the introduction of 3D-modeling tools within one of the leading engineering companies in Scandinavia (Ramboll). The analysis focuses on the changes in knowledge creation and transfer both within the company and in inter-organizational relations. The analysis points towards a need to change the business model as the projecting part of the technical engineering service becomes standardized.

The second chapter describes the changes which are taking place in the printing business due to the advent of e-services. It tells the story of Lexmark, a printer manufacturer that has recently created differentiated offerings to its business customers. In the case of Lexmark, this repositioning of offerings has been enabled by e-services. Here, the e-services consist of the Lexmark Fleet Manager system which monitors the use and availability of the equipment and makes suggestions on how to improve the printing processes on the customer site. The case ends with a description of the actual challenges that Lexmark is currently facing.

The last chapter of this section focuses on the theme of e-service innovation in financial electronic markets. The chapter covers the theories of "technology bundling" and how bundling creates value-added in servicing electronic markets. More specifically, this chapter looks at innovations created through e-service bundling for online brokers connected to various financial electronic markets. The proliferation of different e-trading systems raises the question of which systems provide better service to online stock traders. The objective of this chapter is to show that several innovations in broker e-services are critical in the following areas: how order processes are efficiently managed in financial e-markets; how responsive e-trading systems are in handling trading rules and regulations; how different systems address unique niches in financial e-markets; and how to improve systems stability and reliability.

Section Four deals with governmental e-services or e-government and includes five cases.

The first case of this section discusses the development and management of e-services at Roskilde University, Denmark. The services in question can be distinguished according to purpose into products meant for administration, communication, education, and integration. The chapter discusses several examples of e-services from the point of view of adoption of technological innovation. Further, it is argued that participatory design and voluntary adoption are factors favorable to, but also challenging to the adoption of e-services. The technical and organizational integration of e-services are also touched upon, as is the importance of maintaining a creative environment for developing the services. The chapter concludes by outlining some challenges to the continued diffusion of e-services in the organization.

The second chapter reports the findings of a case study of e-services adoption at research libraries. The case under consideration is Roskilde University Library (RUB), a research library supporting learning activities at Roskilde University. The research focuses on the main issues that RUB had to deal with in the process of adopting e-services and the future challenges that e-services provide for the organization. The chapter also presents the consequences of e-services adoption for Roskilde University Library organization, its business model, and the relationships with customers, publishers (providers of knowledge), and other research libraries in Denmark.

The third chapter presents a case dealing with the experience of e-procurement implementation promoted by the Italian Local Healthcare Public Agency (LHA) of Viterbo. This case is particularly interesting for the comprehensive design of the e-procurement system, the differentiation of the adopted tools, the long-lasting experimentations (since 2000), and the multiple solutions implemented or in progress. In this case the use of e-procurement tools is seen just as one aspect of a deep reorganization of the entire supply process and the initiatives were followed by a detailed assessment of their outcomes. The chapter examines in detail the history and key features of this experience up to the ongoing project aimed at a wide e-procurement implementation. A framework of healthcare spending characteristics is also introduced together with taxonomy of e-procurement tools in public healthcare sector.

The fourth chapter discusses the Healing Touch project which started after the tsunami disaster in Tamilnadu to address the healthcare needs of the survivors through information technology. The project provided mental health support to the victims near their place of residence. This project was sponsored and managed entirely by NGOs and the local community NGOs were directly trained to manage their own health problems after the natural disaster. The success was linked to the intensive pre and post execution work done. Some problems faced were related to a general lack of awareness and nonpenetration of IT in the community in the disaster area. If people are using IT in their day to day work, adoption of telemedicine and other e-services will be far simpler after a disaster.

The last chapter of this section and the book describes a project conducted at the University of North Dakota that has had the purpose of transforming the delivery of government services to citizens located in rural areas. The chapter points to the need of rural and reservation residents to receive better government services. In spite of the best efforts of the Social Security Administration, a vast number of Native Americans living in rural and remote areas have had their access to program information and social benefits limited by distance, economic, and cultural challenges. As an offshoot of work in telemedicine and rural outreach, staff members of the Centre for Rural Service Delivery collaborated with the Social Security Administration and the Indian Health Service to create the first video link connecting a hospital to a Social Security Office. The social benefits of Video Service Delivery (VSD) have been measured by the number of citizens who use video access to seek answers to questions and to make application for benefits each year. Since it went live, the link has resulted in more than 300 completed applications for disability benefits or income supplements. That total is more than 50 times the number produced through conventional service delivery. The service impact includes increased application completion rates, accelerated claims processing, and increased third party assistance in the application process.

REFERENCES

Hoffman, K.D. (2003). Marketing+MIS=E-Service. *Communications of the ACM, 46*(6), 53–55.

Ihlström Eriksson, C., Kalling, T., Åkesson, M., & Fredberg, S. (2008). Business models for mobile news media: Exploring the e-newspaper case from content provider and consumer views [Special issue on e-services]. *Journal of Electronic Commerce in Organizations, 6*(2).

Rust, R.T. (2001, May). The rise of e-service. *Journal of Service Research, 3*(4), 283–284.

Scupola, A. (2008). Editorial [Special issue on e-services]. *Journal of Electronic Commerce in Organizations, 6*(2).

Scupola, A. (2008). Conceptualizing competences in e-service adoption and assimilation in SMEs [Special issue on e-services]. *Journal of Electronic Commerce in Organizations, 6*(2).

Travica, B. (2007). Virtual organizing of e-commerce (Guest Editorial Preface). *Journal of Electronic Commerce in Organizations, 5*(4).

Yee, G. (2006). *Privacy protection for e-services*. IGI Global.

Acknowledgment

The writing and production of this book has been a long and interesting process, in which many people have collaborated. Some people have participated more directly, others more indirectly. The editor would like to thank all the authors that have expressed an interest in the book's first call for papers and could not get their article published in the book due to the acceptance rate of circa 30%.

The editor also would like to thank the companies that have been willing to provide information to write a case about them with or without their name being disclosed.

In addition the editor would like to thank the authors of cases or chapters included in this book that also served as referees for articles written by other authors. I also would like to acknowledge the help of many anonymous reviewers that have contributed to the success of this book. Without their help, time, support, and constructive comments, this project could not have been satisfactorily completed.

A further special note of thanks goes also to all the staff at IGI Global, whose contributions and timely support throughout the whole process from inception of the initial idea to final publication have been invaluable. Among IGI Global staff, deep appreciation and gratitude goes to Kristin Klinger for believing and supporting me in this project.

Special thanks also go to the colleagues of the project on e-services from my university and Technical University of Denmark for the fruitful discussions that are the basis of this project.

In closing, I wish to thank all of the authors for their insights and excellent contributions to this book.

Finally, I want to thank my husband and children for their love and support throughout this project.

Ada Scupola, PhD
Editor,
Roskilde University, Denmark
June 2008

Section I
Issues and Challenges
of E–Services

Chapter I
Services, E–Services, and Nonservices

Anders Henten
*Center for Communication, Media and Information Technologies (CMI),
Aalborg University, Denmark*

EXECUTIVE SUMMARY

This chapter examines the provision and co-development of electronic services, content, and applications at the conceptual level. There is focus on the provision of services electronically (e-services) and the development of user-produced electronic content and applications (nonservices). The chapter points at codifiability, digitization, and interpretation as three crucial conditions for the development of e-services and nonservices. Codifiability is the basic prerequisite, but even if knowledge is codifiable, it does not necessarily follow that it can be entirely digitized or that it will be interpreted in the same manner in different contexts. Regarding implications, an important issue is whether the development of e-services and nonservices leads to specialization and/or convergence in the production and marketing of informational services. Is there reason to anticipate that the production and marketing of informational services will develop differently from other production areas with respect to the implications of technology on the combination of specialization and convergence?

INTRODUCTION

The research issues examined in this chapter are what the major conditions for the development of e-services and nonservices are and what the implications are with respect to specialization and/or convergence in the provision and development of e-services and nonservices. The starting point of the chapter is to define services in order to be able to discuss what e-services and nonservices are. Following these definitional sections, the conditions for and the implications of the development of e-services and nonservices are discussed. The conditions are related to the codification of informational services, as these are the types of services that can be entered on digital media and transported on communication networks and constitute the services in question in this chapter. The implications are discussed in relation to the organizational changes, which, on the one hand, will result from the development of e-services and nonservices and, on the other hand, may also be important preconditions for their growth.

BACKGROUND

During especially the past two to three decades, services have increasingly come to the fore in social sciences. Consequently, discussions on the concept of services have erupted time and again, from Hill (1977) to Chesbrough and Spohrer (2006). The present chapter, however, does not venture into a long-winded definitional exercise of the service concept but stays with the basic definition of services. In contrast to goods, which can be separated from the immediate producers and sold on an anonymous market, services are not anonymous (Henten, 1994). Consumers will know who the immediate producers are (or will at least have the possibility to do so). It is often said that services are produced and consumed simultaneously and, therefore, require face-to-face contact between the producers and the consumers in the production/ consumption phase. This may not always hold entirely true, but the consumption will at least start right after the end of production – as in the case of repair work.

The basic definition of services has nothing inherently to do with whether the product is material or immaterial. The repair work of a plumber, for instance, is material in nature, but is a service. Indeed, information and communication technologies (ICTs) affect all kinds of goods and services with respect to their transaction on the market (e-business). However, in the case of data, information and knowledge services (informational services), it is the service itself which is affected. With ICTs, it is possible to enter data,

information and knowledge (to the extent it can be codified) on digital media and use communication networks for transportation. This means that data, information or knowledge services increasingly can be separated from the immediate producers and sold on anonymous markets. They become goods in a sense. Formerly, paper was the primary physical medium for turning informational services into goods. Presently, electronic media increasingly dominate.

At the same time, for some categories of goods, producers seek to customize their products to meet the individual choices of customers (Sundbo, 1997). One of the most heralded examples is Dell and their use of Internet to receive information from customers regarding their specific computer configuration choices (Dell, 2000). Furthermore, a wide variety of services surrounding the goods, e.g. after sales services and information services, are developed in order to provide a better customer experience and a more personalized/customized environment. Nevertheless, most goods will remain mass-produced and maintain their anonymous character.

To the extent that this develops, it could be claimed that there is a degree of convergence between goods and services enabled by the use of digital communications. As always, there is no sharp and unequivocal dividing line between goods and services. The most important thing in the context of the present chapter, though, is the trend regarding informational services to acquire elements of the basic characteristics of goods concerning separation from the immediate producers and anonymity.

SETTING THE STAGE

E-Services

Having briefly discussed what services are, we now turn to e-services, i.e. electronic services.

One of the first academic papers defining the term e-services was written by Tiwana and Balasubramaniam in 2001. In this paper, they define e-services:

We view e-services as Internet-based applications that fulfil service needs by seamlessly bringing together distributed, specialized resources to enable complex, (often real-time) transactions. Examples of e-services include supply chain management, customer relationship management, accounting, order processing, resource management, and other services that are electronically delivered through the Internet. (Tiwana & Balasubramaniam, 2001, p. 1)

Their paper is about software and the trends towards selling software as a service—often, actually called Software as a Service (SaaS) today. It should be noted that the term service in this conception is not entirely the same as in the previous section of the present chapter. Service in the SaaS concept means that software vendors develop software applications and host and operate the applications for the users. Users pay not for owning the software, but for using it. Tiwana and Balasubramaniam call this e-service.

However, the general use of the term e-service is closer to the e-service concept developed by Hewlett-Packard. As in the case of the e-business concept, which was first coined by IBM, the term e-service was also originally developed by an IT company, Hewlett-Packard. According to WhatIs.com:

E-services, a business concept developed by Hewlett Packard (HP), is the idea that the World Wide Web is moving beyond e-business and e-commerce (that is, completing sales on the Web) into a new phase where many business services can be provided for a business or consumer using the Web. Some e-services, such as remote bulk printing, may be done at a Web site; other e-services, such as news updates to subscribers, may be sent to your computer. Other e-services will be done in the background without the customer's immediate knowledge. (http://searchcio.techtarget.com/sDefinition/0,,sid19_gci535452,00.html)

This conception of e-services is wider than SaaS. It encompasses informational services offered to the end users (e.g., news updates) in addition to the services "done in the background without the customer's immediate knowledge," that is, back-office operations.

In its understanding of the term e-services, the present chapter is in line with the conception developed by Hewlett-Packard. This is the most common use of the term and is not limited to software but includes all services delivered digitally. This applies whether the services are delivered to end users (B2C) or to business users (B2B). In a paper written by Piccinelli and Stammers (2001), working for Hewlett-Packard, an e-service is defined as *"any asset that is made available via the Internet to drive revenue streams or create new efficiencies."* This definition is sufficiently broad and, at the same time, narrow, in the sense that it excludes services that cannot be delivered via the Internet.

This means that the kinds of e-commerce, where goods or services are marketed and sold on the net but cannot be delivered (i.e., transported) on the Internet, are excluded from the e-service concept. It must be services that can be entered on digital media and therefore transported on digital networks in order to be included in the e-service concept.

Nonservices

Nonservices may not be the best of concepts, but it emphasizes one important aspect of user-produced content and applications, namely that we are not dealing with services commercially offered by service providers to users, business, or residential. We are dealing with applications and content developed by users in (partly) noncommercial relationships.

There is nothing inherent in the term *service* itself that necessarily indicates a commercial relationship. The word service has a very long history and has changed meaning with changes in social relations in society (Illeris, 1996). There are expressions, which indicate a noncommercial connotation of the word *service*. "To render a service," for instance, means to help someone or to do somebody a favor, that is, to do something for free. However, in an economic context, the term *service* describes a commercial relationship between somebody selling a service and someone buying a service. This is why the term *nonservice* is used here to emphasize that far from all activities facilitated by digital communications are commercial. If all activities of exchanging data, information, and knowledge on the Internet are subsumed under the term *e-service*, there will be a danger that one forgets the noncommercial parts of such activities.

Presently, there is an increasing amount of activities on the Internet, where noncommercial relations constitute (at least part off) the foundation. This applies to elements in the so-called Web 2.0 developments (O'Reilly, 2007), where users upload and exchange content and applications, which are at the disposal of other users without any fee to the producers of the content and applications. The term *prosumer* originating from Toffler (1980) has been used to reflect this phenomenon, but is not the most fortunate term, as it is a contraction of two words, producer and consumer, and therefore connotes a commercial relationship with the word consumer. Wikipedia is one of the most well-known examples of these kinds of activities. Social computing is a better term to reflect such activities (Charron, Favier, & Li, 2006).

The fact that the core of an activity is noncommercial does, however, not mean that the context in which it grows is noncommercial. The platforms on which users exchange videos and pictures, for instance, can be set up by commercial entities or entities that turn into commercial operations. The business models for such platforms are continuously under development, but if successful, they may be sold as in the case of YouTube. There is thus a complex relationship between commercial and noncommercial activities, a kind of symbiosis.

In fact, there is nothing new in this. People have "always" been involved in activities where they jointly help each other in noncommercial manners. For instance, sports clubs and other kinds of leisure activities have often been and are still developed in this way. Such social activities also live in a kind of symbiosis with commercial activities, for example, in football clubs that have professional as well as amateur departments. The new thing is the digital platform and the massive size and global character of some of these activities.

CURRENT CHALLENGES

Conditions and Implications

The present section examines conditions for and implications of the development of e-services (and nonservices). The conditions are concerned with the causes and the implications with the effects. However, as in other social science research, cause and effect very much depend on the perspective. In the present case, there are, for instance, implications on business organization of the development of e-services, but such organizational changes can also be the preconditions for the development of e-services.

Two conditions and implications are dealt with here:

- Codification of knowledge
- Organizational changes regarding specialization and convergence

Before examining these two issues more in depth, the obvious condition—the development of information and communication technology (ICT)—needs to be mentioned. The Internet, and more specifically the Web, is a necessary precondition for e-services, but is far from a sufficient condition. Other factors include codification of knowledge and organizational changes.

The necessary technologies are, furthermore, in constant development. The Internet consists of a wide range of technologies, which are continuously developed and supplemented with new technologies. The Web, for instance, is essential for most e-services today, but did not exist until the beginning of the 1990s. Moreover, compression technologies are vital for the development of video material on the Internet. Technologies are developed to meet the demands from newly arising services. As in the case of conditions for and implications of e-services, there is a co-development and co-determination of the different elements and levels in the development of technology and other factors (social, economic, etc.).

The present chapter puts emphasis not on the technology basis for e-services, but on "soft" conditions for the development of e-services regarding the nature of informational services. The codification of informational services is, in this context, the basic condition (*sine qua non*) for the development of e-services. On the implications side, the fundamental question concerning the organization of the provision of services as an outcome of the application of new technologies is approached by means of the question regarding specialization and convergence.

Codification of Knowledge

In the first part of this chapter, the concept of "data, information, and knowledge" is used. However, there is an important difference between data, information, and knowledge. While the data concept denotes the simple elements, information denotes a more complex structure of data elements put into context, whereas knowledge constitutes an even more complex phenomenon, namely an understanding of relationships between different data elements, that is, a conceptual framework. A persuasive conceptualization of "data, informa-

tion, and knowledge" is that knowledge is a tool used to turn data into information, meaning that knowledge is used as a framework for putting data into context transforming it into information (Valentin & Hansen, 2004).

Such a conceptualization emphasizes the unique character of knowledge. It draws a fundamental line of division between knowledge, on the one hand, and data and information, on the other. Data are the raw material; knowledge is the tool; and information is the product. This language taken from manufacturing is used here on purpose, as it provides an instructive association to the development of manufacturing, where machines are developed to substitute manual labor. In the early days of industrialization, knowledge on the ways in which goods were produced manually was extracted from the immediate producers and was built into machines mechanizing production. Manufacturing knowledge was codified, so to speak. This development still takes place today.

In relation to services of an informational character, the same issue is raised. To what extent is it possible to extract and codify knowledge and use it in the production of information for digital distribution? As in the case of manufacturing, codified knowledge can be entered on/imbedded in machinery (in the case of informational services, ICT) and used in the production of informational services and, furthermore, distributed on markets by means of ICT. There is a business-to-business (B2B) as well as a business-to-customer (B2C) aspect. Codified knowledge on how to process and distribute informational services can be sold to businesses (business services) and can also be sold to end users (customer services). In both cases, the question raised here is the degree to which knowledge can be codified, entered on ICT, and sold on markets as informational goods.

In discussions on the codifiability of knowledge, the issue of tacitness is invoked (Cowan, David, & Foray, 2000; Polanyi, 1958). The question of codifiability concerns the degree to which tacit knowledge can be turned into explicit and codified knowledge. The discussion thus focuses on the different kinds of knowledge and the differences in the codifiability of different types of knowledge. The question is also the degree to which codified knowledge can be entered on digital media for processing and transmission. Furthermore, the question is the extent to which codified and digitized knowledge is interpreted and understood in the same manner in different contexts, companies, cultures, and so forth. And, in connection to this, whether digitized knowledge can "stand on its own," or whether it needs interpretation or other kinds of authoritative implementations.

There are thus, at least, the following basic issues to take into consideration when discussing the codifiability and digitization of knowledge:

- Codifiability
- Digitization
- Interpretation

There are differences in the codifiability of different types of knowledge. This applies to the objects of the different branches of the sciences, although the concept of science itself denotes codification. The natural and technical sciences have a greater degree of codifiability than the social and humanistic sciences. It also applies in business practices, which is of greater interest here. Certain types of know-how in production and marketing are more easily codified than others. Furthermore, there are different kinds of informational services being sold. Banks provide a good example of this. The basic services provided by banks, for example, payment services, are data services. In addition, banks provide customers with information on different facts and developments in the financial markets. Finally, banks also offer advice and consultancy to customers (knowledge services). This last type of service is less codifiable or at least less codified than the two other types of services. This, however, is also an example of the possible lack of interest of banks in codifying

all types of services. Banks may have an interest in maintaining a close personal relationship with their customers in order to lock them in.

The issue of digitization is concerned with the potential for distributing knowledge on digital media. Even if knowledge is codified, it is not certain that it can be distributed on digital media. Or rather, it is not certain that the service, which includes the digitized knowledge, can be sold digitally. All the knowledge that can be codified and put on a piece of chapter, for instance, can of course also be entered on digital media. However, this does not mean that it can be sold as an all-digitized service. Legal services, for instance, are based on the laws and other legal documents. Still, lawyers have very profitable businesses, as customers seek their advice and their experience in handling legal matters. Another example is the buying and selling of real estate. All legal documents and other kinds of information related to the buying and selling of real estate can be codified and digitized. However, real estate agents still make money on the intermediation of these processes. A major reason is that buyers and sellers of real estate do not have sufficient confidence in their own handling of these affairs. They need an intermediary with experience in these matters (Hagedorn-Rasmussen, 2006).

This issue is closely related to the last-mentioned question of interpretation. Customers need an interpretation of the facts and documents. Such interpretations can, of course, be written down and are written down in, for instance, textbooks for teaching. However, an overview of the different kinds of interpretations requires experience, which is what professionals offer. But this is not the only question related to interpretation, which is important in connection with the transfer of digitized knowledge. When different people and different organizations cooperate on producing an informational service, there will be different interpretations of the codified and digitized information. This will be even more apparent if dealing with people from different countries or cultures.

The implication is that the production and marketing of knowledge is limited to contexts in which there is a match of interpretation. Engineering consultancy services in the house building area provide a good example: Local offices of engineering consultancy companies are often essential, as the requirements and environments are different from country to country (Henten, 2005).

Organizational Changes

While the former subsection clearly is concerned with important conditions for the development of e-services (and nonservices), the present subsection is on the implication side. However, organizational changes may also be the prerequisites for the development of e-services.

The organizational changes dealt with here are related to the specialization vs. convergence of business functions as an effect of the development of e-services. This applies to B2B as well as B2C services. The question is whether the potential to deliver information services digitally leads to a greater degree of specialization among business enterprises or whether a greater degree of convergence will take place. Or rather, how will the combination of specialization and convergence develop? It is not a one-way street; developments in both directions can easily take place at the same time.

It should be emphasized that the focus is not on technological convergence. In this field, there are and have been strong trends towards convergence—the convergence between IT and telecommunications and the convergence between interactive communication and broadcasting. The technological convergence is the technology basis for the Internet and thus also for e-services. What we are interested in here is the classical business economic question on the specialization and convergence of business functions as a consequence of the use of new technologies. Now that a common platform for the delivery of a wide range of services is established—the Internet—will this lead to a greater degree of convergence of business areas that hitherto have been apart, or will it lead to more specialization?

In general, the history of the application of technology in businesses points in direction of a greater degree of specialization. To the extent that the comparison between the use of technology in manufacturing and the use of ICT in services is valuable, one would expect more specialization and an increasing development of new business areas. However, it is too soon to pass a final judgment on this with respect to the development of e-services. In the media area, there are clearly tendencies towards convergence (Jenkins, 2006). Media companies seek to deliver content on different media platforms and to go beyond the platforms that they have used up until now. At the same time, many new companies enter the media industry offering a wide range of intermediate services. Furthermore, entirely new content media are established based on the Internet such as YouTube and Facebook. These new services and applications build on content delivered by the users and constitute a totally new type of development, and this applies not only to media-like applications but also to the different kinds of wikis based on the contribution of the users, where the Wikipedia encyclopedia is the most well-known example.

If going beyond the media area, the picture is even more unclear. Portals of different kinds constitute a type of convergence as seen from the customer point of view. However, behind such portals there will be a large number of specialized business enterprises. Furthermore, most e-services will not be offered via portals. The Internet will be the general marketplace for such services, and there will be an increasing specialization of companies offering different elements of services and the many new services that Internet enables. The expectation is, therefore, that e-services will be part of a trend towards greater specialization, but presented to users on a converged digitized market place, the Internet.

CONCLUSION

The research issues examined in this chapter are what the major conditions for the development of e-services and nonservices are and what the implications are with respect to specialization and/or convergence in the provision and development of e-services and nonservices. The chapter points at codifiability, digitization, and interpretation as three crucial conditions for the development of e-services and nonservices. Regarding implications, the chapter points at the issue of specialization and/or convergence in the production and marketing of informational services.

In order to examine these issues, the chapter starts out by defining the concept of services and to discuss what e-services and nonservices are. E-services encompass all informational services (data, information, and knowledge) and software delivered on digital networks to users. However, not all e-services are commercial. Presently, there is a range of digital applications, which are provided by the users and are put at the disposal of other users for free. In the chapter, these applications are called nonservices to emphasize their noncommercial character.

Some of the most important conditions for the development of e-services and nonservices are concerned with the codifiability of knowledge. However, even if knowledge is codifiable, it does not necessarily follow that it can be entirely digitized or that it will be interpreted in the same manner in different contexts. Digitization and a common interpretative context is, therefore, also important for the development of e-services and nonservices.

Whether the development of e-services and nonservices leads to more specialization or convergence in the production and marketing of informational services is an open question. However, the likelihood is that the production and marketing of informational services will develop in a manner similar to other production areas with respect to the implications of technology on the combination of specialization and convergence. This means that specialization will presumably be the main development trend.

Finally, it should be emphasized that the development of e-services not only depends on the potentials in terms of digitization and with respect to codifiability. It also depends on the actual demand of users and customers. And, it depends on the incentive for producers to digitally market their services. In some cases, producers prefer and give emphasis to a direct and personal relationship for business reasons.

REFERENCES

Charron, C., Favier, J., & Li, C. (2006). *Social computing: How networks erode institutional power, and what to do about it*. Forrester Research.

Chesbrough, H., & Spohrer, J. (2006). A research manifesto for services science. *Communications of the ACM, 49*(7), 35-40.

Cowan, R., David, P.A., & Foray, D. (2000). The explicit economics of knowledge codification and tacitness. *Industrial and Corporate Change, 9*(2), 211-253.

Dell, M. (2000). *Direct from Dell: Strategies that revolutionized an industry*. New York: Collins.

Gershuny, J., & Miles, I. (1983). *The new service economy: The transformation of employment in industrial societies*. New York: Praeger.

Hagedorn-Rasmussen, P. (2006). Making sense of "e-knowation": Exploring the relationship between emerging strategy, innovation and entrepreneurial nets of critical capabilities and resources (Working Paper No. 8). Lyngby: E-Service Project.

Henten, A. (1994). *Impacts of information and communication technologies on trade in services*. Lyngby: Technical University of Denmark.

Henten, A. (2005, October 25–26). *Internationalisation of knowledge services: The case of engineering consultancy services – Ramboll.* Presentation at the Nordic Conference on Innovation and Value Creation in the Service Economy, Oslo, Norway.

Hill, T.P. (1977). On goods and services. *Review of Income and Wealth, 23*(4), 314–339.

Illeris, S. (1996). *The service economy: A geographical approach.* Hoboken: John Wiley and Sons.

Jenkins, H. (2006). *Convergence culture: When old and new media collide.* New York: NYU.

O'Reilly, T. (2007). What is Web 2.0: Design patterns and business models for the next generation of software. *Communications & Strategies, 65,* 17–37.

Piccinelli, G., & Stammers, E. (2001). *From e-processes to e-networks: An e-service-oriented approach.* Retrieved June 1, 2008, from http://www.research.ibm.com/people/b/bth/OOWS2001/piccinelli.pdf

Polanyi, M. (1958). *The tacit dimension.* New York: Doubleday.

Sundbo, J. (1997). Management of innovation in services. *The Service Industries Journal, 17*(3), 432–455.

Teece, D.J. (1980). Economies of scope and the scope of the enterprise. *Journal of Economic Behavior & Organization, 1*(3), 223-247.

Tiwana, A., & Balasubramaniam, R. (2001, March). *E-services, problems, opportunities, and digital platforms.* Paper presented at the 34th Hawaii International Conference on System Sciences.

Toffler, A. (1980). *The third wave.* Bentham Books.

Valentin, F., & Hansen, P.V. (2004). *Udvikling af videnservice* [Development of knowledge service]. Copenhagen: Nyt Teknisk Forlag.

ENDNOTE

[1] The chapter is based on work performed in connection with a Danish research project on e-services, "'E-service: Knowledge services, entrepreneurship, and the consequences for business customers and citizens," 2004–2007, http://www.eservice-research.dk. The author would like to thank the other project participants for the ideas that they have contributed to this chapter. The author alone, however, bears responsibility for the chapter.

Chapter II
Developing Measures and Standards for the European Electronic Signatures Market

Ioannis P. Chochliouros
Hellenic Telecommunications Organization S.A. (OTE), Greece

Anastasia S. Spiliopoulou
Hellenic Telecommunications Organization S.A. (OTE), Greece

Tilemachos D. Doukoglou
Hellenic Telecommunications Organization S.A. (OTE), Greece

Elpida Chochliourou
General Prefectorial Hospital "Georgios Gennimatas", Greece

ABSTRACT

The European Authorities have promoted a specific and innovative framework for the use of electronic signatures, allowing the free flow of electronic signature-related products and services cross borders, and ensuring a basic legal recognition of such facilities. The core aim was to promote the emergence of the internal market for certification products, mainly intending to satisfy various requirements for the proper use and immediate "adoption" of electronic signature applications related to e-government and personal e-banking services. Thus, a number of technical, procedural, and quality standards for electronic signature products and solutions have been developed, all conforming to the requirements imposed by the EU regulation and the relevant market needs. In the present work, we examine the role of standardization activities for the promotion of several needs of an "open" European market based on the effective usage of e-signatures, and being able to affect a great variety of technological, business-commercial, regulatory, and other issues. In any case, the transposition of legal requirements into technical specifications (or business practices) needs to be harmonized at a European member-states' level in order to enable adequate interoperability of the final solutions proposed. Appropriate technical standards for the sector can help to establish a presumption of conformity that the electronic signature products following or implementing them comply with all the legal requirements imposed, in the background of the actual European policies. Thus we discuss recent European and/or national initiatives to fulfil such a fundamental option. The European Electronic Signature Standardization Initiative (EESSI) has been set up under the auspices of the European Commission for the carrying out of a work program aiming at the development of standards (be it technical specifications or policy practices) that would facilitate the implementation of the basic legal instrument (the "Electronic Signatures Directive"). Two major streams of possible standards-setting work have been determined, covering: (i) Qualitative and procedural standards for the provision of certification services and (ii) technical standards for product interoperability. We identify (and evaluate at a primary level) the basic components/modules of EESSI's specific results, already developed and offered in the market either as technical regulations and/or as recognized standards, with respect to essential requirements imposed by the European regulation. We also discuss relevant "feedback" already gained from various market areas and we focus on challenges for further implementation, progress, adoption, and development, especially in the framework for the promotion of converged broadband (Internet-based) communications facilities. It is important for the market that expected standardization work takes into account new technological developments as, in the future, users will move their e-signature key from device-to-device in a connected world. The added value of standards in the e-signatures sector, for both end users and assessing parties (judge, arbitrator, conformity assessment body, etc.) is of extreme importance for the future of the European electronic communications market.

INTRODUCTION

The digital technological landscape has changed significantly during the past decade. New communication technologies, new media, the Internet, and devices carrying new functionalities are expected to meet consumers' demand for seamless, simple, and user-friendly digital tools providing access to an extended range of services and content (i2010 High Level Group, 2006). In fact, electronic communication via open networks such as the Internet has been remarkably increased and expanded, on a scale unimaginable some years ago. As a consequence, electronic communication networks and information systems have been developed exponentially in recent years and are now an essential part of the daily lives of almost all European citizens (European Commission, 2002); in addition, they both constitute

fundamental "tools" to the success of the broader European economy in the international scenery (Chochliouros & Spiliopoulou, 2005).

In particular, networks and information systems are converging and becoming increasingly interconnected, thus creating a variety of potential opportunities for all categories of "players" involved. This rapid expansion concerns all sectors of human activity, whether business, public services, or the private sphere. Actually, global networks have truly become the "lifeblood" of our societies and economies: An overwhelming number of employees use a mobile phone, a laptop, or a similar device to send or retrieve information for their work. Furthermore, in multiple cases, such information can represent a considerable value, for instance, describe a business transaction or contain technical knowledge (Lalopoulos, Chochliouros, & Spiliopoulou, 2004).

Despite the many and obvious benefits of the modern electronic communications development, this evolutionary process has also brought with it the worrying threat of intentional attacks against information systems and network infrastructures (European Commission, 2000). As cyberspace gets more and more complex and its components more and more sophisticated, *especially due to the fast development and evolution of (broadband) Internet-based platforms*, new and unforeseen vulnerabilities may emerge.

Moreover, as Internet becomes ubiquitous for all business and personal communications, the sensitivity and economic value of the content of information transmitted is highly increasing (Shoniregun, Chochliouros, Laperche, Logvynovskiy, & Spiliopoulou, 2004). The economic damage caused by network and/or service disruptions is becoming larger. Unfortunately, due to the transnational and borderless character of modern information systems, it is possible to launch an attack from anywhere in the world, to any place, at any time. This constitutes a severe threat (PriceWaterhouseCoopers, 2001) to the achievement of a safer information society and to an area of freedom and security, and therefore requires a "proper" and immediate response at the level of the European Union (EU). In particular, the economic burden imposed by various illegal actions on public bodies, companies, and individuals is considerable and threatens to make information systems more costly and less affordable to all potential users. Therefore, as so much depends on networks and information systems, their secure functioning has nowadays become a key concern, especially for the smooth operation of both internal EU market and society (European Commission, 2001).

BACKGROUND: THE NECESSITY FOR ENHANCED SECURITY

Development of a Proper Strategic Framework

As already pointed out, communication infrastructures have now become a "critical" part of the backbone of modern economies. Users should be able to rely on the availability of information services and have the confidence that their communications (and data) are safe from unauthorized access and/or modification. Thus, security is a major global challenge that has recently come to the fore due to world events and societal changes and it has therefore become an "enabler" for e-businesses and a prerequisite for privacy (Chochliouros & Spiliopoulou, 2006). Innovative solutions relying on emerging technologies are replacing previous "traditional" security approaches: the former may involve the extensive use of encryption and "digital signatures," new access control and authentication tools, and software filters of all kinds.

Ensuring secure and reliable information infrastructures and corresponding (offered) facilities not only require a range of technologies but also their correct deployment and effective use to respond to practical needs. At the European level, a variety of legislative action (Chochliouros & Spiliopoulou, 2003b; Weber, 2002) has mainly taken the form of measures especially in the fields of the protection of the fundamental right to privacy and data protection, together with electronic commerce (and other relevant electronic services) and electronic signatures (Kamal, 2005). (In the context of the present work, e-services can be considered as those providing the specific needs of businesses conducting commerce on the Internet by using Web technology to help businesses streamline processes, improve productivity, and increase efficiencies.) To adopt European legislation is sometimes a challenging task; but to put it into real life and in real business conditions is an even bigger challenge.

The practical application of e-communications in various spheres of activity, and specifically in that of electronic commerce, depends on the efficient removal of any "obstacles" to the expected harmonized development (Chochliouros & Spiliopoulou, 2004). These "obstacles" can be described as probable insecurities typical to "open" networks; that is, messages can be intercepted and manipulated, the validity of documents can be contested, and personal data can be illicitly collected and several forms of communication can be used for illegal purposes. Electronic commerce and many other applications of the information society will only develop if confidentiality can be guaranteed in a user-friendly and cost-efficient way. Therefore, it is necessary to create a secure environment that will enable the establishment of an information society that will safeguard the public against misuse, and the development of e-commerce on bases at least as assured as those which currently govern paper currency transactions in the business world.

To this aim, the international practice/experience has suggested two fundamental goals: digital signatures and encryption (European Commission, 1997; Richards, 2000). The first guarantees the identity of the user and the origin of the message (authentication), while the second protects against illegal interference (integrity) and ensures the confidentiality of communications. The regulation of this area had to be approached with a clear overall vision: on the one hand, there is a need to proceed with flexibility so as not to hamper technological advances and their applications while, *on the other hand*, the fundamental principles of the EU should be preserved including, *among others*, consumer protection, a level playing-field in terms of competition, free movement of services, and mutual recognition. General rules have to be established, leading to greater confidence in electronic commerce but providing guarantee that it remains flexible and open enough to allow for new technological developments.

Consequently, both electronic communication and commerce (European Parliament & Council of the European Union, 2000b; Ford & Baum, 2001) necessitate proper solutions and related services allowing data authentication. However, divergent rules with respect to legal recognition of electronic signatures and the accreditation of certification-service providers in the EU may create a significant barrier to the use (and growth) of e-communications and e-commerce.

The development and use of authentication products and services is still in progress, even at the global level. Up to now, several systems existed, which all made use of authentication for commerce, administration, and public services; however, it was necessary to create and to endorse a complete "set" of internationally agreed industry standards (or technical specifications) for their use. Without such standards, it is impossible to provide a common level of security, recognized as "valid for use" at national/regional level, even less at international level (Dempsey, 2003).

Open networks such as the Internet are of increasing importance for worldwide communication. They offer new ways of doing business, such as teleworking and virtual shared environments, and they offer opportunities for communication between parties which may not have pre-established relationships. Electronic signatures open up opportunities to exploit the (broadband) Internet for secure document exchange, for purchase requisitions, contracts, and invoice applications. To date, the most common form of electronic signature is the "digital signature." For the problem of authentication and integrity of data, digital signatures can provide a solution creating a proper framework at the European level to ensure mutual compatibility and to encourage the development of a range of certification arrangements that will suit different applications between public bodies and citizens (Kaufman, 2002).

It is quite important for the EU not only to guarantee practices and/or measures for the effective adoption of such digital signatures, but to establish appropriate procedures in the field of standardization and product which are interoperable with other international ones, or (at least) have a common interface with them. The aim for such an initiative is to encourage all sectors of society, and particularly the European industry, to design, develop, and endorse commonly accepted standards not only at national level but also at international level (bearing in mind the importance of ensuring that such standards comply with best practice and the state-of-the-art) (Dumortier, Kelm, Nillson, Skouma, & Van Eecke, 2003).

The Basic European Regulatory Initiatives

The "digital signature" is a digital code that can be attached to an electronically transmitted message that uniquely identifies the sender (Aalberts & Van der Hof, 1999). Like a written signature, its purpose is to guarantee that the individual sending the message really is who he or she claims to be. Digital signatures are based on public key technology (Chochliouros, Chochliouros, Spiliopoulou, & Lambadari, 2007), a special form of encryption invented in the 1970s which uses two different keys. Due to this specific usage, this form of encryption is also known as asymmetric cryptography. One key is kept secret (the so-called "private key") whereas the other key is made publicly available (the so-called "public key"). Both keys are generated simultaneously and they are collectively known as a "key pair." Once a message has been encrypted using one of them, it can only be decrypted by the other key. To be effective, digital signatures must be unforgeable. There are a number of different encryption techniques to guarantee this level of security. A signature is not part of the substance of a transaction, but rather of its representation or form. Digital signatures identify and authenticate the originator of the information. They allow the receiver to ascertain the identity of the sender and

to determine (and verify) whether the message has changed during transit.

The Internet has created a borderless space for information exchange, and the keyword for the deployment of corresponding applications in all sectors of the worldwide economy is trust. Rapid technological development and the global character of all underlying platforms (and infrastructures) impose the requirement/necessity for an effective approach, adequately "open" to various technologies and services, and capable of authenticating data electronically (Kamal, 2005; Shoniregun et al., 2004).

Consequently, a very important and identifiable challenge (ISO, 2005; OECD, 2004) is to exploit Internet for secure document exchange, originating from various thematic areas. Recognizing that Internet's expansion and progress in e-commerce offer an unrivaled occasion for economic integration, after appropriate consultation procedures the EU has very early endorsed the *"Electronic Signature Directive"* (hereinafter as the "Directive") aimed at ensuring the proper functioning of the internal European market in the field of electronic signatures by creating a harmonized and appropriate legal framework for their use (European Parliament & Council of the European Union, 2000a). A clear European Community framework regarding the conditions applying to e-signatures can strengthen confidence in, and general acceptance of, the new corresponding technologies.

The Directive establishes a set of detailed criteria, which form the basis for en effective legal recognition of electronic signatures and create an open environment and infrastructure for secure transactions, while it promotes interoperability of related products and/or similar facilities. More specifically, it intended to create a suitable framework for electronic signatures and certain certification services, in order to ensure the proper functioning of the European marketplace (thus avoiding several divergent national laws in the area). Without any doubt, as a result of international experience, global electronic communication and commerce are dependent upon the progressive adaptation of international and domestic laws to the rapidly evolving technological infrastructure (Commission of the European Communities, 2005) ensuring conditions for a proper functioning of the market and supporting interests of all actors involved.

The Directive also identifies requirements that have to be met by service providers supporting e-signatures and prerequisites both for signers and verifiers. These obligations need to be supported by detailed technical standards and open specifications which also meet the requirements of European business, so that products and services supporting electronic signatures can be known to provide legally valid signatures, thus furthering the competitiveness of European business in the international market arena.

Transpositions of legal requirements into technical specifications (or business practices) need to be harmonized at a European member states' level in order to enable interoperability of electronic signature-creation products and cross-border availability of all related services, to the extent possible. Simultaneously, the Directive's wording is wide enough to prescribe security requirements that should be met by electronic signature-creation systems and products, but without mandating the use of a specific technology, thus preserving the sense of technical neutrality, which composes a core axis of the present European regulation. For an extensive range of issues enounced in the approach performed, that is, from the "electronic signing" process to business applications and policies supporting the e-signature creation (e.g., supply of certification services), the corresponding regulatory requirements need to find a more concrete "echo" in several business practices. A means to achieve this coherence between law and practices is by the efficient adoption and usage of standardization processes.

STANDARDIZATION ACTIVITIES FOR ELECTRONIC SIGNATURES

Reliable electronic signatures are essential in the creation of open markets, enabling the development of cross-border trust services and increasing competitiveness, with consequent benefit to service providers, manufacturers, and, *ultimately*, the whole user community (Treasury Board of Canada Secretariat, 1999).

The European Authorities have taken various initiatives to stimulate further standardization and interoperability in the area, while efforts have also been performed at the level of the member states. The Directive lays down a number of functional requirements that cannot be addressed through law only. More specifically, the Directive identifies several requirements for qualified certificates, qualified Certification Service Providers (CSPs), and security-creation devices. In addition, it allows the European Commission to establish and publish references of generally "recognized standards" for e-signatures products, under the scope of these conditions. Therefore, national legislation needs to presume compliance with the relevant prerequisites/requirements, when one of these products meets the reference standards. Such "recognition" could for instance be achieved if the standards in question become finally widely accepted in the market practices, because of their undisputable added value, their wide availability, cross-border acceptability, and so forth (Boyd & Mathuria, 2003; Feghhi, Williams, & Feghhi, 1998).

In order to guarantee wider acceptance of any proposed standards, a broad range of participants has been involved in the relevant activities, including: different departments and agencies of national governments, individual corporations, industry associations, civil society organizations, intergovernmental organizations at the regional and global levels, and other international groups and organizations, some of which are multipartite while others may represent a single stakeholder group.

The work of the European Committee for Standardization/Information Society Standardization System (CEN/ISSS) and the European Telecommunications Standards Institute (ETSI) in providing technical specifications and guidance material for their implementation and market adoption was hence "decisive" to the future of e-commerce, to provide timely standards permitting full and efficient implementation of a commonly adopted framework. These two authorized standardization bodies work in close cooperation with each other and with other standardization organizations around the world as appropriate. Their work follows a number of core principles, mainly including openness, transparency, consensus, effectiveness, and relevance.

In fact, industry and the European standardization bodies together with service providers, vendors, users and consumers, national authorities, and/or other interested organizations have all joined under the auspices of the Information and Communication Technologies Standards Board (ICTSB) to identify and to analyze, *in a coherent manner*, the exact Europe's standardization needs in the sector (Sherif, 2006).

Several standardization initiatives had already been launched at the national, regional, and international levels by organizations and industry fora. Worthy of mention were the activities of the International Chamber of Commerce, the ILPF (Internet Law Policy Forum), the IETF (Internet Engineering Task Force), the W3C (World Wide Web Consortium), and the ABA (American Bar Association) standardization activities. In January 1999, therefore, to initiate and coordinate the necessary standardization effort, a new initiative was launched (i.e., the European Electronic Signature Standardization Initiative, or EESSI), bringing together industry, market players, public authorities, and legal and technical experts (http://www.ict.etsi.org/EESSI_home.htm). Its basic task was to develop the standardization activities required to enable electronic signatures in a coherent manner (particularly in the business environment) and to monitor the implementation of a proper work program to meet this need and to harmonize specifications at the international level to maximize market take-up (Nilsson, Van Eecke, Medina, Pinkas, & Pope, 1999). Three key areas were identified:

- Quality and functional standards for CSPs;
- Quality and functional standards for signature creation and verification products; and
- Interoperable standardization requirements.

The initiative had no desire to "reinvent the wheel," and, *wherever possible*, new standards were built on existing specifications from the International Telecommunication Union (ITU), the International Organization for Standardization (ISO) and the IETF.

In the fast moving domain of information and communications technologies, CEN/ISSS was responsible for the part of the work program dealing with quality and functional standards for signature creation and verification products, as well as quality and functional standards for CSPs (http://www.cenorm.be/isss/Workshop/e-sign/Default.htm).

Several related responsibilities have been focused on the following distinct issues:

- security requirements for trustworthy systems and products;
- security requirements for secure signature creation devices;
- signature creation environment;
- signature verification process and environment; *and*
- conformity assessment of products and services for electronic signatures.

Various EESSI deliverables have been published as CEN Workshop Agreements (CWA) and ETSI Technical Specifications (TS). Since a number of valuable documents have been published in this area, national supervisory authorities can now make use of these specifications, to facilitate the proper functioning of their markets. Many countries are now promoting, using, or planning to use several of these specifications. More specifically, the interoperability standards developed by ETSI have also been accepted as "de-facto standards" by multiple market players, although further work is still needed to enhance interoperability at different approaches.

Within ETSI, the Electronic Signature Infrastructure (ESI) Working Group has promoted a variety of corresponding activities (http://portal. etsi.org/esi/el-sign.asp). Its core responsibilities under EESSI have been focused on the subsequent areas:

- The use of X.509 public key certificates as qualified certificates (ITU, 2001);
- Security management and certificate policy for CSPs issuing qualified certificates;
- Security requirements for trustworthy systems used by CSPs issuing Qualified Certificates;
- Security requirements for signature creation devices;
- Signature creation and verification;
- Electronic signature syntax and encoding formats (occasionally in XML);
- Technical aspects of signature policies; *and*
- Protocol to interoperate with a Time Stamping Authority.
- In certain cases, apart from the above context, there is the additional possibility to examine signature policies for extended business models, together with harmonized provision of CSP status information.

Each of these thematic categories of standards addresses a range of requirements including those of Qualified Electronic Signatures as specified in relevant EU Directive (*article 5.1 of the Directive*). However, they also address general prerequisites related to the proper and the effective use of e-signatures for business activities and for realizing various forms of e-commerce (which all fall into the category of *article 5.2 of the Directive*). Such a variation in requirements may be identified in the standards either as different levels or different options (European Parliament & Council of the European Union, 2000a).

The standardization work is still ongoing in a number of areas, with emphasis given in the fundamental thematic domains covering:

- The development of certification services (*according to the provisions of Annexes I & II of the Directive*); and
- Work on signing process and signature creation products (*according to the provisions of Annexes III & IV of the Directive*).

More specifically, the former category includes standards describing, *among others*:

- Policy requirements for certification authorities issuing qualified certificates (ETSI, 2006d)
- Profile for qualified certificates (ETSI, 2006a)
- Electronic Signature Formats (ETSI, 2007a)
- Time Stamping Profile (ETSI, 2006b)
- Security requirements for trustworthy systems managing certificates for electronic signatures (CEN Workshop Agreement, 2003a; 2003b)
- XML advanced electronic signatures (ETSI, 2006c)
- International harmonization of policy requirements for CAs issuing certificates (ETSI, 2005)
- Signature policies report (ETSI, 2002a)
- Policy requirements for time stamping authorities (ETSI, 2003)
- Provision of harmonized Trust Service Provider status information (ETSI, 2002b)
- XML Format for signature policies (ETSI, 2002c)

- Policy requirements for certification authorities issuing Public Key Certificates (ETSI, 2007b)

In the context of effort performed on signing process and signature creation products are included the following works:

- Guidelines for the implementation of secure signature-creation devices (CEN Workshop Agreement, 2004a)
- Secure signature-creation devices (CEN Workshop Agreement, 2001; 2004b)
- Security requirements for signature creation applications (signature creation process and environment) (CEN Workshop Agreement, 2004c)
- Procedures for electronic signature verification (CEN Workshop Agreement, 2004d)
- Conformity assessment guidance (CEN Workshop Agreement, 2004e), where work that has been realized includes general approach, provision of certification services, security of certificate management systems, procedures for signature creation (and verification), and provisions for secure signature creation devices

EESSI's deliverables have been developed on Public Key Infrastructure (PKI) and related certificate techniques. PKI technology is known by the industry as a reference tool for digital signature (Chochliouros et al., 2007). It is however clear that other technologies are relevant and consideration is already being given to these. EESSI has put all its effort towards the definition of operating procedures and security environment assisting users and trust service providers in the implementation of electronic signature applications. The produced deliverables contribute to fundamental objectives of the EU strategic framework as: *on the one hand*, they propose to providers of trust products and service solutions for compliance with the critical requirements of

the basic European Directive in the area, thus contributing to a harmonized implementation of electronic signatures in the EU (in respect of the free movement of goods and services in the internal market); *on the other hand*, they contribute to the creation of an open, market-led environment for the availability of interoperable products and services, thus enabling the development of cross-border trust services with a view to increasing competitiveness and favoring exploitation of services in the internal market for the benefits of the whole user community.

EESSI's activities have been well publicized outside Europe, links have been established with various fora and consortia worldwide, and representatives of international organizations participated in several among its working groups. With the detailed publication of a full set of standards, EESSI has fulfilled its mandate and consequently ICTSB decided to close EESSI WG in October 2004. However, standardization work in the area is still ongoing and carried out by various European bodies, mainly on the basis of the results performed by the previous corresponding effort. A great part of the relevant work has been considered as the basis for solutions already applied in several national legislative regimes (i.e., in Italy and in Germany).

The Impact of Standardization Activities in the Sector

With convergence effects in the electronic communications sector, the marketplace has fundamentally changed: the monolithic world of the past has been replaced by a heterogeneous technology development and standards environment and new complex relationships have arisen between networks and business models as well as contractual and strategic business relationships, often at a global level, between all "key players." Standardization consortia (and/or fora) become a common practice in the sector and some of the suggested standards have reached large market acceptance, challenging the role of the formal European Standardization Organizations. In order to respond to new market requirements, the standardization structures were flexible and able to evolve quickly (De Vries, 2006).

It is widely recognized that one of the impediments to electronic commerce is the lack of standards to support the use of electronic signatures and certificates. The EU standardization initiatives for supporting e-signatures addressed two major aspects of openness: one was to support fast and easy establishment of trust between parties who desired to do business online; the other option was to take care of the technical compatibility of services and components. Such a context can support new business relationships, while it "minimizes" risks involved with investments by corporations and/or by private users. An open environment is favorable for public services to the citizen and for all kinds of business activity.

Thus, partnership/collaboration of all relevant stakeholders is always regarded as "essential" to the successful standardization of electronic signatures. By involving all interested parties, a common and harmonized framework can be agreed and interoperability, at least within Europe, can be ensured (European Commission, 2003). As already mentioned, the e-signatures Directive allows the European Commission to establish and publish reference numbers of "generally recognized standards" for several corresponding products. Consequently, compliance with the requirements laid down in the Directive when an e-signature product meets those standards is presumed.

In the context of a Decision published by the European Commission in July 2003 (European Commission, 2003), there were particular references to CEN standards for the requirements related to the creation of qualified electronic signatures. The validity of these CWAs was initially expected to expire after three years of their publication, with the possibility for further temporal extension, *if needed*. In the meantime,

other standards could also be developed and accepted, as long as they could be considered as being "generally recognized standards." In this framework, it is important for the market that future standardization work takes into account new technological developments as users will move their e-signature key from device to device in a digitally connected world.

The purpose of the original EESSI initiative was to ensure that the legal requirements imposed by the (commonly accepted) European legal framework should be implemented by workable, interoperable solutions, to develop effective market solutions and underpin the development of e-business in Europe, on the basis of a proper consensus among all actors involved, representing public authorities, industry, and the private sector.

The initiative was an open and neutral platform, bringing together expertise from different fields and regions and supporting "co-regulation" initiatives. "Co-regulation" represents a sharing of responsibilities between public authorities and private market players: This is particularly important for the e-economy, as the new information society services require a high level of trust and security, and this in a business environment where technologies are rapidly changing. In this circumstance, the suggested standards can all be taken into account as a practical effort for developing detailed technical rules on how qualified e-signatures have to be made and become applicable. These rules need to become essential part of the national legal framework, if progress and efficiency is expected.

In order to support a "wider" acceptance, international standards adopted and/or developed by industry had to avoid the need for detailed regulations, *to the extent possible*. As necessity of standards was (and still is) urgent, reference to existing recognized international standards has to be preferred to the development of new standards, wherever possible. The complete effort in the area has represented the first coordinated initiative on a large scale in Europe, being led by formal standardization bodies that attempted to provide an agreed framework for an open, "market-oriented" implementation of the corresponding legal requirements, through a consensus-based approach.

Without any doubt, under the current circumstances practical guidance and technical specifications are necessary to help the private sector and the public authorities to put into practice the legal EU framework in a clear, well-organized, efficient, and cost effective manner (European Parliament & Council of the European Union, 2000a). The e-signatures Directive is, *by definition*, "technology neutral." Standards, however, are not. Thus, they have to be structured upon specific business models that are considered to be as relevant. At the same time, security aspects must be fully respected to give legal recognition to any suggested electronic signatures and, *simultaneously*, to be conformant to specific national conditions. Taking these requirements together, the suggested standards must be adequately open and internationally agreed. They have to be satisfactorily flexible to cover different business models and to provide quite secure solutions. These basic criteria are fully met by the recent European standardization works, including EESSI's works.

The added value of the European standardization system is to ensure the transparency, openness, inclusiveness, and accountability of the consensus-building process for creating standards for adoption and use (Chochliouros & Spiliopoulou, 2003a). As a consequence, all efforts performed for the development of a series of proper "guidelines" for an efficient e-signatures standardization are more than "simply important" for the internal European market and have a growing contribution to different policies and thematic areas such as: sustainable development; global trade; avoidance of market fragmentation, European governance, *and*; support of several strategic initiatives. In any case, it is essential to develop, as widely as possible, measures based on existing technical solutions, representing the "state-of-the-art" and, *most importantly*, a wide consensus among market players (European Commission, 2005, 2006).

Building strong user commitment is one of the key requirements for successful standardization in the e-signatures sector. For this reason, it would be essential that EESSI deliverables are as widely disseminated and promoted as possible (for example, making these deliverables available for downloads from the Internet can also be an important matter). In addition, guidelines for practical implementation can further help in testing and certifying secure software European-wide in a consistent manner. This cannot only support the creation of an internal market for the corresponding facilities, but it can provide immediate response to current challenges, due to the fast development of various (global) e-commerce activities. The entire initiative has been well performed, in order to be more open to direct industry participation and more internationally oriented for secure business solutions, supporting the European approach for security in the international literature.

Many countries are now promoting, using, or planning to use several of the EESSI deliverables. Recent works (such as Commission of the European Communities, 2006; Dumortier et al., 2003; Hayat, Leitold, Rechberger, & Rössler, 2004) provide a detailed overview of the state in the European environment, demonstrating that significant progress has been realized on the basis of EESSI's works. (In these references, exact informative data is listed, correlated to the specific national legislation. Further information about the current status of the implementation of the e-signatures Directive at national level, the existing regulatory framework, and exact depiction of all appropriate progress for each separate member state can be found at http://ec.europa. eu/information_society/eeurope/2005/all_about/ security/esignatures/index_en.htm.)

There is a strong requirement for technical interoperability standards for electronic signature functions in an open and competitive marketplace, to achieve interoperability between products and services. In fact, users want standardized and interoperable products to enable them to buy different components from different vendors, while vendors prefer standards to enable them to sell products on an international market.

Interoperability depends on standardization, but standardization cannot be the only and unique answer. The lack of common standards in a converged area (like the sector of e-signatures) is an inhibitor to its development. However, variable and competing standards can also raise serious concerns. The interoperability standards developed by ETSI have been accepted as "*de-facto*" standards by many European actors, although further work may still be necessary to promote their actual use, as it may be probably "unwise" to integrate such standards into the legal framework at a very early stage. When different national authorities set different standards as to what attributes are required for an electronic signature before it will be considered enforceable, businesses face daunting practical difficulties in using e-signatures for transactions nationwide and internationally. Any lack of technical interoperability at national and at cross-border level causes a severe obstacle for the market acceptance of e-signatures. This has resulted in many "isolated" islands of e-signature applications, where certificates can only be used for one single application. EESSI has worked on the promotion of interoperability and has supported the definition of specifications that will encourage the emergence of interoperable competitive solutions; but most of the EU member states have specified national standards in order to promote the option for enhanced interoperability; for example, the ISIS-MTT specifications in Germany (Giessler & Lindemann, 2003) aimed at creating technical interoperability between the related e-signatures products.

Anyway, according to the actual European legislation, the responsibility for the recognition of electronic signatures remains with the national authorities, whether common standards exist or not. This may occasionally led to conflicts (and case law) about various kinds of e-signatures, while national laws can be enacted, *in several instances,* with various security requirements with regards to authentication issues, and so forth. Thus, legislation ranges from a "minimalist" approach that simply authorizes the use of electronic signatures in very limited circumstances, to legislation that establishes some evidentiary presumptions and default provisions that parties can contract out of, to a very formal and highly regulatory approach governing the manner in which digital signatures may be used and certification authorities may operate (Hayat et al., 2004; Van Eecke, Pinto, & Egyedi, 2007).

From an EU perspective, national legislation with differing requirements risks holding back the effective establishment of the internal market especially in areas which depended on e-signature related products and services. Avoiding disruption of the internal market in an area considered as "critical" to the future of electronic transactions in the European economy is at the basis of the proposed harmonization measures at all levels. The European Commission sees a clear need to further encourage the development of these services/applications and therefore to monitor market and technological developments. Thus, particular emphasis is given on the interoperability and cross-border use of e-signatures. The European Commission has recently announced that will encourage further standardization work in order to promote the interoperability of all corresponding systems within and across borders and the use of all kinds of technologies for qualified e-signature in the single market (Commission of the European Communities, 2006).

With the globalization of trade and the (expected) growth of e-commerce, the flexibility and the ability of national law to deal with contracts concluded in cyberspace are severely tested. There is a widely held belief that the law is slow moving and not able to properly cope with the demands of modern technology. But standards such as the EESSI deliverables have proved that they can help EU member states to work towards interoperable and mutually recognized solutions, able to support market expansion, conformingly to the national legislation systems. EESSI standards may spur the use of e-signatures and will help European countries to "transpose" effectively, from a legal point of view, the basic EU common regulatory provisions of the (e-signature) Directive. International experience has demonstrated that only standards that are widely used can have an essential impact on the market. Thus, the aim of standardization in the domain is to "push the market forward," while standards have to remain voluntary and flexible (European Commission, 2004; Van Eecke et al., 2007).

CONCLUSION

To make fullest use of the opportunities offered by the Internet, secure electronic signatures are essential to verify the authenticity and integrity of a communication activity. In fact, security is a key priority for e-business, e-procurement, and e-government in the global digital environment. Electronic signatures can now be used in a large diversity of circumstances and applications, resulting in a wide range of new services and products. It is so expected that online purchasing, e-marketplaces, and e-procurement will further promote the use of e-signatures, in parallel with the immense Internet penetration affecting international businesses between various players, mainly from the private sector. Electronic signatures can be also used in the public sector within national and European Community administrations and in communications between such administrations and with citizens and economic operators (for example, in the public procurement, taxation, social security, health, and justice systems).

The definition of e-signatures products and services will not be limited to the issuance and management of certificates, but will also encompass any other service and product using, or ancillary to, electronic signatures, such as registration services, time-stamping services, directory services, computing services, or consultancy services. In fact, e-signatures increase the (state's and/or private and/or public) businesses' efficiency by ensuring trusted and secure end-to-end electronic processes. A reliable system of electronic signatures that work across intra-EU borders is vital to safe electronic commerce and the efficient electronic delivery of public services to businesses and citizens, in the context of a remarkably converged world.

The European Union has promoted effective several regulatory measures, mainly on the basis of the "e-Signatures Directive." These initiatives have even influenced international standardization initiatives as well as other legal and technical activities, *to a great extent*. All EU member states have now implemented the general principles of this fundamental legislative tool, and the EU rules that all member states have transposed into their national laws make e-signatures legally recognized on their territory. For e-commerce to develop and flourish, both consumers and businesses must be confident that their transaction will not be intercepted or modified, that the seller and the buyer are "who they declare," and that transaction mechanisms are available, legal, and secure. However, for promoting practical solutions to current market needs, it is necessary to support specific technical solutions of the wider possible acceptance. The solution may be through the adoption and the endorsement of appropriate standards, created on the basis of the common EU practice, as those created in the context of the EESSI initiative. For Europe to benefit fully from the information society, standardization is an important prerequisite. The traditional standards environment, in the face of the sheer pace of technological innovation and changes in market demands, is responding to the challenge. The EESSI deliverables came in the form of an implementation model (technical specifications or guidelines) with the double objective to satisfy the requirements of the e-signatures Directive and to propose effective answers to market needs in the current timeframe.

The full work performed in the scope of the European standardization entities to fulfill the requirements imposed by the European regulation has achieved remarkable effects to facilitate a consistent and coherent implementation for validity and cross-recognition of e-signatures. Current open issues in the area of electronic signatures are European interoperability, European coordination of supervision, European accreditation schemes, European Root Authority, and sustainable business models; but EESSI standards have been a first important step towards the solution of these open issues. Several solutions for specific corresponding requirements have been already adopted in the market and have been implemented to a wide area of activities at national level, thus supporting the development towards an "*information society for all citizens.*"

REFERENCES

Aalberts, B., & Van der Hof, S. (1999). *Digital signature blindness: Analysis of legislative approaches toward electronic authentication.* Tilburg, The Netherlands: Tilburg University. Retrieved June 1, 2008, from http://www.buscalegis.ufsc.br/busca.php?acao=abrir&id=15433

Boyd, C., & Mathuria, A. (2003). *Protocols for key establishment and authentication.* Berlin/Heidelberg, Germany: Springer-Verlag GmbH & Co.

CEN Workshop Agreement (2001). *CWA 14168: Secure signature-creation devices.* Brussels, Belgium: CEN (European Committee for Standardization).

CEN Workshop Agreement (2003a). *CWA 14167-1: Security requirements for trustworthy systems managing certificates for electronic signatures* (Part 1: System security requirements). Brussels, Belgium: CEN.

CEN Workshop Agreement (2003b). *CWA 14167-2: Cryptographic module for CSP signing Operations with backup: Protection profile (CMCSOB-PP).* Brussels, Belgium: CEN.

CEN Workshop Agreement (2004a). *CWA 14355: Guidelines for the implementation of secure signature-creation devices.* Brussels, Belgium: CEN.

CEN Workshop Agreement (2004b). *CWA 14169: Secure signature-creation devices "EAL 4+."* Brussels, Belgium: CEN.

CEN Workshop Agreement (2004c). *CWA 14170: Security requirements for signature creation applications.* Brussels, Belgium: CEN.

CEN Workshop Agreement (2004d). *CWA 14171: General guidelines for electronic signature verification.* Brussels, Belgium: CEN.

CEN Workshop Agreement (2004e). *CWA 14172: EESSI conformity assessment guidance. General introduction.* Brussels, Belgium: CEN.

Chochliouros, I.P., Chochliouros, S.P., Spiliopoulou, A.S., & Lambadari, E. (2007). Public key infrastructures (PKI): A means for increasing network security. In L.J. Janczewski & A.M. Colarik (Eds.), *Cyber warfare and cyber terrorism* (pp. 281–290). Hershey, PA: Information Science Reference.

Chochliouros, I.P., & Spiliopoulou, A.S. (2003a). European standardization activities: An enabling factor for the competitive development of the information society technologies market. *The Journal of The Communications Network (TCN), 2*(1), 62–68.

Chochliouros, I. P., & Spiliopoulou, A.S. (2003b). Innovative horizons for Europe: The new European telecom framework for the development of modern electronic networks and services. *The Journal of the Communications Network (TCN), 2*(4), 53–62.

Chochliouros, I.P., & Spiliopoulou, A.S. (2004). Potential and basic perspectives of the European Electronic Commerce (e-Commerce) Directive for the Effective Promotion of Modern Business Applications in the Internet (article in Greek). *Telecommunications Audit and Law of New Technologies Magazine, 1*(4), 502–535.

Chochliouros, I.P., & Spiliopoulou, A.S. (2005). Broadband access in the European Union: An enabler for technical progress, business renewal and social development. *The International Journal of Infonomics (IJI), 1*, 5–1.

Chochliouros, I.P., & Spiliopoulou, A.S. (2006, August 30–September 02). Privacy protection vs. privacy offences in the European regulatory context: The cases for interception of communications and the retention of traffic data. In Federation of telecommunications Engineers of the European Union (Ed.), *Proceedings of the 45th International Congress: "Telecom Wars—The Return of the Profit,"* Athens, Greece (pp. 197–203). Athens, Greece: FITCE.

Commission of the European Communities (2005). *Communication on i2010: A European Information Society for growth and employment* [COM(2005) 229 final, 01.06.2005]. Brussels, Belgium: Commission of the European Communities.

Commission of the European Communities (2006). *Report on the operation of Directive 1999/93/EC on a community framework for electronic signatures* [COM(2006) 120 final, 15.03.2006]. Brussels, Belgium: Commission of the European Communities.

Dempsey, J.X. (2003). Creating the legal framework for ICT development: The example of e-signature legislation in emerging market economies. Washington, DC: Center for Democ-racy and Technology. *Information Technologies and International Development (ITID), 1*(2), 39-52. Washington, DC: Center for Democracy and Technology. Retrieved June 1, 2008, from http://www.internetpolicy.net/e-commerce/20030900esignature.pdf

De Vries, H.J. (2006). IT standards typology. In K. Jakobs (Ed.), *Advanced topics in information technology standards and standardization research, 1*, 1–26.

Dumortier, J., Kelm, S., Nillson, H., Skouma, G., & Van Eecke, P. (2003). *The legal and market aspects of electronic signatures: Study for the European Commission* (DG Information Society, Service Contract No. C28.400). Brussels, Belgium: The Interdisciplinary Centre for Law & Information Technology & Katholieke Universiteit Leuven. Retrieved June 1, 2008, from europa.eu.int/information_society/eeurope/2005/all_about/security/electronic_sig_report.pdf

European Commission (1997). *Communication on ensuring security and trust in electronic communication: Towards a European framework for digital signatures and encryption* [COM(97) 503 final, 01.10.1997]. Brussels, Belgium: European Commission.

European Commission (2000). *Communication on creating a safer information society by improving the security of information infrastructures and combating computer-related crime—eEurope 2002* [COM(2000) 890 final, 26.01.2001]. Brussels, Belgium: European Commission.

European Commission (2001). *Communication on network and information security: Proposal for a European policy approach* [COM(2001) 298 final, 06.06.2001]. Brussels, Belgium: European Commission.

European Commission (2002). *Communication on eEurope 2005: An information society for all* [COM(2002) 263 final, 28.05.2002]. Brussels, Belgium: European Commission.

European Commission (2003). *Communication decision 2003/511/ERC of 14 July 2003 on the publication of reference numbers of generally recognized standards for electronic signature products in accordance with Directive 1999/93/EC of the European Parliament and of the Council* [Official Journal (OJ) L175, 15.07.2003, pp. 45–46]. Brussels, Belgium: European Commission.

European Commission (2004). *Communication on the role of European standardisation in the framework of European policies and legislation* [COM(2004) 674 final, 18.10.2004]. Brussels, Belgium: European Commission.

European Commission (2005). *Communication on more research and innovation: Investing for growth and employment: A common approach* [COM(2005) 488 final, 12.10.2005]. Brussels, Belgium: European Commission.

European Commission (2006). *Communication to the Council, the European Parliament, the European Economic and Social Committee and the Committee of the Regions, on Bridging the Broadband Gap* [COM(2006) 129 final, 20.03.2006]. Brussels, Belgium: European Commission.

European Parliament & Council of the European Union (2000a). *Directive 1999/93/EC of the European Parliament and of the Council of 13 December 1999 on a community framework for electronic signatures* [Official Journal (OJ) L13, 19.01.2000, pp. 12–20]. Brussels, Belgium: European Parliament & Council of the European Union.

European Parliament & Council of the European Union (2000b). *Directive 2000/31/EC of the European Parliament and of the Council of 8 June 2000 on certain legal aspects of information society services, in particular electronic commerce, in the internal market (Directive on Electronic Commerce)* [Official Journal (OJ) L178, 17.07.2000, pp. 1–16]. Brussels, Belgium: European Parliament & Council of the European Union.

European Telecommunications Standards Institute (2002a). *ETSI TR 102 041 V1.1.1 (2002-02): Signature Policies Report*. Sophia-Antipolis, France: ETSI.

European Telecommunications Standards Institute (2002b). *ETSI TR 102 030 V1.1.1 (2002-03): Provision of harmonized trust service provider status information*. Sophia-Antipolis, France: ETSI.

European Telecommunications Standards Institute (2002c). *ETSI TR 102 038 V1.1.1 (2002-04): TC Security - Electronic Signatures and Infrastructures (ESI); XML format for signature policies*. Sophia-Antipolis, France: ETSI.

European Telecommunications Standards Institute (2003). *ETSI TR 102 023 V1.2.1 (2003-01): Electronic signatures and infrastructures (ESI); Policy requirements for time-stamping authorities*. Sophia-Antipolis, France: ETSI.

European Telecommunications Standards Institute (2005). *ETSI TR 102 040 V1.3.1 (2005-03): Electronic signatures and infrastructures (ESI); International harmonization of policy requirements for CAs issuing certificates*. Sophia-Antipolis, France: ETSI.

European Telecommunications Standards Institute (2006a). *ETSI TS 101 862 V1.3.3 (2006-01): Qualified certificate profile*. Sophia-Antipolis, France: ETSI.

European Telecommunications Standards Institute (2006b). *ETSI TS 101 861 V1.3.1 (2006-01): Time stamping profile*. Sophia-Antipolis, France: ETSI.

European Telecommunications Standards Institute (2006c). *ETSI TS 101 903 V1.3.2 (2006-03): XML advanced electronic signatures (XAdES)*. Sophia-Antipolis, France: ETSI.

European Telecommunications Standards Institute (2006d). *ETSI TS 101 456 V1.4.2 (2006-12): Electronic signatures and infrastructures (ESI);*

Policy requirements for certification authorities issuing qualified certificates. Sophia-Antipolis, France: ETSI.

European Telecommunications Standards Institute (2007a). *ETSI TS 101 733 V1.7.3 (2007-01): Electronic signatures and infrastructures (ESI); CMS Advanced Electronic Signatures (CAdES).* Sophia-Antipolis, France: ETSI.

European Telecommunications Standards Institute (2007b). *ETSI TS 102 042 V1.2.4 (2007-03): Electronic Signatures and Infrastructures (ESI); Policy requirements for certification authorities issuing public key certificates.* Sophia-Antipolis, France: ETSI.

Feghhi, J., Williams, P., & Feghhi, J. (1998). *Digital certificates: Applied Internet security.* Addison-Wesley.

Ford, W., & Baum, M. (2001). *Secure electronic commerce* (2nd ed.). Upper River Saddle, NJ: Prentice Hall.

Giessler, A., & Lindemann, R. (2003, July 29). *ISIS-MTT compliance criteria* (Version 1.1). Berlin, Germany: T7 & TeleTrusT. Retrieved June 1, 2008, from teletrust.de/fileadmin/files/ag8_isis-mtt-compliancecrit-v1.1.pdf

Hayat, A., Leitold, H., Rechberger, C., & Rössler, T. (2004, August 10). *Survey on EU's electronic-ID solutions* (Version 1.0). Vienna, Austria: Secure Information Technology Center (A-SIT). Retrieved June 1, 2008, from www.a-sit.at/pdfs/A-SIT_EID_SURVEY.pdf

i2010 High Level Group (2006, December). *The challenges of convergence* (Discussion paper). Brussels, Belgium: European Commission. Retrieved June 1, 2008, from http://ec.europa.eu/information_society/eeurope/i2010/docs/i2010_high_level_group/i2010_hlg_convergence_paper_final.pdf

International Organization for Standardization (2005). *ISO/IEC 17799: Information technol-ogy: Security techniques: Code of practice for information security management.* Geneva, Switzerland: ISO.

International Telecommunication Union (2001). *ITU-T recommendation X.509 (2000)/ISO/IEC 9594-8: Information technology: Open Systems Interconnection: The Directory: Public-key and attribute certificate frameworks.* Geneva, Switzerland: ITU.

Kamal, A. (2005). *The law of cyber-space.* Geneva, Switzerland: United Nations Institute of Training and Research (UNITAR).

Kaufman, C. (2002). *Network security: Private communication in a public world* (2nd ed.). Prentice Hall.

Lalopoulos, G.K., Chochliouros, I.P., & Spiliopoulou, A.S. (2004). Challenges and perspectives for Web-based applications in organizations. In M. Pagani (Ed.), *The encyclopedia of multimedia technology and networking* (pp. 82–88). Hershey, PA: IRM Press.

Nilsson, H., Van Eecke, P., Medina, M., Pinkas, D., & Pope, N. (1999, July 20). *Final report of the EESSI Expert Team.* European Electronic Signature Standardization Initiative (EESSI). Retrieved June 1, 2008, from http://www.ictsb.org/EESSI_home.htm

Organization for Economic Coordination and Development (2004). *Digital delivery of business services (JT00162724).* Paris, France: OECD.

PriceWaterhouseCoopers (2001). European Economic Crime Survey 2001. *European Report.* Retrieved June 1, 2008, from http://www.pwcglobal.com

Richards, J. (2000). The Utah Digital Signature Act as a "model" legislation: A critical analysis. *The John Marshal Journal of Computer & Information Law, XVII*(3).

Sherif, M.H. (2006). Standards for telecommunication services. In K. Jakobs (Ed.), *Information technology standards and standardization research*. Hershey, PA: Idea Group Publishing.

Shoniregun, C.A., Chochliouros, I.P., Laperche, B., Logvynovskiy, O., & Spiliopoulou, A.S. (2004). *Questioning the boundary issues of Internet security*. London: e-Centre for Infonomics.

Treasury Board of Canada Secretariat (1999). *Digital signature and confidentiality: Certificate policies for the Government of Canada public key infrastructure* (Government of Canada (GOC), PKI Certificate Policies version 3.02).

Van Eecke, P., Pinto, P., & Egyedi, T. (2007, July). *EU study on the specific policy needs for ICT standardisation* (Final Report, Ref. ENTR/05/059). Brussels, Belgium: DG Enterprise, European Commission. Retrieved June 1, 2008, from http://www.ictstandardisation.eu/

Weber, R. (2002). *Regulatory models for the online world*. Zurich, Switzerland: Schulthess Juristische Medien.

Chapter III
Quality Assessment of Digital Services in E-Government with a Case Study in an Italian Region

Flavio Corradini
University of Camerino, Italy

Alberto Polzonetti
University of Camerino, Italy

Barbara Re
University of Camerino, Italy

ABSTRACT

The quality assessment of e-government services is more and more emerging as a key issue within public administrations. Ensuring a proper quality of digital services is mandatory to satisfy citizens and firms' needs and to accept the use of ICT in our lives. We propose a methodology for quality assessment that takes e-government quality features into account. We also define a reference model to provide a single quality value starting from a set of service parameters. To validate our approach we assess the goodness of the 'TecUt' shared services management system.

INTRODUCTION

Information and communication technologies (ICTs) are widely used within public administra-tions. In this context, e-government refers to the "use of ICT in public administrations combined with organizational changes and new skills in order to improve public services and democratic processes and strengthen support to public policies" (Commission of the European Communities, 2003, p. 7). These technologies allow governments to improve both the delivery of government services to citizens and the interactions with the business and the industry world. Digital government services represent one of the most critical areas of the whole service domain and several definitions are available in the literature (see, for instance, Elmagarmid & McIver, 2001; Tiwana & Ramesh, 2001) and references therein). In a broad sense, they can be thought as the provision of service, including pure services or tangible physical products, over electronic networks such as the Internet (Rust & Lemon, 2001). In particular, digital government services encapsulate public administration functionalities and informative resources making them available through the use of digital interfaces.

The growing diffusion of e-government requires services with high standard level of quality. Nowadays, quality of services is a hot topic of research. There is a very extensive research activity towards quality assessment in different application domains such as software development, multimedia applications, networking, mobile computing, real time and embedded applications, and so forth. According to the International Organization for Standardization, the term "quality" is intended as all the features of an entity (resource, service, and tool) that influence its capability to satisfy declared or implied needs (ISO, 1994).

Unfortunately, quality of services receives little attention by the e-government research community (see Papadomichelaki, Magoutas, Halaris, Apostolou, & Mentzas, 2006) and references therein for a review on quality dimensions in e-government services). Within the application domain of our interest—e-government—we could rephrase the above definition of quality as "all the features of digital services in public administrations that influence their capability to satisfy declared or implied citizens and firms' needs."

Certainly, quality in e-government plays a significant role. A proper quality of digital services is mandatory to satisfy citizens and enterprises' needs, to accept the use of information and communication technology in our lives as well as improve "government management."

In this chapter, we propose a framework to analyze the quality of digital services in e-government. Our methodology takes e-government quality features into account and is composed by three different phases: (i) quality definition, (ii) quality measurement, and (iii) quality interaction. We define (within the first phase) a comprehensive quality model. It is based on a taxonomy of four parameters subcategories related to services and their implementation (e-government, presentation, behavioral, and infrastructural). Our main efforts were to identify those parameters and their relationships that are necessary to assess the quality of e-government services. For each parameter, we pursue a proper analysis to determine the more appropriate metrics and measurement procedures. At the same time, we define a mathematical model that aggregates the detected parameters values into a single one. The model plays a fundamental role allowing a high abstraction level of the problems description and a formal background of the applicative solutions so to avoid possible structural mistakes and inaccurate descriptions.

To validate our approach, we rely on an existing shared services management system—the so-called TecUt portal (www.tecut.it), a portal developed in collaboration with one of the Italian regions, the Marche Region (Corradini, Sabucedo, Polzonetti, Rifón, & Re, 2007). In more details, we have considered the TecUt digital services and we have compared the quality of services (with the same functionalities) provided by several Italian Municipalities to discover those that are more suitable to users requests.

The rest of the chapter is organized as follows. The second section provides a comprehensive understanding of the case study. The third section introduces related works that have somehow contributed to the development of our work. The fourth section presents our methodology for quality assessment taking into account e-government quality features, while the fifth section introduces service quality model based on taxonomy of parameters related to service and its implementation. The sixth and seventh sections propose the measurement model and the mathematical model, respectively. Finally, the eighth section introduces experimental results, and the final section completes the chapter with conclusions and future work.

BACKGROUND

Several Italian Regions have been involved to implement e-government solutions to increase interactions between public administrations and citizens/enterprises by means of ICT infrastructures. To reach such a goal, key aspects of services distribution have been taken into account (authentication, accounting, discovery, etc.). According to the investigation on one-stop government (Corradini, Forastieri, Polzonetti, Riganelli, & Sergiacomi, 2005), the UeG group (Unicam e-Government research group) and the Marche Region public administration have developed the TecUt portal (Corradini et al., 2007), a fully integrated government portal for shared and standardized municipalities services. TecUt supports activities of small and medium municipalities providing a "gateway" between citizens/enterprises and public administrations. It allows a rapidly access to services by means of a single access point.

A global vision of the Marche Region stakeholders includes financial arrangements and aggregations, enterprises, banks, and citizens. This clearly boosts the national and international chances to increase relations with public administrations (PAs) and drives advanced ways to improve standards of living. As a matter of fact, the Marche Region is among the first places in Italy as far as welfare, cohesion, and competitiveness are concerned. At the same time Marche Region is characterized by a lot of small municipalities that are not able to support the fully digital services distribution. TecUt represents an opportunity to e-government diffusion in such an environment.

RELATED WORK

In application domains such as marketing, e-commerce, bioinformatics, and multimedia, the literature on quality of services contains interesting approaches. All of these contributions somehow influenced the development of our work, though we differ from them significantly. As far as we know, our chapter is the first attempt to introduce a comprehensive methodology for quality assessment of e-government digital services focusing on the role of users and ICT technologies. In our opinion, an in-depth analysis of quality literature gives us the necessary input for both the definition of the methodology for quality assessment and related models. In this section we essentially concentrate our attention on those papers that have more directly contributed to the development of our work. We put together domain and implementation related aspects focusing on the role of ICT in the services provision.

Starting from government quality literature, we identify two main areas of interest:

- **Organizational performance:** CAF (CAF Resource Center, 2006), Balanced Scorecard (Kaplan & Norton, 1992), Six Sigma (De Feo & Barnard, 2005), and Baldrige Criteria (Baldrige National Quality Program, 2006);
- **Site quality:** SiteQual (Webb & Webb, 2004), Portal Usage Quality (Lin & Wu, 2002), IP-Portal (Yang, Cai, Zhou, & Zhou, 2005), Norwegian Approach (Jansen & Olnes, 2004), and G-Quality (Garcia, Maciel, & Pinto, 2005).

Regarding organizational performance, the authors mainly discuss the role of organizations while services play a marginal role. The authors define quality models but do not introduce ICT and implementation related aspects. Our approach takes into account organization elements for the identification of implicit relationships in the e-government domain but also focuses on the distribution of digital service and related issues. On the other hand, item (ii) above, the site quality area, introduces facilities to measure the quality of Web site focusing on the e-government front-end aspects. We refer to this stream of research for the definition of parameters and metrics related to the front-end layer of the services. Indeed, the evaluating and monitoring of digital government services must take into account aspects like adaptability, accessibility, and so on. The introduction of a proper client site represents a fundamental part of e-government services distribution. Regarding the e-government domain, we also mention e-government in a Thai approach (Sukasame, 2004). This latter presents a conceptual framework and some factors (content, linkage, reliability, ease of use, and self-service) affecting the e-service provided on the Web portal of Thailand's government. Unfortunately, it does not introduce a complete discussion on the objective assessment of digital services quality.

Interesting works done within services marketing literature have been taken into account, such as SERVQUAL (Parasuraman, Zeithaml, & Berry, 1998). The marketing literature always states that services quality perceptions are important elements of customers' satisfaction. The e-government setting heavily relies on technological and domain dependent constraints. Interesting suggestions also came from the business management domain with a special focus on quality policies (see Seth, Deshmukh, & Vrat, 2005 and references therein). In particular, Yang and Jun (2002) introduce a business service quality model that underlines the role of users (purchaser and nonpurchaser). Also in this setting their satisfac-

tion plays a role. In the e-government domain, of course, we do not rely on business executives but the customers' perception of services quality is crucial. Santos (2003) introduces a model of e-quality, to achieve high customer retention, customer satisfaction, and profitability for the organizations in e-business. He proposes a model of e-service quality that takes into account static and dynamic parameters.

Unfortunately, none of the presented models proposes a complete set of parameters and a specific process for run time measurement. It has to be said that the literature on marketing and business contributed to our approach on the subjective part of the assessing methodology. They are useful to investigate the users feeling on the services.

Related to the technological aspects, we underline the role of Web services as the most common implementation of digital services. In Ran (2003), Farkas and Charaf (2003), and Maximilien and Singh (2004), there is a first approach to define nonfunctional aspects in Web services discovery. From these works we have selected interesting parameters. In particular, Ran (2003) suggests an UDDI quality extension as solution for Web services discovery. In such a way, during the discovery phase, functional and nonfunctional service aspects are introduced. In Farkas and Charaf (2003), a software architecture is proposed to provide Web services with high quality. They implement a quality of service (QoS) broker for services discovery to reflect quality parameters stored in UDDI. Maximilien and Singh (2004) discuss the standard lack of description of nonfunctional attributes needed for Web services discovery. They propose an ontology-based framework to describe quality in order to improve the stakeholders' interaction. Moreover, in Cardoso, Sheth, and Miller (2002); Menascé (2004a, 2004b); and Zeng, Benatallah, Dumas, Kalagnanam, and Sheng (2003), a quality composition approach is investigated. Unfortunately, they consider a short list of quality parameters that are meaningless for e-government application domain and do not introduce a formal measurement and assessment process.

In Nahrstedt, Xu, Wichadakul, and Li (2001) and Tsetsekas, Manitias, Funfstuck, Thoma, and Karadimas (2001), QoS is introduced in a middleware domain. In Nahrstedt et al. (2001), the authors discuss QoS middleware information able to support quality-based applications like streaming and e-commerce. This work presents key aspects about service quality introducing application and process quality information at low abstraction level. In Tsetsekas et al. (2001), a middleware that drives service presentation to the users is proposed. It allows description and selection of QoS parameters and related resources preemptive reservation. In general, distributed applications and their quality provide several hints to quality of services in e-government.

Finally, Menascé (2003) and Corradini et al. (2004) introduce digital service quality in e-commerce and bioinformatics, respectively. They propose an approach for domain related quality investigation and parameters modularization. In Menascé (2003), a QoS controller is introduced.

It uses aggregated metrics to take into account performance parameters. In particular, a QoS controller continuously supervises e-commerce sites and fixes the best configuration to achieve the quality objectives. Corradini et al. (2004) proposes a quality model for biomedical service discovery using a MAS approach and in particular matchmaker functionalities. This is an agent contacted by other agents which want to obtain the best service for specific task. In order to ensure the best quality service to the client, the matchmaker communicates with the QoS certification authority that provides a quality level to each registered service.

QUALITY ASSESSING METHODOLOGY

We propose a methodology suitable for quality assessment of digital services. Our methodology (Figure 1) takes into account e-government quality features and relies on the following activities: (1) development of a quality vocabulary, (2) formalization of the measurements, and (iii)

Figure 1. E-government quality assessing methodology

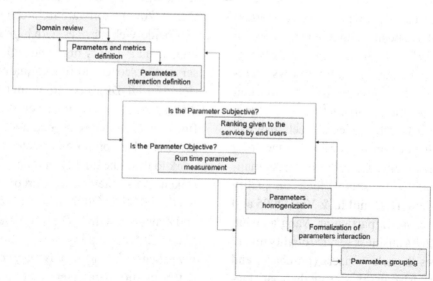

definition of a quality aggregation function. We can also cycle through the methodology activities to propose the more accurate solution for quality assessment.

The first phase—quality definition—refers to the identification of parameters and related metrics starting from a review of the e-government domain. This phase defines a comprehensive e-government quality model. We have investigated the domain at different abstraction levels and we have developed a quality vocabulary. We consider parameters as usability, attraction, availability, and execution time (just to cite a few). In particular, we split the parameters into two sets of the same importance: subjective parameters and objective parameters (see, for instance, Shewhart, 1980) that describe quality in term of subjective and objective parameters in the manufacturing domain. The former is conditioned by individuals experience or knowledge and by personal mental characteristics or states, whereas the latter is individual independent. Related to metrics, we define a unit of measure that is in line with a specific procedure for quality measurement. In this phase, we also find parameters dependences to measure dynamic relationships among them and overall quality.

The second phase—quality measurement—refers to the formalization of the measurements. We have introduced a model that allows a suitable abstraction level of the problem description and a formal background of the applicative solutions so to avoid possible structural mistakes and inaccuracies. The model is scalable with respect to the considered set of parameters. Starting from the parameters taxonomy previously detected and the classification in subjective and objective parameters, we investigated on a proper measurement model. In particular, subjective parameters are measured using ranking given by the end users to a specific service. A rank is based on the user profiles and the user preferences and is collected starting from a sample of population (Devore, 1995). The target of population and the number

of people to interview are critical aspects. If you do not interview the right kinds of people, you might not meet your goals. We define a sample group composed of 30 people aged 25–45. At the same time, objective parameters are measured performing an automatic run-time monitoring.

Finally, the third phase—quality interaction—introduces a mathematical model to define a quality function and assess a quality value starting from the sets of parameters. The model relies on parameters homogenization, interaction, and grouping. In particular, homogenization of the input is useful to reason over different metrics (for instance, time-based measurements need to be aggregated with security-based boolean measurements or some other metrics). The homogenization takes also into account whether a given parameter grows in a proportional or in an inverse proportional way with respect to the overall quality measurement. Interaction between different parameters is also considered by the mathematical model. In such a way we can take into account how parameters influence each others (for instance, how trust parameter influences usability, Bedi & Banati, 2006). Finally, the proposed model groups parameters and manages them with different importance.

QoS CRITERIA OF QUALITY MODEL

In this section we present the parameters of our quality model able to assess the quality of services. They can be classified in a taxonomy of four subcategories (Table 1): (1) *e-government parameters* that take into account how digital services of public administrations are perceived by the final users, (2) *presentation parameters* that analyze front-office services with respect to the final users needs, (3) *behavioral parameters* that describe the implementation of back-end services, and (4) *infrastructural parameters* related to the basic infrastructures enabling digital services.

At this stage of presentation we do not introduce the further classification related to subjective and objective parameters because we give them the same importance.

Service Related Aspects

As previously mentioned service parameters are split in two parts: (1) e-government and (2) presentation.

In the e-government group we introduce the following items. *Popularity* considers the amount of population interested to the service as well as the utilization frequency with respect to time and the number of interactions between government and users. *Usability* considers easiness of learning the service and easiness to benefit of the service information. Moreover, we introduce *attraction* and *multicanality* to detect e-government maturity. Attraction measures the users' incentive to use online services rather than traditional ones (offered by public administrations through off-line channels), while multicanality points out service distribution solutions (Web, mobile computing, etc.). We also consider *internationalization* that refers to the languages used for service description and distribution and *reputation* that represents the service trustworthiness. We introduce *originality* and *contents* that are related to service contents quality. Originality focuses on the service innovation level, while contents indicate public administrations capabilities to provide useful and proper information. *Legality* represents laws and norms that regulate the provision and the service user fruition. A further significant parameter is *domain security* that measures the process and information control level. *Trust* represents the level of confidence among stakeholders in the services execution. This parameter involves citizens, enterprises, public administration employee, software agents, and organization focusing the attention on proper skills and tasks. At the same time a digital service underlines privacy and communication security levels. A proper service distribution allows a certain level of trust and promotes the service utilization. Moreover, *promoting e-democracy* represents a useful parameter to evaluate the impact of a service on the society. This supplies a quantitative value to show how a service can promote digital citizenship. Namely, the set of practices of ICT used by citizens to take part to political choices at any level. The presence of forums, FAQs, mailing lists, and so forth, related to the service has a good impact on the value of this parameter. Finally, we consider the *completeness* of a service, representing the e-Europe levels. It is evaluated starting from different way to interact with the services. An high level corresponds to a complete online service presence to perform proper transactions.

About front-end related aspects, we take into account *cost, accessibility,* and *adaptability.* The cost parameter measures the mean amount of money involved in a complete service transaction, capturing the economic condition of the service use. It summarizes every cost related to the service provision such as execution price and pricing model. Accessibility measures the users' easiness to detect and to use the needed service capabilities. It is particularly relevant related to disadvantaged people. Finally, adaptability evaluates the service capacity to change (or be changed) and make itself suitable for a new context.

Implementation Related Aspects

As well as service parameters, the implementation parameters are split in two parts: (3) behavioral and (4) infrastructural.

Table 1. QoS categorization for digital e-government service parameters

Service	e-Government
	Presentation (front-end)
Implementation	Behavioral (back-end)
	Infrastructural

In the first group, we introduce *interoperability* levels achieved by the services. It represents the amount of cooperative work between consumer applications, software agents, and services in different development environments that implement and deploy procedures. From this perspective, the use of standards affects service interoperability. It is measured by *supported standard/regulatory*. Moreover, *applicative security* represents the security level of Web services introducing authentication and authorization policies and procedures. *Integrity*, about data and transactions, is another important element. It measures service ability to prevent unauthorized access to—or modification of—computer programs or data. It remarks on the ACID properties: atomicity, consistency, isolation, and durability (Gray, 1981). At the same time, *robustness/flexibility* measures the service capabilities to work correctly even when invalid, incomplete or conflicting inputs occur. It is affected by service stability in terms of its interface and/or implementation.

About infrastructure parameters, we analyze the following items. *Availability* represents how the service is available when a client attempts to use it. *Performance* represents how fast a service request can be completed. It measures the speed in completing tasks using service response time, latency, and execution time. *Scalability* refers to the capability of increasing the service capacity in terms of operations or transactions processed in a fix time. Moreover, *scheduling* refers to the quality level of the service assigning resources. *Throughput* represents transfer rate for information in a given time interval. It is measured using Successful Execution Request and Successful Execution Rate. Finally, *reliability* represents the ability of a service to perform its required functions under stated conditions for a specified period of time.

QUALITY MEASUREMENT

In this section we present measurement algorithms and we focus on a representative subset of parameters. The parameters are chosen according to the classification in the previous section.

Terminology and Algorithms

The measurement model refers to the following elements.

- Σ is the set of digital e-government services that we would like to monitor, where S, R, V range over Σ.
- Π is the set of parameters in our quality model, where par_1, par_2, par_3 range over Π.

Over parameters and services we need a couple of predicates. Assume $par \in \Pi$ and $S \in \Sigma$. Predicate $qt(par, S)$ indicates whether parameter par can be measured for service S (or, in other words, par is relevant for service S). As an example consider security parameters are introduced when sensible data are involved in a service behavior. Predicate $PAR(par)$ indicates whether parameter par can be measured for all services in Σ ($PAR(par) = true$ if $qt(par, S) = true \quad \forall S \in \Sigma$). For instance, usability parameter is related to all the services in e-government domain.

- T is the set of time instances, where t_1, t_2, t_3 range over T. Of course, we assume an ordering among time instances in a discrete time domain. Ω denotes the set of time intervals. They take the form (t_1, t_2), where $t_1, t_2 \in T$ (and $t_1 \le t_2$). Time is needed in a quality assessment framework due to the dynamic environment.
- Λ is the set of service locations, where loc_1, loc_2, loc_3 range over Λ. A spatial environment for quality measurements allows an overview of the services context (Lee & Helal, 2003).

35

Assume $S \in \Sigma$, $t \in T$, and $loc \in \Lambda$. We can measure the parameters in a fixed time instance and in a spatial location according to the following algorithm. Parameters measurement represents the input of the mathematical model described in detail in the "QoS Assessment Model" section.

```
MeasureAlgorithm (S, t, loc) {
QoS = list of array
Q = array
for all par if qt(par, S)
Q.addElement = measure (par, S, t, loc)
end for
QoS.addElement = Q
}
```

Array Q stores the measurements of the parameters related to a service. The list of array QoS stores the measurement of the parameters related to the service S and all the digital government services measured in different time by the algorithm. Starting from the measures, we define upper bound using the following algorithm.

```
UpperBoundAlgorithm (par, QoS) {
Ub(par) = 0
for all QoS.element
if (QoS.Q (par) > Ub(par)) then
   Ub(par) = QoS.Q (par)
end for
return Ub
}
```

Finally, the parameters trend is represented by *Tr(par)*. It assumes value true or false depending on the behavior related to the overall quality value: proportional parameter in the former case, inverse proportional parameter in the latter one. In other words:

• the parameter trend is positive (true) if whenever the overall quality at t_1 is bigger than the

overall quality at t_2 then the value of *par* in t_1 is bigger than the value of *par* in t_2, and

• the parameter trend is negative (false) if whenever the overall quality at t_1 is smaller than the overall quality at t_2 then the value of *par* in t_1 is bigger than the value of *par* in t_2.

Of course, the above considerations on measurements and trends at time instants apply also at time interval.

Measured Parameters

This section proposes the measurement on a subset of parameters related to the "measure" procedure in the "measure" algorithm. The service response time (*rt*) (6.2.1) measures the delay (at client site) between sending a request and receiving response.

$$rt = t_{clientReceive} - t_{clientSend} \qquad (6.2.1)$$

The service execution time (*et*) (6.2.2) measures the time needed to process service instructions. In particular, it measures the delay between request reception and response forwarding by the service. The measure is executed at service site.

$$et = t_{serviceSend} - t_{serviceReceive} \qquad (6.2.2)$$

The service latency (*lat*) (6.2.3) measures the delay between sending a request and receiving a result at client site, without taking into consideration the execution time of the service.

$$lat = rt - et \qquad (6.2.3)$$

The service reliability (*rel*) (6.2.4) measures ability to perform required functionalities under stated conditions for a fixed period of time. In (6.2.4), $F(S)$ indicates the number of executions that the service has not been successfully completed within the interval t_1, t_2 interval.

$$rel = \frac{F(S)}{t_2 - t_1} \qquad (6.2.4)$$

The service successful execution request (*sereq*) (6.2.5) is the number of service requests completed successfully in a given time interval. In (6.2.5), $N_C(S)$ indicates the number of times that the service has been successfully completed within the interval t_1, t_2.

$$sereq = \frac{N_C(S)}{t_2 - t_1} \qquad (6.2.5)$$

The service successful execution rate (*serat*) (6.2.6) is the rate of service requests successfully completed in a given time interval related to the executed requests. It is related to the successful execution request. In (6.2.6), $N_C(S)$ indicates the number of service executions that has been successfully completed in the interval t_1, t_2 while $N_{Cmax}(S)$ indicates the maximum number of executions that the service is able to complete with success within the same time interval. $N_{Cmax}(S)$ can be computed starting from $N_C(S)$ and $F(S)$.

$$serat = \frac{N_C(S)}{N_{C\max}(S)} \qquad (6.2.6)$$

The service availability (*ava*) (6.2.7) represents capability to reply immediately to the users requests. In (6.2.7), $T_A(S)$ is the total amount of time where the service is available during the interval t_1, t_2 and it is computed through service site measures. If $T_A(S) = t_2 - t_1$, then we have the maximal availability.

$$ava = \frac{T_A(S)*100}{t_2 - t_1} \qquad (6.2.7)$$

The service attraction (*att*) (6.2.8) represents the users incentive to use online services rather than traditional ones. Different end users may have different opinions on the same services. The value of the attraction is computed using the (6.2.8) formula and it is defined as the average ranking given to the service by end users. In (6.2.8), $R_i(S)$ is the *i*-th end-user ranking on the service attraction and *n* is the number of time that the service has been graded in t_1, t_2 time interval.

$$att = \frac{\sum_{i=1}^{n} R_i(S)}{n} \qquad (6.2.8)$$

Finally, the service reputation (*rep*) (6.2.9) represents trustworthiness of the service. It is measured using an approach similar to that one used in attraction assessment. In (6.2.9), $G_i(S)$ is the *i*-th end-user ranking on service reputation and *n* is the number of time that the service has been graded in t_1, t_2 time interval.

$$rep = \frac{\sum_{i=1}^{n} G_i(S)}{n} \qquad (6.2.9)$$

Given the above consideration, quality parameters can be aggregate using the mathematical model explained in "QoS Assessment Model" section. In this way we can associate to a specific service a single quality value starting from quality measurements on a set of heterogeneous parameters.

QoS ASSESSMENT MODEL

In this section we introduce our mathematical model for QoS quantification of e-government digital services. The model provides an assessment, after three normalization phases, of the quality level for a digital service. Starting from a set of quality parameters, the model estimates a value in the [0...100] range. This model is inspired by Liu, Ngu, and Zeng (2004), but we introduce further elements like data homogenization and parameters interaction. In detail, (i) homogenization of the input is useful to reason over different e-government parameters metrics and behavior. The homogenization takes into account whether a given parameter grows in a proportional or inverse proportional way with respect to the overall quality measurement. For example, infrastructure related criteria measured against time needs to be aggregated with security parameters measured with boolean values, or some other metrics, and if the quality of infrastructure grows up, then the quality of security also grows up. At the same time, we introduce (ii) interaction among parameters to measure dynamic relationships. In such a way we can take into account how parameters influence each other (for instance, usability parameter influence on service trust).

Input of the Model

Let S be a service. The mathematical model uses the following input parameters.

- $Q = (q_1, q_2, ..., q_n)$ is an array of n natural numbers representing the measured value of parameters (*par*) related to the service S. Each q_i, for $1 \leq i \leq n$, is collected during measurement process and represents a specific view of the service.

- $Z = (z_1, z_2, ..., z_n)$ is an array of n boolean values used in the normalization phase. It is defined starting from *Tr(par)*. Each z_i, for $1 \leq i \leq n$, assumes a value as in (7.1.1).

-

$$z_i = \begin{cases} 1 & \text{if the } q_i \text{ parameter in } Q \text{ grows in proportional way with respect to the overall quality value;} \\ 0 & \text{if the } q_i \text{ parameter in } Q \text{ grows in inverse proportional way respect to the overall quality value.} \end{cases}$$

(7.1.1)

- $C = (c_1, c_2, ..., c_n)$ is an array of n not zero natural numbers used during the normalization process. It is defined starting from *Ub(par)*. Each c_i $1 \leq i \leq n$ represents the upper bound of the q_i parameter in Q vector. The C elements are bound to parameter analysis and they depend on the specific

Figure 2. QoS assessment model phases

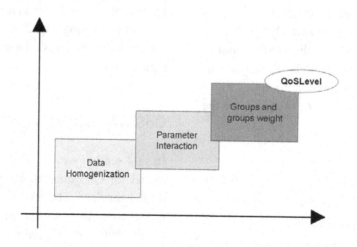

metrics used to express them and on the methodology for the measurements.

- MI is a matrix of $[0...1]$ values composed of n rows and n columns. It shows the interaction level between parameters in Q. Each $m_{i,j}$, for $1 \leq i, j \leq n$, assumes a value as it follows:

$$m_{i,j} = \begin{cases}]0...1] & \text{if } q_i \text{ and } q_j \text{ interact} \\ 0 & \text{if } q_i \text{ and } q_j \text{ not interact} \end{cases}$$

(7.1.2)

In particular, in the MI diagonal all the values are 0 to represent a not relevant interaction of a parameter with itself. For instance, cost parameter cannot interact with itself in the same spatial-temporal location.

- D is a matrix of boolean composed of n rows (representing the parameters) and l columns (that refers to the number of quality groups). D is used to group the parameters with similar features. Each parameter can take part to one and only one group. The matrix complies with the followed constraint.

$$\forall i \; 1 \leq i \leq n \; \sum_{j=0}^{l} d_{i,j} = 1 \qquad (7.1.3)$$

In particular, we indicate groups cardinality using h_i.

- $W = (w_1, w_2, ..., w_l)$ is an array of l natural numbers with each w_i $1 \leq i \leq l$ that indicate the weight of the specific group i. Moreover, the array complies with the following constraint

$$\sum_{i=1}^{l} w_i = 100.$$

The weights can be also associated to parameter if and only if the groups are composed of only one of them.

Figure 2 shows the phases to evaluate the overall service quality.

Phases of the Model

Phase 1: Data Homogenization. As a first step, let Q, Z and C be the input. We introduce a normalization function f_1. It takes triples of the form (q_i, z_i, c_i), where q_i, z_i, c_i are the i-th elements of the arrays Q, Z, and C respectively, and returns a value in the range $[0...100]$. We obtain a new array Q' of elements $q_i' = f_1(q_i, z_i, c_i)$. The formal definition of function f_1 is proposed in (7.2.1).

$$f_1(q_i, z_i, c_i) = z_i \left(\frac{q_i * 100}{c_i} \right) + (1 - z_i) * \left(100 - \frac{q_i * 100}{c_i} \right)$$

(7.2.1)

Phase 2: Parameters Interaction. In the second phase we consider the interaction factors of the quality parameters. We obtain, using (7.2.2), the interaction factor φ_k $\forall k$ such that $1 \leq k \leq n$.

$$\varphi_k = \frac{\sum_{j=1}^{n} m_{j,k}}{n-1} \qquad (7.2.2)$$

The proposed interaction factor does not take into consideration recursive impact on parameters; as matter of fact MI is a matrix with null diagonal elements. Moreover, each element q' must be normalized to obtain a new arrays Q'' (its elements will be denoted by $q_1'', q_2'', q_3'', ...$) using function f_2 in (7.2.3). It takes pairs of the form (φ_i, q_i') where φ_i and q_i' are the i-th interaction factor and element of the array Q' respectively.

$$f_2(\varphi_i, q_i') = \varphi_i q_i' \qquad (7.2.3)$$

Phase 3: Grouping and Group Weight. At this point we introduce the possibility to group the parameters and manage them as groups with different importance (exploiting to this purpose the matrix D and array W). In the first step of this phase we use matrix D and we obtain a new array G (its element will be denoted by $g_1, g_2, g_3, \ldots$ range over G) of QoS values for each group with $G = Q''D$.

Finally, it is possible to evaluate an overall quality value for a service considering the *QoS-Level* function showed in (7.2.4). It takes triples of the form (g_i, h_i, w_i) where g_i and w_i are the *i*-th elements of the arrays G and W respectively and h_i is the cardinality of *i*-th group. It gives a value in the range $[0\ldots100]$.

$$QoSLevel(g_i, h_i, w_i) = \frac{\sum_{i=1}^{l} \frac{g_i}{h_i} * w_i}{\sum_{i=1}^{l} w_i} \quad (7.2.4)$$

EXPERIMENTATION

In order to examine the effectiveness of our quality approach we carried out a set of simulations to study step-by-step the impact factor of the digital e-government services parameters on quality.

TecUt is an ASP.NET Web application running on IIS6 (Windows Server 2003 Environ-

ment). The server is a Pentium IV 3.0GHz with 1Gb of RAM located inside the Marche Region Demilitarized Zone.

In this section we present the most important experimental results related to the

1. behavior of some service parameters under growing amount of stress;
2. dependence among parameters;
3 behavior of the overall quality of service value starting from a subset of parameters, in this case we have verified also parameters and interaction variation;
4. global trend of the quality function.

The specific service under experimentation in the TecUt portal is the "Residence Certificate" request. It is used to certify personal information with respect legal residence/domicile.

Parameters Behavior

We perform parameters measurement to under stress service. The outputs of measurement are represented in the following graphs. We immediately observe that the successful execution request behavior is proportional to the number of service invocations that are done simultaneously. Parameter behavior depends on the lack of time

Figure 3. Service successful execution request

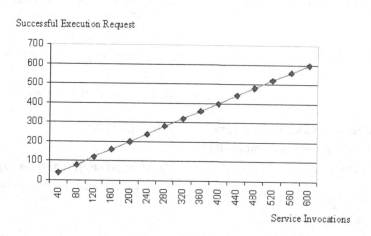

Figure 4. Service execution time distribution

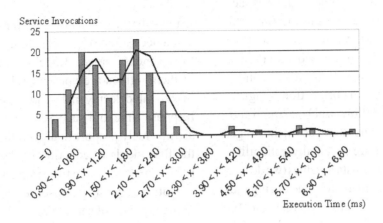

Figure 5. Service latency distribution

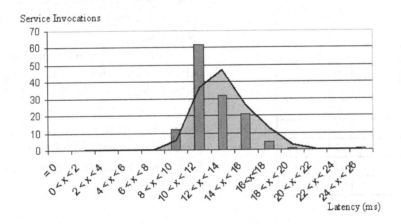

Figure 6. Service response time distribution

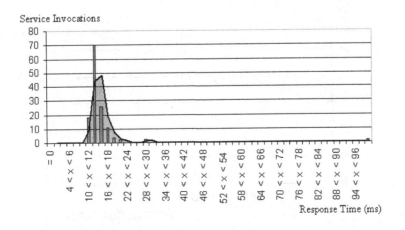

constraints (meant as upper bound on the service execution) on the execution time of the service. In this case all the service requests are satisfied (Figure 3). We also observe service execution time, in the range 0.3–3 milliseconds (Figure 4) and latency in the range 10–16 milliseconds. Their distribution follows a normal trend (Figure 5). Also response time follows a normal trend and shows a stable behavior, its values are in the range 6–24 milliseconds (Figure 6). Finally, reliability and availability assume constant values (we do not observe fault and types mismatch) and during the measurements service was always achievable. In general, a good quality level and stable behavior characterize the service, thanks to a proper service context and a good connectivity level.

Parameters Dependence

In this subsection we observe different kinds of dependences among objective parameters presented in the measurement model. We mention some of them; others are not very relevant or will be investigated deeply in the future. We observe that response time and successful execution request are inversely proportional, and the increasing of the first yields a reduction of the second. Also latency and execution time impact the successful execution request; we observe some waving due to the growing of service requests. The growing of service requests and the complexity of service behavior play a fundamental role. Moreover, response time is related to latency and execution time in a proportional way. Their decreasing reduces the response time of the services, and vice-versa.

Finally, we also individualize dependences between successful execution request and reliability-availability. Service faults (or mismatch) bring out a successful execution request reduction. Moreover, reliability and availability grow in inverse proportional and proportional way related to successful execution request respectively.

Table 2. Quality variation

Interaction value	QoS
1	56,33
0,88	49,57
0,84	47,60
0,24	13,52
0,1	5,63
0,00001	0

Figure 7. Quality variation

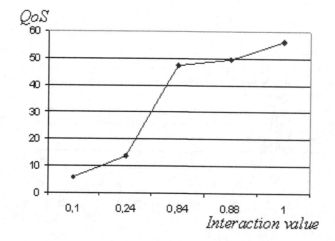

Figure 8. Quality Distribution—Low interaction

Figure 8. Quality Distribution—Low interaction

Figure 9. Quality Distribution—High interaction

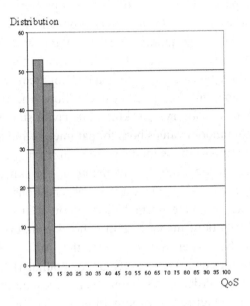

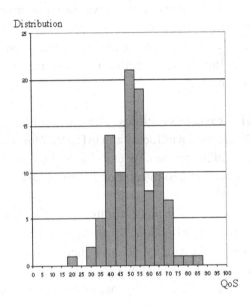

Experimental Result Related to a Specific Service

In this section we introduce our quality approach to TecUt "Residence Certificate" and we analyze two quality parameters: availability and response time.

- $Q = (350, 120)$ represents parameters values in particular availability (measured in minutes) and response time (measured in second).
- $Z = (1, 0)$ introduces trend relations between overall quality and individual parameter. We underline that quality grows in a proportional way respective to availability value and in an inversely proportional way respective to response time value.
- $C = (1440, 600)$ proposes the upper bound of the two parameters; in particular a service can be available at most for 1440 minutes and the delay allow to receive a valid response from the service is 600 seconds.

- MI shows a positive and symmetric interaction between the considered parameters.

$$MI = \begin{pmatrix} 0 & 0,84 \\ 0,84 & 0 \end{pmatrix}$$

- D represents the groups; in our case it is meaningless; and each parameter represents a group.
- $W = (40, 60)$ shows the weight given by the users to availability and response time.

Starting from this set of input, the output value of *QoSLevel* is 47,60. We observed parameters and interaction variations.

First case, availability. We observe a variation of availability values from 350 to 1460 minutes. Availability grows in a proportional way respect to the value of *QoSLevel* and we expect an increase of the quality value. Indeed, the quality rises from a value of 47,60 to 70,13.

Second case, response time. We observe a variation of response time values from 120 to 300 seconds. Response time grows in an inversely proportional way respective to the value of *QoSLevel* and we suppose a decrease of the quality value. Indeed, the overall quality changes from 47,60 to 32,39.

Third case, interactions. The experimental results are shown in Table 2 and in Figure 7 for some values of interaction. We can observe that quality is proportional to interaction function value.

Moreover, the model limits interaction function to nonzero values. It represents the lower bound of the quality. Overall quality is next to zero when the interaction function is next to zero. This means that quality parameters choice on non-interactive parameters is not very good to analyze the overall quality of the service. More generally, in e-government domain we underline the importance of interaction to reach the full users' satisfaction.

General Considerations

We would also like to observe the quality behavior by introducing random values as inputs. The following cases are proposed:

(a) We analyze the behavior of quality function observing the variation of quality parameters by fixing all the other model entities.
(b) We analyze the behavior of frequency distribution of the quality values starting from random values both for parameters and for other inputs of the model.
(c) We analyze the quality frequency distributions underlying the role of parameters interactions (we observe bound behaviors).

After several experiments we were able to assess the QoS trend. Experiments in item (a) above show a linear trend of QoS value. It increases or

decreases steadily with respect of the parameters trend. We take into account the properties of the parameters; some of them are proportional whereas others are inversely proportional with respect to the quality value (i.e., the quality increases if the execution time decreases and/or the usability increases). The behavior of frequency distribution of the quality values follows a normal trend. We observe this kind of behavior starting from random values both for parameters and for other inputs of the model in item (b). Taking into account the central limit theorem, the sum of large and independent quality observations has an approximate normal distribution (Gaussian Distribution) under certain general conditions. Finally, in item (c) it is clear that parameters interactions affect quality upper bound. If the interaction decreases the quality level assume low values (Figure 8), while with height interaction also the QoS values increase (Figure 9). Finally, we observe with low interactions a close quality frequency distribution, while it is stretched to a normal trend with high interactions. The increase of parameters interaction support the goodness of our approach; as matter of fact, the e-government process is influenced by different dependent factors.

CONCLUSION

We have presented a methodology to assess the maturity of digital government services in public administrations. In our opinion, quality assessment of services, together with a shared service management system as TecUt, represents the main element to monitoring services capabilities and implement optimal resources allocation saving time and costs.

Nonfunctional services aspects awareness and specific measurement and assessment models allow complete and fine services governance. Our final aim is to improve people trust and access to e-government services through a dynamic ICT infrastructure that responds quickly to changing needs.

Quality approaches, which are discussed in detail in the "Background" section, present a global view of the problem. Most of them do not introduce both domain and technology related features. These aspects are usually discussed separately. Some works focus also on the role of users and introduce subjectivity users experiences in service utilization but do not merge them with objective ones. Vice versa works in that the objective quality aspects do not take into account users roles. Moreover, they usually define metrics but only a few of them introduce careful measurement on the detected parameters. The closest approach to this work is Sukasame (2004) about e-government in Thai. Unfortunately, it does not introduce neither a complete list of quality parameters nor specific and careful measurement activities. It focuses only on subjective parameters and does not introduce a complete discussion on the assessment of quality of digital services. As previously mentioned, this work presents the first attempt to introduce a complete assessment methodology for quality of e-government digital services focusing both on the role of users and ICTs. In such a way, we combine different aspects in a formal and homogeneous way.

Our methodology, together with the formal treatment, provides several benefits. First of all it allows a certain level of confidence on the service capabilities and enhances reliability and efficiency of inspection procedures. We can analyze (i) the behavior of parameters under growing amounts of stress, (ii) the dependence among parameters related to government domain, and (iii) the behavior of the overall quality of service. We can also control parameters value, interactions, upper bound, and the trend of overall quality.

Starting from the set of experimentation carried out on the TecUt portal, we observe a good quality level of the services. In practice, we have effectively noticed a stable behavior. The main reasons are related to services location and connectivity level. The quality value indicates the maturity of the services and it is also useful to analyze offered solutions (on the hand of service providers). Public administrations can plan the development of new services and the adaptation of existing ones by using the results of the application of this kind of quality assessment. However, the most important result, after the application of quality assessment, is the utilization improvement of the TecUt services (62%). In this way TecUt trustworthiness is improved.

We plan to extend this work taking into consideration dynamic aspects related to quality of services. We are going to introduce more e-government parameters to extend the goodness of the models. In particular, we are going to refer also to those parameters that cannot be measured in an objective way but that rely on data collected from the evaluations given by end users. At the same time, we must study complexity reduction algorithms for the proposed mathematical model. This kind of algorithm will be able to maintain the models' expressivity.

REFERENCES

Baldrige National Quality Program (2006). *Criteria for performance excellence*. Retrieved June 8, 2008, from http://www.quality.nist.gov/

Bedi, P., & Banati, H. (2006). Assessing user trust to improve Web usability. *Journal of Computer Science, 2*(3), 283–287.

CAF Resource Center (2006). *Common assessment framework*. Retrieved June 8, 2008, from http://www.eipa.nl/CAF/CAFmenu.htm

Cardoso, J., Sheth, A., & Miller, J. (2002, April). Workflow quality of service. In *Proceedings of the IFIP Tc5/Wg5.12 International Conference on Enterprise Integration and Modeling Technique: Enterprise Inter- and Intra-Organizational Integration: Building International Consensus*, Valencia, Spain (pp. 303–311).

Commission of the European Communities (2003). *The role of e-government for Europe's future* (Communication from the commission to the council, the European parliament, the European economic and social committee, and the committee of the regions). Brussels.

Corradini, F., Ercoli, C., Merelli, E., & Re, B. (2004, November). An agent-based matchmaker. In *Proceedings of WOA04 Sistemi Complessi e Agenti Razionali*, Torino, Italy (pp. 150–156).

Corradini, F., Forastieri, L., Polzonetti, A., Riganelli, O., & Sergiacomi, A. (2005, February). Shared Services Center for E-Government Policy. In *Proceedings of the 1st International Conference on Interoperability of eGovernment Services (eGov-Interop'05)*, Geneva, France (pp. 140–151).

Corradini, F., Sabucedo, L.A., Polzonetti, A., Rifón, L.A., & Re, B. (2007, September). A case study of semantic solutions for citizen-centered Web portals in eGovernment: The TecUt Portal. In *Proceedings of the 6th International EGOV Conference 2007, DEXA*, Regensburg, Germany (pp. 204–215, LNCS).

De Feo, J.A., & Barnard, W.W. (2005). *JURAN Institute's Six Sigma breakthrough and beyond: Quality performance breakthrough methods*. Tata McGraw-Hill Publishing Company Limited.

Devore, J.L. (1995). *Probability and statistics for engineering and the sciences*. Duxbury Press.

Elmagarmid, A.K., & McIver, W.J. (2001). Guest editors' introduction: The ongoing march toward digital government. *IEEE Computer, 34*(2), 32–38.

Farkas, P., & Charaf, H. (2003). Web services planning concepts. *Journal of WSCG, 11*(1).

Garcia, A.C., Maciel, C., & Pinto, F.B. (2005, August). A quality inspection method to evaluate e-government sites. In *Proceedings of the 4th International EGOV Conference 2005, DEXA*,

Copenhagen, Denmark (pp. 198–209, LNCS).

Gray, J. (1981). The transaction concept: Virtues and limitations. In *Proceedings of the 7th International Conference on Very Large Data Bases*, Cannes, France (pp. 144–154).

ISO (1994). *ISO 8402: Quality management and quality assurance* (Vocabulary, 2nd ed.). Geneva: Author.

Jansen, A., & Olnes, S. (2004, June). Quality assessment and benchmarking of Norwegian public Web sites. In *Proceedings of the 4th European Conference on E-government*, Dublin.

Kaplan, R.S., & Norton, D.P. (1992). *The balanced scorecard: Measures that drive performance*. Harvard Business Review.

Lee, C., & Helal, S. (2003). Context attributes: An approach to enable context-awareness for service discovery. In *Proceedings of the 2003 Symposium on Applications and the Internet, SAINT* (p. 23). IEEE Computer Society.

Lin, S., & Wu, C. S. (2002, January). Exploring the impact of online service quality on portal site usage. In *Proceedings of the 35th Annual Hawaii International Conference on System Sciences (HICSS'02)*, Maui, Hawaii (pp. 2654–2661).

Liu, Y., Ngu, A.H., & Zeng, L.Z. (2004, May). QoS computation and policing in dynamic Web service selection. In *Proceedings of the 13th International World Wide Web Conference on Alternate Track Papers and Posters*, New York (pp. 66–73).

Maximilien, E.M., & Singh, M.P. (2004). A framework and ontology for dynamic Web services selection. *IEEE Computer Society, 8*(5), 84–92.

Menascé, D.A. (2003). Automatic QoS control. *IEEE Computer Society, 7*(1), 92–95.

Menascé, D.A. (2004a). Composing Web services: A QoS view. *IEEE Computer Society, 4*(6), 88–90.

Menascé, D.A. (2004b). Response-time analysis of composite Web services. *IEEE Internet Computing, 8*(1), 90–92.

Nahrstedt, K., Xu, D., Wichadakul, D., & Li, B. (2001). QoS-aware middleware for ubiquitous and heterogeneous environments. *Communications Magazine, IEEE, 39*(11), 140–148.

Papadomichelaki, X., Magoutas, B., Halaris, C., Apostolou, D., & Mentzas, G. (2006). A review of quality dimensions in e-government services. In *Proceedings of the 5th International EGOV Conference 2006, DEXA*, Krakow, Poland (pp. 128–138).

Parasuraman, A., Zeithaml, V.A., & Berry, L. (1998). SERVQUAL: A multiple-item scale for measuring consumer perceptions of service quality. *Journal of Retailing, 64*(1), 12–40.

Ran, S. (2003). A model for Web services discovery with QoS. *SIGecom Exchange, 4*(1), 1–10.

Rust, R.T., & Lemon, K.L. (2001). E-service and the consumer. *International Journal of Electronic Commerce, 5*(3), 85–101.

Santos, J. (2003). E-service quality: A model of virtual service quality dimensions. *Managing Service Quality, 13*(3), 233–246.

Seth, N., Deshmukh, S.G., & Vrat, P. (2005). Service quality models: A review. *International Journal of Quality & Reliability Management, 22*(9), 913–949.

Shewhart, W. (1980). *Economic control of quality of manufactured product.* American Society for Quality.

Sukasame, N. (2004). The development of e-service in Thai government. *BU Academic Review, 3*(1), 17–24.

Tiwana, A., & Ramesh, B. (2001, January 3–6). e-services: Problems, opportunities, and digital platforms. In *Proceedings of the 34th Annual Hawaii International Conference on System Sciences (HICSS-34)*, Maui, Hawaii (pp. 3018). IEEE Computer Society.

Tsetsekas, C., Manitias, S., Funfstuck, F., Thoma, A., & Karadimas, Y. (2001). A QoS middleware between users, applications and the network. In *Proceedings of the 8th International Conference on Advances in Communications and Control*, Crete, Greece.

Webb, H.W., & Webb, L.A. (2004). SiteQual: An integrated measure of Web site quality. *Journal of Enterprise Information Management, 17*(6), 430–440.

Yang, Z., Cai, S., Zhou, Z., & Zhou, N. (2005). Development and validation of an instrument to measure user perceived service quality of information presenting Web portals. *Information Management, 42*(4), 575–589.

Yang, Z., & Jun, M. (2002). Consumer perception of e-service quality: From Internet purchaser and non-purchaser perspectives. *Journal of Business Strategies, 19*(1), 19–41.

Zeng, L., Benatallah, B., Dumas, M., Kalagnanam, J., & Sheng, Q.Z. (2003, May). Quality driven Web services composition. In *Proceedings of the 12th International Conference on World Wide Web*, Budapest, Hungary (pp. 411–421). ACM Press.

Chapter IV
Self–Service Systems:
Quality Dimensions and Users' Profiles

Călin Gurău
GSCM – Montpellier Business School, France

ABSTRACT

The evolution of information technology applications has changed the landscape of the service industry, offering the possibility of customer empowerment through self-service applications. Considering the main three streams of research already applied in the study of self-services, this chapter investigates customers' perceptions about eight dimensions that characterise the quality of the self-service experience. On the other hand, the study attempts to analyse the influence of the self-service users' profile (gender, Internet usage experience, and online self-service usage experience), and to provide specific insights about the needs and wants of various categories of customers.

INTRODUCTION

In the last 15 years, the evolution of information technology applications has changed the landscape of the service industry. The implementation of self-service technology has created new service channels and procedures. Nowadays, clients can conduct bank transactions through automated teller machines (ATM) or on the Internet (online banking), make reservations or purchase tickets through online kiosks, check-in automated hotels, or use self-scanning systems in retail stores (Bobbitt & Dabholkar, 2001). The integration of self-service technology with Internet applications has increased even more the convenience of information-rich services; the customers can now access the service from their homes or offices, 24 hours a day, without geographical limitations.

On the other hand, the introduction of effective **self-service systems** allows companies to automate the repetitive elements of services, concentrating their resources and personnel on more personalised aspects of the company–customer relationship, and thus providing more added-value to their clients. However, the implementation of this strategy requires more than the introduction of self-service applications. These **self-service systems** need to be tied-in with employee-related policies and procedures. These internal procedures must insure that the customer can rely on virtual assistance when using a self-service interface and that can feel comfortable in a range of transactions without human intervention (Kotler, Armstrong, Saunders, & Wong, 2002).

The production and consumption of services have specific characteristics that permit **customer empowerment** but, on the other hand, create challenges related with customer satisfaction and with customer's perception regarding service quality. By comparison with products, the services are (Zeithaml, Bitner, & Gremler, 2002a):

1. **Intangible:** Services cannot be seen, tasted, felt, heard, or smelled. This makes evaluating service quality very difficult and potential consumers look for visible indicators of quality.

2. **Inseparable:** Services are produced and consumed at the same time and cannot be separated from their providers. Provider and client must interact for the service to occur and therefore both parties become part of the service provided.

3. **Variable:** As consumer and producer are both part of the service, the quality of services may vary greatly depending on who provides them and when, where, and how they are provided. Marketers must therefore take steps towards achieving quality control amongst their service providers.

4. **Perishable:** Services must be consumed as they are provided and cannot be stored for later use. This becomes a problem if demand fluctuates and service opportunities are missed. Marketers must develop strategies to either keep demand constant or provide the equivalent supply of service to match the fluctuating demand.

5. **No transfer of ownership:** Services cannot be owned by the user. Marketers therefore should develop strategies to enable consumers to recall the quality of service they received.

The introduction of online self-services has changed the way in which companies relate to their customers. This new technology eliminates firm's personnel from the service interface, replacing it with software applications that can be accessed through real-time Internet connection. On the other hand, the **self-service system** gives additional responsibilities to the customer, who will initiate, generate, and consume the service interacting directly with software applications. However, this additional responsibility is not necessarily perceived as negative by the involved customers. In fact, many studies have shown that customers, and especially online service users, enjoy having a greater degree of control over the service they require. The self-service systems might permit a better customisation of the online service, resulting in improved satisfaction for the user.

On the other hand, the lack of a direct relationship with an employee might represent a disadvantage for customers that prefer direct human interactions. The dialogue with an employee might add a personal quality to the service provided, and can provide quick and flexible solutions when things do not go as planned. All these factors, together with the propensity of customers to adopt a new technology, can significantly influence the adoption and frequency of use of a specific online self-service.

The purpose of this exploratory study is to identify the quality dimensions that influence customers' perceptions about online self-service systems. On the other hand, considering that these perceptions can vary from one customer to another, the research attempts to identify the sociodemographic characteristics that influence the perception of online self-service quality dimensions and their practical use, creating the basis of a general customer profiling. After a brief but comprehensive presentation of the streams of research that are relevant for the study of self-service systems, the chapter presents the research objectives of this research project, as well as the methodology applied to collect primary and secondary data. These results obtained from data analysis are then presented and discussed in direct relation with the defined research objectives. The chapter ends with a summary of the main findings and with propositions for future research.

ONLINE CUSTOMER SELF-SERVICE: PREVIOUS RESEARCH

Customer empowerment through self-service technology is a new but fertile field of studies. Previous research on this topic can be categorised into three main streams:

a. the **innovation diffusion theory** – although many self-services offered online were previously provided into the physical environment, the application of self-service technology can be considered an innovation;

b. **consumer readiness** to adopt the online self-service technology; and

c. **e-service quality** and customer satisfaction, which studies the self-service dimensions that are considered essential for online service quality.

Considered from an empirical point of view, these research streams complement each other well; the diffusion theory considers customers' perceptions about the characteristics of online self-services before and during the trial phase,

the consumer readiness framework analyses the personal capacities of online users, and, finally, the e-service quality-customer satisfaction theory emphasises customers perceptions during and after the interaction with self-service systems.

The **innovation diffusion theory** was formulated by Rogers (1962) and applied in a large number of projects (Gerrard & Cunningham, 2003). Rogers (1995) defined five main characteristics of innovations that influence their adoption rate by the population:

1. Relative advantage represents the additional benefit offered by the innovation in comparison with the existing offer on the market. The research conducted on the adoption of banking self-services identified as sources of relative advantage economic benefits (Black, Lockett, Wiklofer, & Ennew, 2001; Loudon & Delle Bitta, 1993; Polatoglu, & Ekin, 2001), convenience (Black et al., 2001; Loudon & Delle Bitta, 1993; Polatoglu, & Ekin, 2001), performance (Polatoglu, & Ekin, 2001), and independence, eliminating the need to rely on others (Black et al., 2001).

2. Compatibility is the consistency of the innovation with existing values, past experiences, and needs of the potential adopters. For example, familiarity with the Internet and online applications was identified as an essential factor for customers' willingness to adopt online self-service technologies (Black et al., 2001).

3. Complexity – the level of difficulty of the innovation will influence its speed of adoption. In the case of online self-service technology, this dimension can be related either with the simplicity and/or friendliness of the Web interface or with the user's level of capability (Black et al., 2001; Hewer & Howcroft, 1999; Polatoglu, & Ekin, 2001; Rotchanakitumnuai & Speece, 2003).

4. Trialability is the capacity to interact with the innovation. Trialability is essential to transmit

firsthand information about self-service applications and facilitate consumers' learning about the use of the new technology (Hewer & Howcroft, 1999).

5. Observability is the degree of innovation visibility within the society at large, or in a social/professional group. This dimension is not always applicable to characterise the adoption of online self-services, because in most cases the interaction between the customer and the online applications is not visible to other users (Black et al., 2001; Gerrard & Cunningham, 2003). However, the organisation that attempts to introduce a new self-service on the Internet may increase its observability by actively promoting and demonstrating the use of this service.

Another determinant of customer's readiness to adopt innovations is the perceived level of risk (Holak, 1988; Labay & Kinnear, 1981; Lockett & Littler, 1997; Ostlund, 1974). Many studies have outlined that the online environment is considered more risky than the physical market (Pavlou, Liang, & Xue, 2007). This perception can represent an important deterrent for the adoption of self-services, especially when the online process implies a transaction—buying a flight ticket, or an online transmission of confidential information—online banking operations.

Consumer readiness to embrace the self-service technology is explained in the academic literature by three main variables:

1. **Role clarity:** Since traditionally the services were produced through the interaction between a customer and a specialised employee, the adoption of self-service technology requires customer empowerment and a modified consumer behaviour. Role ambiguity for staff or customers can create important problems for the introduction of new services (Easingwood, 1986), and limits the capacity of consumer to participate in the co-production of services (Larsson & Bowen, 1989). Meuter, Bitner, Ostrom, and Brown (2005) have also investigated the relationship between **role clarity** and self-service system trial.

2. **Motivation:** Intrinsic and extrinsic **motivation** were identified as essential factors for the successful introduction of online self-service technology (Barczak, Ellen, & Pilling, 1997). Some customers welcome a higher degree of empowerment, because they find the participation in the co-production of services intrinsically attractive (Bateson, 1985; Dadholkar, 1996; Rogers, 1995; Schneider & Bowen, 1995). On the other hand, the customers might be motivated by specific extrinsic advantages, such as price discounts, time saving, or convenience (Dadholkar, 1996; Schneider & Bowen, 1995).

3. **Ability:** The online environment in general and the self-service system in particular may require specific personal skills. A complex or unfriendly Web site interface can transmit to the customer the fear that she/he will not have the **ability** to interact with the system, and therefore prevent her/him to engage in a proactive behaviour (Jayanti & Burns, 1998; Meuter et al., 2005).

The theories of **e-service quality** are based on the traditional **SERVQUAL** model (Parasuraman, Berry, & Zeithaml, 1988). This model is based on extensive research conducted by Parasuraman, Zeithaml, and Berry (1985) and Parasuraman et al. (1988) who initially identified ten determinants of service quality: tangibles, reliability, responsiveness, competency, courtesy, communication, credibility, security, access, and understanding the customer. These dimensions were later reduced to five features, using factor analysis: tangibles, reliability, responsiveness, assurance, and empathy.

The specific characteristics of the Internet have required a significant adaptation of these quality dimensions to online services. Zeithaml, Parasuraman, and Malhotra (2001) and Zeithaml et al. (2002b) have identified a series of **e-service quality** dimensions: reliability, responsibility, access, flexibility, ease of navigation, efficiency, assurance/trust, security, price knowledge, site aesthetics, and customisation/personalisation, developing on their basis the e-**SERVQUAL** model. Yang et al. (2003) have investigated the quality of e-retailing services, identifying three additional dimensions: convenience, continuous improvement, and collaboration. Another study of Jun and Cai (2001) in the context of Internet banking services has found six main dimensions of online systems quality: content, accuracy, ease of use, timeliness, aesthetics, and security.

A model, developed by Curran and Meuter (2005), explains how customers decide whether to use a self-service technology. They identified four elements that can be used as predictors of attitudes toward self-service systems: ease of use, usefulness, need of interaction, and risk. The study demonstrates that self-service systems should be useful and easy to handle, but also that these dimensions are not enough to insure customer satisfaction. Analysing **self-service systems** such as ATMs and phone banking, the authors conclude that there is room for improvement in the design and functionality of this service technology.

Bateson (1985) explored the factors that determine a customer to choose a do-it-yourself option (including self-service alternatives), or the traditional service delivery system. The findings indicated that time (consuming time), control (control over the received service), effort (the effort made to access the service), and dependence (depending or not on another person) are the most important elements that influence the decision to use a specific service system. The customers that preferred the self-service option emphasised that time and control represent essential factors for their choice. The importance of personal control was confirmed by Meuter, Ostrom, Roundtree, and Bitner (2000) and Meuter, Ostrom, Bitner, and Roundtree (2003) that demonstrated that many perceived benefits of the self-service technology can be linked with this dimension.

A study conducted by Lee and Allaway (2002) attempted to verify if the manipulation of personal control over a new self-service technology leads to predictable changes in the way consumers perceived the risk associated with this technology. An additional objective was to verify if the specific dimensions of personal control (predictability, controllability, and outcome desirability) contribute equally to variations in perceived risk, perceived value, and adoption intention. The results showed that an increased sense of control over the self-service technology reduces perceived risk, heightens perceived value, and stimulated the intention to adopt and use self-service technology. This study also stated that marketers should evaluate six issues in relation to their self-service system: (a) whether the Web site is easy to understand for new customers, (b) whether the potential adopters are able to predict the benefits before using the service, (c) whether the customers can adapt the service to their personal preferences, (d) whether the customers can change their usage level/involvement with the system, (e) how desirable the benefits are of using the self-service technology from the customers perspective, and (f) if potential adopters have enough knowledge and skills to successfully self-service systems.

According to the Boston Consulting Group, there are three important issues that a company must take into account when implementing an online **self-service system**. The online site must be like a professional off-line salesperson: (a) it should inspire trust and provide solutions to consumer's problems; (b) must be entertaining, and (c) should create a community of interest, by allowing customers to actively interact with the site.

Despite these projects focused on self-service technology, this topic still has many unknown elements. Expressing this problem, Gournaris and Dimitriadis (2003) stated that few academic efforts have been devoted to the identification of the criteria used by customers to assess a Web's portal quality. This study attempts to fill in this knowledge gap, investigating the quality dimensions used by customers to shape their perception about online self-service systems.

RESEARCH METHODOLOGY

Considering the existing research in the area of online self-service systems, the following research objectives have been defined for this study:

1. To define the quality dimensions that may influence consumers' perceptions of online self-service systems.
2. To evaluate the importance of these quality dimensions for online self-service users.
3. To investigate the way in which personal characteristics of users influence their perception about the quality dimensions of online self-service systems.

The research was only focused on the self-service systems that involve online transactions and payments, such as travel booking, online retailing, or online insurance, which involve a certain level of risk.

In order to answer these research objectives, both secondary and primary data have been collected and analysed. In the first stage of the research process, a series of academic and professional articles dealing with the subject of self-service systems and with the quality dimensions of online services have been accessed and consulted, in order to identify the specific quality dimensions that influence the perception of online customers. On the basis of this secondary research (Bateson, 1985; Curran & Meuter, 2005, Lee & Allaway,

2002; Meuter et al., 2000, 2003; Parasuraman et al., 1985, 1988; Zeithaml et al., 2001, 2002b), the following dimensions have been identified:

- **Perceived level of security:** The level of risk perceived by a customer using an online self-service system.
- **Flexibility:** The possibility of the client to change options during his/her with the self-service system without restarting the whole process.
- **Personalisation:** The possibility to adapt the self-service systems with personal options, depending on the country, the way information is displayed, personal preferences, and so forth.
- **Information about pricing conditions and fees:** The clarity and completeness of the information provided by the self-service Web site regarding the pricing conditions and fees of the service transaction.
- **Tools for problem solving:** The self-service Web sites provide specific information/solutions to the users that encounter problems during the service transaction.
- **Web page design:** The attractiveness and logic of the self-service Web page interface.
- **Personal contact:** The possibility to contact an employee who can help in problem situations.
- **Trial/demo before using the actual service:** The self-service Web site provides a trial/demonstration of the client interaction with the self-service system, helping him/her to understand the functioning of the online self-service system, without concluding a real transaction.

The definitions of these eight quality dimensions have been refined through face-to-face interviews with 15 online self-service users and their validity was also verified through the answers obtained to the main questionnaire survey. In the second stage of the research project, a questionnaire was applied to 250 respondents contacted in the Internet area of London and Edinburgh airports. From these, 228 respondents have answered all the questions, providing usable data. The questionnaire contained two main parts: a first one asking for information about the personal profile of the respondent (gender, age, education level, profession, frequency of using the Internet, frequency of using self-service systems), and the second part in which the respondent was asked to evaluate the importance of the eight quality dimensions, using a 5-item Likert scale (very low importance, low importance, medium importance, high importance, very high importance). Another two open-ended questions have been included at the end of the questionnaire, asking the respondents to indicate specific problems they encountered during their interaction with online self-service systems, and to provide any other comments related to this topic. The collected data was analysed using the SPSS software.

GENERAL DEMOGRAPHICS

52.2% of respondents were males and 47.8% females. In terms of age, 18% were between 18 and 25 years old, 56.1% were between 26 and 35 years, and 25.9% between 36 and 50 years old. 46.5% of respondents had a high-school education level, and 24.5% were university graduates. The professions of respondents were very diverse, 18.8% being students, 21.5% working as administrative staff, and 6.6% having a managerial function. 5.3% declared themselves profession entrepreneurs or self employed.

97 respondents (42.5%) indicated a high frequency of Internet usage (every day), 65 respondents (28.5%) could be defined as medium frequency users (3 to 5 times a week), while the remaining 66 (29%) were low frequency users (1–2 times a week). The large majority of respondents are using regularly online **self-service systems** (159 respondents, 69.7%), which means that they access online self-service applications more than three times a week, while the (69 respondents, 30.7%) rest are using these systems only occasionally (1–2 times a week).

THE IMPORTANCE OF QUALITY DIMENSIONS

The data presented in Table 1 indicate the level of importance of the eight quality dimensions considered in this study, as well as the standard deviation of the received answers.

The security of the **self-service system** was considered by respondents as the most important quality dimension. This result is logical considering the subject of this study—self-services permitting online transactions, and therefore transmission of personal data and money transfers. The capacity of the Web site to provide clear and

Table 1. The medium importance of the quality dimensions of online self-service systems

Quality dimension	Level of importance	Standard deviation
Security	4.8	0.402
Flexibility	4.1	0.55
Personalisation	3.74	1.002
Information	4.64	0.48
Tools for problem solving	4.24	0.484
Web page design	3.6	0.831
Personal contact	3.58	1.078
Trial/demo	2.68	0.942

complete information about the products/services offered, the transaction and the procedure of money transfer is also considered very important, with a mean value of 4.64.

The respondents also show a specific concern in relation with crises situations and the tools for problem solving—level of importance of 4.24. They also prefer to deal with flexible self-service system, which permit them to change their options during the transaction, without restarting the whole process—level of importance of 4.1.

Personalisation, Web page design, and the personal contact have very similar levels of importance, with medium to high importance levels, and finally, the existence of a trial/demo application was considered as the less important quality dimension, with a level of only 2.68. This result can be partially explained by the fact that many respondents were experienced users of online self-service systems, for which the trail/demo application has lost its utility. On the other hand, this low level of interest for demonstrations can be the consequence of users' tendency to use repeatedly sites that they already know. These two explanations were confirmed by the answers provided by some respondents to the open-ended questions. They indicated that they are already very familiar with these Web sites, and with the general procedural logic of **self-service systems**, and therefore, they do not consider the trial/demo application as important for them. However, they emphasised that such facility can be very useful when accessing a new self-service system, because it can significantly reduce the perceived risk of the transaction and accelerate the learning process.

The standard deviation of the answers provided by respondents for personal contact, Web site personalisation, and the availability of a trial/demo application is quite high, which might indicate the existence of various clusters of users with different preferences. These elements are explored in more detail in the following section.

THE INFLUENCE OF CUSTOMER'S PROFILE ON THE IMPORTANCE OF QUALITY DIMENSIONS

The gender of respondents seems to have a very little influence on the perceived importance of the online self-service quality dimensions (see Table 2). It is easy to see that the differences are insignificant, as they are also very close to the general values presented in Table 1.

The frequency of Internet usage has a significant influence on the perceived importance of a few quality dimensions (see Table 3). The lower the online expertise of respondents is, the higher is the importance associated to security, information, Web page design, the existence of a trial/demo application, and especially, to the possibility to contact a person for additional advice. The impersonal nature of the Internet interaction can create a perception of high risk to the less experienced Internet users, who feel the need to be helped and supported by a customer service employee. On the other hand, the frequency of the Internet usage seems to have little influence on the need for personalisation, or for problem solving tools.

The trend is reversed for the perceived importance of flexibility and personalisation. These results can be explained by the specific demand of experienced Internet users for highly customised online interfaces and services. In their case, the difference between two sites offering the same service can be made by the level of personalisation and flexibility embedded in the Web interface.

The data presented in Table 4 show the differences between regular and occasional users in the way they perceive the importance of various quality dimensions. The level of importance associated with some dimensions is significantly influenced by the expertise of the respondent. The occasional users are much more concerned than the regular users regarding the level of information presented on the Web site (4.97 in comparison with 4.5), the Web page design (3.93

Table 2. The influence of gender on the perceived importance of quality dimensions

Gender/quality dimension	Males	Females
Security	4.78	4.82
Flexibility	4.11	4.09
Personalisation	3.71	3.77
Information	4.65	4.64
Tools for problem solving	4.24	4.23
Web page design	3.59	3.61
Personal contact	3.56	3.6
Trial/demo	2.7	2.66

Table 3. The influence of the online expertise of respondents on the perceived importance of quality dimensions

Frequency of Internet usage/quality dimension	High frequency	Medium frequency	Low frequency
Security	4.75	4.77	4.89
Flexibility	4.18	4.14	3.95
Personalisation	3.8	3.71	3.68
Information	4.58	4.57	4.82
Tools for problem solving	4.27	4.22	4.21
Web page design	3.53	3.6	3.71
Personal contact	2.84	3.54	4.71
Trial/demo	2.42	2.89	2.85

Table 4. The influence of the online self-service expertise of respondents on the perceived importance of quality dimensions

Frequency of online self-service usage/quality dimension	Regular users	Occasional users
Security	4.72	4.99
Flexibility	4.07	4.17
Personalisation	3.72	3.78
Information	4.5	4.97
Tools for problem solving	4.21	4.29
Web page design	3.46	3.93
Personal contact	3.49	3.78
Trial/demo	2.33	3.48

in comparison with 3.46), the availability of a personal contact (3.78 in comparison with 3.49), and the level of security implemented by the service Web site (4.99 in comparison with 4.72). The highest difference in the perceived importance is found in relation with the trial/demo application, occasional users evaluating this dimension at 3.48,

while regular users rank it as a low to medium importance (2.33).

The logical explanation of these differences is the higher level of risk perceived by the occasional users in relation with online **self-service systems**, because of their reduced transactional experience. In this situation, they are trying to find and apply strategies for risk reduction, which include elements provided by the online **self-service system**, such as the information provided by the Web site, the Web site design, the trial/demo application, and the possibility to contact an employee for additional information.

On the other hand, it is interesting to note that the differences between the two groups of users are much smaller in relation with the flexibility of the **self-service system**, and the available tools for problem solving. Unfortunately, it is difficult to explain these differences with the available data. Further qualitative research may develop a detailed profile of consumers' behaviour during their interactions with online **self-service systems**.

CONCLUDING REMARKS

The findings of this exploratory study demonstrate that the importance associated with various quality dimensions that characterised the online self-service systems is variable. This variation is introduced by the specific elements that define consumers' profile, and which influence their perceptions and online behaviour.

The gender seems to have a very small influence on the perceived importance of these quality dimensions, which means that this variable cannot be effectively used for segmenting and targeting the population of users. On the other hand, both the frequency of Internet usage and the respondents' expertise in using online self-service systems produce significant differences in the perception of quality dimensions. As a rule, the less experienced users feel more insecure in their interaction with **online self-service systems**, looking for specific elements that can support and reassure them: increased transaction security, more information, the possibility to contact a customer support service, or to use before the real transaction a trial/demo application. The companies implementing **online self-service**

systems should take into account these specific requests and provide additional customer support in the first stages of the interaction. Although this strategy is difficult to apply, since the same site is accessed by customers with various levels of expertise, a possible solution is to increase the flexibility of the Web interface, and to permit an increased customisation of the service offer, that can be defined by every online user in direct relation with his/her needs, preferences, and level of expertise. This can increase significantly the level of control perceived by the customers, which, according to other authors, represents an important determinant of consumer satisfaction (Lee & Allaway, 2002; Meuter et al., 2000).

The findings of this study can be useful both for academics and for professionals. On one hand, the results can be used to refine the existing framework of analysis regarding online self-service systems. However, the statistical analysis of quantitative data is not enough to provide an in-depth understanding of consumers' perceptions and use of online self-service systems. This analytical approach has to be complemented with qualitative studies, in which individual case studies can be developed to illustrate the specific interaction between individuals and self-service systems.

On the other hand, these results can provide for companies important insights into the way in which the quality of online **self-service systems** is evaluated by various categories of customers, and the measure in which this evaluation will influence the user choice and behaviour. These elements are essential in the online environment, where any minor problem can encourage the customer to search for another service provider. The specific characteristics of the Internet empower the customer, who can easily search, using specialised software applications, other similar firms with more effective self-service systems.

This study has a number of limitations determined by the applied research methodology. The sample of self-service users is quite small, and the collected data had mainly a quantitative nature. The complexity of users' interactions with online **self-service systems** can hardly be fully explained through a statistical analysis of quantitative data. Future research projects should complement this approach with qualitative studies of online consumer behaviour, investigating at the same time strategic process applied by companies for the design and implementation of effective online self-service systems.

REFERENCES

Barczac, G., Ellen, P.S., & Pilling, B.K. (1997). Developing typologies of consumer motives for use of technologically based banking services. *Journal of Business Research*, *38*(2), 131–139.

Bateson, J. (1985). Self-service consumer: An exploratory study. *Journal of Retailing, 61*(3), 49–76.

Black, N.J., Lockett, A., Wiklofer, H., & Ennew, C. (2001). The adoption of Internet financial services: A qualitative study. *International Journal of Retail & Distribution Management, 29*(8), 390–398.

Bobbitt, L.M., & Dadholkar, P.A. (2001). Integrating attitudinal theories to understand and predict use of technology-based self-service. *International Journal of Service Industry Management, 12*(5), 423–450.

Curran, J., & Meuter, M. (2005). Self-service technology adoption: Comparing three technologies. *Journal of Services Marketing, 19*(2), 103–113.

Dabholkar, P.A. (1996). Consumer evaluations of new technology-based self-service options: An investigation of alternative models of service quality. *International Journal of Research in Marketing, 13*(1), 29–51.

Easingwood, C.J. (1986). New product development for service companies. *Journal of Product Innovation Management, 3*(4), 264–275.

Gerrad, P., & Cunningham, J.B. (2003). The diffusion of Internet banking among Singapore consumers. *International Journal of Bank Marketing, 21*(1), 16–28.

Gournaris, S., & Dimitriadis, S. (2003). Assessing service quality on the Web: Evidence from business-to-consumer portals. *Journal of Services Marketing, 17*(5), 529–548.

Hewer, P., & Howcroft, B. (1999). Consumers distribution channel adoption and usage in the financial services industry: A review of existing approaches. *Journal of Financial Services Marketing, 3*(4), 344–358.

Holak, S.L. (1988). Determinants of innovative durable adoption: An empirical study with implications for early product screening. *Journal of Product Innovation Management, 5*(1), 50–69.

Jayanti, R.K., & Burns, A.C. (1998). The antecedents of preventative health care behavior: An empirical study. *Journal of the Academy of Marketing Science, 26*(1), 6–15.

Jun, M., & Cai, S. (2001). The key determinants of Internet banking service quality: A content analysis. *International Journal of Bank Marketing, 19*(7), 276–291.

Kotler, P., Armstrong, G., Saunders, J., & Wong, V. (2002). *Introduction to marketing* (2nd ed.). London: Pearsons Education, S.A.

Labay, D.G., & Kinnear, T.C. (1981). Exploring the consumer decision process in the adoption of solar energy systems. *Journal of Consumer Research, 8*(3), 271–278.

Larsson, R., & Bowen, D.E. (1989). Organization and customer: Managing design and coordination of services. *Academy of Management Review, 14*(2), 213–233.

Lee, J., & Allaway, A. (2002). Effects of personal control on adoption of self-service technology innovations. *Journal of Services Marketing, 16*(6), 553–572.

Lockett, A., & Littler, D. (1997). The adoption of direct banking services. *Journal of Marketing Management, 13*, 791–811.

Loudon, D.L., & Della Bitta, A.J. (1993). *Consumer behaviour: Concepts and applications* (4th ed.). New York: McGraw-Hill.

Meuter, M.L., Bitner, M.J., Ostrom, A.L., & Brown, S.W. (2005). Choosing among alternative service delivery modes: An investigation of customer trial of self-service technologies. *Journal of Marketing, 69*(2), 61–83.

Meuter, M.L., Ostrom, A.L., Bitner, M.J., & Roundtree, R.I. (2003). The influence of technology anxiety on consumer use and experience with self-service technologies. *Journal of Business Research, 56*(11), 899–906.

Meuter, M., Ostrom, A., Roundtree, R., & Bitner, M. (2000). Self-service technologies: Understanding customer satisfaction with technology-based service encounters. *Journal of Marketing, 64*(3), 50–64.

Ostlund, L.E. (1974). Perceived innovation attributes as predictors of innovativeness. *Journal of Consumer Research, 1*(2), 23–29.

Parasuraman, A., Berry, L.L., & Zeithaml, V.A. (1988). Servqual: A multiple-item scales for measuring consumer perceptions of service quality. *Journal of Retailing, 64*(1), 12–40.

Parasuraman, A., Zeithaml, V.A., & Berry, L.L. (1985). A conceptual model of service quality and its implications for future research. *Journal of Marketing, 49*(4), 41–50.

Pavlou, P.A., Liang, H., & Xue, Y. (2007). Understanding and mitigating uncertainty in online exchange relationships: A principal-agent perspective. *MIS Quarterly, 31*(1), 105–136.

Polatoglu, V.N., & Ekin, S. (2001). An empirical investigation of the Turkish consumers' acceptance of Internet banking services. *International Journal of Bank Marketing, 19*(4), 156–165.

Rogers, E.M. (1962). *The diffusion of innovations*. New York: The Free Press.

Rogers, E.M. (1995). *The diffusion of innovations* (4th ed.). New York: The Free Press.

Rotchanakitumnuai, S., & Speece, M. (2003). Barriers to Internet banking adoption: A qualitative stud among corporate customers in Thailand. *International Journal of Bank Marketing, 21*(6/7), 312–323.

Schneider, B., & Bowen, D.E. (1995). *Winning the service game*. Boston: Harvard Business School Press.

Zeithaml, V.A., Bitner, M.J., & Gremler, D.D. (2002a). *Services marketing* (3rd ed.). New York: McGraw-Hill.

Zeithaml, V.A., Parasuraman, A., & Malhotra, A. (2001). *A conceptual framework for understanding e-service quality: Implications for future research and managerial practice* (MSI Working Paper Series No. 00-115, pp. 1-49). Cambridge, MA: MSI.

Zeithaml, V.A., Parasuraman, A., & Malhotra, A. (2002b). Service quality delivery through Web sites: A critical review of extant knowledge. *Journal of the Academy of Marketing Science, 30*(4), 362–375.

Chapter V
Online Journalistic Services:
Are Digital Newspapers Complementary to Traditional Press?

Carlos Flavián Blanco
University of Zaragoza, Spain

Raquel Gurrea Sarasa
University of Zaragoza, Spain

ABSTRACT

The new online communication has had a considerable impact on the activities of the newspaper industry. As a result, analysis of the duality of journalism has aroused increasing interest. This chapter analyses the readers' behavior in relation to digital and traditional media. We identify the main reading motivations and the behavior patterns in each medium. Besides, we examine the possible relationship between readers' objectives for reading and the choice of each channel. The results confirm that the electronic and traditional channels are compatible, but suggest that it is necessary to take the process of differentiation in order to enhance this complementarity, meeting readers' needs in different circumstances and combining effects to raise loyalty to a newspaper.

INTRODUCTION

The constant development of the Internet and the growing spread of its use in the business environment are producing notable changes in the way relationships are established between a company and its sphere of operations. In fact, the impact of the Internet in recent years has been such as to change conventional conceptions of certain activities and businesses. This process of change is particularly notable in the case of services characterized by high levels of intangibility and an increasing presence in the digital media. Indeed, it seems reasonable to think that the characteristics of the digital media could well suppose important advantages for the distribution and sale of services.

Newspaper publishing is one of the activities that has been most affected by the development of the new medium. The appearance of the new digital media has brought far-reaching changes in this sector (Bush & Gilbert, 2002). These changes will foreseeably increase in the future. Also, Internet technology is rapidly changing the way and the aims with which readers consult newspapers. Definitely, the new medium involves enormous advantages for journalistic services in terms of both supply and demand. Due to these advantages, there is a proliferation of electronic newspapers and these are among the services most avidly sought by Internet users (AIMC; 2006; Media Contacts, 2007; Newspaper Association of America, 2005).

Bearing in mind all the above, there is a clear duality of information distribution channels. In this way, readers have the possibility of using both mediums for reading news. This fact has led some fears at the possibility of cannibalistic effects between digital and traditional medium. In this context, the analysis of readers' behaviour shows a growing relevance for e-journalistic firms. So, the aim of this chapter is to identify and characterize reading behaviour patterns in both channels; as well as to study the key attributes that motivate the use of online vs. printed newspapers.

NEWSPAPER BUSINESS ON THE INTERNET

The majority of print newspapers are developing their digital versions with the use of the online communication and the new medium. These processes involve relevant changes in the press business. We could note a transformation at the organizational level, the creation of a specific language, and a new multimedia environment. Also, the Internet has involved changes in access, production, and circulation of the information.

All these imply the arrival of new challenges and opportunities that they will have to face very soon (Dans, 2000; Flavián & Gurrea, 2006). Indeed, editorial offices are working in a different way and with a quicker pace compared to the traditional medium (Greer & Mensing, 2003).

The speed with which news reaches the reader, the low cost of distributing information, the opportunity to establish more direct contact and interact with users, and the possibilities to personalize the journalistic offer are noticeable trends. Besides, the electronic channel allows for updating the news immediately and showing links to other information sources. Moreover, we must note that the Internet combines the three basic advantages of the radio, the press, and the television. In fact, this new medium presents the immediacy of the radio, the wide and deep information offered by the press, and the impact of the images in television. All these aspects allow configuring a complete journalistic offer.

All these advantages have involved a growth in the supply of digital news. There are currently over 4,000 digital newspapers worldwide (Editor & Publisher, 2006; World Newspapers Online, 2007) (see Table 1). All these journalistic firms have contributed to implement definitively the virtual business as a real communication media. The growth of this new distribution channel is spectacular. In fact, the Internet has reached 50 million people during four years (Nielsen/NetRat-

Table 1. Digital newspapers around the world (Source: World Newspapers Online (2007))

GEOGRAPHIC AREA	
Canada	394
United States	1226
Latin America	443
Europe	824
Middle East	129
Africa	181
Asia	299
Oceania And Antarctica	87

ings, 2007); meanwhile the radio and the television have needed 38 and 13 years, respectively. Also, some studies point out the good situation of the sector and its expectations. More specifically, the World Association of Newspapers (2005) analyzes the strategic developments and opportunities in the press industry. It indicates that the growth of Internet use will involve higher levels of digital news audience. This fact will positively affect the press sector development and results.

The electronic dailies offer not only current news, but also a large range of additional services that could increase the perceived value by the readers. Among these services, we must point out the access to back issues, forums and chats, search engines, classifieds, weather forecast and alert, and RSS services, which provide readers the main news daily with a fast and easy access. These services offer daily alert services through e-mail. Moreover, some newspapers offer the possibility of personalizing these alerts, their contents, and the moments for receiving the breaking news.

From the demand side, digital news and newspapers are among the services most avidly sought by Internet users (Newspaper Association of America, 2005). According to Nielsen (2003) and AIMC (2006), news sites and digital newspapers are among the most widely demanded and visited Web sites among Internet users. Kaye and Johnson (2004) affirm that the main aim of users accessing the Internet is to read breaking news and search for up-to-the-minute information (83.7%), only exceeded by the use of e-mail. Moreover, the Pew Research Center for the People and the Press (2000) affirmed that one in three Americans visited online newspapers and anticipated sharp growth in the number of users consulting current news items on these sites. Similarly, Media Contacts (2007) affirmed that 61% of Internet users read electronic newspapers.

Nevertheless, it is necessary to explain the development of new divisions of the digital press business. First, the news search engines (e.g., Googlenews.com, news.yahoo.com) have had an important success in the last years because they simply search and read news. Second, it is a fact the growing success of the Weblogs as current news providers. Indeed, there are over 30 million in the world, according to Mediabriefing (2005). These sites offer current information with reflections and opinions. The readers could participate and complete the information, playing an active role. So, the new generation of readers, associated to the newspapers 2.0, want not only to see and read, but also to create and participate.

DIGITAL NEWSPAPERS AND READERS' BEHAVIOUR

In spite of the major importance associated with this sector, there are few studies from the demand perspective, which study the real motivations and behaviour of readers, given the opportunity of buying or consuming goods and services in each of the channels (Black, Lockett, Ennew, Winklhofer, & McKechnie, 2002; Flavián & Gurrea, in press). In fact, most of the research in this direction tackles individual aspects, such as frequency, type, and moments of use of digital channels for reading the latest news, or the demographic characteristics of digital newspaper readers (e.g., Dans, 2000; D'Haenens, Jankowski, & Heuvelman, 2004; De Waal, Schönbach, & Lauf, 2004).

Nonetheless, research exists which could be a starting point, since this analyzes the attitudes and preferences of consumers towards the electronic channel in different sectors (e.g., Krampf & Griffith, 2003; Mattila, Karjaluoto, & Pento, 2003; Richard & Chandra, 2005). In the context of the communication media, Cai (2003); Ferguson and Perse (2000); and Dimmick, Kline, and Stafford (2000) define a digital medium as a functional alternative as compared to other traditional communication media. However, due to the constant changes of the journalistic business, it is necessary to analyze this topic identifying the readers' behaviour patterns and the main motivations that lead the choice of digital newspapers vs. the traditional format.

Identification of Reading Motivations: Special Reference to Qualitative Studies

In order to identify the key variables that lead to reading digital newspapers, the first step was the review of the specialized literature and the search for scales which could be adapted to this context of analysis. Nevertheless, there is an important but scarce body of literature related to the analysis of readers' behaviour on the Internet. Thus, it was necessary to take the problem further by undertaking a series of preliminary qualitative studies. This research allowed knowing in detail the context of our analysis.

In fact, in the last years, the qualitative research is increasing its importance (Carson, Gilmore, Perry, & Gronhaug, 2001; Szymanski & Hise, 2000). This fact is explained by the great utility that it represents for the hypothesis generation process in an exploratory stage previous to the final research (Miles & Huberman, 1994; Strauss & Corbin, 1998). The qualitative analysis allows knowing the consumers' ideas, perceptions, and attitudes in depth (Berg, 2004; De Ruyter & Scholl, 1998;), as well as to identify and characterize possible consumer behaviour patterns (Srinivasan, Anderson, & Ponnavolu, 2002). Definitely, the qualitative studies as research technique present unquestionable advantages because they allow knowing emotional and behavioural aspects which it was not possible to analyze on quantitative researches (Carson et al., 2001; Das, 1983; Silverman, 2004).

In this context, we must indicate that there is no overall model that allows us to identify the main aims that lead readers to consult the newspapers and to explain the choice of the digital press vs. the conventional format. In this line, with the aim of analyzing the individuals' reading behaviour in an exploratory way, it is convenient to propose the carrying out of a series of qualitative studies in the first stage of the research.

More specifically, the first phase consisted of a series of focus groups, and in the second phase, in-depth interviews of digital newspapers' readers were conducted. These tasks had a duration of 9 weeks, from February to April 2006. As reflected in Table 2, after the organization and the beginning of the research, we elaborated the discussion guide in the second week. For that, we took as a reference some research studies related to this subject that offer basic structures and recommendations (Carson et al., 2001; Silverman, 2004). These authors pointed out the need of planning a discussion draft for the session, that is, the main subjects to comment on and the time assigned for each of them (Gaskell, 2000). Nevertheless, this task must be planned flexibly, respecting the informality and naturalness of the focus groups. This discussion guide had the following basic parts: introduction, preparation, analysis, key questions, and final summary.

Between the third and the sixth week, the focus groups were carried out. More specifically, the information was transcribed and analyzed. These tasks were done by the session's moderator, who is the person that was in contact with participants. This person noted each comment, expression, as well as the emphasis of the participation. The focus groups' results were the basis for developing the in-depth interviews from the fifth to eighth week.

Finally, the last two stages were focused on the conclusions of the research. For that, we used the "descriptive-interpretative" strategy (Silverman, 2004), which is one of the most frequent techniques considered in the social sciences. This strategy implies the elaboration of summaries of answers that are illustrated with literal interventions of participants.

Table 2. Planning of qualitative studies

	Week 1	Week 2	Week 3	Week 4	Week 5	Week 6	Week 7	Week 8	Week 9
Planning and beginning	■	■	■						
Discusión guide		■							
Selection of participants and focus groups			■	■					
Transcription of focus groups					■				
Data analysis					■				
Focus groups' results						■			
In-depth interviews						■	■	■	
Transcription of interviews						■	■	■	
Data analysis							■	■	
Interviews' results								■	■

Focus Groups

Following the suggestions of Edmunds (1999), the first step consisted of defining and bringing together three focus groups (24 participants) with the aim of familiarizing ourselves more deeply with the subject and making an initial approach to the attitudes and behaviour of newspaper readers. This methodology is quite usual (Carson et al., 2001), and it is recommended for the exploratory stages in a research (Fern, 2001; Millward, 1995).

The profile of the sample selected for the focus groups was representative of our target public (Internet users). The sample was divided in three groups according to the level of users' experience on the Internet. This allows us to make an initial approach to the attitudes and behaviour of newspaper' readers (De Ruyter & Scholl, 1998), as well as the possible development of their perceptions. A discussion guide was produced using a questioning route approach. A moderator led the participants through each 60–100 minutes discussion session. Specifically, the main goals of the focus groups were the following:

a. To identify the factors that motivate online and traditional press readership: aims, needs, motivations, and stimulus.
b. To identify the press readership behaviour patterns on both channels: frequency, duration, situation, and moments.
c. To identify possible relationships between the reading motivations and the choice of each type of newspapers.

The results of the focus groups were enormously useful in fleshing out the scope of our research and progressing with the work, in that they highlighted the importance of certain factors that have not been considered in detail in the existing literature.

In-Depth Interviews

As a second stage, we also held a series of in-depth interviews with a sample of 30 readers of digital newspapers, with varying profiles and who had no professional connection with the issue that concerned us. The profiles of these readers were similar to those of the typical Internet user profile.[2] These interviews were conducted face to face with a duration of between 15 and 30 minutes.[3]

We must point out the semistandardized character of the interviews. In this way, there are two main options for carrying out an interview: the standardized interview (inflexible and descriptive) and the nonstandardized interview (flexible and no planning) (see Figure 1). However, we decided to follow a combined structure. In this line, as well as raising the questions of the interview's guide, we could change the conversation to other important and new aspects.

The main goal of these interviews was to analyze in-depth the most relevant conclusions of the focus groups. In this way, interviewees were asked about the variables that were identified in the previous phase.

Taking into account the theoretical contributions on the literature and the results of the qualitative studies, it was possible to identify five key motivations for reading a newspaper nowadays. These motivations are the following:

- **Knowledge of current news**. It seems a logical fact that the reading of a newspaper is a consequence of the readers' intention to gain knowledge about current news (e.g., "*I read the newspapers with the aim of being informed about matters occur*" (Interviewee 2). In this line, McQuail (1987), Kaye and Johnson (2004), and Lin (2002) argue the importance of this motivation in the newspaper reading. Consequently, reading a newspaper becomes a way to know information and acquire culture. Moreover, reading news led readers to talk about the news with friends or family. These aspects are coherent with theoretical and no contrasted proposals of McCauley and Nesbitt (2003) or Eighmey and McCord (1998). Moreover, this aspect was remarked by participants in qualitative studies as a key reading motivation ("*Reading a daily helps you to obtain information related to current events.... Also, this allows you to talk about the news with your colleagues and friends* (Interviewee 15).

- **Search for specific information**. The Internet is playing an important role in search processes (e.g., Savolainen & Kari, 2004). In fact, the digital medium presents important possibilities for searching specific data (Bush & Gilbert, 2002; De Waal et al., 2004), such us the existence of search engines.

Figure 1. In-depth interview structuration (Source: Adapted from Berg (2004))

STANDARDIZED INTERVIEWS	NONSTANDARDIZED INTERVIEWS
- Most formally structured - No deviations - Specific wording - No adjusting of level of language - No clarifications or additional questions - Similar to questionnaire on paper	- Completely unstructured - No set order to any questions - No set wording to any questions - Level of language may be adjusted - Possible clarifications - Possible adding and deleting questions

Besides, many of the readers interviewed in the qualitative study affirm that they sought specific data in the newspaper, such as stock prices, sports results, and so on (e.g., *"I use to search the results of the football competition many times"* (Interviewee 9); *"I think that the newspaper is very useful if you are interesting in acquiring informations. For example, my brother always pays attention to the quotations on the stock exchange* (Interviewee 22); *"The hoarding that appears in the newspaper is very great... And also the television programmes to see what television broadcasts tonight* (Interviewee 24).

• **Search for updated news.** Another reason for reading a newspaper is the desire to keep abreast of breaking news (i.e., the latest events), or to follow current affairs (Rathmann, 2002). This phenomenon was demonstrated by the pattern of Internet use in the wake of recent world events (e.g., 11-S terror attacks). Some of the statements of the interviewees point out this aspect: *"When events such as terrorist bombs occur, people read the press in order to know what is happening"* (Interviewee 1); *"I follow the general elections through the television and the newspapers. On television, the information reaches you more speedily, but then I read the newspaper to know what is more interesting to me* (Interviewee 6).

• **Leisure/Entertainment.** Kang and Atkin (1999) and McQuail (1987) point out the relevance of entertainment as one of the main reasons that motivates the use of services on the Internet. In the newspaper sector, many of the readers affirm that they begin reading information in the newspaper to entertain themselves or pass the time (Bouwman & Van de Wijngaert, 2002). Some of the affirmations that illustrate this motivation are the following: *"I have a good time when reading the newspaper during*

some minutes. Meanwhile, I know what is happening around the world" (Interviewee 10); *"Yes, the newspaper is consulted at my home when there is nothing to do. This is, for pass the free moments"* (Interviewee 21).

• **Habit.** Finally, Kang and Atkin (1999) explain the role of habit for the use of the Internet. In the press business, a significant segment of newspaper readers has a habit acquired over time (Len Ríos & Bentley, 2001) and generally associated with a given time of day (e.g., *"All my family read the newspaper everyday"* (Interviewee 11); *"I think that many people, I too, read the newspaper as a daily costume. I specially read the press at the weekend, with the breakfast* (Interviewee 13). In this situation, they read the newspaper almost systematically (e.g., *I turn all pages of the newspaper, although I don't read it fully. I use to see the main heads and then, I read the most interesting news* (Interviewee 17).

READERS' BEHAVIOUR PATTERNS: THE CHOICE OF DIGITAL VS. TRADITIONAL NEWSPAPERS

Previous literature confirms that a significant proportion of readers of dailies in the printed medium are also readers of the digital versions (Rathmann, 2002). It seems reasonable that readers use each channel in order to satisfy different goals or needs. In this line, there are two major theories which explain the behaviour of the reader of news (Marath, Shepherd, & Watters, 2002; Watters, Shepherd, & Burkowski, 1998). First, reading may take place to satisfy a need for specific information, which implies the search for up-to-date information (Dozier & Rice, 1984). Second, reading could also be the consequence of the search for general information, without it being necessary to find any specific information.

This type of reading is related to entertainment and leisure (Stephenson, 1967).

Moreover, the advantages of each channel could affect the patterns of reading the press. More specifically, it seems reasonable to postulate that if the aim for reading the press is to obtain current news or specific information on some particular aspect, this reading takes place on the Internet. In this way, it is possible to take full advantage of the different search tools it provides: access to a great amount of information (Frazier, 1999) in an immediate manner (Görsch, 2002); ease comparisons (Alba, Lynch, Weitz, Janiszewski, Lutz, Sawyer, & Wood, 1997; Brynjolfsson & Smith, 2000); cost savings related to the search for information (Frazier, 1999); lesser duration of this process; and minor effort needed to access (Geyskens et al., 2000). Thus, when the reader bases his action on achieving an objective, reading becomes a planned and rapid task, restricted to the search for the required information (eMarketer, 2002). It seems reasonable that this model of news readers' behaviour should occur at times associated with their jobs. In fact, according to eMarketer study (2002), 67% of users visit news Web sites during working hours.

The readers are also motivated by the updating of news (Lin, 2002; Rathmann, 2002). This is due to the immediacy and updates that are key features of the Internet closely bound up with breaking news (Brown, 2000; Chyi & Lasorsa, 2002). This fact was clearly demonstrated by the pattern of Internet use in the wake of recent world events such as the September 11 terrorist outrage (Kim, Jung, Cohen, & Ball-Rokeach, 2004) and the March 11 train bombing in Madrid.

In contrast, due to the format of conventional newspapers and the association of the traditional press with times of leisure, its reading is more in-depth and relaxed. According to Marath et al. (2002), reading physical newspapers is a casual, spontaneous, and unstructured activity. In this way, Bogart (1992) pointed out that reading on paper is relaxed and detailed, especially on weekends. Print newspapers are therefore usually read at moments related to leisure and entertainment.

FINDINGS

These proposals have been tested with the data collected by way of an online survey. The questionnaire was published on a Web site designed specifically for the purposes of our research. Information was sent to various distribution lists associated with a range of subjects, and banners were placed on the Web sites of electronic newspapers in order to disseminate the existence of our research. The digital newspapers were selected according to the amount of users and the audiences (Nielsen/NetRatings), as well as according to the quality criterions offered by Google search engine.

We obtained 253 questionnaires completed by readers of both printed and digital newspapers. The interviewees had a profile that we have fixed as the target public of our research: digital and traditional newspaper readers at a medium or high frequency. The representative nature of the sample could be guaranteed by the similarity of the profile of the interviewees with the sample profile achieved because it showed similarities to recent AECE (2005) and AIMC (2006) samples of Internet users. The majority of the interviewees were male, aged between 25 and 34, and highly educated with over 5 years' experience with computers and Internet use. This is therefore a very interesting sample to work with, whose responses will provide high quality information, given that these are not new users who might behave more erratically than more experienced users.

Thus, in order to approach the analysis of the different aspects which might have a bearing on the analysis of newspaper reading behaviour, we ran a T test on mean differences for paired samples. For this purpose, the questionnaire posed a series of aspects which would characterize the typology of newspaper reading by the respondent.[1] The results highlight that reading newspapers on the Internet is characterized by being focused on specific subjects, fairly rapid, particularly in the initial moments before going deeper into news of major interest and news linked to work. By contrast, the press in traditional format is read more thoroughly, in a more relaxed manner, is more detailed, and associated with free time (Table 3). Therefore, it is possible to defend the existence of a clear duality of newspaper reading behaviour in physical and digital environments.

In this way, Table 4 indicates that different habits exist for reading traditional/digital newspapers. More specifically, traditional newspapers are mostly read on weekends, while digital press is read more on working days. Besides, the most of the interviewees read conventional newspapers all days or several times a week. On the other hand, 76.7% of the sample read electronic newspapers with a higher frequency.

Besides, we can confirm that there are significant differences between the most valued attributes of a digital newspaper and a traditional daily.[2] We also ran a T test on mean differences for paired samples (see Table 5). More specifically, immediacy, accessibility, and free charge are the most relevant attributes for electronic press; while writing style is very important in traditional press. Nevertheless, there are three attributes that do not present significant differences between channels: editorial firm's reputation, sources' quality, and sources' reliability. These results are reasonable since those aspects are important for any reader, regardless of whether she read digital or traditional press.

Table 3. Behavior patterns

	Differences Averages Digital/Traditional
TRADITIONAL NEWSPAPERS	
Focus your attention on specific information	-1.36 **
Focus your attention on specific topics	-0.84 **
Read fairly fast	-0.91 **
Skim and scan initially, focusing your attention later on news of greater interest	-0.30 *
Read at moments associated with job	-1.52 **
DIGITAL NEWSPAPERS	
Read all types of news in a newspaper	0.69 *
Read entire newspaper	0.78 **
Read in a relaxed manner	1.08 **
Read in a detailed manner	0.78 **
Read in free time	1.46 **
Read at home or outside the workplace	1.57 **

Note: *"*"significant coefficients to level 0.05; "**"significant coefficients to level 0.01*

Table 4. Reading the newspaper: weekdays and frequency

When do you read more newspapers?	Working week		Weekend	
TRADITIONAL NEWSPAPER	30.8%		69.2%	
DIGITAL NEWSPAPER	78.4%		21.6%	

Newspaper reading frequency	Several times a day	All days	Several times a week	Sometimes	Hardly ever
TRADITIONAL NEWSPAPER	0.9%	37.6%	35.1%	21.9%	4.5%
DIGITAL NEWSPAPER	36.6%	40.1%	15.1%	6.3%	1.9%

Table 5. Newspapers' attributes

	Differences Averages Digital - Traditional
TRADITIONAL NEWSPAPERS	
Writing style	-0.27*
DIGITAL NEWSPAPERS	
Immediacy/Update	2.16*
Free charge	2.58*
Convenience	0.48*
Design	0.63*
Accessibility/Interactivity	2.14*
Readers' services	0.57*

Note: ""significant coefficients to level 0.01*

Table 6. Reading motivations: channel choice

DIGITAL NEWSPAPERS	TRADITIONAL NEWSPAPERS
Knowledge of current news Search for specific information Search for updated news	Leisure – Entertainment Habit

Moreover, the results of the previous qualitative studies enable us to confirm an association between the different reading motivations and the channel that readers choice for reading or consulting the newspapers (see Table 6).

First, the results of the qualitative studies show that the majority of readers, who want to obtain knowledge about current events and specific news, are focusing their attention and interest to the digital newspapers more and more (Kaye & Johnson, 2004; Lin, 2002). The importance of attributes such as the convenience, immediacy, and availability of the Internet justifies this fact. Indeed, these characteristics are key factors that explain the use of the Web (Lin, 2002). Definitely, the readers valuate the main characteristics of the new medium positively, so the interest in digital dailies is increasing in the last time.

Similarly, users who are particularly interested in learning to keep abreast of up-to-the-minute news will read newspapers online (Rathmann, 2002) because the immediacy and updates are key features of the Internet and closely related to with breaking news (Chyi & Lasorsa, 2002).

Consequently, the interest in the updated news is a goal associated with reading the digital rather than the traditional press.

In contrast, due to the format of conventional newspapers and the association of the traditional press with times of leisure, its reading is more in-depth and relaxed. The readers interviewed declare that one of the objectives for reading most closely associate with the traditional medium is entertainment in free time. This reading is more extensive, detailed, and relaxed compared to reading in a digital environment. Thus, the entertainment would have a negative influence on reading digital newspapers because it would be likely to motivate reading the traditional physical press.

Finally, the results of the qualitative studies suggest that reading frequently takes place as a result of a daily habit. This is a habit of reading the newspaper at given times of day or in certain situations (bus, restaurant, sofa, etc.). Many of the interviewees remark that they read the traditional newspaper out of a habit they had acquired over time. They would not stop this action as a result of the publication of digital newspapers. These results are consistent with the findings of Len Ríos and Bentley (2001). In this way, reading the press out of habit is important to explain the use of traditional formats for news delivery. In this case, the readers usually look over the full newspaper. Thus, the authors should not link this motivation to reading newspapers in the digital medium but rather with reading traditional newspapers.

As a consequence, it is possible to propose the existence of a clear duality of newspaper behaviour patterns. Rapid searches for news or job-associated current information characterize online newspaper reading, while in-depth and detailed reading, associated to leisure time, characterizes printed newspaper reading.

CONCLUSION AND MANAGERIAL IMPLICATIONS

This chapter underlines the growing importance of the electronic medium for the development of journalistic services. Also, taking into account the growing relevance of the analysis of the duality of information channels, this case explores reading behaviour patterns in online and traditional contexts.

In view of the results obtained, we may observe that the new channel presents considerable opportunities for the newspaper industry. For example, the digital medium is very convenient for specific information needs because searches can be carried out at any time and on any day throughout the year. The new electronic channel also benefits from attributes such as the possibility of continual updates, personalization, and immediacy in the distribution of breaking news.

As a consequence of the clear duality of patterns, it seems reasonable to propose that the e-newspapers are complementary to the traditional press. In fact, it seems probable that if the printed version and the digital version of one same news-

paper are positioned adequately, readers would thus perceive these services as complementary products meeting the same generic need, that is, obtaining current information, but with varying features for use in different contexts. Thus, reading the printed version of a newspaper may be more advisable for eyesight than the digital version and it may also be preferred when the reader has more time, or is interested in reading a major part of the content of the newspaper. Alternatively, reading a digital newspaper may be preferred if what the reader is looking for is a general brief overview of the news of the day; if he is looking for the latest information which has not been published in the printed version; or if only a few specific facts are sought.

In this way, the offer of a digital newspaper should provide substantially different features from that of the printed version of the same paper, in such a way that the two products are clearly differentiated and fit more closely the preferences of different consumer groups and their motivations or needs. Logically, this differentiation of form should be based on the different peculiarities or advantages these media provide. Specifically, we must note the relevance of the steadily updating of news, the speed of distribution, the use of multimedia resources, the matter of availability of previous issues, or the interaction between newspapers and users. If companies exploit these aspects, it will be possible to calm the fears associated with readers' cannibalism between the electronic and conventional media.

This would have significant implications for management. Thus, e-journalistic firms should achieve a high level of complementarity between both offers, according to the progressive readers' segmentation. This allows ruling out some of the fears in the newspaper sector at the present moment, characterized by high levels of uncertainty as regards the possibility of exploiting the virtual service simultaneously with the traditional channel. In fact, the main aspects which justify digital newspaper reading should be considered by management personnel in this type of news medium in order to promote its use.

Besides, journalistic firms should make efforts in the analysis and knowledge of readers' needs. This action could be easier through the electronic channel because it is possible to track users' behaviour on a Web site. Anyway, the knowledge of readers' needs and goals could be a starting point for developing marketing strategies. Thus, firms would offer readers what they want at any given place and moment. Moreover, the use of two distribution channels simultaneously could allow individuals to reach a more complete offer and satisfy their needs by using the preferred channel.

Nevertheless, it must be admitted that although initially the Internet was simply considered a new medium for distributing a limited version of the printed newspaper, more and more publishers are bearing in mind the new opportunities which this medium offers and are developing more specific products which differ from the printed versions. In fact, journalistic firms could find a new source for its development by taking advantage of the Internet possibilities. In this way, this e-service could have undoubted future opportunities.

In this regard, we may mention some possible future research lines, such as the possibility of including new explanatory motives in the model to describe reading behaviour. Moreover, the results of this study could be extrapolated to other contexts where the new digital scenario raises doubts about potential cannibalization between channels. It would also be useful to analyze the possible moderating effects of certain variables, such as readers' experience or familiarity with the Internet. In fact, it seems reasonable that a great evolution of the reader behaviour will occur in a short time, according to the fast development of the sector.

REFERENCES

Alba, J., Lynch, J., Weitz, B., Janiszewski, O., Lutz, R., Sawyer, A., & Wood, S. (1997). Interactive home shopping: Consumer, retailer and manufacturer incentives to participate in electronic marketplaces. *Journal of Marketing, 61*, 38–53.

Asociación Española de Comercio Electrónico (AECE) (2005). Retrieved June 2, 2008, from www.aece.org

Asociación para la Investigación de Medios de Comunicación (AIMC) (2006). Retrieved June 2, 2008, from www.aimc.es

Berg, B. (2004). *Qualitative research methods for the social sciences* (5th ed.). Allyn & Bacon.

Black, N., Lockett, A., Ennew, C., Winklhofer, H., & McKechnie, S. (2002). Modelling consumer choice of distribution channels: An illustration from financial services. *International Journal of Bank Marketing, 20*(4), 161–173.

Bogart, L. (1992). *The state of the industry.* In P. Cook, D. Gomery, & W. Lichty (Eds.), The future of news (pp. 85–103). Washington, DC: The Woodrow Wilson Center Press.

Bouwman, H., & Van de Wijngaert, L. (2002). Content and context: An exploration of the basic characteristic of information needs. *New Media & Society, 4*(3), 329–353.

Brown, M. (2000). Bringing people closer to news. *Adweek, 41*(40).

Brynjolfsson, E., & Smith, M.D. (2000). Frictionless commerce? A comparison of Internet and conventional retailers. *Management Science, 46*(4), 563–585.

Bush, V., & Gilbert, F. (2002). The Web as a medium: An exploratory comparison of Internet users versus newspapers readers. *Journal of Marketing Theory and Practice, 10*(1), 1–10.

Cai, X. (2003). Is the computer a functional alternative to traditional media? *Communication Research Reports.*

Carson, D., Gilmore, A., Perry, C., & Gronhaug, K. (2001). *Qualitative research in marketing.* London: Sage.

Carson, D., & Perry, C. (2001). *Qualitative marketing research.* Sage Publications.

Chyi, H., & Lasorsa, D. (2002). An explorative study on the market relation between online and print newspaper. *The Journal of Media Economics, 15*(2), 91–106.

Dans, E. (2000). Internet newspapers: Are some more equal than others? *The International Journal on Media Management, 2*(1), 4–13.

Das, T.H. (1983). Qualitative research in organisational behaviour. *Journal of Management Studies, 20*(3), 311.

De Ruyter, K., & Scholl, N. (1998). Positioning qualitative market research: From theory and practice. *Qualitative Market Research: An International Journal, 1*(1), 7–14.

De Waal, E., Schönbach, K., & Lauf, E. (2004, May 12–15). *Online newspapers: A substitute for print newspapers and other information channels?* Paper presented at 6th World Media Economics Conference, Canada.

D'Haenens, L., Jankowski, N., & Heuvelman, A. (2004). News in online and print newspapers: Differences in reader comsumption and recall. *New Media & Society, 6*(3), 363–382.

Dimmick, J., Kline, S., & Stafford, L. (2000). The gratification niches of personal e-mail and the telephone. *Communication Research, 27,* 227–248.

Dozier, D., & Rice, R. (1984). Rival theories of electronic news reading. In *The new media* (pp. 103–128). London: Sage Publications.

Editor & Publisher (2004). Retrieved June 2, 2008, from www.editorandpublisher.com

Edmunds, H. (1999). *The focus group research handbook.* Chicago: NTC Business Books.

Eighmey, J., & McCord, L. (1998). Adding value in the information age: Uses and gratifications of sites on the World Wide Web. *Journal of Business Research, 41,* 187–194.

eMarketer (2002). El impacto de Internet en la prensa. In J. Cerezo & J. Zafra (Eds.), *Cuadernos sociedad de la información.* Fundación Auna.

Ferguson, D.A., & Perse, E.M. (2000). The World Wide Web as a functional alternative to television. *Journal of Broadcasting & Electronic Media, 44*(2), 155–174.

Fern, E. (2001). *Advanced focus group research.* London: Sage Publications.

Flavián, C., & Gurrea, R. (2006). The choice of digital newspapers: Influence of readers goals and user experience. *Internet Research, 16*(3), 231–247.

Flavián, C., & Gurrea, R. (in press). Exploring the influence of reading motivations on perceived substitutability between digital and traditional newspapers. *International Journal of Market Research.*

Frazier, G.L. (1999). Organizing and managing channels of distribution. *Journal of the Academy of Marketing Science, 27*(2), 226–240.

Gaskell, G. (2000). Individual and group interviewing. In M.W. Bauer & G. Gaskell (Eds.), *Qualitative researching with text, image and sound: A practical handbook.* Londres: Sage.

Geyskens, I., Gielens, K., & Dekimpe, M. (2000). *Establishing the Internet channel: Short term pain but long term gain?* (Working Paper). E-Business Research Center.

Görsch, D. (2002). *The impact of hybrid channel structures on the customer purchase process: A research outline* (Working Paper). E-Business Research Center.

Greer, J., & Mensing, D. (2003). *The evolution of online newspapers: A longitudinal content analysis, 1997–2003*. Paper presented at the meeting of the Association for Education in Journalism and Mass Communication, Kansas City, MO.

Kang, M., & Atkin, D. (1999). Exploring the role of media uses and gratifications in multimedia cable adoption. *Telematics and Informatics, 16*, 59–74.

Kaye, B., & Johnson, T. (2004). A Web for all reasons: Uses and gratifications of Internet components for political information. *Telematics and Informatics, 21*, 197–223.

Kim, Jung, J., Cohen, E., & Ball-Rokeach, S. (2004). Internet connectedness before and after September 11 2001. *New Media & Society, 6*(5), 611–631.

Krampf, R., & Griffith, D. (2003). Print and online catalogs: The influence of communication mode on consumer information processing. *Journal of Marketing Channels, 10*(1), 25–39.

Len Rios, M., & Bentley, C. (2001). *Use of online news site: Development of habit and automatic procedural processing*. Paper presented at the AEJMC Conference.

Lin, C. (2002). Perceived gratifications of online media service use among potential users. *Telematics and Informatics, 19*, 3–19.

Marath, A., Shepherd, M., & Watters, C. (2002). *Adaptative user modelling for filtering electronic news*. Paper presented at 35th Annual Hawaii International Conference on Systems Sciences (vol. 4).

Mattila, M., Karjaluoto, H., & Pento, T. (2003). Customer channel preferences in the Finnish banking sector. *Journal of Marketing Channels, 10*(1), 41–64.

McCauley, T., & Nesbitt, M. (2003). *The newspaper experience study*. Retrieved June 2, 2008, from http://www.readership.org/consumers/data/newspaper_exp.pdf#search=%22mccauley%20y%20nesbitt%202003%22

McQuail, D. (1987). *Mass communication theory: An introduction* (2nd ed.). Londres: Sage.

Mediabriefing (2005). Retrieved June 2, 2008, from www.mediabriefing.com

Media Contacts (2007). *Online press consumption*. Retrieved June 2, 2008, from www.media-contacts.com

Miles, M., & Huberman, A.M. (1994). *Qualitative data analysis: An expanded sourcebook* (2nd ed.). Sage Publications.

Millward, L. (1995). Focus groups. In G.M. Breakwell, S. Hammond, & C. Fife-Scha (Eds.), *Research methods in psychology* (pp. 304–324). London: Sage Publications.

Newspaper Association of America (2003). Retrieved June 2, 2008, from www.naa.org

Nielsen, J. (2003). Usability 101. Retrieved June 2, 2008, from www.useit.com/alertbox/20030825.html

Nielsen/Net Ratings (2007). Retrieved June 2, 2008, from www.nielsen-netratings.com/

Pew Research Center for the People and the Press (2000). Retrieved June 2, 2008, from www.people-press.org

Rathmann, T. (2002). Supplement or substitution? The relationship between reading a local print newspaper and the use of its online version. *Communications, 27*, 485–498.

Richard, M., & Chandra, R. (2005). A model of consumer Web navigational behavior: Conceptual development and application. *Journal of Business Research, 58*, 1019–1029.

Savolainen, R., & Kari, J. (2004). Placing the Internet in information source horizons. A study of information seeking by Internet users in the context of self-development. *Library & Information Science Research, 26*(4), 415–433.

Silverman, D. (2004). *Qualitative research: Theory, method and practice* (2nd ed.). Sage Publications.

Srinivasan, S., Anderson, R., & Ponnavolu (2002). Customer loyalty in e-commerce: An exploration of its antecedents and consequences. *Journal of Retailing, 78*, 41–50.

Stephenson, W. (1967). *The play theory of mass communication*. Chicago: The University of Chicago Press.

Strauss, A., & Corbin, J. (1998). *Basics of qualitative research: Techniques and procedures for developing grounded theory* (2nd ed.). Sage Publications.

Szymanski, D., & Hise, R. (2000). E-satisfaction: An initial examination. *Journal of Retailing, 73*(3), 309–322.

Watters, C., Shepherd, M., & Burkowski, F. (1998, February). Electronic news delivery

project. *Journal of the American Society for Information Science, 49*(2), 134–150.

World Association of Newspapers (2004). *Shaping the future of the newspaper: Analysing strategic developments and opportunities in the press industry* (Strategy report 4.1: Profiting from digital, pp. 19–23).

World Newspapers Online (2007). Retrieved June 2, 2008, from www.worldnewspapersonline.com

ENDNOTES

[1] The interviewees were selected according to their similitude to the typical Internet user profile offered by recent studies (AECE, 2005; AIMC, 2006). More specifically, the majority of interviewees were male, aged between 25 and 34 years, well educated, and had over 5 years' experience with computers.

[2] This work has been funded by the Spanish Ministry of Science and Technology (SEC2005-4972; PM34); the Aragon Government (S-46) and Fundear.

[3] Interviews were recorded with the interviewees' permission.

[4] Readers were asked to indicate their degree of agreement or disagreement with the statements, through a Likert scale of 7 points, from (1) Totally disagree to (7) Totally agree in each medium.

[5] Readers were asked to valuate different attributes of a newspaper, through a Likert scale of 7 points, from (1) Not important to (7) Very important in each medium

Section II
Cases on Business–to–Consumer E–Services

Chapter VI
Profightstore.com:
Developing an Online Store for the Niche Market

Mirjana Pejic-Bach
Faculty of Economics & Business—Zagreb, Croatia

Miran Pejic-Bach
Dux Sport d.o.o., Croatia

ABSTRACT

This chapter explores the possibilities for small and medium-sized enterprises (SMEs) to find their way to success in e-business. The basic assumption of this chapter is that the Internet allows SMEs to access the niche markets which have not previously been accessible to them. We are presenting a case study of one Croatian online store developed as a portal which targets the niche market and our focus is on the following issues: subcultures as niche markets, criteria for selecting suppliers, developing a new brand, designing an online store as a portal in order to attract visitors, and opportunities for growth. The authors hope that presenting this particular case will help small companies to take into account niche markets when designing their online stores, but also it will help researchers to further explore niche markets as a possible business strategy for SMEs while entering the e-commerce arena.

INTRODUCTION

The development of the Internet and e-commerce as interrelated phenomena has given small and medium enterprises (SMEs) a new opportunity to present themselves to the global market, both to business-to-consumer (B2C) and business-to-business (B2B) markets. However, it is not realistic to expect SMEs to be able to compete on the mainstream markets with major players like Fortune 500 companies. Therefore, most SMEs found their way to success in e-business by entering niche markets (Barnes, Hinton, & Mieczkowska, 2004).

Firms that pursue niche market strategy are able to make extra profit (Porter, 1998). Those firms focus on the smaller part of the market which is growing fast and which is not yet captured by other firms. The Internet allows SMEs to access the niche markets which have not previously been accessible to them.

The objective of this chapter is to present the process of developing an online store, developed as portal, for targeting the niche market. The case study approach will be used (Yin, 2003) to answer "how" an online store that targets the niche market was developed and marketed, and "why" niche market strategy was used. The focus of the case study is on the contemporary phenomenon according to which small firms use the Internet as a medium to enter a particular market and to even outmatch the existing competitors who have already established a strong competitive position on the "brick and mortar" market. In addition, the purpose of the case study is to clarify some uncertainties surrounding both the development of online stores by SMEs and to use the established online store for entering niche markets:

- Could a particular subculture be used as a market niche?
- What are the criteria for selecting suppliers?
- Should the firm sell the existing brands or try to develop its own brand?
- What are the most efficient ways of attracting visitors to the online store?
- What is the influence of design on the shopping habits of visitors to the online store?
- Should the firm try to open another online store in order to "scare away" competition?
- What is the possible income from selling advertisements?
- What are other opportunities for growth?

BACKGROUND

The development of modern national economies relies not only on big corporations, but also on SMEs which are often an important generator of growth. In Croatia, for instance, in 2006 there was a total of 72,000 companies, 93% of which were SMEs. The Government of the Republic of Croatia stressed in its strategy of economic development entitled "Croatia in the 21st century" that SMEs were the main generators of economic development. However, in the era of globalisation SMEs stand the smallest chance of survival, so that one may rightfully question how realistic it is for Croatian SMEs to fulfil such high expectations set by the creators of economic policy. It has been shown in the last couple of years that Croatian SMEs stagnate due to increased competition and higher client demands. On the other hand, the Internet economy fosters the remarkably speedy growth of the national economy because it allows SMEs to direct their marketing strategy toward dislocated markets at smaller business costs. The use of advanced information technologies makes it possible to establish personalised contacts with buyers within the Internet economy, which improves the quality of customer relations. In addition, the growth of e-commerce allows SMEs to achieve competitive advantage if they manage to adjust in a timely manner to the changes of the Internet market. It should also be mentioned that in the Croatian economy, significant growth is recorded in tourism, but also in retail trade. Finally, the Internet users perceive online sales and advertising as increasingly important factors in making their buying decisions (Malic-Bandu, 2006).

The Croatian Internet market (Gfk, 2006) is characterised by a significant number of firms with Web pages which are mainly used as marketing channels. It should be mentioned that only a small number of firms use Web pages as their delivery and selling channel. The number of Internet users in Croatia is one million (45% of the population older than 15), and the total value of e-commerce transactions was over 60 million euros in 2006. According to several researchers (Gfk, 2005), the typical Internet users in Croatia include people from urban areas who have access to the Internet. In contrast, this is true only for a smaller percentage of people from rural areas. Most Internet users come from the Croatian capital city—Zagreb and towns on the Adriatic coast. Approximately one third of men have access to the Internet, and the same is true only for one quarter of women. Finally, the majority of the users are people younger than 35.

Profightstore.com is an online store established in 2003. It sells equipment for combat sports, which are competitive contact sports where two combatants fight against each other using certain rules of engagement, typically with the aim of simulating parts of real hand to hand combat. Examples of combat sports are: boxing, sports wrestling, and mixed martial arts. The firm was established by the owner who is himself familiar with combat sports and who understands combat sports culture very well. At the time when the firm was established, the owner worked solely by himself. Today (in 2007) the firm employs two part-time journalists and two office clerks. The management structure is very simple, which is to be expected considering the number of people employed. The owner of the firm is the front man of the firm, and he coordinates journalists and office clerks. The firm is situated in Zagreb, the capital city of Croatia (a country in Southeast Europe).

The organisational culture in the firm is informal, meaning that the people who work in the firm are closely connected with each other. As Profightstore.com has become a well known online portal for combat sports in Croatia, journalists are proud to be a part of the Profightstore.com journalist team. However, one has to be aware that journalists working for Profightstore.com are not professionally trained journalists. Instead, they come from the Croatian combat sports community which gathers around online discussion

groups like nokaut.com. Therefore, working for a well-known portal like Profightstore.com gives them a chance to become widely recognized as combat sports experts. In addition, the owner of the firm has personal experience in training combat sports, which helps in establishing the network of useful contacts.

Setting the Stage

Combat sports are probably the oldest form of men's competition with each other. Different disciplines/arts like boxing, karate, wrestling, judo, and tae kwon do originate from all over the world (Asia, Europe, and America). The common goal of all combat sports disciplines are twofold: to be able to defend oneself from an attacker, and to be able to hurt the attacker in order to make the attacker incapable of further combat. Therefore, combat sports could be defined as systems of codified practices and traditions of training for combat. The most important characteristic of combat sports fans is that they usually practice combat sports by themselves.

Profightstore.com offers equipment for combat sports which have become increasingly popular in the last 10 years with the appearance of vale tudo events in Brazil, PRIDE Fighting Championships in Japan, and Ultimate Fighting Championship (UFC) in the USA. In 2007, the owners of the UFC bought PRIDE which resulted in the merging of those two greatest combat sports shows into one big championship.

The Internet has allowed combat sports fans to become closely connected through Internet online discussion groups (forums), and through regular visits to Web sites with the latest news. Before the emergence of the Internet, combat sports fans could follow news only through specialised magazines and rare bits of news in the mainstream media (TV and sports journals). They could comment on the latest events only with their friends and acquaintances. However, the emergence of Internet forums allowed combat sports fans to participate in asynchronous communication (Powazek, 2002), when users are able to participate at different times in the debate that can last for a longer period of time (Gurstein, 2000). At the same time, there are a number of Web sites which cover combat sports events with prompt commentaries and which offer their content free of charge. Those Web sites have allowed a greater number of people to become combat sports fans, which certainly would not have occurred if only specialised magazines had been available on the market. Therefore, the Internet has enabled more people to become combat sports fans as a result of the emergence of specialised forums and portals.

Virtual communities could be defined as a network of people who communicate with each other electronically and share common interests (Hagel & Armstrong, 1998). Combat sports fans consider forums to be the most popular form of virtual communities. One of the most popular forums is Sherdog Mixed Martial Arts Forum (www. sherdog.com/forum), whereby joining those free communities, members can post topics, privately communicate with other members, start and vote in polls, update contents, and be able to upload video clips, photos, and other special content.

Combat sports fans could be treated as part of subculture, if we define subculture as "a set of people with a set of behaviours and beliefs, which could be distinct or hidden, that differentiate them from the larger culture of the area from which they are a part of" (Loflin & Winogrond, 1976). According to the owner of Profightstore. com, the following elements constitute combat sports subculture in Croatia:

1. *Styling* – Combat sports fans usually train combat sports by themselves. They usually look similar with shaved heads, strong muscles, tight clothes, and quite eager to look like tough guys. The purpose of such styling is to make the fighter look dominant inside and outside the ring. The intention is also to scare the opponent with all possible means so that even the fighter's gaze is very important.

2. *Strength, courage, skill* – combat sports are the best way to express emotional stability and physical readiness. People who practice combat sports aim to enhance their physical ability to their maximum. The best way to test physical readiness is to fight with someone of similar size and strength. Combat sports give athletes an opportunity to test to what extent they are better than other fighters. The greatest challenge is to test if one is emotionally ready. Some fighters will rely more on their strength, and some on their skills. Some do not have strength or skill, but will rely on their courage instead. Those three components are crucial for practicing combat sports. Expressing aggression is not the main goal of practicing combat sports. It is all about two people who compete against each other.

3. *Combat sports and other sports* – The difference between combat sports and other individual sports is not as great as it seems at first sight. Group sports do not have such strong "one-against-another feeling," but rather stress the importance of team spirit. Tennis is also characterised by strenuous practice, physical effort, and pain. However, physical confrontation with the opponent is not as important as in combat sports. To the outside observer, combat seems like violence, but it is competition as in any other sport. Most men possess an impulse to fight with each other, and combat sports give them the opportunity to fulfil this desire.

4. *Who practices combat sports* – It is hard to give a description of a typical person who practices combat sports. Combat sports are practised by different kinds of people: young, old, and with different educational back-

grounds. However, most of them are young males. Another important characteristic of people who practice combat sports is that they work out as hard as any other athlete. It is a common prejudice that people who practice combat sports do not do anything else in their lives and want to earn money "easily" through fighting. Quite the opposite, most people who practice combat sports in their private lives work in different areas. Some of them are even experts in their fields, while most of them seem eager to obtain college education or some other form of education.

5. *Media* – Most men like to watch combat sports fights. Some people will even wake up at 3 a.m. to watch a fight in real time, while other people will read the report on the fight in tomorrow's newspaper. All fans are extremely happy when their hero wins and all the people who watch combat sports fights seek reality in fights. That is why some time ago the reality show called Ultimate Fighter (tv.com, 2007) gained strong media attention. It seems that people want to watch real fighting and really appreciate the efforts of the show participants so that the same dedication is expected in the ring. In the past, movies were important for the popularity of a particular combat sport discipline. However, today there are fighters like Randy Couture or Mirko Filipovic Cro Cop (Ultimate Fighting Championship, 2007) who have a bigger charisma and are more appealing to the media than some actors who played in action movies 20 years ago. Today, media competition is getting stronger and stronger so that fights are not covered only on TV and in the newspaper, but increasingly on the Internet.

Combat sports subculture could be best described if we resort to the description of a typical combat sports fan. He is a young male who trains in combat sports at the neighbourhood club or somebody who regularly practices at home by himself. His look is specific (shaved head, tight clothes, masculine look). He informs himself on combat sports events using the mainstream media and even more so using online portals. He regularly participates in discussions in one or more Internet forums dedicated to combat sports. In private life, he is not violent, but has ability to defend himself in dangerous situations, and the possibility to test his strength with equally strong and capable opponents are very important to him.

According to the facts on the demographic features of Internet users in Croatia, a typical Croatian Internet user is a young male. The owner decided to use that fact at the time when he realised that there was growing demand for online shopping. Four years ago (in 2003) the supply side was rather weak and it was the right time to launch combat sports equipment through the online market. At that time, only two online shops offering combat sports equipment existed, but they did not succeed in attracting a sufficient number of visitors. Those online shops only offered combat sports equipment but did not offer any other additional information.

In addition, combat sports are very popular in Croatia where a strong tradition exists in training world-class combat sports fighters. However, the owner soon realised that it was not enough to just open an online store and expect customers to come shopping automatically. The owner's concept was based on four steps: content, traffic, trust, and selling. The owner believed from the start that people on the Internet were not looking for a particular store, but for information. Therefore, the store was built as an information portal (Chiou & Shen, 2006; Kennedy & Coughlan, 2006) for people interested in combat sports. Good content should attract visitors who will develop trust in the Web site and eventually buy combat sports equipment.

CASE DESCRIPTION

At the time of the development of Profightstore.com (in year 2003), it was widely accepted that digital and information-based products that customers did not have to physically inspect by themselves were the most appropriate for e-commerce (Hsein & Lin, 1998; Poon & Matthew, 2000). Therefore, the owner decided to sell combat sports equipment (gloves, punch bags, etc.) through an online store. He realised that the customers who bought combat sports equipment had a distinct set of needs, and were willing to pay a premium price for high-quality equipment. In addition, none of the existing competitors who also sold combat sports equipment had an online store in combination with a news portal. At the same time, the number of combat sports fans was growing because the Internet had increased the popularity of combat sports and created combat sports subculture. Therefore, the market for combat sports equipment could be defined as a niche market according to the characteristics defined by Kotler (2003). The owner's idea was that the name of the store should indicate its purpose, and that is how the name Profightstore.com was chosen. However, the firm registered another name esport.hr (hr is the Croatian domain) if ever a need for selling other sports equipment appeared.

Finding the Supplier

Different world-known combat sports equipment brands were considered for sales in Profightstore.com. However, the prices were rather high, and profit margins were too narrow. Electronic marketplaces (Ems) were considered as a second source for possible suppliers.

Electronic marketplaces (Chircu & Kauffman, 2001) have great potential of stimulating disintermediation (Shunk, Carter, Hovis, & Talwar, 2007). They connect buyers and suppliers from all over the world who would otherwise have a very small chance of communicating with each other.

Apart from encouraging disintermediation, Ems manage other functions like checking customers' and suppliers' credibility, and checking product quality. First, customers and suppliers give basic information on their credibility in the registration process. Then, the credibility of customers and suppliers is examined through personal contacts of Ems representatives at their headquarters and trade fairs. Finally, providers of credit information and credit reports give information. Dun and Bradstreet provide information mainly on U.S. firms, and FriedlNet provides information on Chinese firms (Duffie & Singleton, 2003). The quality of products offered by suppliers is checked in a similar way. In addition, Ems give additional advice to both suppliers and customers which helps them in conducting secure trade transactions. However, Ems usually do not accept any legal responsibility for lost products, product damage, and non-ethical customers who do not pay for the received products. Finally, contracts that customers and suppliers conclude do not mention Ems.

The owner registered in one of the electronic marketplaces (Ems), that is, Web sites which connect buyers with suppliers, and he announced that he wanted to buy combat sports equipment. Around 20 offers arrived by e-mail, and it took about three months to choose the supplier. The final choice of the supplier was based on several criteria: good communication, good assortment, convenient prices, and no request for a minimum quantity. The owner also checked if the supplier was well-known through some online discussion groups which discuss dishonest suppliers of combat sports equipments. In addition, the chosen supplier sent a trial order. As it seemed that everything was going well, the first bulk of combat sports equipment was ordered in the form of airplane delivery. It was agreed that the goods would be paid 50% in advance, and the remaining amount would be paid as Cash Against Documents, which is "a method of payment for goods in which documents transferring title are given to the buyer upon payment of cash to an intermediary acting for the seller, usually a bank" (Reyndols, 2003).

Developing a New Combat Sports Equipment Brand

The owner decided to sell combat sports equipment under the new brand name PFS (ProFightStore). He also designed a logo for the new brand and sent it to the supplier. In other words, the owner followed embryonic brand orientation which presumes developing its own brand from the start, although this approach is highly risky especially for SMEs (Groucutt, 2006). In developing the brand, the owner relied solely on himself and his own familiarity with combat sports subculture. He examined the design of different combat sports equipment brands but also colours and shapes that combat sports online communities use on popular Web sites. Clear shapes and dark colours have proven to be popular and widely accepted, because they indicate strength and masculinity typical for combat sports subculture. Such an approach, coupled with the owner's passion for the brand, his active role as the entrepreneur as well as his creativity, are a recipe for successful brand management proposed by Frank and Krake (2005). In addition, the decision was made that PFS brand would be priced within the medium-quality price range, which is the usual pricing setting in SMEs (Carson, Gilmore, Cummins, O'Donnell, & Grant, 1998).

Developing an Online Store

The stages of e-commerce development and their characteristics include (Rao Subba, Metts, & Mora Monge, 2003) presence, portals, transactions integration, and enterprise integration. Transactions integration presumes that the Web site offers goods and/or services to potential customers, and that it is possible to order goods through an online store. In addition, two general Web site design strategies

are proposed by Wen, Chen, and Hwang (2001): (1) informational/communicational strategy, which presumes using the Web site as a supplement to traditional marketing, and (2) online transactional strategy which is suitable for companies that use the Web to construct "virtual business" existing only on the Internet and independent from the main business activity. Wen et al. (2001) identify several models of e-commerce Web site design. One of those models is the community model based on user loyalty which emerges from the fact that users invest both time and emotions in the site.

Profightstore.com is designed as a transactions integration online store based on the community model because it is the only Web portal which delivers the latest daily news on combat sports events and intriguing interviews with combat sports fighters. Most visitors access Profightstore.com daily where they read the latest news written in an unbiased and objective tone. Journalists who write for Profightstore.com are instructed not to incorporate their personal opinions if they report on personal conflicts which are frequent in the combat sports world. At the same time, online combat sports forums are more than just a place where visitors exchange information, they are also the "arena" for pursuing personal conflicts. By being objective, Profightstore.com differentiates itself from such trivial issues. However, when reports on fights are given, personal opinions of journalists are welcome. In that way, visitors can be sure that Profightstore.com will give them the most objective view of current personal conflicts in the combat sports community and the juiciest report on the latest fights.

The development of the online store was conducted by a professional provider who offered a convenient price. The owner did not choose the developer who offered the lowest price, but instead he made a decision based on the recommendations of customers who have already established a strong and reliable relationship with the developer. Also, Web stores that the developer had already set up were thoroughly examined in order to detect if the quality and depth of the design were acceptable to the owner's high standards. The store design was made by a professional designer employed by the developer of the online store, following widely accepted standards such as: accessibility, navigation, readability, and download speed (Thelwall, 2000). In addition, Profightstore.com was created with such colours, shapes, and photos that turned it into a place where visitors could encounter virtual experience (Gilmore, 2002). The store is designed as content management system (CMS), which means that the content to the online store is added by journalists and the owner himself.

The store is organised as a portal, and at least several relevant pieces of news are published on the Web site, together with interviews, TV programs with combat sports shows, and other contents (the best fighter, the best fighting club).

The process of ordering goods is very simple. First, customers browse through the offer of combat sports equipment products, and add the products to the basket. When all the goods are added to the basket, customers give their personal information (name, address, contact phone number, and e-mail address). An automatic e-mail is sent both to customers and the selling staff. It is not possible to pay by credit card in this online store. Therefore, customers pay for the goods at the time of either door-to-door or post-office delivery.

Attracting Visitors

The first day of launching Profightstore.com was the day when the first order was made, which indicated that the future was bright for this particular online store. However, things did not go as smoothly as expected. In the beginning, the number of visits was rather small, and the owner realised that although the Web site content was attractive, potential visitors should be additionally informed about Profightstore.com. Therefore, the owner of Profightstore.com pursued three ways of attracting visitors: (1) guerrilla marketing approach through online combat sports community, (2) paid search, and (3) sponsorship of combat sports events and fighters.

Guerrilla Marketing Approach

The owner of Profightstore.com thought it would be unreasonable to use broadcast advertising techniques that appeal to the general public, when he is targeting the niche market of combat sports equipment. Expensive prime time television advertisements would surely be a waste of money, especially because they are unfocused. The only time when TV advertisements would yield results would be TV broadcasts of combat sports fights, but their price is beyond Profightstore.com's marketing budget.

Guerrilla marketing, a term coined by Jay Conrad Levinson, uses "unconventional marketing intended to get maximum results from minimal resources." Some of the guerrilla marketing principles are (Cohen, 2003):

- Setting clear goals and objectives
- Learning the media usage and business habits of your target
- Posting advertisements in the media that reach your target audience
- Using e-mail and virtual marketing
- Alerting the media with the public relations campaign

Therefore, the guerrilla marketing approach was employed to target online discussion groups. This approach was also chosen because of a tight marketing budget. Hagel and Armstrong (1998) point out in their book on virtual communities that great marketing potential lies in the fact that a group of people communicates virtually to each other because of their common interests and, even more importantly, because they trust each other. Most online discussion groups have some kind of administrators or moderators who take care that certain rules are respected, e.g. people should not be offensive to each other; no commercials should be posted on the online discussion group Web site etc.

Profightstore.com has therefore decided to benefit from such great potential of virtual communities and the owner's vision was to use online discussion groups dedicated to combat sports. He made this decision based on his gut feeling, although procedures for estimating the success of an online community could have been applied (Cothrel, 2000). At this point the owner hired several members of such groups. They started to write news for Profightstore.com, and at the same time they mentioned Profightstore.com in their posts in online discussion groups.

Paid Search

Search engines are the most frequently visited Web sites in virtual Internet space. They enable visitors to easily find the content they are interested in. The most popular search engines today have gained their popularity due to their simple design and lack of banner ads. Google, for instance, has based its strategy on innovations, among which paid search stands out as the greatest source of its revenue. It might be mentioned at this point that synonyms used for the term *paid search* are pay-per click, pay for payment, pay-for-performance, paid listing, and sponsored search (Laffey, 2007). However, there are some problems with paid search such as the infringement of trade mark (Tyacke & Higgins, 2004).

Paid search is based on the following four steps (Google, 2007): (1) advertisers choose keywords related to their business; (2) advertisers create the text of the ad by themselves; (3) the ads appear on the search engine next to search results, and (4) visitors can click on the ad in order to make a purchase or because they are curious about the advertiser. Although Profightstore.com is highly rated in search engines, and visitors generally prefer nonsponsored links to paid ads (Jansen, Brown, & Resnick, 2007), the owner started Google Adwords campaign two years ago with great success. This was the result of a very careful keyword selection, and constant monitoring of campaign performance.

Sponsorship of Combat Sport Events and Fighters

Sponsorship in today's world has changed its role from a special form of advertising to an important relationship in which the sponsoring firm and the sponsored subject (person, nonprofit organization, event, etc.) form a strategic alliance (Urriolagoitia & Planellas, 2006). In addition, sponsorship is an important opportunity for operationalising brand strategy (Cliffe & Motion, 2005). As it gained popularity, Profightstore.com became sponsored by numerous combat sports events and fighters. However, fighters and event organisers tend to stress that money is not the main reason for collaborating with Profightstore.com. Instead, they focus on the Web site objective and ability to cover combat sports events in the fastest possible manner.

Change of the Web Site Design

The development of the Web site is a continuous process which should never end. Many technological innovations, user capabilities and needs, competitor actions, and the growth of supporting business reinforce the change of Web design (Waite & Harrison, 2007). Profightstore.com was designed by a professional designer in light colours. After one year the design changed into much darker colours following the model of some world famous combat sports Web sites, like sherdog.com. Surprisingly enough, the number of visits remained the same. However, after such drastic changes in design, the number of orders diminished (fewer orders were made for almost one month after the change). The owner again changed the design to the new one that resembled more the original one. Sales again started to increase. A possible explanation of the decrease in the number of orders was the use of dark colours in combination with white letters, which diminished the visibility of the Web site. However, an important lesson was learned: design should not be changed drastically and suddenly.

Developing One More Combat Sports Online Store

Additionally, the owner of PFS launched another online store with more expensive combat sports equipment brands. However, the store only offered combat sports equipment, and did not have any other additional content that could attract visitors. Google Adwords were not enough to attract more visitors, and sales were infrequent. This online store still exists, but the owner does not plan to improve it any further.

Selling Advertisements

Banner ads were the first form of Internet advertising that appeared on Web sites in the late 1990s. They were priced similarly to TV ads on a flat fee, cost per thousand, or on the basis of audiences (Hoffman & Novak, 2000). After initial enthusiasm with banner ads, the revenue from such advertisements dropped because Web site visitors simply ignored them. However, Profightstore. com succeeds in selling banner ads of combat sports events because of their great design, which gives visitors a genuine feeling of what they will experience in real combat sports events—pure fighting. For now, those banners are designed with as few Flash effects as possible because of the slow Internet connection. The goal is to develop more vivid banner ads as soon as fast Internet connections become more widespread among the Croatian population. Advertisers are given access to Profightstore.com Web-site metrics: number of unique visitors, visitors' countries and search engines, the most popular pages of the Web site, statistics per hours, days, months, and years.

Current Challenges Facing the Organization

The main business objective of the owner of Profightstore.com is to position his store as regional leader with the English version of the Web site as soon as Croatia becomes member of the European Union. (Once Croatia joins the EU, export procedures will be less complicated.) Currently, the majority of visitors of Profightstore.com come from Croatia and neighbouring countries but there is quite a number of visitors from English speaking countries as well despite the language barrier. Therefore, the English version of Profightstore. com is planned in the near future.

Internationalisation is usually connected with larger firms. However, SMEs also use internationalisation as growth strategy, but it is usually successful only if the owner of a small firm is strongly dedicated to it, and has knowledge and resources to conduct it properly. Some common problems that SMEs encounter when trying to internationalise their operations include (Lloyd-Reason & Mughan, 2002): lack of language skills, poor understanding of foreign cultures, poor development of international marketing skills, and skills of other supporting activities (finance, operations, IT, human resources, strategy development). Only if the owner/manager pursues a very strong international orientation of his firm and only if he has well developed skills and resource base of the firm will Profightstore.com succeed in achieving the goal of becoming a regional leader. In addition, the issue of the impact of local culture on the Web site content, design, and structure (Fletcher, 2006) should be taken into account when new Web sites are developed.

Sandy and Burgess (2003) list the following levels of facilitation of Web sites: electronic brochure, electronic brochure and order, electronic brochure and order and payment, and finally, interactive publishing. Currently, Profightstore. com is at the stage of electronic brochure and order and should move to the higher levels of facilitation of Web sites. However, the owner's opinion is that the current facilities of Profightstore.com (news, product catalogue, order) are sufficient for attracting customers, so that he is more oriented on enhancing the number of products offered.

REFERENCES

Barnes, D., Hinton, M., & Mieczkowska, S. (2004). Avoiding the fate of the dotbombs: Lessons from three surviving dotcom start-ups. Journal of Small Business and Enterprise Development, 11(3), 329–337.

Carson, D., Gilmore, A., Cummins, D., O'Donnell, A., & Grant, K. (1998). Price setting in SMEs: Some empirical findings. Journal of Product & Brand Management, 7(1), 74–86.

Chiou, J., & Shen, C. (2006). The effects of satisfaction, opportunism, and asset specificity on consumers' loyalty intention toward internet portal sites. International Journal of Service Industry Management, 11(1), 7–11.

Chircu, A.M., & Kauffman, R.J. (2000). Reintermediation strategies in business-to-business electronic commerce. International Journal of Electronic Commerce, 4(4), 7–42.

Cliffe, S.J., & Motion, J. (2005). Building contemporary brands: A sponsorship-based strategy. Journal of Business Research, 58(8), 1068–1077.

Cohen, N. (2003). Early-stage marketing for start-ups. Retrieved June 3, 2008, from http://www.clickz.com/showPage.html?page=825181

Cothrel, J.P. (2000). Measuring the success of an online community. Strategy & Leadership, 28(2), 17–21.

Duffie, D., & Singleton, K.J. (2003). Credit risk: Pricing, measurement and management. Princeton University Press.

Fletcher, R. (2006). The impact of culture on Web site content, design, and structure. Journal of Communication Management, 10(3), 259–273.

Frank, B.G., & Krake, J.M. (2005). Successful brand management in SMEs: A new theory and practical hints. Journal of Product & Brand Management, 14(4), 228–238.

Gfk (2005). Number of Internet users in Croatia. Retrieved June 3, 2008, from http://www.gfk.hr/press/internet6.htm

Gfk (2006). Citizens and the Internet. Retrieved June 3, 2008, from http://www.gfk.hr/press1/internet.htm

Gilmore, J.H., & Pine., J., II. (2002). Customer experience places: The new offering frontier. Strategy & Leadership, 30(4), 4–11.

Google.com (2007). Learn about AdWords. Retrieved June 3, 2008, from http://adwords.google.com/select/Login

Griffin, T. (1994). International marketing communications. Oxford: Butterworth Heinemann.

Groucutt, J. (2006). The life, death and resuscitation of brands. Handbook of Business Strategy, 7(1), 101–106.

Gurstein, M. (2000). Community informatics: Enabling communities with information and communications technologies. Hershey, PA: Idea Group Publishing.

Hagel, J., III, & Armstrong, A.G. (1998). Net gain: Expanding markets through virtual communities. Boston: Harvard Business School Press.

Hoffman, D.L., & Novak, T.P. (2000). How to acquire customers on the Web. Harvard Business Review, 78(3), 179–183.

Hsein, C., & Lin, B. (1998). Internet commerce for small business. Industrial Management & Data Systems, 3(1), 113–119.

Jansen, B.J., Brown, A., & Resnick, M. (in press). Factors relating to the decision to click on a sponsored link. Decision Support Systems.

Kennedy, A., & Coughlan, J. (2006). Online shopping portals: An option for traditional retailers? International Journal of Retail & Distribution Management, 34(7), 516–528.

Kotler, P. (2003). Marketing management (11th ed.). New York: Prentice Hall.

Laffey, D. (2007). Paid search: The innovation that changed the Web. Business Horizons, 50(3), 211–218.

Lloyd-Reason, L., & Mughan, T. (2002). Strategies for internationalization within SMEs: The key role of the owner manager. Journal of Small Business and Enterprise Development, 9(2), 120–129.

Loflin, M.D., & Winogrond, I.R. (1976). A culture as a set of beliefs. Current Anthropology, 17(4), 723–725.

Malic-Bandu, K. (2006). Electronic media as a key of competitiveness of transition countries. Informatologija, 39(4), 280–285.

Poon, S., & Matthew, J. (2000). Product characteristics and Internet commerce benefit among small businesses. Journal of Product & Brand Management, 9(1), 21–34.

Porter, M.E. (1998). Competitive advantage of nations. New York: The Free Press.

Powazek, D.M. (2002). Design for community: The art of connecting real people in virtual places. Indianapolis: New Riders.

Rao Subba, S., Metts, G., & Mora Monge, C.A. (2003). Electronic commerce development in small and medium sized enterprises: A stage model and its implications. Business Process Management Journal, 9(1), 11–32.

Reyndols, F. (2003). Managing exports: Navigating the complex rules, controls, barriers, and laws. New York: Wiley.

Sandy, G., & Burgess, S. (2003). A decision chart for small business Web site content. Logistic Information Management, 16(1), 36–47.

Shunk, D.L., Carter, J.R., Hovis, J., & Talwar, A. (2007). Electronics industry drivers of intermediation and disintermediation. International Journal of Physical Distribution & Logistics Management, 37(3), 248–261.

Thelwall, M. (2000). Effective Websites for small and medium-sized enterprises. Journal of Small Business and Enterprise Development, 7(2), 149–159.

Tv.com (2007). The Ultimate Fighter. Retrieved June 3, 2008, from http://www.tv.com/the-ultimate-fighter/show/31862/summary.html

Tyacke, N., & Higgins, R. (2004). Searching for trouble: Keyword advertising and trade mark infringement. Computer Law & Security Report, 20(6), 453–465.

Ultimate Fighting Championship (2007). Fighters. Retrieved June 3, 2008, from http://www.ufc.com

Urriolagoitia, L., & Planellas, M. (2007). Sponsorship relationships as strategic alliances: A life cycle model approach. Business Horizons, 50(2), 157–166.

Waite, K., & Harrison, T. (2007). Internet acheaeology: Uncovering pension sector Web site evolution. Internet Research, 17(2), 180–195.

Wen, H.J., Chen, H., & Hwang, H. (2001). E-commerce Web site design: Strategies and models. Information Management & Computer Security, 9(1), 5–12.

Yin, R.K. (2003). Case study research design and methods. London: Sage Publications.

FURTHER READING

Ihlström, C., Magnusson, M., Scupola, A., Tuunainen, V.K. (2003). SME barriers to electronic commerce adoption: nothing changes-everything is new. In G. Gingrich (Ed.), *Managing IT in Government Business & Communities.* (pp. 147-163). Hershey, PA: IDEA Group/IRM Press.

Krug, S. (2005). *Don't Make me Think: A Common Sense Approach to Web Usability.* Indianapolis: New Riders Press.

Grandon EE. Pearson JM. (2004). Electronic commerce adoption: an empirical study of small and medium US businesses. *Information Management,* 42(1), 197-216.

Hedbor, L.D.H. (2005). *Small Business Projects / Internet.* Indiana: AuthorHouse.

Brache, A. & Webb, J. (2000) The eight deadly assumptions of e-business. *Journal of Business Strategy*, 21(3), 13-17.

Aragon-Correa JA. Cordon-Pozo E. The influence of strategic dimensions and the environment on the introduction of Internet as innovation into small and medium-sized enterprises. [Article] Technology Analysis & Strategic Management. 17(2):205-218, 2005 Jun.

Gilmore, A., Gallagher, D. & Henry, S. (2007). E-marketing and SMEs: operational lessons for the future. *European Business Review, 19*(3), 234-247.

Chapter VII
Emerging E–Services in Accounting:
A Longitudinal Case Study

Benita M. Gullkvist
Hanken School of Economics, Finland

ABSTRACT

This chapter analyses and provides an example of the introduction and first years of the management of accounting services and e-services in a professional accounting firm. It argues that e-services, as a result of adoption and use of Web-based digital technology, are slowly emerging within the accounting field. Further, the change to e-services implies a significant change in the business model for professional service providers as well as acceptance and adoption of the new services among customers. Furthermore, the author hopes that by identifying development and learning issues, the case cannot only be used for implementation of similar initiatives within other organizations but will also assist students in their understanding of the process of change and e-service management.

INTRODUCTION

Within many disciplines the utilization of Internet technology has moved traditional business processes to the electronic environment and changed the business models for professional services (Kotler, Hayes, & Bloom, 2002). Web utilization has given many companies "Internet presence" and provided them with opportunities to develop and expand new services. The concept of electronic services, known in short as e-services, has emerged in academic literature and practice. Although the term "e-services" is commonly used in business and information science journals, a generally accepted definition of the concept does not seem to exist (Stafford, 2003). For this study, based on Rust and Kannan (2002), an e-service is defined as "the provision of service over electronic networks"; where in this study the term "networks" implies the Internet.

The objective of this case study is to analyse and provide an example of the introduction and first years of the management of accounting services and e-services in a particular professional accounting firm in order to identify development and learning issues, which can be used for implementation of similar initiatives within other organizations in the future. The focus is on the perceived problems and opportunities in transforming services into e-services as well as the operational and strategic solutions used by the company to solve the emerging problems. The professional accounting firm in this study is a service provider of financial, accounting, and taxation related services for client companies, but not internal or external auditing services. The accounting firm uses information technology both to provide services to the clients and to support its own internal operations for internal administration and accounting. This case study will not distinguish between internal and external use, but will discuss the introduction and utilisation of Internet technology as a whole.

The introduction of e-services and the change in the business model are examined via a longitudinal case study over a period of three years, from 2004 until early 2007. Extensive investigation was undertaken to find an agency that would be among the forerunners in digital accounting systems use, preferably in the post-implementation phase of a Web-based accounting software adoption. Besides being on top of technology, the selection criteria included the researcher having relatively open access to the company for further studies and permission to publish the findings. The case agency was previously unknown to the researcher. Data were collected with multiple semistructured interviews and open discussions being conducted at six-month intervals with the business owner and employees. The data were transcribed, analysed, and codified into themes, and emerging issues were examined. Each interview candidate viewed the findings and was invited to comment on the issues. Further, the researcher had access to company documents and notes but with regard to client confidentiality, full access to all documents was not possible to obtain. Data triangulation (Denzin, 1989) was obtained by comparing feedback, interview data, and participant observation. However, since the research was undertaken by only one researcher, which did not facilitate investigator triangulation, the findings may be subject to bias. Further, data collection was limited to the accounting agency, thus neither the ASP vendor providers' nor the clients' opinions have been investigated.

BACKGROUND

Accounting is about providing useful information to users for decision-making and in a standardised format that allows for comparability and understanding (Wallman, 1997). The users of accounting and business information are both internal, within the enterprise itself, and external, for example the taxation authorities, investors, financial institutions, and auditors.

An enterprise can prepare the financial information itself or purchase the services. In Finland approximately 90% of book-keeping records, financial, and fiscal reporting in companies is provided by accounting agencies (Association of Finnish Accounting Firms, 2006). Finnish companies thus heavily rely on external accounting service providers. The high number should however be compared to the existing large number of small and medium sized enterprises (SMEs) in Finland and in the EU (Ghobadian & Gallear, 1996). Further, the most common category of clients of Finnish accounting firms is micro-entities and small companies (Lith, 2004). Previous research has found evidence that SMEs tend to contract out non-core business functions to service providers due to reasons such as cost savings and lack of expertise (for example, Lacity & Willcocks, 1998). In Finland, like in many other countries, accountancy is legally regulated (subject to the

Accounting Act) and a strong link exists between accounting and taxation. The demand for the accountant's reporting services in small entities has mainly been driven by regulatory requirements (see also Marriott & Marriott, 2000) and, as many owner-managers possess limited financial skills, they do not understand or use the information produced for strategic management purposes (see also Templeman & Wootton, 1987).

The relationship between small company owners-managers and their accountants is primarily an economic one (Marriott & Marriott, 2000). Accounting firms can be characterised as knowledge intensive service organisations, which provide services to clients for a price. The provided services may include book-keeping, accounting, tax returns, payroll calculations, cost and budget control, financial statements, invoicing, business advice and consultation, education, business administration and management services. Of these, book-keeping and preparation of financial statements form the bulk of the business for accounting firms (Association of Finnish Accounting Firms, 2006). According to Statistics Finland there are altogether approximately 3980 accounting agencies in Finland. Most accounting agencies are family-owned micro-entities (Lith, 2004), with an average number of 2.1 employees including the owner (Association of Finnish Accounting Firms, 2006). The market is dominated by small and medium-sized agencies with a market share of 90%, and the number of large accounting agencies is small. Agencies with more than 20 employees account for less than 1% of the total number of

agencies. Small-sized agencies provide work for approximately half of the industry's employees and account for approximately half of the total industry's turnover (Toivonen, 2005). More details on industry's statistics can be found in Table 1.

The accounting firm at the focus of this study, hereafter known as eAgency, is located in a mid-sized town in central Finland. eAgency was established in 2004 through the division of an existing agency (known as OldAgency) into two separate agencies. In the years preceding 2004 the accounting software in use in OldAgency was outdated and in urgent need for renewal. The two owners and business partners of OldAgency set out to investigate possible options. At this point a new Web-based accounting software was launched, and one owner saw many advantages with this type of software compared to other existing technological solutions on the market. However, the other owner was less enthusiastic, stressing potential problems with new software for the agency, staff, and clients. The disagreement about the software resulted in one of the owners leaving OldAgency to establish her own accounting firm, eAgency, on 13 February 2004. Based on a mutual agreement between the business partners, the existing customers of OldAgency were divided between them. Thus, eAgency did not have to acquire new customers for its establishment, but started off with approximately 40 clients, mainly small- and medium-sized local entities from various industrial and service areas.

Since its establishment eAgency has had three full-time employees working alongside the owner.

Table 1. Accounting agency industry's statistics in the year 2003 (Source: Toivonen 2005 based on Statistics Finland)

Accounting Agency Industry	Agencies		Employees		Turnover
	Number	In percent	Number	In percent	in 1000 €
1–4 employees	3576	89.4 %	4557	51.2 %	285 382
5–9 employees	291	7.3 %	1789	20.1 %	97 151
10–19 employees	97	2.4 %	1259	14.1 %	70 863
20 or more employees	35	0.9 %	1304	14.6 %	127 795
Total	**3999**	**100.0 %**	**8909**	**100.0 %**	**581 191**

All three employees and the owner came from OldAgency. This was a decision taken by the employees themselves who reported in the interviews that the move was motivated by mainly personal reasons, either related to the employees' wish to develop their skills or continue to work with this particular owner. In addition to the full-time employees, one or two students worked in 2004 and 2005 during peak seasons. Furthermore, the father of the owner, being a retired accountant, provided support and advice as well as made a keen and experienced debating partner, according to the owner herself. The eAgency owner has over 20 years' experience in book-keeping and accounting related issues and has completed the professional accountant (KLT) exam. All employees as well as the owner are females, which is a typical feature of the industry. Statistics show that the majority, approximately 75%, of the Finnish accounts clerks and book-keepers are female, which is in congruence with international findings (for example, Cooper & Taylor, 2000, p. 576). Further details of eAgency will not be disclosed in order to protect the positions of the participants.

One common problem in SMEs is the scarceness of resources of both the service provider and the client (for example, Davies & Garcia-Sierra 1999; O'Connor & O'Keefe, 1997; Raymond, 1985). The emergence of Web-based accounting applications has provided accounting firms with an alternative to desktop accounting when dealing with their SME customers. A Web-based accounting package is an accounting system that exists on a Web server. Anybody with a browser, an Internet connection and a password can access the system, basically from anywhere. Further, instead of making a large investment in technology, the alternative is that the user pays a smaller monthly fixed rental fee to the service provider; a fee based on the size of the data and/or on the transaction volume. These new leasing possibilities appeared very attractive and eAgency chose to lease access to server and software across the Internet, rather than purchasing, housing, and backing up the

system itself. Thanks to the ASP-solution, the use of NetX eAccounting required no initial investment in software for eAgency or the clients, but a Web browser, and Internet access was needed. According to the owner, the ASP-solution further facilitated a smooth and fast implementation of the system, since the system was already "up and running." The choice of the ASP-solution can also be seen as a strategic change in the management of ICT-technology at eAgency.

Further motives for the change to NetX eAccounting were derived from the business environment. The owner of eAgency was keenly motivated to continue in the accounting business even after 20 years of business experience. The Finnish accounting firm industry has undergone structural changes since the late 1990s and the trend seems to continue. Along with technology, the few big accounting firms have expanded their operations and become even bigger by establishing new offices and/or buying existing local small and medium-sized agencies all over the country. By utilizing the Internet technology and establishing a presence on the Internet the owner of eAgency saw an option to remain in business and a path through which to gain competitive advantage.

The owner was also truly impressed by the NetX eAccounting software and saw potential for her firm through its utilisation. In addition, she was a strong believer in digital accounting. Without undermining the existing service and financial reporting quality, she ambitiously set out to introduce digital accounting and new services to her clients. EAgency as a small-sized agency must without doubt be regarded as one of the Finnish accounting agency pioneers in using Web-based accounting with its SME clients.

Setting the Stage

Since the mid-1990s there has been an ongoing discussion in popular accounting magazines in Finland and among researchers worldwide about the coming electronic revolution of financial accounting (for example, Alles, Kogan, & Vasarhelyi, 2000; Mäkinen, 2000; Olivier, 2000; Sutton, 2000; Vahtera & Salmi, 1998; Vasarhelyi & Greenstein, 2003). Terms such as paperless accounting, e-accounting, Internet accounting and digital accounting have emerged in the media. "Digital accounting" refers to the representation of accounting information in digital format, which then can be electronically manipulated and transmitted (Deshmukh, 2006). Furthermore, digital accounting should be seen as an inter-organizational system, where the service provider, e.g. the accounting agency, co-operates online with customers in providing services. In practice, advances in information and communication technology (ICT) as well as e-business have promoted the use of integrated software solutions, where accounting entries are generated as a by-product of the underlying business transactions (Gottlieb, 1996; IFAC, 2002) or the data on the paper-based source document is captured into an electronic file by a scanner (Alles et al., 2000). The development of electronic bank statements and reference payments in the banking sector as well as the emergence of online banking and electronic invoicing can also be seen as facilitating digital accounting. In addition, the revised Accounting Act in 1997 makes it possible to use electronic data media in transferring, maintaining and storing accounting data (Accounting Act, 1997; Accounting Board, 2000). Further, the taxation authorities have promoted the use of e-forms and e-filing for monthly and annual tax reports.

The owner of eAgency acknowledged the past and on-going discussion in the media about the impact of ICT on business and in particular on accounting. This may also have influenced her business decisions and choice of software. One issue raised in media discussion is that along with the development of ICT, not only would tasks related to recording numerical data essentially decrease and enable the development of new services (Hunton, 2002), but the decrease in work would also compel the accounting industry to

find new tasks in order to safeguard the future of the business (Toivonen, 2004). Lith (2004) noticed that some large accounting firms have developed their supply of advisory services and provide for example ASP-services, for example, hiring out and providing software vendor services to enterprises that prefer to manage their own financial accounts.

As stated above, financial accounts for small companies have in many cases been produced to meet statutory requirements, and thus the relevance and added value of such reports to the business owner has previously been regarded as low. The owner of eAgency had a strong urge and saw great opportunities to change the situation through modern technology. By automating the routine work of accounting data entry and digitizing the accounts, the staff at eAgency were expected to have more time and energy to develop new, customer-oriented services and "to take a closer look at the bottom line of the income statement". In the first interview the owner mentioned the development of management accounting services, where financial information would be presented in a form more likely to be understood and used by the client. Further, a move towards providing additional business advice and consultancy was seen as important because accounting is often the only external expert service that small-scale clients use. However, as Toivonen (2004) points out, adopting the consultative operating method means a very great change and challenge to the content of the expertise in the accounting sector. The know-how it requires is partly even contrary to the traditional skill requirements in this sector, which has emphasised first and foremost accuracy. Further, Kirby, Najak, and Greene (1998) found that the role of the external accountant in the 1990s was narrowly defined for many SME owner-managers, with 70% of respondents using their external accountants for statutory advice and less than half this group, 33%, seeing the role as one of business management advice. Since the SME clients of eAgency may have similar expectations of the provided services, the demand may be low for business advice and consultancy. A change in the SME owner's perceptions may not be an easy task to overcome.

The market for accounting services was expected to grow in the future. Toivonen (2004) found in her research that the interviewees anticipated a growth in outsourcing by large companies in the years to come. Medium-sized and large companies, that have previously managed their accounting and finances in-house would be an important and interesting client group for eAgency, realizable through new technology. Further, eAgency would be able to increase the number of clients without having to increase the number of employees when part of the routine work has been automated. The enterprises themselves usually face an urge to cut administrative costs, and outsourcing their financial administration functions has been seen to render cost benefits. The needs and requirements of large organizations are however different to the traditional preparations of monthly financial and tax statements. Further, differences in international reporting and business regulations may also cause a need for additional know-how, if the enterprise operates on the international market.

New players, such as software houses, banks and consulting firms, have been seen to enter the accounting field and whilst not providing accounting services as such, they do offer complementary support. Further, intense cooperation between legal firms, accounting firms and banks has also been noticed (Toivonen, 2004). The heavy reliance on information technology in many firms has also strengthened the cooperation with software vendors regarding system maintenance and development. Emerging standards for electronic invoicing indicate an even stronger move towards digital accounting in the future. Further, online banking has grown in strength. A keen debate regarding taxation authorities introducing more demanding requirements for companies to file information electronically could be seen in 2004 in the media.

As a whole, there seemed to be a positive market for e-services in 2004 and Web-based accounting solutions were expected to dramatically change financial accounting practice.

CASE DESCRIPTION

Establishing a new business is a demanding task, even for someone with previous business experience. In addition, knowing that the first half of the financial year is the high season for accounting firms, it is understandable that the eAgency employees and owner had a trying time in early 2004. The implementation and management of the NetX eAccounting system and the transfer of accounting data of existing clients from the old software into NetX eAccounting came at the same time as the closing of the books and the preparations of clients' annual accounts in most client companies. However, as mentioned previously, the NetX eAccounting system was, according to the owner and the employees, easy to implement and learn. It was implemented over a two-week period with the aim of fully embedding it within the organization by the end of the first half year of operation. Further, the data transmission between the two systems was carried out using spreadsheets, thus ensuring that very little data entry work was actually carried out manually with regards to data transfer between the previous system and NetX. The closing of the accounts for the year 2003 was, if possible, completed in the old system, before the data, e.g. Opening Balances of the General, Purchases and Sales Ledger, were transferred into NetX eAccounting.

The first three years of the new agency could best be described as a time of constant development of the business model and provided services. Being a small-sized agency with limited resources, the owner's strategy was to advance little by little. Some of the major changes in operations have been summarized in Table 2 and they will be thematically discussed below.

Technology

One of the first issues for eAgency in early 2004 was the creation of the eAgency website. The role of the website was not only to function as an advertising medium, but to provide an interactive medium and platform for new services. The website was designed by a local ICT entrepreneur with some help from the ASP-vendor. Further, the clients needed to have access to the software.

EAgency adopted a web-based application for accounting and financial administration called NetX eAccounting. Compared to the previous system used by OldAgency, the change was huge.

The previous accounting software was a standard package application that maintained accounting records in a local network. Daily system maintenance was taken care of by the staff and since no major up-grades had taken place during the few years before, big problems had not emerged. The clients brought paid invoices, receipts and similar source documents approximately one or one and a half months after the conclusion of the month. The accountants keyed the data into the accounting system and delivered the statutory reports within due time. NetX eAccounting presented new opportunities to integrate finance and accounting services within and across clients

Table 2. Some major changes in e-agency's operations during the first years

Year 1: 2004	New Web site creation
	Software training (eAgency)
	Marketing of new service concept & business model
	Expanding the market (region --> country)
	Standard start-up procedure with new clients developed
	Marketing of digital accounting
	Pilot user agreement with software vendor
	Development of new pricing model
Year 2: 2005	Intensive marketing campaign (old clients)
	Long-term goal set to focus only on digital accounting-clients
	Additional functions of the software utilized
	Client training package, e.g., new sales product developed
	Invoice scanning increased
	Computer-based time-management system for internal use developed
Year 3: 2006	Lease of additional software
	Packaging of services (3 different sales products)
	Improvements in staff ergonomics (tools for electronic environment)
	Services ordering via the Web facilitated
	Client communication via e-mail & Web emphasized
	Alliances with legal firm & auditor formed
	eAgency's client billing outsourced
	Pilot project with medium-sized client (link to client's ERP system)
	eAgency filed for debt rescheduling
	Owner on sick leave

and markets. Data and information on business transactions or electronic bank statements were automatically transmitted into NetX eAccounting. Thus, manual data entry tasks were expected to decrease. Further, the latency in reporting was expected to improve, since data entries take place on transaction (recording of orders, invoices etc.) or shortly afterwards (payments on electronic bank statements). Moreover, Internet technology facilitates work from anywhere, thus providing new possibilities for eAgency to expand the business and serve customers all over the country and even internationally.

The features of NetX eAccounting software truly fascinated the owner, her father, and the employees. With a simple browser, the client can access the accounting system, check accounts, information, make entries, pay bills, and run ad hoc reports. Further, via the direct link to the client's bank statement, transactions on the bank statement are automatically entered into NetX. In 2004 approximately 70% of the traditional data entry tasks were automatically managed by NetX. The figure had grown to approximately 90% by the end of 2006, since NetY, an additional software solution that has been adopted, includes a feature which facilitates "system learning." Approximately 30% of the reference payments needed to be checked due to missing data in late 2004, but the figure has now decreased considerably and mismatches or missing references are nowadays rare. The use of new technology resulted in a major change in the routine work of the employees, whose tasks since computers were first utilised had consisted mainly of manual data entries. However, since the software was newly designed, there were still some missing features and modules. The software was for example not designed for production companies, since the production and material handling modules had not been created. This was not a major problem for eAgency, because most of their clients did not need this module. Even so, the owner of eAgency decided to join the NetX team as a pilot tester and

user of new software upgrades in late 2004 to further improve the functionality of NetX. This cooperation continued until early 2006. Further, the owner was on occasion engaged in promoting digital accounting and used eAgency as an example with new customers in marketing campaigns organised by the ASP vendor. In addition, a pilot project with a medium-sized e-commerce company was launched in late 2006, where a link was built between the client's information system and NetX for accounting purposes. The link facilitates automatic daily data transfer of confirmed sales orders from the client's system into NetX. The rest of the process, for example, accounting and payment related issues, are thereafter handled in NetX. Although the technical details were demanding to handle, the project came through and this gave eAgency confidence and appetite for more similar projects.

The NetX eAccounting solution, though targeted at the SME market segment, turned out to be too limited for medium-sized companies. The owner of eAgency made the decision to lease an additional, similar but more advanced application in 2006, also targeted at SME enterprises. According to the Web site, this Web-based application NetY includes economy, material, service, project, communication, time, and quality features. For example, in 2006 NetY facilitated the adoption of Web-based ordering of services in eAgency.

Although standards for electronic invoicing emerged in the early 2000s, the existence of e-invoices in practice has been progressing very slowly in Finland. This implies that most of the source documents, except bank statements, are paper-based and eAgency has been "forced" into invoice scanning in order to make use of NetX's and NetY's features. The invoice scanning is, upon agreement, either performed by eAgency or by the client. Invoice scanning for very small entrepreneurs is not considered cost effective and is thus rarely carried out. More recently, eAgency has outsourced the purchase invoice scanning process to a third-party vendor.

NetX and NetY are considered well-functioning and secure information systems by the owner and employees of eAgency. During the interviews the staff recalled few failures when accessing the Internet and software. The authentication service is the same as the banking industry uses and considered very reliable. In spite of this, the eAgency staff has identified a certain reluctance among their clients to place accounting details online. Lack of trust in technology and its ability to perform properly has also been noted in previous research (Hart & Saunders, 1997; Parasuraman, 2000) and can constitute a major barrier to the adoption of e-services among clients. Further, previous research has also presented evidence of limited access and use of Internet technology, in particular among small entrepreneurs (Toivonen, 2004). This was also recalled by eAgency among its clients.

Market and Customers

The business idea of e-services needed to be sold to the SME market. Although there had been an ongoing discussion about digital accounting in popular accounting magazines and newspapers, the adoption and use of similar technology in other accounting agencies or enterprises and the knowledge of the systems in SMEs was very limited in 2004. Mainly large, internationally operating companies had similar technology already in use. Thus, eAgency not only promoted their own services, but also acted as a local and regional pioneer in marketing digital accounting. Eight clients, of the 40 at eAgency had adopted a complete online accounting service by the end of the first year of operation. This may seem a small number but it was considered somewhat satisfactory by the owner. Considering all the other changes that were being undertaken during the year, there was little time for active marketing of the new services. The Web site of eAgency included information and a contact form for possible new clients.

For new and existing clients, the client's business processes had to be identified in the client's business environment and the best solution for adopting the accounting software planned and mapped out. In the beginning, the owner took care of this task herself. After half a year, she realized that the start-up procedures for new clients needed to be organised better and developed a standard routine procedure for this (including forms to be filled out, time schedules, interviews, and site visits). Moreover, the start-up procedure took time to work through, depending on the size of the client's business operations. Thus, the owner realised that mastering the implementation of all clients at the same time (at the end of the financial year) and by herself would not be possible. She made a time schedule and long-term implementation plan, based on the closing time of the clients' books. This plan set out to realise an intensive market campaign in 2005. The general idea was not only to have as many of the existing clients as possible adopting complete online accounting, but also to attract new clients. In addition, one of the employees was taught how to carry out the start-up procedure. Also, a follow-up on the start-up routines was implemented and performed within six months of the client's adoption. A similar subsequent check was also performed after any major changes in the client's business operations.

In spite of the intensive push to make digital accounting attractive, only a handful of the existing clients adopted the full service package for each passing year. However, some new clients were targeted; some from outside the former market region. In 2006, eAgency had in total 70 clients, including consultancy clients derived through the owner's father's auditing practice. However, many of the old clients still preferred traditional accounting services, where the accountant entered data manually into the accounting system. This resistance in adopting the services (and the software) was recognised primarily during the first two years of operation. At the end of the third year the owner noticed that the demand for e-services had grown and that the accounting firm actually attracted new customers, who explicitly asked for digital accounting. In particular small entrepreneurs did not consider the characteristic feature of self-services in the online accounting model as very attractive. Customers' innovation adoption behaviour has also intrigued researchers for decades. The problem with selling self-services could also be due to the fact that the relationship between eAgency and the existing clients is long-term and the manner of operation has been standardised over the years. The partners have been accustomed to do their share in the accounting process. Previously the entrepreneur (client) has paid for the work to be done by the agency. Why should he now have to do it himself and still pay for it, when he had the option to buy the service in the traditional way?

Services

It could be said that the service innovation process at eAgency already started when the eAgency owner made the decision to adopt Web-based accounting technologies. She recognised a need for strategic development and had a strong desire to implement digital accounting. The owner therefore had a clear vision of change in services from the beginning. However, the change in the operations was not the absolute answer to the needs of clients, something that could also be derived from the difficulties eAgency has had in promoting e-accounting services to them.

One new feature in the emerging e-services is, as already stated, the introduction of self-services. The client is granted password-protected access to the data and financial reports via the software vendors' Web site. He can follow the accounting information in real-time, check financial status, and analyse the accessible information. To some extent (according to the customer agreement) he is expected to update the data himself, for example, by entering orders, sales, or accounts for purchase

invoices and/or paying bills. Further, he can run ad-hoc reports and narrow down (drill-down) the data to check for further details. This is all considered part of the traditional accountant's work.

The owner set out to broaden the content of the services provided by eAgency. She developed three different service packages for the clients to choose from. They are targeted for different types of clients and depending on the contents, priced differently to suit the enterprise. The degree of self-services varies in the packages, as does the amount of business and accounting advice. The client can also buy additional business advice or consultancy. Previously provided services, such as discussions about the result or sales, have been priced and are included in the service package. Further, the client is expected to make a reservation for the discussion time on the Web. The idea of buying business advice has however not attracted eAgency's small entrepreneurs, but has been well welcomed by the medium-sized companies. In 2005 the owner also developed two training packages, one for new clients and one for more advanced operations. The training packages are sold separately. Telephone advice on software use is available for free up to three times for a new client, after which he is advised to call a service number. Other new services include preparing budgets and forecasts for the client and providing technical, legal, or financial advice in cooperation with other business partners.

The services of eAgency were mainly developed through conscious innovative efforts by the agency's owner and based on the wish to reengineer eAgency's operations using Web-based technology. It could be said that the services developed were rarely radical, but small improvements, combinations of existing elements, and modifications were made to traditional services. Many innovations came from daily business activities and from the interaction with customers and other business partners as well as participation in seminars. Further, some of the emerging services may be classified as traditional services and some seen as new, for example, e-services in an accounting context. Also, the nature of the developed services were not primarily technological, but consultancy and business advice. Table 3 provides a classification and an overview of the emerging services in eAgency.

According to Boyer, Hallowell, and Roth (2002) a critical component of self-sourcing involves the benefits to consumers and businesses. Consumers must perceive value in conducting their transactions online. Benefits can include 24-hour access to data and information, more detailed information, or easier access to services. The developed e-services of eAgency have so far principally been of interest to medium-sized and large clients, which see an opportunity not only to reduce costs but also to acquire real-time information about company finances and to integrate the accounting process into their business processes. A further understanding of the client's business processes and organisation would most likely also enhance the development and customisation of services in the future. Further research is needed on what the clients really want (Yrjölä, 2003). A deeper understanding of the client's business and strategies would also mean that the service needs are perceived in a more comprehensive way (Toivonen, 2004, p. 173).

Internal Operations of eAgency

The change in business operations created a need to change the pricing model of provided services to the clients. The old pricing model was based on the number of source documents entered into the accounting system. A new pricing model, based on time and provided services, had to be introduced. In order to gain a realistic view, the owner carried out time studies to clarify how much time was spent on various activities and services. Further, the NetX eAccounting ASP-vendor charges for the use of the application based on the number of transactions (variable expense) as well as a monthly fixed rate. The NetY ASP-vendor invoices a fixed sum each month. Thus the invoice sent to the client includes a charge for the use of software based on the ASP-vendor's bill and for provided services by eAgency, stated on separate lines. To manage client billing more effectively, eAgency outsourced its own billing in 2006. Further, an internal time-management system was taken into use in eAgency in 2005. The aim was to better organise and manage time spent on various activities and to be able to manage the clients' bookings of consultancy and business advice online.

Having the clients to do part of what previously was the job of eAgency has changed the boundaries of eAgency. The owner says that "the distinction between what is our job and the client's job is no

Table 3. Emerging services and e-services

	SERVICES	e-SERVICES
Emerging New Services	Client Training in Software Use	Client Self-Services
	Standard Client Start-Up Procedure	Web-based Ordering of Services
Development of Traditional Services	Client Training in Accounting Management Accounting Services	Accounting Information via the Web

longer crystal clear." This is one of the reasons why the start-up procedure is very important with all new clients. Discussions and agreements on "who does what" have to be undertaken and rules established from the beginning and included in the contract. Further, the change has resulted in closer relations between the clients and eAgency. This was expected and corresponds with previous research findings in e-business models (Upin, Beckwith, Jennings, Chen, & Schaeffer, 2000). Furthermore, the new business strategy involved external technical expertise. Keen cooperation with the software vendor was emphasised in the initial phase, but also in developing the packaged e-services. In addition, alliances with a law firm and an authorised auditor were formed in 2006 to provide more advanced and qualified professional services to the clients.

Management and Employees

The owner's enthusiasm for digital accounting and leadership is considered to have played a key role in the deployment of the e-service strategy, something that is consistent with the integration of technology in previous research (Armstrong & Sambamurthy, 1999; Chatterjee, Grewal, & Sambamurthy, 2002). During the interviews the owner stood out as an outgoing, innovative, and skilled person, who also supported the employees in changes related to their tasks and working conditions. Further, extending the traditional business model and developing a consumer-focused e-service strategy required risk-taking abilities. She has also received full and strong support from her father in the development process of new services and work processes.

Prior to the adoption of NetX, the owner and employees of eAgency had experience in Internet use, but none of them were familiar with digital accounting in practice. The formal training in software use was brief and further knowledge was gained by working with the software. Using NetX eAccounting was considered very easy by

all employees and minimal additional training was required after adoption. However, the work of tester of new upgrades was quite demanding and as it was carried out in addition to the normal workload, it took its toll. The owner's hard work and high ambitions in combination with a feeling of failure in awakening the clients' interest in digital accounting and new services led to stress and she went on long-term sick leave in 2006. She returned to work in early 2007, having been almost one year away from her work responsibilities. During most of this time development stood still, which is understandable considering the limited resources of the small-sized agency and the fact that the development had mainly come from and depended on the owner.

The focus of the accountants' work has moved from the production of financial records and statements to providing new forms of services, such as providing consultation, education, and analytical services for the clients. Daily accounting tasks are carried out on the Internet in real-time, if possible. Monthly financial statements are no longer prepared and printed out on paper (if not specifically requested and paid for), but the information can be accessed by the client himself. Moreover, financial reporting is perceived as real-time (however not completely in practice) and the interface more "user-friendly," both by eAgency and the clients, according to the owner. Further, no decrease in the quality of provided financial information has been allowed, rather the opposite is promoted as eAgency has introduced adjustments to monthly reports for small entrepreneurs in order to provide relevant and useful information.

The transformation of the tasks has also changed the skills and competences needed to approach the new tasks and technology. Current tasks are perceived as being more demanding but also more meaningful. The possibility to work from home has not yet been adopted by the staff of eAgency.

Business Model

The business model of eAgency has changed. The importance of service management has increased and focus has moved from the production of financial records and statements to handling the relationship with the customers. In the case company the key elements of service management have been on creating new service products and designing and managing service processes. Activities such as deliveries of financial information and invoice recording no longer exist in their previous form, but have become customer-oriented and hopefully value-adding services. To keep existing customers and attract new ones, service customisation was emphasised resulting in new service packages and a developed pricing model. An overview of the evolved changes in the business model is provided in Table 4.

Current Challenges Facing the Organization

The introduction and adoption of the new service model by the SME clients of eAgency took much longer than anticipated and the number of clients that were initially targeted has not yet been reached. In early 2007 the total number of eAgency clients was 50, of which 21 had adopted various stages of digital accounting, from using an electronic bank statement to completely digitalising their accounting books. The decline in the total number of clients between 2006 and 2007 is due to the fact that the consultancy clients, which the owner's father had brought with him to eAgency, could no longer be served since he had turned 70 years old and his auditor authorisation was up. Thus, the net increase in clients between 2004 and 2006 was approximately 10.

Reasons for the perceived failure in attracting clients' interest in e-services could probably be derived from customers' readiness for self-services or their lack of trust in technology. Further, technological innovations are still emerging and technical standards do not exist in all respects. Also the growth of electronic invoicing has been much slower than anticipated (Gullkvist & Ylinen, 2006); up to 17% domestically in 2006 according to a recent survey, and has not yet reached a critical mass. Moreover, most e-invoices are sent and received by large companies and in B2B business. Furthermore, although the Association of Finnish Accounting Firms has clearly expressed its beliefs in and preference for digital accounting, the owner feels that efforts and actions to support and promote the accounting industry's transition to digital accounting have been poor. Disappointment with the association's strategy and role in the transition process has also made eAgency reappraise its membership of the Association. Moreover, the number of agencies belonging to the Association is approximately 700 out of a total

Table 4. Changes in the business model

Traditional Business Model "FACTORY"	New Business Model "SERVICE MANAGEMENT"
Input–Output Process	Emphasis on Output
Highly standardized service product	Move towards customized services
Handling data entry & transactions	Handling control & relationships
Information quality	Information + service quality
Expert skills (accounting & taxation)	Expert + business + communication skills
Automation -> efficiency & productivity -> cost reduction -> higher profits	Automation & Customer satisfaction -> revenue & higher profits

of 3980 agencies in Finland, which implies that the majority of the Finnish accounting agencies are not members. The nonmembers therefore do not receive correspondence from the Association nor are they subject to quality requirements and the ethical guidelines for accounting firms called "Good Accounting Practice" that the Association publishes. The slow transition among Finnish accounting agencies towards digital accounting may also have affected the general opinion and clients' demand for and acceptance of e-services. Further, the slowly growing demand for e-services and new consultancy services has made it difficult for eAgency to fully utilise employees' work capacity derived from less manual work. Thus, it would be possible for eAgency to take on more clients or provide additional services, if there was customer demand.

Pricing new and traditional services in the new business model has been a challenge for eAgency. The existing clients are very price conscious and would not accept a rise in what they have been charged previously, especially since one of the arguments for the transition to digital accounting has been that it reduces costs and provides a more efficient way of handling administrative and accounting activities. Thus, the total fee on the client's invoice has had to remain on the same level as before or rather decrease. Nowadays, however, a large part of eAgency's client invoices includes charges that eAgency pays to the ASP and other service providers. Further, although the margin on e-services is, according to the owner, higher than on traditional accounting services, the high proportion of existing traditional clients in eAgency has had a negative effect on the total margin. The books of so-called traditional clients are prepared in the traditional way; for example, one of the accountants enters the data manually into NetX or NetY. This is a time-consuming procedure, which is neither cost-effective nor supported by the current pricing model. Hence, eAgency's operating margin and net margin have slightly decreased. The margins are however

expected to grow again as clients move over to e-services and full digital accounting and new ways of working in the digital environment become routine. A strategic decision needs to be taken on the future of the old clients that refuses to move to full digital accounting. One solution would be to ask the clients to turn elsewhere to continue receiving traditional accounting services. Another solution would be to raise the fees for these services, which would most likely have the same effect on the client relationship.

Furthermore, the owner says that although she has tried to track down all tasks performed to the clients in the digital environment, she still has a feeling that the employees of eAgency spend time doing tasks that they do not get paid for, for example, activities that are not included in the client's invoice. She mentions examples such as archiving accounting material in electronic form on behalf of the client, providing the client's auditor with financial data and statements on a CD/DVD disc, or providing him password access. The technological environment and increased cooperation with software vendors and banks in doing start-up routines with new clients are services that are difficult to price, but which are complicated and time-consuming. Since eAgency wants to attract new clients and it is understood that clients compare eAgency's prices to agencies providing traditional services, she feels that she has not been able to fully invoice all start-up tasks and administrative services.

The sluggish advance of the new business model and services has caused financial difficulties for eAgency and an urgent need to raise new or additional revenue and capital. In mid-2006 eAgency filed for debt rescheduling. The application and debt rescheduling plan were processed and approved by the district court in early 2007. After returning back to work from her sick-leave, the owner, with renewed strength, started tackling the existing traditional clients in order to persuade them into digital accounting and self-services. Thanks to raised project funding, the clients would be able to receive a small compensation for possible investment or transition costs, which she hopes will motivate them to adopt digital accounting. The owner has also considered some future ways to increase revenue.

One possible future development of eAgency, considered by the owner in an interview in early 2007, is to focus mainly on medium-sized and large companies in the future. The outsourcing trend appears to be expanding and there is potential to reach new clients in the medium-sized category. Medium-sized and large companies are also believed to be more interested in additional consultancy services and e-services than small-sized entrepreneurs, something that would increase revenue. The project in late 2006, where NetX was linked to the client's system, is one proof of the increasing trend towards outsourcing accounting and financials. Further, the owner considers e-commerce companies as a very attractive client group. Since they operate on the Internet themselves, they have no or low barriers to using a Web-based accounting system. She has plans to locate Finnish e-commerce companies for an advertising campaign. Another target group, that seems to be heading for outsourcing but still in its very initial stages, is the public sector. Entering the outsourcing market would also create a need for advanced services and possibilities to charge for provided services. However, the current staff may not have the experience needed for such an adventure and further training or recruitments may be needed, which would lead to greater costs.

Additional revenue could further be gained through selling consultancy services to other accounting agencies that have started to adopt digital accounting. Being a pioneer in the digital accounting field, the owner has extensive experience compared to other agencies. However, providing advisory and consultancy services to competitors may on one hand turn out to be to eAgency's disadvantage, since eAgency may lose its competitive advantage. On the other hand,

however, an increase in the number of agencies providing e-services may result in an increase in the awareness and knowledge of such services among the clients and provide the critical mass of clients and demand needed to make these services profitable. At the moment, the owner of eAgency does not consider competition among similar e-service accounting agencies to be hard. In the region where eAgency operates there is only one other agency providing full digital accounting services and, in the whole country, mainly mid-sized and large agencies advertise digital accounting services.

Increased differentiation and segmentation would further advance opportunities for eAgency and could include greater development of advisory services and e-services. According to some surveys undertaken in recent years, the clients expect the accounting agencies to provide even more consultancy services in coming years. Also, e-services are expected to grow in popularity and one reason may be recent changes in pricing; for example, e-services are becoming cheaper than traditional accounting services. A possible development of existing online financial reports would be to customise products, which could include client-specific data and could be purchased by the client on a "click and add to the basket" principle. Also interactive online consultancy services could be developed. However the demand and market for these kinds of services is not known.

CONCLUDING REMARKS

This case study provides an insight into emerging services as well as the challenges faced and efforts taken within the service practice of a small-sized accounting firm when adopting Web-based technology. The case presented here supports the conclusion that the accounting field does respond to new technological innovations, although the process of change may seem slow and gradual. Further, small businesses such as the accounting agency profiled in this study are well suited to adopt and use available third party Web services without needing to align and coordinate technological infrastructure. In addition, the level of technology skills necessary to manage the new software was low, thus making it very suitable for the small eAgency with few ICT resources. Moreover, the use of a Web-based software facilitated the move towards digital accounting and development of e-services.

This case study also illustrates that the pace of change in services in eAgency is an ongoing and indeed long-term process. The process of change is not yet complete and will most likely never be. Further, the process can be seen as a learning process for both the clients and eAgency. The adoption of Internet technology in eAgency enabled a change in the business model, the development of new innovative products or services and strengthened the competitive advantage of the company. However, pricing of self-services and e-services is not considered easy and the profitability of eAgency has taken a bad turn. Furthermore, the clients' interest in these kinds of services has been growing very slowly. However, recent growing interest in digital accounting and e-services has been noted. In an interview in October 2007, the owner proudly states that the number of clients has grown to 57, of which 30 (53%) have adopted e-services to some extent with the remaining 27 clients still using traditional services.

Despite the problems and current challenges facing eAgency, the owner still has high expectations of digital accounting and Web-based technology. However, the existing clients' acceptance of the new business model and readiness for self-services would have to change in order to turn failure into success, otherwise new customers or markets would have to be found. Managing e-services in eAgency has not only been about inventing and applying a new business model and new services, it has also been about managing change in organisational structure and culture, tasks and processes, technology, and people (both in-house as well as business partners). Further, it has involved significant new risks. With regards to the starting point of eAgency in 2004, considerable changes have taken place. It is reasonable to say that the case company has achieved many goals. However, taking full advantage of the Web-based technologies would provide even further opportunities to extend business and accounting with regard to information, communication, distribution, and transactions.

REFERENCES

Accounting Act (AA) 1336/30.12.1997.

Accounting Board (2000, May 22). *Yleisohje Koneellisessa Kirjanpidossa Käytettävistä Menetelmistä.*

Alles, M., Kogan, A., & Vasarhelyi, M.A. (2000). Accounting in 2015. *The CPA Journal, 70*(11), 14–20.

Armstrong, C.P., & Sambamurthy, V. (1999). Information technology assimilation in firms: The influence of senior leadership and IT infrastructures. *Information Systems Research, 10*(4), 304–327.

Association of Finnish Accounting Firms (2006). Data retrieved July 2007 from http://www.taloushallintoliitto.fi/

Boyer, K.K., Hallowell, R., & Roth, A.V. (2002). E-services: Operating strategy—a case study and a method for analyzing operational benefits. *Journal of Operations Management, 20*(2), 175–188.

Chatterjee, D., Grewal, R., & Sambamurthy, V. (2002). Shaping up for e-commerce: Institutional enablers of the organizational assimilation of Web technologies. *MIS Quarterly, 26*(2), 65–89.

Cooper, C., & Taylor, P. (2000). From Taylorism to Ms Taylor: The transformation of the accounting craft. *Accounting, Organizations and Society, 25*, 555–587.

Davies, A.J., & Garcia-Sierra, A.J. (1999). Implementing electronic commerce in SMEs: Three case studies. *BT Technology Journal, 17*(3), 97–111.

Denzin, N.K. (1989). *The research act.* Englewood Cliffs, NJ: Prentice Hall.

Deshmukh, A. (2006). *Digital accounting: The effects of the Internet and ERP on accounting.* Hershey, PA: Idea Group.

Ghobadian, A., & Gallear, D.N. (1996). Total quality management in SMS's. *Omega, 24*(1), 83–106.

Gottlieb, M.M. (1996). Electronic transactions: Their impact on financial reporting. *International Advances in Economic Research, 2*, 146–150.

Gullkvist, B., & Ylinen, M. (2006). E-accounting systems use in Finnish accounting agencies. In M. Seppä, M. Hannula, A.-M. Järvelin, J. Kujala, M. Ruohonen, & T. Tiainen (Ed.), *Frontiers of E-Business Research 2005.* Tampere.

Hart, P., & Saunders, C. (1997). Power and trust: Critical factors in the adoption and use of electronic data interchange. *Organization Science, 8*(1), 23–42.

Hunton, J.E. (2002). Blending information and communication technology with accounting research. *Accounting Horizons, 16*(1), 55–67.

IFAC (2002). *E-business and the accountant.* Retrieved June 4, 2008, from http://www.ifac.org/

Kirby, D., Najak, B., & Greene, F. (1998). *Accounting for growth: Ways accountants can add value to small businesses.* London: ICAEW.

Kotler, P., Hayes, T., & Bloom, P. (2002). *Marketing professional services: Forward thinking strategies for boosting your business, your image and your profits* (2nd ed.). Paramius, NJ: Prentice Hall Press.

Lacity, M., & Willcocks, L. (1998). An empirical investigation of information technology sourcing practices: Lessons from experience. *MIS Quarterly, 22*(3), 363–408.

Lith, P. (2004). Tili- ja tilintarkastustoimistojen liikevaihto kasvu-uralla. *Tilisanomat, 1,* 21–25.

Mäkinen, L. (2000). Tilitoimistoala murroksessa. *Tilisanomat, 5,* 45–50.

Marriott, N., & Marriott, P. (2000). Professional accountants and the development of a management accounting service for the small firm: Barriers and possibility. *Management Accounting Research, 11*(4), 475–492.

O'Connor, G., & O'Keefe, B. (1997). Viewing the Web as a marketplace: The case of small companies. *Decision Support Systems, 21*(3), 171–183.

Olivier, H. (2000). Challenges facing the accountancy profession. *The European Accounting Review, 9*(4), 603–624.

Parasuraman, A. (2000). Technology readiness index (TRI): A multiple-item scale to measure readiness to embrace new technologies. *Journal of Service Research, 2*(4), 307–320.

Raymond, L. (1985). Organizational characteristics and MIS success in the context of small business. *MIS Quarterly, 9*(1), 37–52.

Rust, R.T., & Kannan, P.K. (2002). *E-service: New direction in theory and practice.* Armonk, NY: M.E. Sharpe.

Stafford, T.F. (2003). E-services. *Communications of the ACM, 46*(6), 26–28.

Sutton, S.G. (2000). The changing face of accounting in an information technology dominated world. *International Journal of Accounting Information Systems, 1,* 1–8.

Templeman, J.G., & Wootton, C. (1987). *Small business: Management information needs.* London: Charter Institute of Management Accountants.

Toivonen, M. (2004). *Expertise as business: Long-term development and future prospects of knowledge-intensive business services.* Doctoral dissertation, Helsinki University of Technology, Laboratory of Industrial Management (Series 2004/2, Espoo).

Toivonen, M. (2005). *Taloushallinnon palvelut.* Toimialaraportti ennakoi liiketoiminta-ympäristön muutoksia. KTM:n ja TE-keskuksen julkaisu.

Upin, E.B., Beckwith, M.J., Jennings, C.L., Chen, B.Y., & Schaeffer, K.B. (2000). *B2B: Building technology bridges outside the four walls of the enterprise.* FleetBoston Robertson Stephens Inc.

Vahtera, P., & Salmi, H. (1998). *Paperiton Kirjanpito.* Jyväskylä.

Vasarhelyi, M., & Greenstein, M. (2003). Underlying principles of the electronization of business: A research agenda. *International Journal of Accounting Information Systems, 4,* 1–25.

Wallman, S.M.H. (1997). Commentary: The future of accounting and financial reporting (Part IV: "Access" accounting). *Accounting Horizons, 11*(2), 103116.

Yrjölä, E. (2003). Kilpa kovenee, kirjanpitäjä. *Talouselämä, 1,* 4446.

Chapter VIII
eInsurance:
Developing Customer–Friendly Electronic Insurance Services from the Novel Project Perspective

Aki Ahonen
OP Bank Group Central Cooperative, Finland

Jarno Salonen
VTT Technical Research Centre of Finland, Finland

Raija Järvinen
National Consumer Research Centre, Finland

Jouni Kivistö-Rahnasto
Tampere University of Technology, Finland

ABSTRACT

The chapter introduces an innovative organizational logic for developing and designing electronic services especially in the context of financial services, such as insurance. Furthermore, a novel electronic insurance service concept for consumers is introduced in the chapter. The authors argue that development of electronic service solutions for the use of financial sector formerly rather conducted in an organization may well be executed through a multi-organizational project-based working logic. In fact the chapter establishes that the multi-organizational project-based logic results in a more creative outcome. Hence, the authors hope that the chapter encourages both academics and especially practitioners within the insurance business sector to take steps towards more collaborative working practices in order to generate more creative electronic service solutions for customers.

BACKGROUND

Insurance companies globally have put effort into developing electronic insurance services especially for nonlife and health insurance. Even though the importance of the Internet as a channel for business-to-consumer insurance services has grown, according to research (e.g., Ahonen & Salonen, 2005; Järvinen, Eriksson, Saastamoinen, & Lystimäki, 2001) the Internet is still used mainly for information acquisition purposes. In contrast, the actual service transactions (e.g., buying and reporting a claim) are performed in person or via phone with an insurance officer or independent broker.

In order to increase customers' willingness to use electronic insurance services, a few critical issues need to be taken into consideration. First of all, customers usually need to contact the insurance company only once or a few times a year. Second, in the same way as all current Web-based electronic services, also electronic insurance services are based on self-service principles. This means that physical service contact is not available for the customers and instead they have to rely on their own know-how and skills in order to get their service needs fulfilled. For the above-mentioned reasons, it is more difficult for the customers to start operating in the electronic environment than in the physical service environment.

In spring 2002 some Finnish academics involved in research on insurance business expressed their concern regarding the lack of customer orientation in the case of the electronic insurance services available on the Internet. They raised a question: "How do we get electronic insurance services closer to customers?" A discussion about launching a research and development project for the purpose of increasing the customer (i.e., user) friendliness of electronic insurance services was begun.

Not more than a few months later the discussion had spread to insurance business practitioners when the above-mentioned question was raised also in public seminars and at other events by academics. Both academics and representatives of the business world realized they share a common concern with regard to developing electronic insurance services that better respond to customers' needs.

The cooperation between academics and businessmen started by preparing a research plan, and after a year a public research and development project was launched. The project was entitled "eInsurance 1" and was carried out between August 2003 and December 2004. The project also engendered a follow-up project with the similar but more extensive objective of enhancing the customer friendliness of electronic insurance services (eInsurance 2), which was executed between June 2005 and February 2007.

In this chapter, research and development activities of electronic insurance services included in these two projects are introduced and discussed. Although research results gained through the two eInsurance projects provide valuable information for practical business, the main focus of this article is, however, on the part of the project dealing with development. In particular, attention is paid to introducing the developed electronic insurance service concept for consumers called "Safety and Insurance Advisor" since it is the most fundamental practical result of the two eInsurance projects. The developed service concept is totally new in both Finnish insurance markets and internationally.

Now one could ask: "Why describe research projects and their results in order to provide a case for developing electronic services in an organization?" We can provide many distinct reasons. First, since the projects had received public funding,[1] we considered it our duty to publicly report all results. Second, the two eInsurance projects were not only research projects but also *development projects* aiming at developing concrete electronic service concepts for the use of the insurance industry. In fact the eInsurance projects were, and still are, pioneering projects in examining and developing electronic insurance services in Finland as a whole. Third, basic project organization was the same in both projects. Previously, these kinds of development activities have been performed internally within insurance companies. This case provides an example of how the development of electronic insurance services can be performed in cooperation with several distinct organizations. Hence, this case is an interesting example also from the organizational point of view.

The chapter is structured as follows: the second section provides essential background on the scope of the eInsurance projects and project organization. The most important result of the two projects, namely the electronic service concept "Safety and Insurance Advisor," is introduced in the third section. The execution of the projects (functionality of the project organization and the gained results) as well as future challenges regarding project organization are assessed in the fourth section. Concluding remarks are presented in the final section.

SETTING THE STAGE

Electronic Insurance Services and Consumers

A shift from product-based economy to service economy occurred some 20 years ago (see, e.g., Fitzsimmons & Fitzsimmons, 2006). Later, service orientation was also extended to the electronic environment, such as the Internet. Earlier, the terms most used to describe the operations and/or transactions executed on the Internet were "e-commerce" or "e-business." After the millennium and the so-called hype era of the Internet, online service providers generally started to pay more attention to customers. However, as physical service contact is missing in the electronic service environment, customers' operations are based on self-service logic (e.g., Ahonen, 2007; Meuter, Ostrom, Roundtree, & Bitner, 2000). Therefore,

it is of the utmost importance that there should be real benefit-providing services available for customers in the electronic service environment, and not just bits and pieces of information from here and there forming the content of the electronic services.

Concerning the utility and attractiveness of electronic insurance services, a recent survey (Peura-Kapanen, Nenonen, Järvinen, & Kivistö-Rahnasto, 2007; see also Peura-Kapanen & Järvinen, 2006) concerning consumers' risk perceptions reveals that 77% of Finnish consumers value most of all the opportunity to compare various insurance types on the Internet. However, this kind of service is not commonly available, although at least in Sweden, Estonia, and the Netherlands there is a portal which allows the comparing of insurance prices. The other services consumers prefer on the Internet are examples of accepted and un-accepted claims (73%), price calculators (71%), electronic claim applications (58%), and the opportunity to check and update their personal insurance policies (52%) (Peura-Kapanen et al., 2007).

According to the survey by Peura-Kapanen et al. (2007) and the qualitative study by Peura-Kapanen and Järvinen (2006), most consumers have visited the Web sites of insurance companies and mostly they have been seeking price details or information on insurance types. Especially consumers complained that prices have been difficult to find or to compare. Because of this, many of them still prefer personal service provided by branch offices. In addition, they value interaction with insurance specialists since insurance policies typically are considered complicated by customers. In fact, many consumers even avoid insurance matters because of their complicated nature (see, e.g., Järvinen & Heino, 2004). As a consequence of this, only 80% of Finnish consumers have home insurance and the number of home insurance owners has decreased during recent years, at least in the Finnish market.

As in many other service fields, signs of the development towards *electronic services* started to emerge after the millennium. Insurance companies in many advanced insurance markets, for example, in U.S., UK, Germany, and the Nordic Countries, started to offer possibilities for online purchasing. In addition, reporting a claim online became possible at least in the Nordic countries.

Concerning the design of Web sites, development steps were taken to construct a more comprehensible and appealing operating environment for customers. Especially many online insurance service providers, for instance, within the British insurance market, have adopted a more lively and non-insurance-like approach in the development of their electronic insurance service environments. These firms prefer fresh and lively colours instead of dark and matter-of-fact ones, and use illustrative—in some cases even animated—pictures on their Web sites. These types of service providers can be found at least in American, British, and German markets.[2]

The utilization of visual elements has been welcomed also among Finnish customers (e.g., Ahonen, 2007). Since insurance services often are perceived as complex and confusing, visual elements are seen as a way of facilitating customers' operations in the electronic service environment. However, until now, Finnish insurance companies have preferred the more *conservative and matter-of-fact approach* in offering electronic insurance services. More precisely, they have put a large amount of unstructured information on the Web sites and neglected the use of visual aids, such as colours and pictures, in making the electronic service content more comprehensible for customers.

The starting point in planning the eInsurance projects was that insurance services, and also other financial services, are generally considered complex services. Complex services are defined as "services that consist of many attribute values per attribute, which are often tailor-made, infre-

quently purchased, more difficult to comprehend, and require in general assistance during the decision-making process" (Vroomen, Donkers, Verhoef, & Franses, 2005, p. 38). Considering the fact that electronic services are based on self-service logic, the complexity of service makes it even more challenging for a customer to use such electronic services. With this in mind, the preliminary guideline for planning the essential scope of the eInsurance projects took into account the fact that since insurance is not easy for customers to comprehend, the electronic service environment should be designed in a way which makes it easy and appealing to use and thus, provides customers with better possibilities to become more familiar with electronic (insurance) services.

Insurance is considered one of the most intangible services (e.g., Majaro, 1983). The intangible nature of services usually makes it easier to shift them to the Internet. However, the complexity of the insurance services may hinder the frequent use of electronic services. Instead, customers often require individual and personal service provided by insurance specialists. Following from this, customers use the Internet for gathering information, but after this stage they still prefer to discuss with the specialists before making their final decision (Järvinen & Heino, 2004). These habits create great challenges for insurance services on the Internet. Therefore, insurance companies should start to develop their Internet services by following the logic of their customers and use more concrete elements, such as visualization, in order to make these abstract services as tangible as possible.

Whereas Internet services are usually quite standardized, in the case of insurance services customers' needs are not uniform. Therefore, electronic insurance offerings should at least be mass customized (Järvinen, Lehtinen, & Vuorinen, 2003). One way to approach this issue in the electronic service environment is to offer insurance cover consisting of various elements that customers can choose and pick from according to their personal requirements. However, many customers are afraid of buying insurance on the Internet since they may choose the wrong insurance type or insufficient cover (Peura-Kapanen & Järvinen, 2006). Therefore, electronic insurance services have to take account of the customers' actual life situation and automatically take care of the minimum cover on behalf of customers.

We have discussed above the necessity to approach the development of electronic insurance services from a new and more customer-friendly perspective. This idea has been the central principle in both eInsurance projects. In the next two subsections the construction of both projects is discussed from both the organizational and functional point of view.

eInsurance 1: Electronic Insurance Business (2003–2004)

Back in 2002, the insurance sector was generally interested in putting more effort into adopting electronic services. Although the hype of the Internet was already over, the new communication channel was still seen to have great potential for offering services. *Enthusiasm* might be a felicitous expression to describe the attitude of both business and scientific communities towards electronic services back then. Hence, there existed a favourable basis for constructing a temporary organization with the aim of designing and executing a research and development project. For instance, there was no need to inveigle companies to participate and also funding for the project was easily obtainable.

The core of "eInsurance" organization was constructed in 2003 and comprised one university, one public research organization, and two insurance companies. By August 2003, after complementing the organization with a few additional participants, the final project consortium consisted of four corporate participants, one university, and one public research organization. Furthermore, the Federation of Finnish Insurance Companies

participated in the project management team. From a research point of view, the participating university embraced a business approach while the participating public research organization complemented the business approach by providing technical competence for the use of the research consortium.

Both participating insurance companies can be considered key players in Finnish insurance markets. Approximately 2000 employees work in these companies (in Finland). The two other corporate participants were software companies. One of them can be considered one of the leading software providers in the Finnish financial markets and especially insurance business markets. The company has approximately 100 employees in Finland, but it also has business operations in other Nordic countries and in the Baltic countries. The other software company is a "small business" company which was established in 2001 and specializes in identity and access management in online services.

The efficiency of a new organization might be hindered, for instance, by the lack of cohesiveness of the organization as well as of established working practices. However, this was not perceived as a problem in this case since there already were earlier existing personal relationships between the project members. Thus, an existing core for collaboration encouraged also new members of the established organization to work in collaboration with each other.

Further, the coherency of the brand new organization was moulded through collaborative meetings and a few "kick off" events already before the launch of the first development project in August 2003. More importantly, however, the motivation to gain new information and to design and develop new electronic insurance service concepts for the use of customers provided a good basis for the cohesiveness and functionality of the organization.

From the operational perspective, the project organization was supervised by the *project management team* (11 members), consisting of executive-level members from each participant organization. In addition, an *operative team* was established to be responsible for concrete research and development activities conducted through the "eInsurance" project. The operative team, in which the middle management of the companies and researchers worked in collaboration, consisted of nine members.

The most crucial practical objective of this first eInsurance project was to develop an *electronic service concept for consumers following a logic based on visualizing information.* As a result, a service concept called "insurance cover evaluator" was introduced in January 2005.

eInsurance 2: Novel Electronic Insurance Services (2005–2007)

For the follow-up project, entitled "eInsurance 2: Novel Electronic Insurance Services," the basic philosophy remained the same, but the approach was extended to cover altogether four research themes: *service business and usability, safety and risk management, jurisprudence,* and *technological* environment. The organization was slightly updated to fulfil the requirements of the project in terms of competence and professional knowledge. The research participants in the first eInsurance project (one university and one public research organization) also formed the core of the eInsurance 2 project. In addition, the consortium was complemented with another university and another public research organization. Thus, altogether four research parties participated in the eInsurance 2 project.

One of the two participating insurance companies from the first eInsurance project showed clear interest and motivation to work in a collaborative project-based organization and so continued also in the second project. Similarly, the larger of the software companies was willing to participate in the second project. In addition, another software company specialized in developing IT solutions

and consulting joined in the consortium of the eInsurance 2 project. Hence, altogether three companies participated in the second eInsurance project.

The operational functionality was arranged in the same way as in the first project and comprised the project management team and the operative team. In addition, four research teams were created within the operative team in order to facilitate the research activities within the research themes (service business and usability, safety and risk management, jurisprudence, and technological environment).

The objective of the eInsurance 2 project was *to support customers during the insurance transaction process by developing a comprehensive electronic insurance service environment that is combined with the insurance customership life cycle.* As the most important development result, a service concept called "safety advisor" was introduced. Actually, the result of the first project (insurance cover evaluator) and the "safety advisor" were combined into an entity called "safety and insurance advisor." The overall concept was introduced in March 2007 and it provides customers with safety information related to their living environment and suggests various insurance cover alternatives. The "safety and insurance advisor" is presented more thoroughly in the next chapter.

Describing the Main Results of the Project

It was commonly agreed in the project organization that an electronic insurance service environment would need demonstrative and facilitating features in order to be able to better respond to the needs of customers operating according to self-service logic. Otherwise, electronic insurance services would remain sparsely used since customers perceive them as complex and confusing. Thus, the guiding philosophy of design and development was to create a more illustrative, appealing and easy-to-use service concept for the electronic insurance service environment and thereby to engage consumers more in the electronic insurance service environment.

What was said above naturally raises a question: "What does this mean in reality?" The eInsurance project team decided to emphasize visualization in the electronic insurance service environment in which information is traditionally presented in the form of text (and lots of it!) explaining insurance cover and terms, and thereby to make the electronic insurance service environment more appealing and comprehensible for customers to use. As a starting point for the development work, we utilized the customer service life cycle model (Ives & Mason, 1990) depicted in Figure 1.

Throughout both eInsurance projects, the *main attention* was paid to the *first* (requirements) and the *second* (acquisition) *phases* of the life cycle. The first eInsurance project focused especially on specifying the possible need for insurance cover for consumers. In turn, the main focus of the eInsurance 2 project was on providing a tool for facilitating the acquisition of possible insurance cover by offering customized and visualized information on safety and insurance for consumers. The developed electronic service concept, called "safety and insurance advisor," is introduced in Section 3.1.

The eInsurance Service Concept

The eInsurance service concept called the "safety and insurance advisor" was developed in two separate phases. The first part of the service, called the "insurance cover evaluator," was developed in the first eInsurance project during 2003 and 2004, and the second part, called the "safety advisor," was the result of the second eInsurance project executed during 2005 and 2007. The overall service concept is an Adobe Shockwave[3] application that can be accessed through the project Web site.[4] The selected application type enabled the development of a suitable graphical user interface and the use of an external database that provided easy-to-update storage for information used by the safety and insurance advisor.

Ahonen, Salonen, Kivistö-Rahnasto, Järvinen, and Silius (2007) have illustrated the structure and different functions of the overall service concept in Figure 2. The figure has been divided into three horizontal sections describing the information given by the customer (input level), the four different functions of which the service concept consists (functional level), and the output provided to the customer in each function (output level).

User interaction is carried out by using the mouse in a graphical user interface, in which the

Figure 1. Customer service life cycle (Ives & Mason, 1990, p. 59)

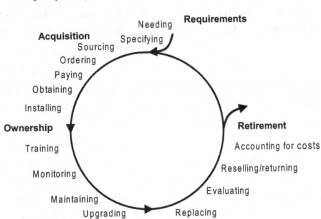

Figure 2. Structure and phases of eInsurance service concept (Ahonen et al., 2007, p. 13)

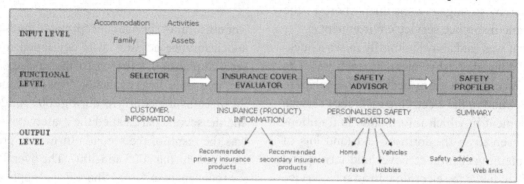

customer either selects an object (e.g., choosing a housing type on the screen to describe his living conditions by clicking with a mouse) or uses drag and drop to combine objects with each other (e.g., choosing family members to describe his living situation by dragging appropriate family members to the selected house). In addition, the service also provides information in balloons that appear when the user moves the mouse cursor over certain objects (e.g., family members). In the following sections we provide a more detailed description of the service concept and its functions.

"Selector" Function

The first phase of the service concept is a "selector" function that collects information about the customers' living environment in order to provide a suggestion regarding suitable insurance products to customers along with tailored safety information. Customers are asked to provide information on the following topics:

- **Accommodation** (apartment house, row house, detached house);
- **Family members** (male, female, teen, child, pet);
- **Assets** (vehicles, valuables, summer cottage, forest, etc.);
- **Activities** (travel, hobbies).

The user interface and the overall appearance of the service concept are illustrated in Figure 3. The service content has been translated into English in order to provide a better understanding of the service. The other phases of the selector function keep to the same graphical appearance in order to maintain ease of use throughout the service concept.

"Insurance Cover Evaluator" Function

The second phase of the service consists of the insurance cover evaluator function that lists the selections made earlier by the customer and combines them with insurance types suitable for each selection (e.g., family member, asset). The insurance types have been divided into the following two categories:

- **Primary insurance types:** the most common and therefore highly recommended types for the selected living environment (e.g., car, home, and travel insurance);
- **Secondary insurance types:** optional, but useful types for the selected living environment (e.g., all-risk car insurance, health, and sports insurance), especially for customers who want full insurance cover against risk.

By selecting an object from the list containing the customer's selections, the customer is provided

Figure 3. eInsurance service concept: selecting family members (Adapted from Ahonen & Salonen, 2007)

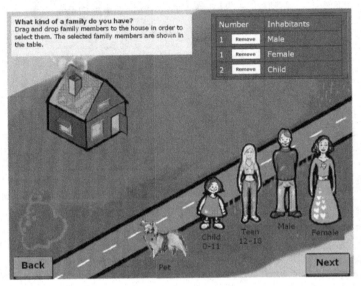

with information about the insurance type related to that certain (selected) object. The combination of customer selections and insurance types clarifies the relationship between them and provides a better understanding of household insurance cover as a whole. The information can also be printed out and used as reference when contacting the insurance company or an independent broker.

"Safety Advisor" Function

The third phase of the service consists of the safety advisor function. This function combines the earlier customer selections with examples of accidents and hazards which may occur within the customers' living environment. The customer can acquire safety information about four different topics within his or her living environment: home, vehicles, travel, and hobbies. The graphical user interface provides several scenarios within each topic, for example, a fire in the kitchen (Figure 4) or losing one's luggage during a trip abroad. The individual scenarios are described both in written and graphical (some including animation) form and they include the following information:

- **What might happen?** (a scenario of an accident or hazard that might happen);
- **How to avoid the damage?** (how to prevent the accident and/or minimize the damage);
- **In the case of damage** (how does insurance apply in this situation and what kind of issues must be considered in making an insurance claim);
- **Did you know...** (statistical, instructional, and/or other information related to the scenario).

The service concept provides customers with customized information by adjusting itself according to their earlier selections. In other words, a family with children receives a scenario and safety information appropriate to their living circumstances which is different from that of a single person or a couple with no children. This supports the research results gained from the eInsurance projects which emphasized the personality and topicality of the insurance and safety information provided to customers.

Figure 4. eInsurance service concept: a screenshot of the safety advisor (Ahonen et al., 2007, p. 15)

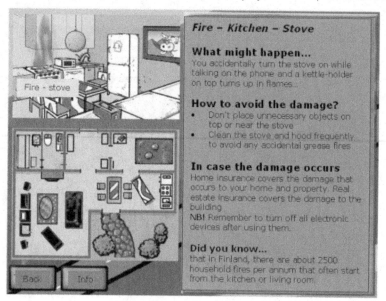

Experiences from the Development of the Service Concept

Since the transformation from industrial to service society in the late 20th century and the introduction of electronic commerce, the term "innovation" has become more related to service development. In this regard, we reflect the development activities conducted during the eInsurance projects through the lenses of innovation. Among others, Fitzsimmons and Fitzsimmons (1994) and Trott (2005) have discussed two common models of innovation, called "technology push" and "market pull." The models provide two alternative processes for innovative development. The difference between the two models lies in the initiator of the process, the "technology push" model being initiated by technology-based research and development performed by an organization while the "market pull" model is initiated by a need noticed by the organization within the target and/or other market.

Following the insights of Trott (2005), the service development process in the first eInsurance project followed the "technology push" linear model of innovation. The initial service concept innovation was developed on the basis of the questionnaire surveys, interviews, and other background information collected from the industrial business partners and external resources in 2003 and 2004. During the development phase in mid-2004, the project partners participated in the development process by commenting on the draft structure and proposed contents of the service during the project meetings. In addition, the project partners evaluated the first prototypes of the service concept to be developed and provided feedback, especially on the terms used in the service as well as on other content. During the service concept publication phase in December 2004, the service was evaluated by selected members of the organizations participating in the project. After the publication of the service concept in January 2005, an electronic questionnaire form was generated to collect feedback from the end users of the services, that is, ordinary insurance company customers.

In this regard, we have adapted Trott's model to fit the scope of the eInsurace 1 project. The reformed model is illustrated in Figure 5. It describes the development process of the insurance cover evaluator and also the methods used during the development of the service concept for collecting the required information in different phases of the project.

Development of the second part of the service concept (safety advisor) began in early 2006 by gathering requirements and ideas from the various project participants. As stated above, the project organization had changed substantially as the number of research organisations had doubled. The industrial business partners consisted of one insurance company and two software companies, of which one was completely new.

Due to the already published service concept and some further development work performed by the insurance company participating in the second project, there was a lot of already existing

information to support the new service innovation ideas. Therefore, the process of developing the second part of the service concept changed from the "technology push" to the "market pull" model (Trott, 2005) in the eInsurance 2 project. The (internal) marketing phase began in the spring of 2006 when a team of three key members within the project conducted interviews in all of the participating organizations in order to make a list of their needs and ideas related to the service concept. In addition to the previous interviews, an internal workshop was organized in March 2006 for the project participants. The main objectives of the workshop were to disseminate information about the current project results and to collect information for the development of the forthcoming service concept. The initial innovation behind the service concept was formed in mid-2006 on the

Figure 5. The linear model of innovation within the e-iInsurance 1 project (adapted from Trott, 2005, p. 23)

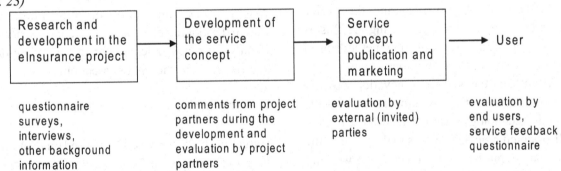

Figure 6. The linear model of innovation within the e-iInsurance 2 project (adapted from Trott, 2005, p. 23)

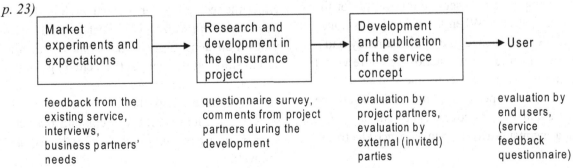

basis of the feedback from the existing service and the project (especially business) partners' needs that were listed during the interviews and the internal workshop.

Even though the eInsurance 2 project had begun in 2005, the main results that supported the initial service concept innovation and defined the content further were collected in summer 2006 when a large questionnaire survey was targeted to a focus group of 800 consumers. At the same time, also other research work was performed to support the concept development. The participants provided comments for the draft models of the service concept at specific meetings that were organized monthly from September to the end of 2006. In the beginning of 2007, the overall service concept including both insurance cover evaluator and safety advisor, and called safety and insurance advisor, were published internally and evaluated by the project partners. Before the publication of the service concept in March 2007, the service concept was also evaluated by external (invited) parties. The reformed model by Trott illustrated in Figure 6 describes the service concept development process during the eInsurance 2 project and the supporting methods used during the development activities.

All in all, the service innovation process changed between the two eInsurance projects from the technology push-oriented to the market pull-oriented model. This was mainly due to the fact that during the first project, there were no existing case examples of electronic insurance services, and therefore the information from the market was insufficient to provide enough support for developing a new service innovation for the insurance sector. When the second eInsurance project was launched, the market already had a practical example of a functioning, more visual electronic service for consumers. The service had been developed on the basis of the insurance cover evaluator service concept by one of the participating insurance companies. Since electronic

services within other market areas were already more developed, the project development team was able to collect insights from both the end users and the industrial business partners. This information was used to support the development of the second part of the service concept.

Assessing the Utility of eInsurance Projects

Having described the background and introduced the eInsurance case, we consider it essential to evaluate how the development activities conducted during the two projects contribute to the field of electronic services. Our particular interest naturally focuses on the field of insurance business.

In this chapter we continue with the innovation approach by evaluating the utility of the two eInsurance projects. First, the benefits of the developed service concept (safety and insurance advisor) are discussed in the first subsection. In the second subsection, a more extensive view is provided, and the eInsurance projects are discussed as an example of organizational innovation in developing electronic insurance services. Finally, current challenges for the organization are discussed in the final subsection.

Service Innovation Perspective

Garcia and Calantone (2002) grouped innovations into five categories. First, *radical innovation* involves a new technology (or service: authors' comment) that changes the current market infrastructure. Second, *new innovation* changes either the technology or the market. Third, *discontinuous innovation* is radical or really new innovation depending on how much and how fast the innovation changes the technology or the market. Fourth, *incremental innovation* is based on current technology that offers new features, benefits, or improvements to existing markets. Fifth, *imitative innovation* challenges the original innovation.

The main innovation of the eInsurance project is the safety and insurance advisor. To our knowledge, the developed service concept is new for the insurance market as a whole. It offers a radically new approach for customers to chart not only personal needs for insurance but also personalized information of safety management and on how to avoid risks. The safety and insurance advisor is based on existing technology, but its user interface is more visual and entertaining than the traditional interfaces of electronic insurance services. In addition, the safety and insurance advisor has influenced the insurance market in general by opening a new communication channel between customers and insurance companies. On that basis, we suggest that the insurance selector can be considered a real new or even radical innovation. On the other hand, the insurance selector influences the insurance business marginally at the macrolevel, even though it is radically a new concept. From the insurance business point of view, the safety and insurance advisor can be considered an incremental innovation.

Furthermore, in our opinion the Customer Service Life Cycle Model by Ives and Mason (see Figure 3) provides a felicitous approach to assessing the utility of the safety and insurance advisor. However, the model had to be refined to fit the scope of electronic insurance services. The adapted model is depicted in Figure 7.

The first phase of the life cycle is called *requirements* (i.e., recognizing the need). The main purpose of the insurance cover evaluator concept was to make it easy for customers to recognize their insurance needs. The main function of the insurance cover evaluator is to collect background information about the customer's life situation (i.e., housing, family, property, hobbies, traveling, etc.) and provide the customer with an insurance cover solution suitable for his or her life situation.

The second phase of the life cycle is called *acquisition*. The safety advisor makes use of the information provided by the customers on the insurance cover evaluator and provides them with customized information concerning risks and other safety-related issues as well as on how

Figure 7. The insurance service life cycle and the new Web services (adapted from Kivistö-Rahnasto, Ahonen, & Salonen, 2006, p. 8)

to prevent them in their own environment. In addition, the safety advisor provides customers with information on how insurance types relate to the previously mentioned risks and includes statistical data and/or other useful information on safety measures and products that can be found on the Internet.

As Figure 7 indicates, the overall service concept (safety and insurance advisor) covers a great proportion of the customer service life cycle in the electronic insurance service context. Hence, the safety and insurance advisor can be considered as a valuable step in bringing electronic insurance services closer to consumers' mindset.

Organizational Perspective on Innovations

At the beginning of the article we emphasized the unique, or at least diverging, nature of eInsurance organization from the perspective of developing electronic services in the insurance context. In the insurance business area, service development has mainly consisted of utilizing technology, that is, transferring existing traditional services to the electronic environment instead of developing completely new service concepts. On the other hand, consumers do not necessarily expect very much from insurance services since they are used only occasionally.

From the point of view of service providers this has lead to a very limited and somewhat restricted orientation towards service innovations, which might result in new ideas with large market potential being rejected automatically since such ideas would require a change in the standard processes and/or culture of the organization. This tendency might, in turn, also diminish customers' willingness to accept innovations. However, the research organizations often have a perspective which is contrary to that of business life, because their organizational culture supports entrepreneurship and innovativeness, but often they lack the resources needed to complete a project. Hence,

research organization projects often have as their objective the developing of a service concept instead of a commercial product or service, since marketing and other business operations aiming at commercializing the developed service concept require such resources that research organizations usually do not have.

The research organizations provided competencies within the areas of technology and consumer research which supported especially the idea-generation phase of the project. The corporate partners, on the other hand, provided general information, target groups (e.g., customers) and a marketing perspective on the project which the research organisations lacked. In addition, the corporate partners provided resources by funding a part of the project, whereas the main funding was granted by the national funding agency.

Uncertainty about the results is often characteristic of research and development projects aimed at creating innovations. This was the case also in the two eInsurance projects. The uncertainty at the beginning of the project caused a certain amount of strain especially for insurance companies. After the participating organizations had learned to rely on the established working practices, tolerance of uncertainty increased.

However, many innovative ideas never see the light of day since the working climate might set certain norms of behaviour which hinder the creativeness of individuals and thus also that of the overall organization. The objective of the two eInsurance projects was to provide a new basis for innovative ideas that might otherwise have been rejected within the insurance company's own research and development (R&D) department. The developed concepts were tested by ordinary users in order to obtain sufficient information on the functionality of the developed service concept(s) before decisions regarding further development and commercialization of the concept(s) were made by the participating corporate partners.

The corporate partners expressed their satisfaction with the appropriateness of organizational structure of the two eInsurance projects for developing electronic insurance services. As one of the most fundamental benefits of this structure, the corporate partners emphasized the freedom to focus on creating innovative electronic service solutions. The organization of the eInsurance projects was perceived as very creative by business partners since it allowed even humorous and far-out ideas to be put forward by participants without having to worry about the disapproving reactions or financial pressure from the firm, as they would often have to in the case of internal projects. As the corporate members of the project expressed, the eInsurance projects, although temporary, enabled the corporate partners to break away from their daily routines and concentrate on being innovative. Also, several members of the project management team expressed the opinion that it was incredible how well the participating members, especially within the operative team, blended to form a cohesive and functional entity.

The project members assumed different roles in the innovation process. As O'Connor and McDermott (2004) have suggested, a radical innovation requires multiple roles, such as those of *idea generator, opportunity recognizer, champion, project leader,* and *project alumni.* They underline that the idea generator and opportunity recognizer are usually different persons. They also emphasize the role of project alumni, some of whom are acting in the project team in leadership roles, regardless of any eventual change in their actual functions within the companies where they are employed during the project (see also McDermott, 1999). In a business–university alliance it is important to pay attention to "cultural gaps" regarding for example the publication of results, long-term vs. short-term project benefits, and ownership of Intellectual Property Rights (IPR).

In the eInsurance projects, various roles of innovators can be found. Representatives from the university and the public research organization which participated in both projects can be considered as *idea generators* since they form the ultimate core of the two eInsurance projects. Although they were not officially *project leaders,* they acted as such in practice by ensuring that everything went as intended. Further, The Finnish Funding Agency for Technology and Innovations (Tekes) as well as the corporate partners and public research organizations can be considered *opportunity recognizers.* The members of the project management team in both projects can be considered as *champions,* but also as *project alumni.* Some members might have participated officially in the first project but not in the second project. Despite this, these members still might have been "unofficially available" for the second project.

To conclude, the virtual eInsurance project organization that involved different cultures, information, and individuals supporting each other provided a functional and fruitful environment for the development of electronic insurance services. Many corporate partners even commended the working methods followed in the projects and the prevailing encouraging and open atmosphere within the organization. In this respect, we warmly recommend a similar collaborative organizational model for organizations in the process of designing and developing (electronic) service innovations. On the basis of our experience, we argue that in terms of developing new and innovative electronic services, such as safety and insurance advisor, the above-mentioned *eInsurance projects can be considered, if not a global, at least a national organizational innovation in the Finnish insurance research and development context, since there is no tradition of joint projects in nonlife insurance R&D functions.*

Current Challenges Facing the Organization

One of the major challenges facing the case organization relate to the further development of the concept within the corporate partner organizations. In order to commercialize the service concept, the information collected by the project organization during the project has to be successfully transferred to the R&D and marketing departments of the participating companies. This is often performed by assigning department representatives to the project team or otherwise interacting with them during the different phases of the project. Information transfer has been performed by reporting the research results via (academic but also practical) publications during and after the project. In addition, a summarizing report on the research results and other findings from the project is being written. The report describes the most crucial results of both projects and lists corresponding reports and/or articles that provide further information.

Despite the positive results of both research projects, the project team discovered that the insurance companies as well as their customers are perhaps not yet ready for novel electronic service concepts. This might be due to the shift towards the electronic environment that the insurance companies are currently undergoing and also to the fact that consumers have just recently started to use the electronic insurance services available to them more actively.

However, as the first eInsurance project proved commercialization of the innovative service concepts within the insurance industry cannot be achieved in a month—not necessarily even in a year. Despite this, the first eInsurance provided a clear message that insurance companies are interested in developing their electronic services, although in their own quiet way. As concrete evidence of this, one of the two participating insurance companies launched an electronic service for their private customers (i.e., consumers) which is based on the logic of the insurance cover evaluator service concept one and a half years after the first eInsurance project had ended.

CONCLUDING REMARKS

This article aims at describing research and development activities for bringing electronic insurance services closer to customers' mindset. These activities comprised two eInsurance projects carried out between 2003 and 2007. As a result, an electronic service concept that supports consumers in their insurance service transactions was developed.

So, how does the developed service concept bring electronic insurance services closer to consumers' mindset compared with existing services? First, the safety and insurance advisor introduces a *visual interface*. Consequently, the information content is more appealing and comprehensible for customers. Second, the service concept is *demonstrative*. The relationship between different insurance products and possible risks related to customers' lives are illustrated by means of the safety and insurance advisor. Third, the service concept is adaptive, providing *customized insurance information* for customers. The service concept collects information and adjusts it to the consumers' life circumstances, thus providing them with a basic understanding of insurance-related issues.

All in all, the safety and insurance advisor introduced a novel approach to offering electronic insurance services to consumers. The service content is made more appealing and comprehensible to customers and thus they are provided with better prerequisites to use electronic services based on self-service logic.

From the organizational point of view, both eInsurance projects were successful. They were well organized and they started and ended on schedule. Even though the budget was strict, the project teams managed to keep approximately within its limits. In addition, both projects provided all the research items agreed in the plan and developed the pilot versions of the tool called safety and insurance advisor for use in the electronic insurance environment. Moreover, one of the participating insurance companies further developed the insurance cover evaluator after the eInsurance 1 project and launched it on their Internet pages in 2006.

The push and pull models adapted from Trott (2005) illustrate well the processes involved in eInsurance projects. The customer service life cycle by Ives and Mason (1990) guided the work from its early phase and as a result of the projects we were able to present the insurance service life cycle that was introduced earlier in this article. As shown above, the developed safety and insurance advisor covers a great proportion of the insurance service life cycle, but mainly covers the requirement and acquisition phases. Other phases (e.g., ownership and retirement) were not included in the eInsurance projects.

More generally, in the financial sector electronic banking reduced the bonds between customers and their banks since changing the banking service provider after a competitive online bidding on a mortgage is made easy for the customers. With the development of electronic services, this situation will apply also to insurance companies in the near future. In any case, the development of electronic insurance services will follow the other players in the financial sector by proceeding slowly rather than rapidly. However, perhaps some day we may see a comprehensive electronic insurance service environment that covers all the different phases of the customer service life cycle. At least we believe so.

REFERENCES

Adobe. (2007). Adobe Shockwave Player. Adobe Systems Incorporated. Retrieved June 5, 2008, from http://www.adobe.com/products/shockwaveplayer/

Ahonen, A. (2007). *From complex to simple: Designing a customer-friendly electronic insurance service environment.* Dissertation, Tampere University.

Ahonen, A., & Salonen, J. (2005). *eInsurance: Kohti asiakaslähtöisempää sähköistä vakuutuspalvelua* [eInsurance: Towards a more customer-oriented electronic insurance service]. Tampere, Finland: VTT Industrial Systems.

Ahonen, A., Salonen, J., Kivistö-Rahnasto, J., Järvinen, R., & Silius, K. (2007, April 26–28). *eInsurance: Novel services in the electronic environment.* Paper presented at the Innovation in Services Conference, Berkeley, CA. UC Berkeley Tekes.

Ahonen, A., & Windischhofer, R. (2005). The Web performance of different types of online insurance providers: A wake up call to traditional insurance providers. In Zhao, Xiande, Liu, & Baoding (Eds.), *Proceedings of the Fifth International Conference on Electronic Business (ICEB2005)* (pp. 245–252). Hong Kong: The Chinese University of Hong Kong.

Fitzsimmons, J., & Fitzsimmons, M. (1994). *Service management for competitive advantage.* McGraw-Hill.

Fitzsimmons, J.A., & Fitzsimmons, M.J. (2006). *Service management: Operations, strategy, information technology* (5th ed.). New York: McGraw-Hill.

Garcia, R., & Calantone, R. (2002). A critical look at technological innovation typology and innovativeness terminology: A literature review. *Journal of Product Innovation Management, 19,* 110–132.

Ives, B., & Mason, R.O. (1990). Can information technology revitalize your customer service? *Academy of Management Executive, 4*(4), 52–69.

Järvinen, R., Eriksson, P., Saastamoinen, M., & Lystimäki, M. (2001). *Vakuutukset verkossa: Vakuutusyhtiöiden tarjonta ja kuluttajien odotuk-*

set (Research paper report no. 7) [Insurance on the Web: The offerings of the insurance companies and the expectations of consumers]. Helsinki: National Consumer Research Centre.

Järvinen, R., & Heino, H. (2004). *Kuluttajien palvelukokemuksia vakuutus: ja pankkisektorilta* (Publications 3/2004) [Consumer experience from insurance and banking sectors]. Helsinki, Finland: National Consumer Research Centre (English summary).

Järvinen, R., Lehtinen, U., & Vuorinen, I. (2003). Options of strategic decision making in services: Tech, touch and customisation in financial services. *European Journal of Marketing, 37*(5/6), 774795.

Kivistö-Rahnasto, J., Ahonen, A., & Salonen, J. (2006). *New service concepts for selecting and evaluating insurance cover within the electronic environment.* Paper presented at the 4th International Conference on Occupational Risk Prevention (ORP), Seville, Spain.

Majaro, S. (1983). Marketing insurance services: The main challenges. In G. Foxall (Ed.), *Marketing in the service industries* (pp. 77–91). London.

McDermott, C. (1999). Managing radical product development in large manufacturing firms: A longitudinal study. *Journal of Operations Management, 17,* 631–644.

Meuter, M.L., Ostrom, A.L., Roundtree, R.I, & Bitner, M.J. (2000). Self-service technologies: Understanding customer satisfaction with technology-based service encounters. *Journal of Marketing, 64*(3), 5064.

O'Connor, G., & McDermott, C. (2004). The human side of radical innovation. *Journal of Engineering and Technology Management, 21,* 1130.

Peura-Kapanen, L., & Järvinen, R. (2006). *Kuluttajien käsityksiä riskeistä, niiden hallinnasta ja sähköisestä vakuuttamisesta* (Publications 7/2006) [Consumer perceptions of risk, risk management and electronic insurance]. Helsinki, Finland: National Consumer Research Centre (English summary).

Peura-Kapanen, L., Nenonen, S., Järvinen, R., & Kivistö-Rahnasto, J. (2007). *Kuluttajien arkipäivän riskit ja turvallisuus. Riskeihin liittyvät käsitykset, turvallisuuden edistäminen ja suhtautuminen sähköiseen asiointiin turvallisuuskontekstissa* [Consumers' everyday risks and safety: Risk-related views, promotion of safety and attitude towards electronic transactions in safety context]. (Publications 8/2007). Helsinki, Finland: National Consumer Research Centre.

Salonen, J., & Ahonen, A. (2007). eInsurance project Web site. Retrieved June 5, 2008, from http://www.einsurance.fi

Trott, P. (2005). *Innovation management and new product development* (3rd ed.). Essex, England: Pearson Education Limited.

Vroomen, B., Donkers, B., Verhoef, P.C., & Franses, P.H. (2005). Selecting profitable customers for complex services on the Internet. *Journal of Service Research, 8*(1), 37–47.

Windischhofer, R., & Ahonen, A. (2004). The effect of physical distribution channels on online distribution channels in the insurance industry: An examination of electronic insurance services on the Internet. In J. Chen (Ed.), *Service systems and service management: Proceedings of ICSSSM'04, Vol. II* (pp. 753758). Beijing: International Academic Publishers/Beijing World Publishing Corporation.

FURTHER READING

De Wulf, K., Schillewaert, N., Muylle, S., & Rangarajan, D. (2006). The role of pleasure in Web site success. *Information & Management, 43*(4), 434–446.

Fitzsimmons, J.A., & Fitzsimmons, M.J. (Eds.). (2000). *New service development: Creating memorable experiences.* Sage Publications.

Froehle, C.M., & Roth, A.V. (2004). New measurement scales for evaluating perceptions of the technology-mediated customer service experience. *Journal of Operations Management, 22*(1), 1–21.

Huang, M.H. (2005). Web performance scale. *Information & Management, 42*(6), 841–852.

Lusch, R.F., Vargo, S.L., & O'Brien, M. (2007). Competing through service: Insights from service-dominant logic. *Journal of Retailing, 83*(1), 5–18.

Meuter, M.L., Bitner, M.J. Ostrom, A.L., & Brown, S.W. (2005). Choosing among alternative service delivery modes: An investigation of customer trial of self-service technologies. *Journal of Marketing, 69*(2), 61–83.

Moon, J.W., & Kim, Y.G. (2001). Extending the TAM for a World-Wide-Web context. *Information & Management, 38*(4), 217–230.

Zeithaml, V.A., Bitner, M.J., & Gremler, D.D. (2006). *Services marketing: Integrating customer focus across the firm.* New York: McGraw-Hill

ENDNOTES

[1] The project was funded by a public organization called Tekes (Finnish Funding Agency for Technology and Innovation).

[2] For a more extensive discussion of the different types of electronic insurance service providers in different insurance markets, see Ahonen and Windischhofer (2005) and Windischhofer and Ahonen (2004).

[3] http://www.adobe.com/shockwave/download

[4] http://www.einsurance.fi

Chapter IX
eBay:
An E–Titan Success Story

Zhongxian Wang
Montclair State University, USA

James Yao
Montclair State University, USA

Ruiliang Yan
Virginia State University, USA

Jeffrey Hsu
Fairleigh Dickinson University, USA

ABSTRACT

eBay provides online marketplaces for the sale of goods and services, online payments, and online communication offerings. Their three primary business segments are: eBay Marketplaces, Payments, and Communications. The Marketplace platform has grown beyond the initial auction platform to include Rent.com, Shopping.com, Kijiji, Craigslist, mobile.de, and Marketplaats.nl. PayPal enables individuals and businesses to easily and securely transact payments. The overgrowth of eBay may have brought about the management problems in a young company that grows so fast. As the eighth largest global retailer, eBay's mission is to pioneer new communities around the world built on commerce, sustained by trust, and inspired by opportunity. Their ability to maintain or enhance this position will depend on their ability to adapt to new technologies while facing increased competition and anticipating customers' needs. This chapter will address management's philosophies, the corporate business model, its challenges, and network relationships, and examine corporate growth to date as well as future horizons.

ORGANIZATION BACKGROUND

History

Pierre Omidyar earned his undergraduate degree at Tuft's University and worked for Apple Computer after graduation. He cofounded Ink Development Corporation, later renamed eShop, which was later bought out by Microsoft (eBay, 2005a).

Subsequently while working for a mobile communication company and inspired by his future wife's Pez collection, Omidyar brainstormed the idea of an online auction where people would be able to trade with each other. In 1995, while keeping his day job he cofounded AuctionWeb with Jeff Skoll, a Stanford MBA graduate. Omidyar created the concept of serving people on the Web, and Skoll provided the business experience to turn the concept into a business (Bunnell, 2001). The company incorporated in 1996, and with the rapid growth of the company the need for additional capital was recognized in the spring of 1997.

During the 1990s, as a result of Silicon Valley's successes, there was a tremendous amount of venture capital available for Internet start-ups, the new "darlings" of Silicon Valley. The computer age was changing its focus from electronic manufacturers to the application of these products to the Web married to business models that promised to change the way people did business. AuctionWeb's person-to-person online trading was provided its initial funding of $5 million from Benchmark Capital. In exchange the venture capitalist group received stock and warrants representing 22% of the company.

In September 1997 the company formally adopted the name eBay, and began to post banner ads on selected sites and ad placement in certain publications. By year end, eBay's revenues topped $350 million and 850,000 registered users. In collaboration with the venture capitalist group the fast growing online auction company began to solicit talents that would allow the company to realize its potential.

Management

The search for a CEO in March 1998 resulted in the recruitment of Meg Whitman. As General Manager of the $600 million Preschool Division of Hasbro, Meg had strong "brand-building" experience. Meg Whitman's employment package included an option to purchase 7.2 million shares of stock, which represented approximately a 6% ownership of eBay which once exercised made the CEO a billionaire.

The new CEO recognized the need for additional strong management to develop the company which was operating in a new and undeveloped business arena. Howard Schultz, chairman and CEO of Starbucks, and Scott Cook, chairman of Intuit, both experienced in successful enterprises in previously undeveloped consumer markets, were brought in as board members (Bunnell, 2001).

Most of eBay's key executives who were first recruited came from the managerial ranks of traditional business: Meg Whitman from Hasbro; Matt Bannick, vice president of customer service, from McKinsey & Company; CFO Gary Bengier from Kenetech Corporation, an energy service firm; and Marketing Senior Vice President Brian Swette from Pepsi-Cola. The philosophy of the company encouraged hiring experienced management with technical know-how in marketing, corporate finance, and human resource management.

Going Public

After an unprecedented growth, in September 1998, the NASDAQ market made an 18% downward adjustment. September 1998 was also the date of eBay's Initial Public Offering. Despite market jitters, the IPO underwritten by Goldman, Sachs, Donaldson, Lufkin & Jenrette, Bancamerica Robertson Stephens, and BT Alex Brown, resulted in the sale of 4,025,000 shares of stock for net proceeds of $66.1 million. During the first day of after-market trading, the price per share rose from $18 to $54 before settling back to close at $48. Nine months after the IPO the share price reached $234.

The Business Model

Mike Malone, editor of Forbes, believes that eBay's success is the outcome of two key decisions: (1) To let anybody sell anything and (2) To take a hands-off approach to user transactions (Bunnell, 2001, p. 36). This philosophy was motivated by the founders' instincts, and this gave their business model infinite scale potential. The following is the application of this philosophy as it has been applied to each of the business segments.

Marketplace

eBay calls itself "the world's personal trading community" (Crowe, 1999, p. B4). eBay has grown from two million users at the end of 1998 to more than 181 million through 2005, with online bidders along identified to have goal-driven, experiential, focused, and opportunistic groups based on their bidding behaviors in consumer-to-consumer (C2C) private value auctions, for example (Hou & Rego, 2007). eBay has established an international marketplace with no peers except a few of the stock and commodity exchanges. eBay's marketplace rationalizes the sale and purchase of used goods. That is to say, eBay always has the maximum numbers of buyers and sellers compared to other markets, all of which are smaller (Sinclair, 2007, p. 6). Buyers enjoy a broad base of goods and services, while sellers are rewarded with high conversion rates. With over two billion searches per month, the company offers selection, value, convenience and entertainment for its buyers. The sellers are afforded the opportunity of maximizing sales and profits through access to a worldwide marketplace and minimal marketing costs. The focus is on convenience for its users. Buyers and sellers are able to search multiple categories and participate in auctions with as little friction as possible.

Online tutorials are provided to guide customers through a simple four step process: register, find stuff, bid, and sell. Placement and success fees are paid by the seller. eBay does not certify the sellers or the quality of their products; it operates on principle of caveat emptor, or let the buyer beware. Their marketplace brings buyers and sellers together creating a huge market for resold goods, allowing the buyers and sellers to find each other and transact business. However, in recognizing the critical importance of trust between buyer and seller, eBay developed marketplace services designed to increase the user's comfort level in dealing with relatively unknown partners in cyberspace. These services are discussed further in the "Trust Factor" section. Additionally, online classified sites, including Kijiji, Marktplaats, and Craigslist, enhance the Marketplace platform and helped situate eBay as number one in C2C classified Web sites worldwide. They service 300 cities in over 30 countries.

Payments

In 2002, eBay acquired PayPal, Inc. in order to provide more satisfying online experiences by eliminating online payment obstacles such as lengthy processing time, inconvenience, and high costs of traditional methods. Initially PayPal offered its account-based system in 38 English speaking countries. Today it is a global leader in online payment solutions in 55 markets with approximately 96 million total accounts, which include 19 million business accounts and 77 million personal accounts with anticipated revenues for 2006 of over $200 million. It is accepted worldwide by merchants on and off eBay. Built on the existing infrastructure of bank accounts and credit cards, it relies on the most advanced fraud protection systems to create a secure real-time payment solution. There are three types of PayPal accounts: personal, business, and premier.

Paypal earns revenues through transaction fees when a business or premier account receives payment, foreign exchange rates of currencies, money withdrawals to a non-U.S. bank, and returns on certain customer balances. Licensing fees are also earned through PayPal debit cards and the PayPal Buyer Credit offering. Perhaps PayPal's most significant corporate return is its synergy with eBay.

Communications

Acquired in 2005, Skype provides free software that enables free VoIP (voice over Internet protocol) between Skype users online. This is actually high quality voice communication to anyone worldwide with an Internet provider. Skype also offers voicemail, instant messaging, call forwarding, conference calling, and Skype video. Skype facilitates real time trading among buyers and sellers. Skype is particularly effective for buyers and sellers in complex transactions, eliminating delays by providing instant clarification through communication. Skype has 75 million members in 225 countries and is considered the worldwide leader in VoIP.

Business Climate

Online sales for the third quarter of 2005 totaled over $40 billion, representing a 22% year-over-year increase (Johnson, 2005a). Interpreted for future sales growth, it was concluded that online sales will enjoy a 14% compound annual growth rate over the next five years, resulting in sales growth from $172 billion in 2005 to $239 billion in 2010 (Johnson, 2005b).

With growth experienced to date and anticipated growth, online sales have become a highly competitive market. Online users have the option to find, buy, sell, and pay for product through a variety of sources. This is not limited to online retailers, but also includes aggregate auctioneers, distributors, liquidators, and import and export companies. The Web has made the global market a much more manageable playing field. eBay has successfully captured 14% of that market in 2005. Over the past five years revenues and net incomes have increased in multiples, and shareholders' equity has increased from $1.4 billion in 2001 to over $10 billion in 2005 (Tables 1 and 2). To remain competitive eBay will need to expend resources in technology and marketing, which will be expensive and may reduce profit margins. However, the success of eBay depends on the development and maintenance of the Internet infrastructure.

SETTING THE STAGE

Initially eBay developed proprietary software capable of supporting scalable user interface and transaction processing which later evolved into a system capable of handling all aspects of the auction process. The system supports the full selling and buying processes, including initial registration for the service, placing bids and managing outbids, listing items for sale, and transaction close. The system also manages various notifications for sellers and buyers, including daily status updates, bid and outbid notices, registration confirmations, account change notices, billing notices, and end-of-auction notices. User registration information, billing accounts, current item listings, and historical listings are maintained and archived for record-keeping and analysis purposes. A search engine regularly updates the titles and descriptions of items, as well as pricing and bidding activity. The seller's billing account is updated every time an item is listed, a feature is selected, or an auction closes with a bid in excess of the seller-specified minimum bid. Electronic invoices are sent to all sellers on at least a monthly basis. The system also supports community bulletin boards and chat areas where users and eBay customer support personnel can interact (eBay, 2005b, p. 10).

Computer systems include Sun database servers running Oracle relational database management applications with a mix of Sun and Hitachi storage devices, along with a suite of Pentium-based Internet servers running the Windows NT and Linux operating systems. For system back up F5 Networks' load balancing systems and select software from Symantec are utilized. The selection and use of these cutting-edge technologies provided faster data transmission and larger volumes of business transactions, which aided eBay to pave its way towards its potentials. This fact was crucially important for such a young and fast growing company since eBay is an entire online company that relies on information technology and information system to achieve its competitive advantage and business objectives.

CASE DESCRIPTION

Little Thinks in a Big Way

As John Little stated, "For some of the people all of the time and for all of the people some of the time, the most convenient way to shop will be on the Web" (Marketing Science Institute, 2006, p. 5). Who would have thought that a small start-up auction company in the 1990s would have emerged to having a market capitalization of over $34 billion? Something as simple as bringing buyers and sellers together from all over the world has made them a successful online community. eBay does not even have to hold any inventory or touch any of its products (Cartwright, 2000). The potential is amazing if you could only imagine the impact it could have on businesses. Companies will have to and already have changed their way of doing business. Every day, we get closer and closer to getting what we want when we want it. Trading on eBay can be something as little as a Pez dispenser to something as big and expensive as a jet.

Although eBay is an online auction and not a retailer, people could not agree with John Little any more. However, eBay should listen to Little's opinion that "peer to peer exchange" is the sleeper (Marketing Science Institute, 2006). eBay members do use a rating system to post transactions in which this information is kept centralized. As noted above, something to think about in the future is a "peer to peer exchange" which is in a decentralized environment in which trust management can be taken advantage of at its best. It will be a much different way of doing business than we are used to today. The obstacle to overcome is that the transactions taken place can be viewed by everyone in the network and reliable information may become questionable (Aberer & Despotovic, 2001). Many people and organizations must rethink our way of conducting business as the globe is becoming one market. eBay is a different animal though. This will be learned in further discussion.

As one of the biggest online communities, eBay has to make sure that they are properly equipped to handle their business. eBay's core infrastructure is provided by Sun Microsystems, a relationship that has existed for over eight years of providing hardware and software to serve their community. Sun Microsystems connects the community of over 160 million users worldwide who are trading more than $1,350 worth of goods every second. eBay has explored ways to lower their costs and increase performance. To assure business continuity, system performance, and sustain their leading position in the field, eBay adopts servers and systems such as Sun Fire X4100 and 4200 plus AMD Opteron processor that allow eBay to meet the demands that their site requires. These advanced technologies also provide eBay's engineering staff with the ability to have insight on the application behavior and operating system performance.

The Trust Factor

A big part of eBay's success has been built on trust. The reason trust is so important is that those who are transacting business are dealing with strangers. To make their users comfortable enough to deal with these strangers and do transactions over the Internet, certain platforms have been put into place. The Feedback Forum allows users to comment on other eBay users and set profiles with ratings. A seller's feedback ratings, reported by other eBay users, can have a measurable effect on his/her auction prices (Lucking-Reiley, Bryan, Prasad, & Reeves, 2007). There is also a SafeHarbor Program (three areas: Investigations, Fraud Prevention, and Community Watch) in place that establishes guidelines for trading and ways to resolve disputes. Reports of misuse are responded to appropriately. The Standard Purchase Protection Program is in place to allow users to communicate with each other on items not received or not as described; however, unresolved items can be submitted as a claim to eBay's Trust and Safety team (eBay, 2005b, p. 5). As an added layer, PayPal offers a Buyer Protection Program which will cover transactions $1,000 or less if the item is not delivered or not as described. This move was needed to combat with shoppers who feel more secure with the traditional retail sites like Wal-Mart (Savitz, 2005).

The Review of Economics and Statistics is a study that examined how important one's reputation was in doing business on online auctions. There were dramatic results that supported the theory that reputation was very important in people's buying decisions. Even if the seller had only a couple of positive reports, the chance of a sale were much greater than if one had negative reports then his or her chances of doing business diminished considerably (Livingston, 2005). Negative feedback ratings have a much greater effect than positive feedback ratings do (Lucking-Reiley et al., 2007). Another study showed that "while impulsive buyers consistently pay high premiums, analytical buyers pay greatly different premiums depending on sellers' reputations" (Kim, 2005, p. 79). Of course, there are those who will dispute the effectiveness of eBay's Feedback Forum. There are those who will argue that honest repeated players will benefit as intended, but there is no legal framework of feedback intermediaries to resolve matters that involves frauds (Rietjens, 2006). Many times it is whom you are buying it from which matters to the customer.

Although eBay lives by their culture of trust, buyers have found that there is reason to beware. The same issues may pop up that you would find when buying something off of a street vendor in New York City. Consumers should beware and companies will need to protect their image from those who are deceitful. Tiffany's is a fine example of this concern. Tiffany's was looking to protect its name because there were many obvious listings of jewelry selling with their name on it but priced extraordinarily lower than the "real deal." In fact, two employees from Tiffany's blocked listings over a 5-month period which resulted in a finding of 73% fakes. eBay has defended them by maintaining that people come to buy and sell on their electronic platform and take the responsibility of verifying those items sold online. eBay is different than retailers and auctioneers who write their catalogue. It is the sellers who write the descriptions, price setup, terms, and collections. eBay's success has been built on trust; therefore it may be wise to make a better effort to prevent such deceit from happening.

Patent infringement lawsuits could also have an effect on trust. Recently this year the Supreme Court ruled unanimously that the federal courts must consider other factors before making an automatic injunction against the patent infringer. The ruling was that traditional principles of equity should be taken into account. At the time, the U.S. District Court had almost forced eBay to shut down their service entirely when they noted that MercExchange would not be harmed if they continued to design around the patent. The Buy

It Now fixed price on their Web site was at stake. This all stems back to when the tiny company from Virginia, MercExchange, had won millions by suing eBay (Holzer, 2006).

Growth Check

For years after the bubble had burst many had wondered when eBay's growth would slow down. A good look should be given as to why eBay has grown successfully. Over the past few years eBay has made dramatic moves into areas which are different from when they first began as an online auction market for collectibles (Savitz, 2005). They acquired PayPal in 2002 which put them in the online payment services category to compete with the credit card companies. In fact, many have predicted PayPal to be a key driver of future growth. eBay has made acquisitions overseas to make a presence outside the United States. In 2005, eBay acquired Shopping.com to gain a stake in the online shopping comparison service market (Savitz, 2005). Their acquisition of Skype, the free voice-over-Internet company, had raised a few eyebrows. However, it may very well prove to be a key move to success being that the future is moving that way and Google, Microsoft, and Yahoo all offer avenues of buyers and sellers to communicate with one another online (Lashinsky & Roth, 2005).

eBay has also added the Buy It Now, which allows for fixed price transactions. Increasingly, people are seeing eBay stores popping up to help sellers of large inventories or slow moving goods. eBay purchased retail listings from Rent.com, a 25% stake in Craigslist's huge electronic bulletin board, and local market classified advertising sites called Kijiji in different countries. Investors have reacted in a negative sense to events such as when the eBay's CEO was interviewed at Disney, but she declined and stayed with eBay. Investors also did not like when eBay increased spending of $100 million to bolster their China expansion. eBay has confessed to interfering with their relation-ship with sellers when they had price increases (Savitz, 2005). Although investors and members may not have valid points, their reaction should always be taken into consideration.

The wild card may prove to be eBay's position in China. There are about 300 million middle class Chinese. That number alone is larger than the entire population of the United States. The good news is that "of the 50,000 or so merchandise categories in which eBay participates, the company accounts for no more than 6% to 7% of overall trade in any single category" (Savitz, 2005, p. 27). It is also interesting to note that there are still some who have never heard of eBay; but there are many more who have heard of it yet never used it. For those who wonder what is sold on it, perhaps the better question would be what is not sold on eBay. It also would not be surprising to see other large businesses besides Vodafone and Thomson Holidays opening stores on eBay.

The Hype about Skype

eBay's acquisition of Skype for $4.1 billion has been questioned by some even though it will give eBay a presence in the free voice-over-Internet market. Lashinksy mentioned in a Fortune article that eBay felt the need to show a 78-page Power-Point presentation to explain the purchase about how they will build Skype into their business. This is a move that eBay felt it had to make being that Google, Yahoo, and Microsoft all have allowed their users to participate (Lashinsky & Roth, 2005). The eBay executives have explained that it will help to promote their three flagship brands: eBay, PayPal, and Net telephony company Skype to all work in unison to boost their revenues (Claburn, 2006). At such a high cost, the company has plans to add Skype into its main site, Rent.com, Shopping.com, Kijiji, PayPal, and a PayPal Wallet for each Skype account. They have a Skype me small button on their site. There is a pay per call advertising service that is using Skype. eBay is also looking at this as a way to expand into China and possibly give Japan another try. In 2005 Skype was adding 166,000 new customers each day. At that time there was 57 million customers where 4 million were using the service at one time (Hof, 2005).

Skype's viewpoint is that communication is natural. It is a way to build a strong word of mouth. It is only a matter of time when people try Skype that they will begin to realize how simple it is to use. Those who use Skype probably want to be able to use it on their mobile phones. It is very common for people to be walking around constantly using their phones. The ability to communicate at any given moment should give good results. From eBay's perspective, acquiring Skype increases their competition and market coverage rather than having them dwindled.

The Missing Link in the Value Chain

The traditional value chain and value system analysis is not appropriate for e-commerce companies. Therefore a different approach is needed for market-space than what was needed for the marketplace. "Knowledge creation and innovation are replacing physical processes as value adding activities. New forms of competitive advantage are gained through the creative application of resources that cannot be readily duplicated" (Cartwright & Oliver, 2000, p. 24). Network relationships are the key factor that adds value to e-commerce. It has gone from a single linear link of two value systems to a system in which firms that compliment each other become allies. Which is why you will find that competitors will create value to a firm while at the same time will be considered in the firm's competitive analysis.

eBay and Google have worked very closely together over the years; however, eBay is beginning to open their eyes and see the search engine giant Google as a serious threat. eBay was one of Google's first customers who advertised with them. To combat this threat eBay has approached

Yahoo and Microsoft to work together as allies. The alarm sounded last year when Google started a classified advertising service which is a direct competition with eBay's online auctions. One way for eBay to work with them would be to agree on advertising more in exchange of gaining access to valuable data that has been collected on their consumers. Another way would be to share technical aspects of their systems to help cross-promote business (Guth & Mangalindan, 2006).

In value cluster analysis it is the activities clumped together which make up the value cluster. For eBay there are activities which are internal such as the auction database, monitoring the auction process, payment process, and online community services. They must also consider those activities of the traditional business model that they are missing, such as shipments, payments, fraud protection, banking services, traffic driven from other Internet portals and hardware support. It is the network relationships which will link the two together. Those firms which compliment their services such as Google are also their competitors. From a strategist's standpoint, eBay must understand their relationship among all the elements in the system to be able to understand how those activities will affect the system and what the response will be from the other members. Therefore, eBay is "part of a competitive system that produces its own change" (Cartwright, 2000, p. 26). eBay and e-commerce have developed the "value web" which has given a totally different approach from the traditional value added approach. eBay has taken cooperative advantage to a different level by building a trust between the merchant and customer in its virtual marketplace. This is a much different approach than the traditional methods used in the real world of highly competitive markets. It is eBay's trust factor that enables this unorthodox approach of having a cooperative culture. They have found it easier to use a cooperative strategy with their customers, stakeholders, and competitors (Cass, 2006).

According to Guth and Mangalindan (2006), eBay is in an interesting position. In view of the fact that Google's search technology is probably the best, eBay chose to run its advertisements on Google. Majestic Research has estimated that eBay has almost doubled its payment for advertising on Google than it does on other search engines simply because eBay knows that Google carries approximately triple the amount of traffic than that of the other search engines. The question to ask is if it is better to form closer ties with Google which should help eBay's business in the short run or divorce their ties with Google being that Google is likely to be a candidate of the biggest threat to eBay in the future. As a result, various offers have emerged from Yahoo, Microsoft, and even Google to have business with eBay. The key business offer is all but advertising. In this new relationship, the company with the best offer may be able to post their clients' advertisements on eBay's auction pages. In return, whoever eBay accepts should also be able to run eBay's advertisements on their sites. No wonder eBay is one of the biggest advertisers on the Web.

CHALLENGES FACING EBAY

In 1997, Jamie Kiggen, director of Internet research for Donaldson, Lufkin & Jenrette, began following eBay when it was still a small private company, as he was impressed with eBay's business model. Though the company was small, it represented a large opportunity combining the scalability of Amazon's model, the ability to grow revenues at a very rapid pace, with the profitability of Yahoo. Kiggen was overwhelmed by the loyalty of the user base and the word of mouth buzz, which would later evolve into the all too common catch phrase, "I got it on eBay." The company was young and fragile (Bunnell, 2001, p. 137) then.

However, eBay developed strategies to preserve its lofty beginnings. Its outsourcing and partnering strategies were to focus on customer oriented issues and market opportunities; minimize investments in fixed assets; and remain small and agile as an organization (Lucking-Reiley et al., 2007). Being a young and small company they would avert the burden of layers of personnel management which would enable them to take decisive action in a fast changing environment.

Since its inception eBay has had to deal with some serious systems' challenges: scaling up to meet exploding demand, technological advancements, and service outages. eBay must continually improve its systems to manage increasing levels of activity and required new features or services (MacInnes, Li, & Yurcik, 2005). Without the ability to upgrade or effectively integrate new technologies, transaction processing systems, security infrastructure, network infrastructure, or databases to accommodate increased traffic or transaction volume, future business success could be in jeopardy. In a business climate of rapidly changing technology, industry standards, services, and products, the future of eBay depends on its ability to adapt effectively and efficiently.

eBay remains steadfast in accomplishing its mission:

- Expanding its user base
- Strengthening brand recognition
- Broadening the trading platform by increased product categories and promoting new ones
- Fostering community affinity
- Enhancing site features and functionality

As Min, Caltagirone, and Serpico (in press) point out recently, as advancements in Internet technology continue to revolutionize today's business practices, it is increasingly more apparent that the Internet has become an integral part of the daily routine. eBay, an e-titan success story has marked its swift and smart steps in e-commerce history.

REFERENCES

Aberer, K., & Despotovic, Z. (2001, November 5–10). Managing trust in a peer-2-peer information system. *Proceedings of the 10th International Conference on Information and Knowledge Management (CIKM01)* (pp. 310–317). New York: ACM Press.

Bunnell, D. (2001). *The eBay phenomenon* (1st ed.). New York: John Wiley & Sons, Inc.

Cartwright, S., & Oliver, R. (2000). Untangling the value Web. *The Journal of Business Strategy, 21*(1), 22–27.

Cass, J. (2006, March 2). What culture does a company need to adopt to use cooperative marketing effectively? *Backbone Media*. Retrieved June 5, 2008, from http://blogsurvey.backbonemedia.com

Claburn, T. (2006). eBay's growth strategy; Community, not acquisitions. *Information Week, 1094*, 26.

Crowe, M. (1999, May 21). eBay Inc.: Going, going, gone! *The Business Journal, 17*(4), B4.

eBay. (2005a) Annual report to shareholders. Retrieved June 5, 2008, from http://investor.ebay.com/annual.cfm

eBay. (2005b). 10K. Retrieved June 5, 2008, from http://yahoo.brand.edgar-online.com/fetchFilingFrameset.aspx?dcn=0000950134-06-003678&Type=HTML

Guth, R., & Mangalindan, M. (2006, April 21). Behemoths' dance: eBay talks to Microsoft, Yahoo about a common foe: Google. *The Wall Street Journal* (eastern), A1.

Hof, R. (2005). No head-scratching at eBay about Skype's potential. *Business Week Online*. Retrieved June 5, 2008, from http://www.businessweek.com

Holzer, J. (2006, May 16). Supreme court buries patent trolls. *Forbes*, pp. 67–68.

Hou, J., & Rego, C. (2007, November). A classification of online bidders in a private value auction: Evidence from eBay. *International Journal of Electronic Marketing and Retailing Issue, 1*(4), 322–338.

Johnson, C. (2005a, November 2). Q3 2005 online sales: Weak, but not a trend for Q4. *Forrester Research, 1*.

Johnson, C. (2005b, September 14). US eCommerce: 2005 to 2010: a five-year forecast and analysis of US online retail sales. *Forrester Research, 1*.

Kim, Y. (2005). The effects of buyer and product traits with seller reputation on price premiums in e-auction. *The Journal of Computer Information Systems, 46*(1), 79–92.

Lashinsky, A., & Roth, D. (2005, October 3). The net's new odd couple. *Fortune, 152*(7), 26.

Livingston, J. (2005). How valuable is a good reputation? A sample selection model of Internet auctions. *The Review of Economics and Statistics, 87*(3), 453–465.

Lucking-Reiley, D., Bryan, D., Prasad, N., & Reeves, D. (2007, June). Pennies from eBay: The determinants of price in online auctions. *Journal of Industrial Economics, 55*(2), 223–233.

MacInnes, I., Li, Y., & Yurcik, W. (2005). Reputation and dispute in eBay transactions. *International Journal of Electronic Commerce, 10*(1), 27–54.

Mangalindan, M. (2005, June 24). EBay aims two new services at merchants looking elsewhere. *Wall Street Journal* (Eastern Edition), B.3.

Marketing Science Institute (2006). Featured academic of John D. C Little. Retrieved June 5, 2008, from www.msi.org/

Min, H., Caltagirone, J., & Serpico, A. (in press). Life after a dot-com bubble. *International Journal of Information Technology and Management (IJITM), 7*(1).

Rietjens, B. (2006). Trust and reputation on eBay: Towards a legal framework for feedback intermediaries. *Information & Communications Technology Law, 15*(1), 56.

Savitz, E. (2005, June 6). Time to bid on: eBay. *Barron's, 85*(23), 25–27.

Sinclair, J.T. (2007). *EBay the smart way: Selling, buying, and profiting on the Web's #1 auction site.* New York: Amacom.

APPENDIX

Table 1. Five-year income statements

(In thousands, except per share amounts)	Year Ended December 31				
	2001	2002	2003	2004	2005
Consolidated Statement of Income Data:					
Net revenues	$748,821	$1,214,100	$2,165,096	$3,271,309	$4,552,401
Cost of net revenues	134,816	213,876	416,058	614,415	818,104
Gross profit	614,005	1,000,224	1,749,038	2,656,894	3,734,297
Operating expenses:					
Sales and marketing	253,474	349,650	567,565	857,874	1,230,728
Product development	75,288	104,636	159,315	240,647	328,191
General and administrative	105,784	171,785	332,668	415,725	591,716
Payroll tax on employee stock options	2,442	4,015	9,590	17,479	13,014
Amortization of acquired intangible assets	36,591	15,941	50,659	65,927	128,941
Total operating expenses	473,579	646,027	1,119,797	1,597,652	2,292,590
Income from operations	140,426	354,197	629,241	1,059,242	1,441,707
Interest and other income, net	25,368	45,428	36,573	77,867	111,148
Interest expense	(2,851)	(1,492)	(4,314)	(8,879)	(3,478)
Income before cumulative effect of accounting change, income taxes and minority interests	162,943	398,133	661,500	1,128,230	1,549,377
Provision for income taxes	(80,009)	(145,946)	(206,738)	(343,885)	(467,285)
Minority interests	7,514	(2,296)	(7,578)	(6,122)	(49)
Income before cumulative effect of accounting change	90,448	249,891	447,184	778,223	1,082,043
Cumulative effect of accounting change, net of tax	--	--	(5,413)	--	--
Net income	$ 90,448	$ 249,891	$ 441,771	$ 778,223	$1,082,043
Per basic share amounts:	$ 0.08	$ 0.22	$ 0.35	$ 0.59	$ 0.79

Items to note: *Although revenues and net income are increasing over the five year period, both gross margin and operating income on a year over year basis have declined, indicating higher costs associated with running the business.*

Table 2. Five-year consolidated balance sheet data

(In thousands, except per share amounts)	As of December 31				
	2001	2002	2003	2004	2005
Cash and cash equivalents	$ 523,969	$1,109,313	$1,381,513	$1,330,045	$ 1,313,580
Short-term investments	199,450	89,690	340,576	682,004	774,650
Long-term investments	286,998	470,227	934,171	1,266,289	825,667
Working capital	703,666	1,082,234	1,498,606	1,826,279	1,698,302
Total assets	1,678,529	4,040,226	5,820,134	7,991,051	11,788,986
Short-term obligations	16,111	2,970	2,840	124,272	--
Long-term obligations	12,008	13,798	124,476	75	--
Total stockholders' equity	$1,429,138	$3,556,473	$4,896,242	$6,728,341	$10,047,981

Table 3. Key metrics (2002–2005)

(In millions)	As of December 31			
	2002	**2003**	**2004**	**2005**
Registered users (1)	61.7	94.9	135.5	180.6
Active users (2)	27.7	41.2	56.1	71.8
Gross merchandise volume (3)	$14,868	$23,779	$34,168	$44,299
Active accounts (4)	7.9	13.2	20.2	28.1
Total payment volume (5)	$7,000	$12,226	$18,915	$27,485

1. Cumulative total of all users who have completed the registration process on one of eBay's trading platforms.
2. All users, excluding Half.com, Internet Auction, and our classifieds Web sites, who bid on, bought, or listed an item within the previous 12-month period. Amount includes users of eBay India since their migration to the eBay platform in April of 2005.
3. Total value of all successfully closed items between users on eBay's trading platforms during the period, regardless of whether the buyer and seller actually consummated the transaction.
4. All accounts that sent or received at least one payment through the PayPal system within the previous three-month period.
5. Total dollar volume of payments initiated through the PayPal system during the period, excluding the payment gateway business, regardless of whether the payment was actually sent successfully, or was reversed, rejected, or was pending at the end of the period.

Figure 1. Four-year stock price comparison vs. Internet competitors (Note: On February 17, 2005 there was a 2 for 1 stock split for eBay)

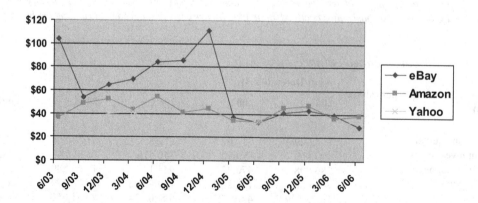

Figure 2. Four-year stock price comparison vs. brick and mortar competitors (Note: On February 17, 2005 there was a 2 for 1 stock split for eBay)

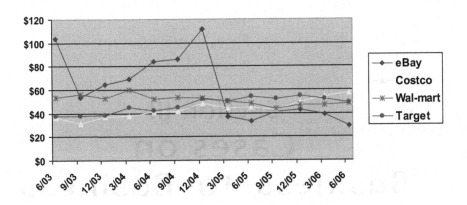

Exhibit 1.

Leading global retailers

Company	FY 2005 Revenue
1. Wal-Mart Stores Inc.	$316B
2. Carrefour SA	$93B
3. Home Depot Inc.	$82B
4. Metro AG	$69B
5. Tesco PLC	$68B
6. Kroger Co.	$61B
7. Royal Ahold NV	$55B
8. Costco Wholesale Corp.	$53B
9. Target Corp.	$53B
10. Sears Holdings Corp.	$49B
11. eBay GMV	$44B
12. Lowe's Companies Inc.	$43B
13. Walgreen Co.	$42B
14. Albertson's Inc.	$40B
15. Safeway Inc.	$38B

Source: 2005 Fortune Global 500 for the Food and Drug Stores, General Merchandisers and Specialty Retailers industries, updated for fiscal year 2005 revenue data publicly reported by each company and converted using the average foreign exchange rate for the respective fiscal year

Section III
Cases on Business–to–Business E–Services

Chapter X
Limitations and Perspectives on Use of E–Services in Engineering Consulting

Hanne Westh Nicolajsen
CMI, Aalborg University, Denmark

Morten Falch
CMI, Aalborg University, Denmark

ABSTRACT

In this chapter we analyse organizational challenges when an engineering consultancy in the building industry integrates information and communication technologies (ICT) in the production and delivery of their services, and discuss how the e-service concept can be applied in this context. The analysis is based on a field study on introduction of 3D-modeling tools within one of the leading engineering companies in Scandinavia (Ramboll). The analysis focuses on the changes in knowledge creation and transfer both within the company and in inter-organizational relations. The analysis points towards a need to change the business model as the project engineering part of the technical engineering service becomes standardized.

INTRODUCTION

This chapter analyses how the use of information and communication technologies (ICT) in an engineering consultancy has led to increasing codification of the knowledge delivered, and how this affects the potential for using the e-service business concept within this particular industry.

Knowledge Intensive Business Services (KIBS), such as engineering consultancy, produce and sell knowledge to other businesses. The knowledge service they sell is often customized to a particular customer and made in interaction with the customer, but builds on in-house expertise from the consultancy. Engineering consultancies must continuously upgrade and develop knowledge if they want to be capable of delivering unique and competitive services. On the other hand it is necessary to reuse the same knowledge in several projects in order to reduce costs. Knowledge management is therefore a key parameter for the success of an engineering consultancy.

The organization of production of engineering consultancy services is like production of other KIBS highly affected by use of ICT. However engineering services cannot be termed e-services in a narrow sense because engineering service is only partly subject to electronic delivery. Engineering consultancy is a complex service involving intensive communication between several parties, including suppliers, contractors, architects, and customers. The end product is to a large extent a physical product in the form of a building. However, the different KIBS involved within this "production" process deliver various knowledge services. The service delivery can thus be seen as a large number of separated deliveries to the building owner (as the primary customer) or to the other partners as "internal customers," which is further complicated through the feedback cycles involving the customer or other parties in the building process. Some of these services may be partly produced or delivered through e-mail communications and other Web-based interaction, others at business meetings, and so forth. It is however unlikely that electronic communication will be able to replace all types of communication in full. The e-service concept must therefore be understood more widely as the use of ICT to produce, collaborate, or deliver parts of the service package. ICT is used both as a means of producing services in the sense of new production tools and for creating an electronic communication infrastructure enabling communication with partners and customers, thus facilitating both production and delivery of services.

This chapter analyses how ICT is used to facilitate intra- and inter-organisational collaboration in production and delivery of engineering consultancy services within the area of building construction. Based on information from a field study of the engineering consultancy Ramboll, the chapter studies how use of ICT affects internal organisational issues in relation to securing future innovations, development of new ways of working, and building and maintenance of staff competences needed. First, the chapter provides background information on the field study and a description of the drivers for introducing ICT systems in provisioning of engineering services. Thereafter a general presentation of Ramboll follows together with a detailed description of its building division. This is followed by an outline on the usage of ICT within engineering consulting. Finally organisational implications and the status of engineering consultancy as an e-service are discussed.

BACKGROUND

For decades the building industry has been characterised by increasing costs, low productivity, and often poor quality. This is in part due to labour intensive production processes in design, projection, and construction, which have proved to be hard to automate. Another problem is lack of coordination between the large numbers of partners involved in building projects. Knowledge that flows between partners from different companies is often limited by lack of common standards, lack of common understanding on how the building process is organised, and the varying division of labour and responsibilities between the partner companies. This results in unnecessary conflicts and errors. In addition the lack of knowledge flow within building projects reduces accumulated learning both across projects and across partners. These problems are reinforced by the temporary character of partnerships within the building industry, where each project in general presents a new partner constellation. Moreover, along with increased competition, the ongoing globalisation taking place in segments of the building industry will further complicate coordination between partners.

The use of ICT in the production of service offers a number of advantages addressing these problems. In general the digitalisation of data used in the design and planning phases enables reuse of data both within the organisation and by collaborating partners. In addition the growth in inter-organisational and intra-organisational networks makes it easier to connect and exchange data and communicate on a more ongoing and direct basis providing for closer collaboration across time and space within and between organisations. Also new ICT based production tools have proved to reduce the need for manpower and have automated some of the processes and at the same time create information, making the content of the jobs more abstract (Zuboff, 1989).

In the building sector both industrial players and governments have become aware of the need to advance implementation of ICT systems in order to address the problems sketched above. Engineering consultancy firms as well as other players in building projects are now more focused on using ICT as a tool to reduce costs and improve quality in order to respond to growing international competition. This is supported by growing maturity of both ICT based design and calculation tools as well as new Web based communication tools. This development is in large part based on learning from other industrial sectors that are more advanced in the use of ICT in their production processes. In order to facilitate this development, since the early 1990s the Danish Government has launched a number of projects including "Project House" and later "Digital Construction." In addition the seven largest companies in the Danish building sector created a sector wide organisation in 2003 called BIPS

(Building, Information technology, Productivity and Collaboration). BIPS is a nonprofit membership organisation of companies that represents all parties within the building trade. The aim of BIPS is to develop collective tools and methods to aid collaboration between all players involved in the construction of buildings. Through BIPS and similar initiatives, the Danish government stimulates the development and integration of ICT based solutions. The government has created a growing awareness of the need for change, and companies are becoming more alert and engage more actively in investments related to the integration of new ICT in the production process.

The use of ICT within the building sector offers a wide range of new possibilities including seamless flow of information within and between organisations. This enables more flexibility in organisation of design and project management in relation to the service production. However realisation of these potential benefits demands agreement on common formats, investments in tools, learning of how to use the tools, adjustment of the qualifications needed as well as changes in the established practices and adjustment of business models in order to comply with new products and changes in production processes. In order to analyse these challenges a field study was conducted in the building division of the Danish engineering consultancy company Ramboll. The field study is further described in Box 1. We investigated the use of ICT systems in the building section of the Danish division. The objective was to analyse how the use of ICT tools (in particular a 3D-modeling system) affected the organisation of work and the business models pursued. Especially the study aimed to study how the use of ICT tools affected creation and dissemination of knowledge within the organisation.

The area of technical engineering consulting was chosen as it is a service area of importance in any economy and at the same time it is a service area with special conditions due to its relation to a physical product and the involvement

Box 1. Facts about the field study

From January 2005 to June 2007, 14 interviews with 10 employees from the building section in the headquarters of Ramboll Denmark were carried out. This information was supplemented by secondary material in the form of internal documents and annual reports. The findings of the study were tested in an interactive finalising workshop session with participation of representatives from Ramboll.

of customer and partners. Ramboll was chosen from among technical engineering companies because the company is specialised in designing unique solutions for prestigious buildings, rather than developing standard solutions used for mass production. The subsequent analysis focuses on the integration of 3D models, as the use of such models highlights a wide range of possibilities and challenges within the organisation as well as the inter-organisational collaboration.

A key challenge is to maintain a reputation for being among the most advanced with regard to technical expertise in building construction. Innovation and knowledge management is therefore crucial for success. The service provided is increasingly dependent on the use of ICT based tools, in which much of the knowledge and know-how needed are embedded. It is therefore a challenge for a company like Ramboll to maintain its position as ICT based design tools are being developed and offered as software packages available on the market. This may potentially enable competitors with less technical expertise to develop technical solutions similar to those offered by Ramboll without having the same level of technical knowledge.

THE BUILDING SECTION IN RAMBOLL

Ramboll has provided technical engineering services for more than 60 years and is a leading player in the Danish market of technical

engineering. In 2003 Ramboll and the Swedish engineering company Scandia Consult merged, and Ramboll developed from being among the top three in the Danish market to become a leading player in the Nordic market with 104 offices in the Nordic region and 21 permanent offices in the rest of the world.

Ramboll group provides engineering, consultancy services, product development, and operation services within the areas of buildings, infrastructure, industrial processes, energy, water and environment, telecommunication, management, and IT.

The organisation in Ramboll reflects three different dimensions: geography, business areas, and technical competences. The first level of organisation reflects mainly national borders; the Ramboll group includes six different companies covering each of the Nordic countries: Denmark, Sweden, Norway, and Finland. In addition, Ramboll Informatics and Ramboll Management are defined as separate companies. Ramboll Denmark generates 42% of the group's revenue. At present, the national offices generally serve their own home markets, but Ramboll intends to strengthen international coordination in order to enable their companies to use their special competencies in the entire Nordic region.

Ramboll Denmark includes both regional divisions and divisions defined by business area. In

Figure 1. Organisation chart of Ramboll

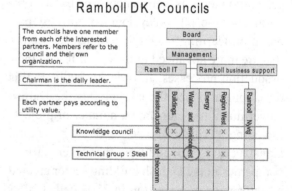

some business areas such as telecommunications the activities are concentrated in one division, while activities in other business areas such as building are distributed among a number of regional offices. However more specialised competences in the building area are concentrated in the building division in Copenhagen.

In addition to this Ramboll has an IT department and a support function supporting the entire organisation). Lately, the number of support staff has been drastically reduced. Instead a number of different councils working across the different sections have been established. However, these councils are embedded in the organisation, as all divisions with an interest in the actual council have a member. The idea is to avoid the costs of having expensive staff functions out of touch with what is going on, and instead let new initiatives grow out of the prioritized needs in and across the different divisions.

The building division in Copenhagen is organised according to technical disciplines such as steel constructions, concrete, electrical installations, and so forth. The blend of geography and professional focus in the departments are seen to provide the best conditions for developing expert knowledge and educating experts. Locating people from the same professional area together gives them daily contact with colleagues from the same discipline and facilitates further development of their competences. This happens, however, at the expense of the coordination between different fields and development of interdisciplinarity within the projects. Other consultancy firms have chosen a structure where offices are defined by market segmentation. In such a structure each

Box 2. Services in the building sector

> • Traditional assignments
> • Overseas consultancy
> • Turn-key projects
> • OPP and BOT

office possesses a broad range of technical expertise, and will be able to carry out many projects without consulting other parts of the organisation; however, they face the challenge of keeping each employee updated within their field of expertise.

In Ramboll, it is thus necessary to involve several parts of the organisation in a project. Therefore Ramboll uses a kind of matrix organisation. Most assignments are defined as projects and a project structure operates across the line structure. Engineers can be allocated to several different projects at the same time. When big and long lasting projects are running such as the Opera House in Copenhagen, many employees are allocated full time and a new department, where project members are placed together during the implementation of the project, is established.

TRADITIONAL BUILDING PROJECTS: PHASES AND PARTNERS

Ramboll consultancy services in building include four different types of assignments (see Box 1). Eighty percent of the business still comes from so-called traditional consultancy projects and design and project engineering of new and unique buildings. Another service area is overseas consultancy following Danish customers in their need to establish buildings in other countries. This is mainly a management assignment and includes identification and recruitment of local companies to do the job. Third, Ramboll provides turn-key projects, where standard solutions such as power plants are provided. In these projects, Ramboll provides everything from design, purchase, construction, inspection, and decommissioning. Last, new types of assignments, such as build-operate-transfer (BOT) projects and private public partnering (OPP), following concepts coming from the UK and the USA, are being introduced. Here maintenance and operation are part of the responsibilities and require Ramboll to assume more financial and operating responsibilities. During the field study it was discovered that it has been possible to avoid involvement in financing of projects through cooperation with pension funds. OPP and BOT imply very different ways of operating and managing the entire project cycle and include several new partnerships. This chapter concentrates on the use of ICT in traditional assignments as they still account for the majority of the services delivered.

Traditional assignments are related to a specific building project. The assignments may vary in size but they are all limited by time. This implies that the organisation continuously must adapt to carry out new tasks. Project groups with participants from line groups are created and closed down, when an assignment is completed.

The first task in a project is to get a contract. Contracts are obtained either through direct negotiation with a potential customer or through public tenders. Ramboll may identify new possibilities

Figure 2. Project phases in a building project

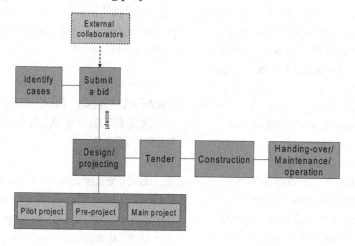

Figure 3. Overview of overlap in competences and need for negotiation of responsibilities

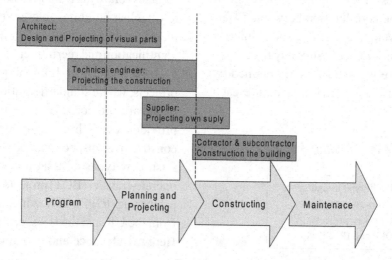

themselves and initiate projects by contacting potential investors and partners. Ramboll may also be contacted directly by customers who know the company from previous assignments or from its good reputation. Following the initial contact Ramboll may prepare a more detailed offer on the project. Sometimes Ramboll gets a contract by winning a public tender either alone or as part of a consortium with external partners. Such consortia will usually include at least an architect firm and an engineering consultancy company.

When the consortium has got a contract the project is designed. In larger projects, this will be done in several phases, where still more detailed solutions are prepared and discussed with other partners and the building owner. Following the preproject phase a tender may be made in order to select one or more contractors to carry out the construction. During the construction phase Ramboll may be responsible for supervision and the management parts of the project. Finally the project is handed over to the building owner. Sometimes a maintenance contract is also included as a separate part of the project.

The role of the engineering consultancy company often varies from project to project. Sometimes the consultancy has responsibilities during the construction phase or during the maintenance/operation phases. These responsibilities may include either carrying out certain tasks themselves, employing somebody else to do it, or supervising the work. However there is a flexible division of work between the architects or the suppliers and the technical engineering company. It is important that the sharing of specific tasks is agreed in detail from the outset, as lack of clarity may otherwise be a constant source of conflicts.

Management of the various partners, each with their own responsibilities, is in itself a big challenge in all building projects. The building process is often described as a stepwise process with a serial relation with some overlap between the companies involved: the output of the archi-

Figure 4. Building project with mutual adjustments

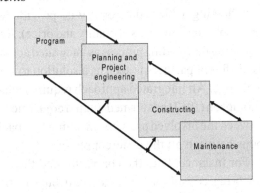

tects in the form of an architectural design or a program (see the lower part in Figure 4) forms the basis for the planning and project engineering work, which includes preparation of a detailed plan with technical solutions considering choices of material, sequences, forces, weights, and so forth, this service is primarily carried out by the engineering consultancy. However, the visual parts of the building such as facades, walls, and the like are often project engineered by the architects. Some suppliers may also carry out the project engineering for the instalment of their own deliveries. In the construction phase, the chosen building contractor and the subcontractors construct the buildings based on the service delivered from the engineering consultancy in the form of detailed descriptions and plans.

When a building project is understood as a process of sequential interconnected phases (Thompson, 1967), this indicates that each phase is thought to present well defined tasks and clear responsibilities separated from other phases, as illustrated in the four phase model presented above. However, describing the building process as a well defined and stepwise process is not without complications, as strong dependencies exist between the different phases and partners. Solutions and choices made by one partner affect possible alternatives and choices to be made by other partners involved in the subsequent project phases. Seeing the building process as sequential phases thus might inhibit some useful knowledge from flowing, which could otherwise provide for better solutions (in terms of quality and price). Approaching the building process as integrated across the different partners is seen as a solution to this challenge. An integrated approach requires what Thompson (1967) has termed mutual adjustments between the involved partners, meaning feedback loops between all the different phases.

For instance, both the contractor and the engineering consultancy should contribute to the design phase with their knowledge on solutions, conditions, and effectiveness of materials and constructions in order to optimise the entire project. The integration of knowledge and agreement on optimal technical solutions is complicated by the division of labour between financially independent partners, each with their own contractual obligations and interests.

USE OF ICT IN ENGINEERING CONSULTING

Digitalisation of administrative processes and work in Ramboll has been going on for quite some time. However it has mainly concerned introduction of Microsoft office tools and other standard tools; more recently internal and external networks have been implemented with applications like project webs, digital library systems, e-mail, and calendar systems as well as administrative systems of different kinds. A digital infrastructure has emerged and much of the communication taking place from ongoing information and exchange of process information has been digitalised, and this has removed some of the time and space limits for interaction within the company and for exchange of information with external partners involved in the same project.

IT has also been used in production tools for quite a while, especially CAD systems are well implemented in the processes for project

engineering for buildings. The early implementation of CAD systems in Ramboll resulted in an estimated reduction of around 80% in the number of technical assistants. Before the introduction of CAD, engineers drafted drawings, which later were refined by technical assistants. Due to the possibility of manipulating and changing in the initial drawings, much of the technical assistant work has disappeared, just as secretarial work did in other sectors. However the introduction of CAD changed working conditions for engineers, as it required the engineers to learn to use computers as part of their work and to complete their own drawings themselves. Still, some calculations of weight and forces were still made outside the CAD system by using pencils and paper. The integration of these systems mainly affected internal work relations within each department, while work relations to other departments and to external partners basically remained unchanged.

Introduction of CAD systems has been followed by introduction of advanced 3D modeling systems. The use of 3D modeling systems has proved advantageous both internally and at the inter-organisational level. However to take advantage of these possibilities some quite major changes are needed within the companies involved. In Ramboll some steps have been taken already, but many considerations and decisions about the future remain unsettled.

3D modeling was initiated by a project on renovation of a plant for water purification. At that time there was a general interest in experimenting with new 3D production systems. However due to the business concept of Ramboll, this type of new investment needed to be justified by specific projects. In the renovation of the water purification plant, 3D modeling was an explicit request in the tender material due to a complicated piping system and fear of collision of pipes. Winning this project provided the necessary goodwill to purchase and to experiment with 3D modeling tools. In 2005 20% of all projects used 3D modeling and a number of opinions existed on how complicated constructions should be to justify use of this method. However in the middle of 2007 it is being used in most projects of a certain size. It is less costly and cumbersome to use now as people have acquired the needed competences through using the system along with process-related experiences and adaptations. The introduction was a bit difficult, the software was expensive, and only a few licenses were purchased in the beginning, making it a limited resource. Second, it was impossible to operate the system without any specific knowledge of it. A few employees were trained in the system and the system was used in a few projects. However after using it for a while it was taken into broader use in all big projects and more licenses were purchased and more people sent on courses.

3D modeling has proved advantageous in a number of different ways, especially combined with calculation modules and CAD systems which have made it a very strong production tool. In addition it can also be combined with a 3D Gypsum printer making detailed plaster models. Or it can be combined with virtual reality technology from the gaming world making it possible to make virtual tours visualising the construction from different angles. The combination of these digital models and the different visualisation tools has improved the work and thus the services along

with the creation of new subservices in a number of different ways:

- Marketing
- Understanding between partners
- Modeling of complex geometry
- Collision control
- Geometry control
- Reuse of data in models
- Reuse of data across partners

Whereas the above advantages (described in details below) are already reality, other advantages are expected in the near future, such as possibilities of compatibility with other systems resulting in new possibilities for time management, resource management, and maintenance management closely linked to the production line.

3D models are a very convincing marketing tool. Many people have difficulties in visualising a spatial construction from drawings and descriptions. The Gypsum printer, which is expensive

Figure 6. Intelligent model of steel tower

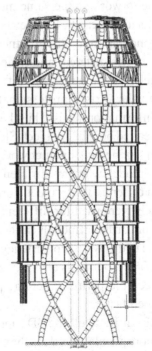

Figure 5. Layered plaster model

to purchase, makes it possible to make plaster models in many layers with a lot of details at a cost of 13 euros.

The model can be cut in pieces or made in parts and opened up to look at the construction inside. In the virtual model people can move around inside a building by using a computer. These kinds of models specifically reveal the spatial consequences of the design and can thus be used to get a feeling of the final result and help in discussing different solutions with the customer. This can thus be seen as an additional service to the customer. Where a virtual tour is an e-service and the plaster model is a service based on ICT used in the production.

The same methods can be used in cooperation with partners in the building process, even though these professionals are trained in using drawings and numbers to visualize the construction in their heads. The solid models help to reveal where construction and design might be problematic because a common model is created which makes it easier to discuss and point at the specific part discussed.

Furthermore Web-based 3D models allow for more people to work on the same model and in addition, this model can be transferred and combined with models from other partners. The 3D model thus unites different angles and interests in the model that can be read in different ways thus serving the various professionals' distinct yet related information needs. Thus the 3D-model acts as a so called boundary object (Star & Griesemer, 1989), connecting distinct worlds through a common model whereby different practices focusing on different issues meet. Formerly, different models were used for different purposes. Now data from different models can be integrated into one, and in this way inconsistency errors can be avoided. The 3D models also provide for data reuse between the partners, helping projects to move on much faster.

Internally in Ramboll the 3D modeling tool allows for more people to work on the same model

at the same time. The 3D programs make the drawings intelligent, it is possible to reuse data around the model, and changes in reused data just need to be changed in one place to become updated throughout the model. It is also possible to copy one part of the model, for instance, the design of a floor into another part (for instance, another floor), or making small changes, which rationalises the project engineering phase tremendously. This method has been used in the project engineering of the 12 stock building in Nuuk, Greenland (see Figure 6). Formerly, reuse also occurred; however in those cases either new calculations were needed or a "too good" solution was reused; that is, it was a balance between material costs and time resource aspects. Today's

Figure 7. Collision control of the Elephant house

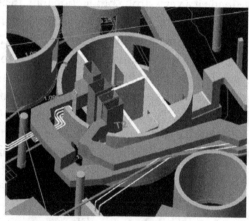

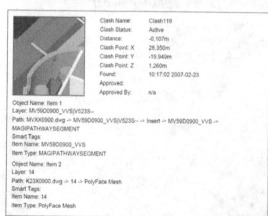

combination with calculation tools has made it possible to design models with greater geometrical complexity, which is an improvement in the technical engineering service that allows for new and geometrically more complex buildings.

Another area of 3D model use is control. Collision control reveals all collisions in the model, for example, if a pipe runs into a wall or another pipe. A whole report of collisions can be made in the system and used to manage the resulting corrections. Another type of control is geometry control, for example, revealing too short beams and other similar inconsistencies. These control types are where the most immediate financial advantages have been found. This is because they reduce almost all these types of faults which are normally not revealed before the construction phase, a factor which is very expensive and time consuming. Again the service delivered from the technical engineering consultancy to the constructor has an improved quality.

However, obtaining these advantages is not without cost as the use of 3D models changes the practice of project engineering. Much more time must be invested before drawings can be made, as a consistent model needs to be drawn first. Second, using the tool requires specific qualifications in using the modeling system. Third, experience and expertise is still highly needed as 3D modeling has some limitations and weaknesses that need to be understood and spotted. The problem here is that the technology is black-boxing part of the process where less understanding and expertise in calculation is needed. The use of 3D modeling for inter-organizational use requires some standardisation or knowledge of the different measures across the different partners as well as common formats to actually make it possible to exchange, read, and understand the models across the different sorts of partner. This is complicated due to the numerous partners in the value chain and the shifting partners from project to project. However the emergence of BIPS has succeeded in supporting these needs by uniting all differ-

ent partners in an organisation working towards these needs.

ORGANIZATIONAL CHALLENGES

The advantages of moving towards the e-service business concept by using ICT in the production and delivery of technical engineering services are numerous. However, as already mentioned, this process is quite demanding and requires major changes in the organisation. Here the demands for change will be further discussed. What we see on an overall level is that the digitalisation and the use of ICT based tools for calculations and presentation of results implies (1) codification of knowledge which (2) results in a move towards standardisation of both processes and final products. These two trends have tremendous impact on the work to be done, the needed qualifications, and not least the core of the business. The impacts on the business models will be discussed in the next section.

So far innovation in technical engineering services in Ramboll happens through experimenting in the production of a service. This means that all service-product innovation takes place in relation to projects. The input for innovation is mainly the competences, knowledge, and creativity of the employees combined with wishes and requests from customers or partners. The management of innovation and knowledge follows what Hansen, Nohria, et al. (1999) call personalisation. In a personalisation strategy the knowledge of the employee is the most important asset as opposed to codification, where knowledge is built into practices or products. With the current development we see a move from personalisation towards codification as a lot of the competencies and thus the knowledge are built into the modeling and calculation systems. This move is not unproblematic according to the theory as it demands less qualified employees.

However the conclusion is not as straight forward as saying that project engineering is becoming a standardised and codified process. The experience in Ramboll so far is that the modeling of the constructions seems easy and straight forward and eliminates the number of people needed due to reuse and manipulation of the data in the system. However, an additional experience is that use of these models in complex buildings does have some severe limitations; they thus need to be drawn or corrected taking forces and other factors into account. This means that highly experienced technical consultants are needed to do the modeling or check the model. We thus reach a different conclusion that less but highly technically competent people are needed (the routine work is taken over by the technology). In addition the project engineering itself is not the whole job. Whereas the standard methods (embodied in software tools) do improve productivity to some extent, the design process can be further facilitated and enhanced if reuse of solutions from different projects is supported, which demands transfer of knowledge. This process is still mainly supported through the employee and his earlier experience; however the modeling tools do open up for implementation of macros for standard solutions. Such use of technology is confronting the values of being a good engineer and point to the differences between definitions of work in a company having a personalisation strategy and those within a company having a codification strategy—different types of employees are needed!

Using a system that black-boxes the process and at the same time calls for high qualifications raises a problem of competence building. Due to increasing use of ICT based modeling tools engineers engage in less assignments and exercises of project engineering. Engineers using the tools need to have an intuitive understanding of the complex relations between the various technical parameters in order to use the tools properly, and to evaluate alternative solutions. Part of this un-

derstanding can only be gained through practical experience, but when still more parts of the design process are being embodied in various modeling tools, it becomes harder for engineers employed in a consulting company to obtain such experience. A competence trap may thus be the result and the companies need to take actions to provide new ways of gaining this knowledge.

If Ramboll decides to make project engineering even more standardised by implementing macros in the system, this may provide an additional opportunity to resolve or reduce the problems related to engineers lacking understanding of the contractors' working conditions. Engineering consultants work on a more abstract level than those responsible for the implementation, and they need to develop an understanding of how the invented solutions will work in practice. In some departments, tours to constructing sites are made to help engineering consultants gain this insight. However, making knowledge flow across the different phases and partners is still a major and unsolved problem. In addition to the internal use of modeling tools and the possibilities of developing macros, there are also visions about integrating knowledge from the different partners, especially knowledge from the constructors. In other words macros on "good" and "workable" solutions should be used instead of newly made solutions which often do not consider construction issues. This would greatly improve the cost of the entire building project; however there are fears about the extent to which such an approach leaves room for creative solutions needed in unique building design and project engineering and that it may undermine project engineering as a unique service that demands high technical engineering competencies.

Making a system with macros that build on the knowledge from different projects and partners will probably restrain the creativity in the work of the technical engineers and make a strong move from personalisation towards codification of knowledge. Such an approach would imply that knowledge development is carried out centrally or becomes more closely linked to an overall coherence.

A final organisational issue limiting the codification of knowledge and thus restraining part of the digitalisation of technical engineering service is the need for local presence. In principle all codified knowledge can be delivered electronically to anywhere in the world, and increasingly digitalised production with the services delivered through inter-organizational networks will therefore facilitate international competition, as is seen for other KIBS. But even though both final and intermediary engineering services to a large extent are delivered as electronic information, local presence is still an important parameter for winning contracts. Local contact is needed to enable good contact with customers and the usually local contractors and suppliers during the project. This is related to issues of trust, cultural understanding, and so forth. Also knowledge of national and local conditions, regulations, and traditions such as weather and working culture is important and it might be difficult to serve a lot of different and dissimilar markets in this respect. These issues are among the reasons for having offices in the different countries and even regional offices within a small country like Denmark.

CHALLENGES TO THE BUSINESS MODEL

Ramboll's building section is specialised in providing consultancy services related to construction of unique buildings, which demands use of innovative design and project engineering. It is therefore crucial for Ramboll to be a leader in using state of the art technologies and in development of new technical solutions. Use of calculation models has had a substantial impact on both productivity and quality, as engineers can develop faster and more complex solutions. The latter is of particular importance for a company like Ramboll, as the

possibility of complex solutions can be turned into highly unique constructions. So far only few direct financial gains have been harvested through standardisation. There is a clear understanding of productivity gains that are mainly due to reduced production time. These gains are used to provide better and more complex solutions, and occasionally to reduce prices. This improves competitiveness, but has no immediate impact on the bottom line.

The use of ICT based calculation models greatly increase possibilities for reuse of data in other projects. It therefore becomes even more important to facilitate knowledge transfer between different projects. Reuse of data across partners is another area where productivity gains can be achieved. However standardised formats for intensive exchange of information with partners are needed at many levels, and include more than agreement on common data formats. It is not easy to develop common standards in an industry with many small and medium sized players. The current trend is that the use of ICT leads towards more standardisation across the building process at the very basic level. Since its creation in 2003 BIPS has worked towards the creation of compatible IT infrastructures, common languages, and well defined partner roles and responsibilities. This supports better and closer collaboration among cooperating partners in building projects. One task has been to develop common formats in order to make it possible to exchange files. Another area of action has been development of tools to settle the division of responsibilities among partners in order to make a better foundation for collaboration by reducing potential conflicts. These agreements can be seen as a way to reduce the need for trust and thus a reduced need for social interaction, which again can be seen as a way to make a foundation for moves towards the creation of e-services.

A strategic disadvantage of the digitalisation of the project engineering process is related to the use of standard models, especially standard models included in commercial software packages available on the market. This service can easily be duplicated by other companies as much of the technical expertise needed for design and project engineering is embodied in the software. Ramboll might thus lose part of its competitive edge. However using these models on complex buildings still requires high project engineering competencies to ensure that models are consistent and to take special conditions not foreseen by the models into account. It is therefore important that Ramboll maintains these competences and also build up new competences which are difficult to duplicate and contribute to better and more sophisticated solutions. Ramboll find itself at a crossroads. Project engineering is expected to become less important for competition and there will therefore be more focus on consulting. In order to stay competitive, new areas of expertise are developed. One example is design of lighting. This has developed into an important market where Ramboll offers highly sophisticated solutions.

Another big challenge is to what degree organisations should allow integration of their production processes with other partners. For the entire building project, there is no doubt that this would lead to overall productivity gains. However it might be difficult for companies involved both to actually realise these gains and to ensure their share of the benefits without losing control of their own part of the production. Especially there is a fear that integration will happen at the expense of the uniqueness and special technical competences provided by an engineering consultancy company like Ramboll. However if Ramboll choose to focus less on project engineering and more on consultancy, this problem becomes less important. One way to solve these problems would be the creation of companies which are able to carry out the entire building project alone or to engage in more stable strategic partnerships or other types of extended enterprises. However due to, for example, insurance, it is often required that certain functions are carried out by separate

independent companies. Moreover integrated companies and stable partnerships will not be as flexible as shifting constellations, where the optimum consortium of partners can be created to win a particular contract.

CONCLUSION

The use of ICT in the production of technical engineering services is changing the services tremendously, along with the practices and competences needed. Ramboll is at a crossroads with regard to project engineering. Despite the need for high competences in technical skills the use of ICT reduces the importance of project engineering for competitiveness, and project engineering is becoming a smaller business area as the number of man hours needed is drastically reduced. Ramboll thus needs to move their focus towards other areas in order to create added value and remain competitive. However, the move towards codification and standardisation of project engineering along with the need for closer integration requires Ramboll and its (shifting) partners to consider how closely they want to integrate. The integration can be on a basic level with use of common formats and ongoing communication. However the integration can also move a step further towards more standardised processes with integration of knowledge from the different types of partner.

Although some processes are becoming more codified and standardised, a substantial part of the processes will not. This will be the case especially for a company like Ramboll that focuses on those processes that require most specialised technical expertise and with most value added. If e-service is defined narrowly as a service, delivered via the Internet or a similar electronic communication infrastructure (as defined in an earlier chapter by Henten), engineering consulting can be provided as an e-service in only few cases. However as noted in the beginning of this chapter, engineering consultancy cannot be seen as (1) one service or (2) a service with one delivery to one customer; rather it is a much more complex service product with several service deliveries and highly complex services with ongoing interaction with a number of players including the building owner and several partners. Some of these separated services are delivered as e-services by using ICT, for example, the virtual models as well as drawings and plans that are communicated to the partners electronically. These e-services are often combined with a meeting to provide further explanation. The use of ICT can thus be seen as a way of providing additional services (the virtual model) or extended services (electronically delivered drawings and plans). In addition multiple examples of improvements in the service have been given, emphasising how the new technology is used in the production of the technical engineering service, including communication with the partners. The knowledge service is improved due to a combination of new tools such as the 3D models, the infrastructure, and common formats that enable more streamlined processes based on interactive communication and sharing and reuse of data between different partners. This can be seen as internal e-services facilitating processes of production in different phases of the building project. Thus if we define e-service as services which are delivered and/or produced using ICT, the answer to whether technical engineering services can benefit from the e-service concept is definitely yes. Technical engineering will never become a full e-service, but many subparts of the service can indeed be delivered as an e-service.

The limitations to becoming a full e-service lie first in the complexity of the product and second in the distributed process involving many partners.

Building a construction is extremely knowledge intensive, part of this knowledge is easy to obtain as it lies within regulations, standardised methods, and so forth; however part of the knowledge is related to the particular situation, that is, the building environment and conditions, which is also knowledge that can be obtained. However part of the knowledge is developed in interaction with the building owner and the other partners; this need for interaction reduces the possibility of a full e-service greatly as it demands ongoing contact to build an understanding of the wishes and possibilities along with trust between project partners. The amount of actors is another issue that limits the possibilities of becoming a full e-service, collaboration requires a division of responsibilities which to a large extent builds on trust, which has so far been developed through interaction. However this need may be reduced when standards on responsibilities are developed further.

REFERENCES

Hansen, M.T., Nohria, N., et al. (1999, March–April). Whats your strategy for managing knowledge? *Harvard Business Review.*

Star, S.L., & Griesemer, J.R. (1989). Institutional ecology, translations and boundary objects: Amateurs and professionals in Berkeleys Museum of Vertebrate Zoology, 1907-39. *Social Studies of Science, 19*, 387–420.

Thompson, J.D. (1967). *Organizations in action.* New York: McGraw-Hill.

Zuboff, S. (1989). *In the age of the smart machine.* Oxford: The Perseus Books Group.

Chapter XI
The Role of E-Services in the Transition from the Product Focus to the Service Focus in the Printing Business:
Case Lexmark

Esko Penttinen
Helsinki School of Economics, Finland

Timo Saarinen
Helsinki School of Economics, Finland

Pekka Sinervo
Lexmark, Finland

ABSTRACT

Today, many manufacturing companies are focusing on their service operations, which are often seen as a better source of revenue than the traditional product business. E-services can accelerate this process by offering companies new ways to control products and monitor equipment from a distance. This chapter describes the changes which are taking place in the printing business. It tells the story of Lexmark, a printer manufacturer that has recently created differentiated offerings to its business customers. In the case of Lexmark, this repositioning of offerings has been enabled by e-services. Here, the e-services consist of the Lexmark Fleet Manager system which monitors the use and availability of the equipment and makes suggestions on how to improve the printing processes on the customer site. The case ends with a description of the actual challenges that Lexmark is currently facing.

BACKGROUND: THEORY SUGGESTS MOVING TOWARDS SERVICES

Management theory suggests that product manufacturers should move downstream closer to the customer and provide different kinds of services along with their tangible products (Oliva & Kallenberg, 2003; Penttinen & Palmer, 2007; Quinn, 1992; Vargo & Lusch, 2004; Wise & Baumgartner, 1999). Manufacturers' traditional value-chain role—producing and selling goods—has become less and less attractive as the demand for products has stagnated throughout the economy (Wise & Baumgartner, 1999). The demand for different kinds of services, on the other hand, has grown considerably. Increasingly, the customers of manufacturing companies are concentrating on their core competencies and, often, do not regard the maintenance of machines as being part of their core business.

Services within the manufacturing business include, for example, maintenance services, condition monitoring services, training services, consultation services, installation services, and documentation services (Oliva & Kallenberg, 2003). Increasingly, these services are in electronic format. As an example of an electronic service, manufacturing companies have innovated information systems that enable condition monitoring from a distance. These systems allow companies to keep an eye on their equipment on the customer site more effectively.

Service industries have grown in importance compared to the agricultural and manufacturing industries. Steady productivity increases in agriculture and manufacturing have meant that it takes ever fewer hours of work to produce or buy an automobile, a piece of furniture, or a home appliance. While productivity has improved, the demand for goods is somewhat capped; people can only consume limited quantities of automobiles, sofas, and washing machines (Quinn, 1992). At the same time, the installed base of products has been expanding steadily in many industries, thanks to the accumulation of past purchases and to longer product life spans (Wise & Baumgartner, 1999). The combination of this stagnant product demand and an expanding installed base has pushed economic value downstream, away from manufacturing and toward providing services required to operate and maintain products (Wise & Baumgartner, 1999).

Many manufacturing companies have learned their lesson and have turned to services in search for growth and increased profitability (Penttinen & Palmer, 2007). Examples of successful companies include the elevator company KONE and the bearing producer SKF (Penttinen, 2007; Penttinen & Palmer, 2007; Penttinen & Saarinen, 2005). These companies have been actively inventing electronic services. For example, SKF has innovated intelligent bearings which report the status of the bearings to SKF. This is done by inserting a sensor to the bearing core which measures the vibration and motion status of the rotating components. These e-services allow SKF to provide maintenance contracts more economically than before. Similarly, KONE has added intelligence to their elevators, allowing a more efficient monitoring of their products from a distance.

Others have not been as successful in making the transition from product manufacturer to service provider. According to Oliva and Kallenberg (2003), there are three successive hurdles to overcome the problems related to the transition from products to services. First, firms might not believe in the economic potential of the service component for their product (e.g., engineers are more excited about building a multimillion-dollar piece of equipment than about a service contract for cleaning it). Second, firms might not have the capabilities and competencies to provide services for their products. Third, firms might fail in deploying a successful service strategy (e.g., Ford Motor Co.'s attempt to enter after-sales services was blocked by its network of independent dealerships) (Oliva & Kallenberg, 2003).

What Are Electronic Services?

In the marketing literature, services have been defined according to the IHIP framework (Zeithaml, Parasuraman, & Berry, 1985). The IHIP framework lists intangibility, heterogeneity, inseparability of production and consumption, and perishability as the distinguishing traits of services. Compared to tangible goods, services are intangible. Services are heterogeneous, meaning that services are customized to individual customers. The production and consumption processes of services cannot be separated. Services are perishable, meaning that it is impossible, for example, to store services for later use. More recently, services have been defined as processes, activities, performances, or changes in the condition of an economic unit. In short, services are the "application of specialized competencies through deeds, processes, and performances for the benefit of another entity or the entity itself" (Vargo & Lusch, 2004, p. 2).

In the case of manufacturing companies' e-services, we define and conceptualize e-services as service systems that enable the dissemination and transmission of information from the manufacturers' products to the manufacturer. At the current case company, the printer manufacturer Lexmark, the core of the company's e-services is the Lexmark Fleet Manager system, which is described later in the chapter.

SETTING THE STAGE: SELLING PRINTERS AND PRINTER CAPACITY TO COMPANIES

In this chapter, we look at the manufacturers of printing machines. We tell the story of Lexmark which has recently turned to services in their B2B activities and launched the e-services concept, Lexmark Fleet Manager system. Increasingly, the turnover of Lexmark comes from services: for example from maintenance services and from

consultation services. The objective of this case study is to familiarize the reader to case Lexmark and to describe the e-services that the company has innovated. The core of the e-services is the Lexmark Fleet Manager system. We will also discuss the transition from products to services taking place in this company. We begin by giving some basic facts of the printing business, then, we introduce case Lexmark and describe how their business model has changed recently. We conclude by listing some key challenges that the company faces.

According to the Gartner Research Group, document handling and printing expenses can amount to 1–3% of a company's turnover. Whereas the other parts of the IT-related activities have often been outsourced outside, printing and document handling activities are the last islands of the IT services that have not been thoroughly considered from the perspective of outsourcing. Generally speaking, relatively little effort has been put to optimizing the printing processes in offices. Procurement processes related to printers and printing material are scattered and seem to fall between the IT side with printers and the office equipment side with copy machines. Even though there is potential for considerable savings, very few companies are interested in optimizing their document handling and printing processes.

When aiming to optimize the printing processes in an office, an important ratio to understand is the ratio describing the number of employees to the amount of equipment within the company. According to Lexmark Finland, currently, this ratio is usually two to one; meaning that there are, on average, two employees per one piece of output equipment (printer, copy machine, fax, etc.). Lexmark has encountered companies, where the ratio has been one to one, meaning that each employee has one printer or copy machine or fax at his/her disposal. In most cases, this represents a considerable waste of resources in offices. Naturally, individual employees have individual printing needs. For example, in some companies, printing may be seen as a critical operation (due to, e.g., confidentiality issues); and therefore, each employee must have his/her own printer. However, in general, we can try to find the optimal ratio of employees per printer; and, according to the Gartner research group, the optimal ratio, in office work on average, is eight to one.

CASE DESCRIPTION: LEXMARK

Lexmark is a manufacturer and supplier of printing solutions including laser and inkjet printers, multifunction products, associated supplies and services. The company employs 13,000 people worldwide and has a turnover of around 4.3 billion euros. Lexmark International Inc. was founded in 1991 when IBM decided to hive off its printing business to retail investors. All business functions from new product development to sales departments were shifted to the new company. Lexmark entered the New York Stock Exchange as an independent company in 1995. Lexmark initially focused on business-to-business (B2B) companies but extended its product range to providing business-to-consumers (B2C) printers in the mid-1990s when ink jet technology came to the market. This case description and the following challenges focus on the B2B activities of the company.

In the B2B activities, during the recent years, we can observe an important change in focus: "In B2B, we printer manufacturers compete over printed papers, not machine sales. It is more important for us to provide MRO (maintenance, repair and operations) products and services for our customers than selling the actual printing machines" (CEO Lexmark Finland). The margins on product sales (namely printers in this case) have decreased sharply lately. This is due to increased competition in the market. The printer market went through a period of rapid change and this was due to the digitalization of office printing. Copy machines moved from the analogical to the digital world. Suddenly, copy machines were able to be used as printers through office networks. Printer manufacturers responded by innovating multifunction products that could function as printers and copy machines simultaneously. Today, in offices, 55–60% of sheets of paper are printed using traditional printers and 45–50% are printed or copied using copy machines. The trend is toward the increasing use of printers. More and more of information can be stored in electronic format, either by originally entering the data in electronic form or by scanning the existing information in electronic format. This favors the use of printers.

The change in the product market described above has affected the focus of the printer manufacturers, including our case company Lexmark. Today, the focus is not in product sales, but, rather, in providing companies service contracts. "By providing service contracts, we can ensure the MRO business for our company" (CEO Lexmark Finland). Under the service contract, the equipment is delivered as part of the monthly contract and the charges are based on the number of printed sheets of paper, or cost per page, and not based on the aggregation of the equipment cost over a period of time.

E-Services: The Fleet Manager System

How to provide these service contracts? For doing this, Lexmark has created new e-service offerings. The core of Lexmark's electronic services is the fleet manager system depicted in Figure 1. It is an information system which essentially monitors the equipment located on the customer site, transmitting automatically updated information on, for example, the number of printed sheets, type of sheets, location of printers and users, and change patterns of use. This information can be used to control the costs on the customer site: by analyzing printing information and by making suggestions on how the printing operations could be optimized on the customer site. The system is located within the customer company provided there are less than 500 devices on the customer site. For global customer companies and for those clients whose number of devices exceeds 500 devices, Lexmark proposes the ARMS system. Here, Lexmark manages the system on a server which is located outside the customer company. Lexmark then provides the customer company a customized view to the system, including all the information the customer wants to see.

The core system, fleet manager, consists of five parts: the Asset Manager, the Billing Manager, the Consumables Manager, the Availability Manager, and the Optimization Manager. The Asset Manager is used to manage the equipment. It identifies and registers the equipment in the customer environment and enables the collection of data from printers and other related equipment. It tracks the life cycle of the equipment and makes suggestions when certain equipment needs to be updated or renewed. The collection of the data is automated, and the data are directly transmitted to the system. The Billing Manager uses the data from the Asset Manager system to produce billing information and reporting analyses based on the number of pages printed at the customer site. The customer can choose from a variety of billing op-

tions: a recurring monthly charge, a monthly per page charge, or a combination of the two.

The Consumables Manager observes the machinery and alerts Lexmark when, for example, the toner level is getting low. The system automatically sends out an e-mail indicating that the machine needs maintenance. The customer can also choose the option that the new spare part is delivered automatically to the customer site. The Availability Manager monitors the device and reports changes in the condition of the machine. It automatically reports the down time of the equipment; and, based on this information, the availability of the printing equipment can be obtained as a service level percentage. For example, the customer can be guaranteed to have a 95% service level, which guarantees that the printer will be available for 95% of the time. The Availability Manager then notifies whether this objective has been achieved or not. The Optimization Manager observes the printing processes on the customer site and evaluates whether the processes could be improved by changing the setup of the equipment. It alerts if some devices are overloaded most of the time and makes suggestions on how such problems could be resolved.

Figure 1. The Lexmark fleet manager system

Differentiated Offerings

Generally speaking, today, the customer usually pays for printed sheets of paper. In 2002, Lexmark launched the concept of "print-move-manage." These three levels can be described as steps toward a more service-oriented market offering. Within the "print-move-manage" framework, each step basically means transferring some responsibility of the functioning of the printers to Lexmark. Moving towards the "manage" part means that Lexmark does more for the company and the company can free its human resources to more productive activities.

Print" relates to the hardware and technical printing solutions that are used for market entry. Here, the main idea is the consolidation of the equipment base. There are many advantages that the customer company can gain by consolidating the printers and the related equipment. First, it is easier to arrange maintenance contracts for the machines when the equipment is more uniform. Second, the MRO (maintenance, repair, and op-

erations) logistics is more efficient whereby the company can compare and choose their MRO suppliers in a more efficient manner. Third, IT support becomes more straightforward when the number of servers and the variety of brands are decreased. Finally, it is easier to take backups when the systems and machinery are consolidated.

"Move" is about combining activities, making the most use of multifunction machines and about scanning documents into electronic format and saving them as well as distributing them electronically. Here, the main idea is about changing the culture of the customer company. For example, by using two-sided printing, the company can save in printing costs but it also has considerable environmental effects. Most of the pollution from paper printing is concretized when the paper is produced. By using two-sided printing, approximately 40% of the negative environmental effects can be avoided. Scanning documents into electronic format and archiving them electronically can further reduce these effects.

Figure 2. Differentiated offerings at Lexmark

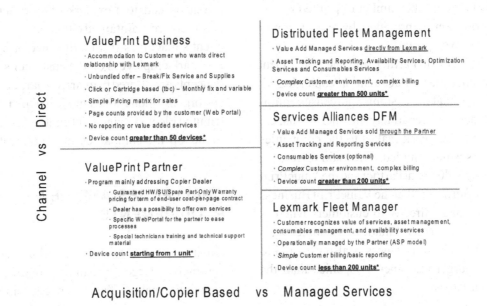

"Manage" is about controlling the output environment: becoming conscious of the costs and trying to find ways to control and lower these costs. For doing so, Lexmark has created differentiated offerings for different customer segments. Figure 2 depicts these offerings. On the left side of Figure 2, Lexmark provides the equipment through dealers. On the right side, Lexmark interacts directly with the customer, delivering equipment directly to the customer, and providing maintenance services and consultation services.

Beginning from the lower left corner of Figure 2, the ValuePrint Partner concept is offered to small companies and organizations through the dealer network. The offering is made primarily to copier dealers, giving them tools and techniques to improve printing processes on their customers' sites. The main idea for Lexmark here is to use the dealer network efficiently by providing the dealers guarantees on hardware, software, and spare part warranties.

ValuePrint Business concept is offered directly to customer companies without the use of the dealer network. Lexmark proposes simple, unbundled offerings without reporting or value-adding services. The main challenge here is to accommodate the offering to customer needs. The billing is based on the number of printed pages; this information is provided by the customer through the Web portal.

The ValuePrint Partner and the ValuePrint Business concepts are acquisition/copier based, which means that the customer purchases equipment and services separately. In other words, the offering that Lexmark makes to the companies and dealers is not bundled. The main difference between the ValuePrint Partner and the ValuePrint Business offerings is that the ValuePrint Business offering is made directly to customers whereas the ValuePrint Partner is made to the copier dealers. The ValuePrint Business is also directed to somewhat larger customer companies than the ValuePrint Partner.

The Lexmark managed services are depicted on the right side of Figure 2. For a simple customer setting with basic reporting, Lexmark proposes the use of Lexmark Fleet Manager. The Lexmark Fleet Manager is essentially an information system and was described in the previous section. Here, the customer recognizes the value of services provided by the Fleet Manager system and is willing to pay for these services. Services Alliances Distributed Fleet Management (DFM) is basically the Fleet Management offering that is made to a more complex customer environment which requires more complex billing processes. The Lexmark Fleet Manager and Services Alliances concepts are made to the market through Lexmark's partners, the application service providers (ASPs).

Interacting directly with customers, Lexmark proposes the Distributed Fleet Management concept which is basically an outsourcing contract in which the customer company can choose from a variety of service levels. The highest service level means that the customer outsources everything from the physical printers to the maintenance and technical support to Lexmark. Here, everything ranging from technical equipment (printers, copying machines, networks, etc.) to technical support is outsourced to Lexmark. These outsourcing contracts are maintained either by controlling the client's machines from a distance or by placing Lexmark employees on the customer site. These concepts are offered primarily to large companies and organizations: for example in Finland, the Distributed Fleet Management contracts are targeted to the top 150 companies and organizations.

CHALLENGES AND NEW REQUIREMENTS

An important challenge in selling the service contracts to large companies is finding the right negotiation partner from the client company. The decision to outsource output management is a strategic one. Therefore, the decision should be taken by top management. In Finland, companies have been criticized for having too few marketing and IT people in their top management. Often, the company names an IT director who is responsible for the IT budget. Usually, the IT director has previously worked as an IT manager and has very seldom had the opportunity to take part in the strategic development of the company. This means focusing on costs and not looking at the big picture of making processes more efficient. Therefore, the customer's decision to outsource or not to outsource is made based on hard numbers and cold facts. It is Lexmark's job to convince the customer that Lexmark will be able to provide the service contracts more efficiently than the customer's own current practices.

Lexmark has recognized that it cannot provide these service contracts on their own: they need to partner with application side partners, outsourcing partners, and other product manufacturers. When providing service contracts for large customer companies, it is essential to try to partner even with competitors such as Hewlett Packard. It would be somewhat arrogant to think that Lexmark alone can provide service contracts for large companies that have tens of thousands of employees. Providing document-handling service contracts for large companies requires more than printers, scanners, and the necessary network to combine the existing equipment. It is about making different kinds of equipment from various product and service providers work well together. This is why Lexmark needs partners, even from the competitor side.

Besides networking with other companies and even competitors, Lexmark has had to re-educate its current staff. The role of sales managers has changed quite dramatically. Today, the sales managers really need to have knowledge of their customers' internal processes, and they need to interact with their customers more than they used to do. Lexmark has put considerable effort in re-educating its sales managers and giving them tools and techniques to deal with the new sales situation.

Transferring Responsibility and Risks

As already mentioned above, when Lexmark proposes these service contracts, it takes more responsibility of the customer's document-handling and printing processes. This brings up the question of risk management. What happens when something goes wrong? Fortunately, printing is very rarely a critical function within a company (although, for example, there are examples of instances where a failure to print out an offer has resulted in losing an important business opportunity). Nevertheless, risks related to product failure and its consequences, for example, are stipulated within the service contract.

The risks for Lexmark include the client's unwillingness to trust Lexmark in improving the document handling and printing processes. This might lead to wasted resources on Lexmark's side without any compensation. What risks might there be for the client? In some companies and organizations in Finland, some service providers have been too ambitious in decreasing the number of printers in the workplace. In other words, the ratio of employees/equipment has been too high. Now, if the client company has taken a 5-year leasing and service contract, it might be very difficult to get it cancelled and to improve the situation.

CURRENT CHALLENGES FACING THE ORGANIZATION

At Lexmark, we can see four main challenges when moving from product focus to service focus. They are related (1) to acquiring of new resources, (2a,b) to convincing the customers and Lexmark employees, (3) to finding the right negotiation partner, (4) to determining the level of service for each customer, and (5) to innovating new e-services.

1. New Resources in the Form of IT Solutions and Human Resources

    As described in the text, the role of the sales manager has changed dramatically. What kinds of innovations could be used to help the sales managers transfer from mere salespeople to consultants who have to understand the client's internal processes and needs and wants? What kinds of IT innovations, besides the asset management system described in the text, could be used?

2a. Convincing the Customers to Purchase Printers As Services

    It is very challenging for Lexmark to find arguments to convince the customer company that it should outsource its printing activities to Lexmark. Very often, taking this decision would mean that the customer company's own staff is made redundant and should be moved to more productive activities. Currently, these arguments are made using hard facts describing how much the company would save in monetary terms if document-handling and printing activities were optimized and made more efficient. What kinds of novel arguments could there be?

2b. Convincing the Personnel of Lexmark and Tackling the Internal Processes

    Besides convincing the customers of the new business deal, there are several internal challenges in the transition. In the past, the Lexmark sales managers were compensated according to their hardware revenue, in other words, the amount of printers they sold to their customers. Today, the situation is reversed. The managers are remunerated according to the revenues from the number of the printed pages that their customers print. The transition has an effect on how the different divisions within the company are evaluated. The CEO must understand that when the company moves to the service focus, some divisions may actually show negative results, even though the overall performance of the company has improved. What kinds of solutions could there be for getting the message through to the personnel? What kinds of new internal performance measurement instruments could the company use?

3. Finding the Right Negotiation Partner in the Client Organization

    Every outsourcing decision is a strategic one, and it should be made by the top management. However, printing process and document-handling optimization is not seen as important activities within the customer companies of Lexmark. Therefore, it is very challenging to get face-to-face meetings with appropriate negotiation partners within the customer company. What kinds of strategies could Lexmark use in order to get the top management interested?

4. How to Determine Whom to Target with the Service Contracts

    Lexmark proposes their Distributed Fleet Management and outsourcing services mainly to large firms, with more than 500 pieces of output equipment (printers, copy machines, faxes, etc.). Smaller firms are not equally attractive to Lexmark because they do not have the critical mass of document-handling and printing needs. Current challenges facing Lexmark include: How to determine what level of service contract is suitable for each customer? What should be the level of service contract offered to large firms/smaller firms? What other determinants than the customer company size should there be?

5. How to Innovate New Services with the Fleet Manager Electronic Information System

    The Lexmark Fleet Manager system currently includes the Asset Manager, the Billing Manager, the Consumables Manager, the Availability Manager, and the Optimization Manager systems. These systems were described in the chapter. What kinds of new innovative systems could Lexmark incorporate to this Fleet Manager system?

REFERENCES

Oliva, R., & Kallenberg, R. (2003). Managing the transition from products to services. International Journal of Service Industry Management, 14(2), 160–172.

Penttinen, E. (2007). Transition from products to services within the manufacturing business. Doctoral dissertation, Helsinki School of Economics, Finland. Retrieved June 5, 2008, from http://hse-publ.lib.hse.fi/FI/diss/?cmd=show&dissid=343

Penttinen, E., & Palmer, J. (2007). Improving firm positioning through enhanced offerings and buyer-seller relationships. Industrial Marketing Management, 36(5), 552–564.

Penttinen, E., & Saarinen, T. (2005). Opportunities and challenges for B2B industrial manufacturing firms: Case SKF. In T. Saarinen, M. Tinnila, & A. Tseng (Eds.), Managing business in a multi-channel world: Success factors for e-business (pp. 117–127). Idea Group Publishing.

Quinn, J. (1992). Intelligent enterprise: A knowledge and service based paradigm for industry. New York: Free Press.

Vargo, S., & Lusch, R. (2004). Evolving to a new dominant logic for marketing. Journal of Marketing, 68(1), 1–17.

Wise, R., & Baumgartner, P. (1999). Go downstream: The new profit imperative in manufacturing. Harvard Business Review, 77(5), 133–141.

Zeithaml, V., Parasuraman, A., & Berry, L. (1985). Problems and strategies in services marketing. Journal of Marketing, 49(2), 33–46.

Chapter XII
Evolution of Online Financial Trading Systems:
E–Service Innovations in the Brokerage Sector

Alexander Yap
Martha and Spencer Love School of Business, Elon University, USA

Wonhi Synn
Martha and Spencer Love School of Business, Elon University, USA

ABSTRACT

This chapter focuses on the theme of e-service innovation in financial electronic markets. The discussion will cover the theories of "technology bundling" and how bundling creates value-added in servicing electronic markets. More specifically, this chapter looks at innovations created through e-service bundling for online brokers connected to various financial electronic markets. The proliferation of different e-trading systems raises the question of which systems provide better service to online stock traders. Many online brokers (e-brokers) now provide low-cost transactions and financial research capabilities, so where is the next level of innovation? The objective of this chapter is to show that several innovations in broker e-services are critical in the following areas: (a) how order processes are efficiently managed in financial e-markets; (b) how responsive e-trading systems are in handling trading rules and regulations; (c) how different systems address unique niches in financial e-markets; and (d) improving systems stability and reliability.

BACKGROUND

Introduction

In this chapter, we start analyzing an entire sector (the brokerage service sector) rather than one particular business organization in order to understand the case studies. The reason for using the entire sector as the *unit* of analysis is that the e-service problems and challenges are similar for the entire sector and is not unique to one organization alone (see next section, which discusses the problem of this sector). More so, the best way to illustrate the e-service innovations of online brokers, we need to relate their unique e-service solutions to the problem facing the entire sector.

E-service in this chapter is defined as the service provided by electronic brokerage systems used to facilitate the buying and selling of publicly traded corporate stocks and financial securities online. If you want to own/buy shares of stocks in companies like Microsoft or IBM, you can trade their shares electronically through e-brokerage systems like Scottrade, E-Trade, and Ameritrade. By trading shares online, you are using an electronic service similar to an online auction system, where sellers and buyers bid for the prices of different stocks and financial securities. Buyers want to get the cheapest prices and sellers want to sell at the highest prices, and the electronic trading systems help them with that objective. This is a critical e-service for the trillion-dollar global financial market, where stocks, futures, options, bonds, foreign exchange, and commodities are traded daily. These electronic brokers do not necessarily own stocks or financial securities. They process the orders electronically by channeling the orders through different networked financial market systems via the New York Stock Exchange, the London Stock Exchange, the Shanghai Stock Exchange, and many other stock exchanges around the world.

Another critical e-service that needs to be defined is the service that assists online investors and traders to make informed decisions whether to buy or sell stocks and when to execute such trade. E-brokers provide bundled e-services like real-time news reports, real-time charting of stock price movements, the demand and supply of stocks, stock analyst ratings, and research on the company's financial health. This is how different e-services are "bundled" to help facilitate critical decisions in electronic financial markets. Different information systems, software applications, real-time databases, and networking technologies are used in the bundling of e-services.

In previous studies (Yap & Lin, 2001), the transaction capabilities of online trading systems as well as their knowledge-based components have been explored. These studies showed that earlier Web-based trading systems took one to three minutes to execute market orders; whereas more current systems can execute orders in one to three seconds. Transaction speed is not the real issue anymore. The real concern is whether traders are getting the "best price" for their trade executions. The demand for financial research and knowledge-base services online also needs to be more innovative to distinguish the uniqueness of e-services provided by different e-brokers. So the issue is what more can e-brokers provide their clients? In what areas can e-service innovation take place in the online brokerage sector? To get an idea of where innovation needs to happen, the problems of the online brokerage sector needs to be defined. Only then can we see how innovations in technologies and its bundling can provide solutions to such problems.

Defining the Problem in the Online Brokerage Sector

The problems with the electronic services provided by most online brokerage outfits are threefold: (1) *Not all systems comply with the U.S. Securities and Exchange Commission (SEC) Trading Require-*

ments (rules and regulations). Most information systems used for financial trading have loopholes in terms of preventing traders and investors from breaking SEC rules and U.S. government laws. This is important because many amateur traders are not familiar with laws governing the trading of financial instruments in U.S. financial markets. Breaking the law could be very costly and may prevent a trader from trading stocks again. This is a very serious problem not adequately addressed by e-service systems in the brokerage sector. (2) *There is a need to connect fragmented financial electronic markets to reflect more realistic stock quotes*. There are financial e-trading systems that are not as broadly networked to different financial electronic markets as other systems. This means that if your online brokerage service is only connected or bundled to two electronic financial markets while another online brokerage service is bundled to eight electronic financial markets, then your online broker's system may not be able to get you the best "buy" and "sell" price for your stocks like the more connected/networked e-brokers can. Many traders have complained that their orders were not executed at the price they wanted, even if they saw that their stocks momentarily hit those price ranges. This happens when an online trading system is only connected to a few electronic markets. (3) *Problem with systems stability and reliability*. Some online brokerage systems are not very stable and reliable, and therefore disrupting e-service more often during the electronic trading process. This is also a very serious problem. Imagine if your stock went down from $21.50 to $17.63 and you could not sell it because your online broker's system was down for three hours. One of the purposes of this study is to test some of the more popular trading systems for more than a year and see how they hold up over time.

Methodology

This research employs the "case research" methodology. The researchers were involved in the actual use of the financial trading system and so data was acquired on a firsthand basis. The research uses the interpretive approach, which is essentially based on the unique experience of the user. The researchers gather the findings from direct experience and day-to-day interaction with the trading systems, its inherent technological features, and the customer support provided by the e-broker when the system is not working properly.

To be able to do an in-depth analysis, the researchers opened four separate accounts so that four different popular e-trading systems can be tested and compared. However, due to limited space in writing this chapter, we can only cover two cases discussing two different e-trading systems. The two cases chosen for this chapter offered the more innovative e-services in the industry at the time of data gathering. Each e-trading system was used for more than a year. More than 50 trades were conducted on each system, with a frequency of at least once each week. Several systems features were explored to see what value it provided the user. Trading online naturally meant that the researchers acquired their information/data firsthand. To validate and confirm some findings, the researchers also engage in dialogues with trading communities through message boards with user reviews.

SETTING THE STAGE

The Strategic Role of IT in the Creation of Electronic Markets: A Theoretical Framework

Ciborra (1993) argued that information technology can be used to lower transaction cost, and in turn, enable the creation of cost-efficient electronic markets. Bakos (1991) emphasized that IT-driven electronic marketplaces can lower the "buyer's search costs" as well as the seller's cost.

Bakos (1998) said that electronic markets lead to a more efficient "friction-free" market, because electronic markets match sellers' offer to the buyers' preferences more efficiently than physical markets. The more buyers and sellers there are in an electronic market system, the smoother (less friction) the market mechanism will be in determining a realistic price for goods and services. If we examine global consumer e-markets with millions of users like eBay, prices of goods or services are realistically determined by the supply and demand forces created by multitudes of buyers and sellers. On the other hand, electronic financial markets have been fragmented into smaller electronic market systems called *Electronic Communication Networks* (ECNs). These financial e-markets have not been as unified, integrated, and as far-reaching as eBay. So, it is not as "friction-less" because price gaps occur in fragmented markets. That is why "arbitrage trading" occurs in financial e-markets. In finance, arbitrage trading is the practice of taking advantage of price gaps/differentials in stocks, options, bonds between two or more financial markets.

Friedfertig and West (1998) enumerated different financial electronic market systems used for trading stocks, to include Instinet, Island, and NASDAQ's Small Order Entry System (SOES). The *National Association of Securities Dealers Automated Quotation System* (NASDAQ) was the first, and as of this writing, the largest electronic stock market. While electronic financial markets have been fragmented, there have been initiatives to start integrating different e-market trading systems. In 2005, NASDAQ acquired Instinet (Ryan, 2005). After that, the Associated Press (2006) reported that the New York Stock Exchange (NYSE) has merged with Archipelago Holdings, a Chicago-based company that owns an electronic market exchange system called ARCA-Ex. The NYSE, a 213-year-old traditional stock exchange, finally adopted its own electronic market system in 2006.

Bakos and Brynjolfsson (2000) argued that the bundling of information goods, systems, and technology is advantageous for service provid-

ers as bundling information goods increases the value of a set of goods to the clients/users of the information systems. The bundling of information goods and systems is reflected in the changes seen in financial markets like the merger of Instincts with NASDAQ and ARCA-Ex with NYSE. The purpose of bundling of information goods enabled by information technology relates to Ciborra (1993) and Malone, Yates, and Benjamin's (1987) arguments that information technology brings down the cost of transaction and coordination in electronic markets. In this study, we believe that e-brokerage firms have bundled different information goods, systems, and technology to make their e-services highly innovative and competitive.

This research looks at two e-brokers and investigates if their online trading systems have been "bundled" in such a way that their system can simultaneously transact and access live data from several financial e-markets. The other aspect of "bundling" that will be studied is how various software applications have been combined to provide a comprehensive electronic service to traders/investors. This research believes that the e-trading system with the best bundled information goods, functions, and systems capabilities will provide the best value to traders/investors.

The Changing Service Environment in the Online Brokerage Sector

Considering that instantaneous transaction speed and financial research are already standard capabilities in most e-brokerage services, systems developers for e-brokers need to recognize other unique innovative e-service capabilities that are really needed in this service sector. The following are critical issues to consider:

Order Process Flow - First, there is the issue of how buy and sell orders are channeled to various electronic trading systems and whether traders are getting the "best price" for their orders. The question is to what extent are online trading systems linked to different electronic markets to process orders and get traders the best price for their orders?

Targeting Niche Markets - Second, what differentiates one e-service from another? In what ways do different systems cater to various types of traders? E-brokers need to take advantage of market segmentation and cater to different types of clients/traders.

SEC Regulation - Third, there have been several changes in government rules and regulations that could penalize online brokerage firms if trader violates those SEC rules. The chapter will determine whether there are some loopholes in the systems that are disadvantageous to traders.

Systems Reliability and Security - Finally, there is an increasing risk of system failure and security breaks. Are trading systems as reliable? How are online brokers providing clients safe guards and fail safe systems?

Current Issues in the Stock Market Prompting Changes in Online Trading Services

The growth of electronic markets has caused market fragmentation as alternate market centers are "balkanizing" the order flow process and encouraging internalization. *Internalization* is the situation where brokers buy the stock from their own internal sources or inventory instead of buying from the larger open market. It is not good for orders to be executed in isolated small markets rather than in bigger, more unified, and networked e-markets. Roberts, Pittman, and Reeds (2000) stated this appropriately in their article.

Recent advances in technology and changes in securities regulation have sparked the development of a growing number of alternative market centers. These market centers include regional exchanges and alternative trading systems.

Advancements in technology and regulatory changes have made it possible for these market centers to attract order flow by offering narrower spreads and improved trading efficiencies, including speedier and more reliable executions... .The SEC is concerned that fragmentation of the markets has caused or will cause too many customer orders to be executed in isolation, rather than interacting with other market orders.

The objective of having an electronic market is providing accessibility to as many market segments as possible; however, the growing fragmentation or balkanization of electronic markets appears to limit the order flow process from reaching a wider market given time execution constraints. Moreover, the larger the volume of the trade, the more difficult it is for the online system to match, buy, and sell volumes.

For example, an online brokerage firm may not find 1,000 shares of stocks being sold lower than $20.20/share in their own e-market system, even though another seller in an alternate e-market center may be selling it at $20.00/share. Due to execution time constraint, the system may be able to get the best bid at the fastest execution within its own internal order flow (that is $20.20) but not across other market centers. So, theoretically, the buyer is forced to pay $20.20 instead of only $20.00 and therefore paying $0.20/share more (or $200 for 1000 shares) due to the inability of an electronic market system to search several other electronic market systems for a better price given the constraint of execution time.

Electronic markets seem to be getting more fragmented due to the proliferation of different electronic trading systems in the form of Electronic Communication Networks (ECNs), such as Instinet and Archipelago. Routing orders across different electronic markets can be inefficient in terms of getting the best price of a stock; hence the temptation of brokers to internalize orders. Traditional markets like NYSE and AMEX behave more like a singular unfragmented market where trading occurs on the floor among a network of human specialist.

Figure 1. Balkanized or fragmented e-markets (left) and unified single market (right)

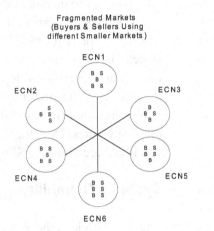

Figure 1 compares and illustrates fragmented markets (such as ECN1 or ECN2) vs. a single market. In fragmented markets, buyers (B) and sellers (S) may not be properly matched. Some markets have more buyers than sellers or vice versa. If an e-trading system just executes orders within one or two ECNs, their clients may not always get the best traded price.

If an online system can access all ECNs, then it gives its clients the opportunity to access a bigger e-market. In effect, it is unifying all smaller e-markets to a single e-market.

Diversifying E-Services by Targeting Niche Markets

There are different types of traders or investors in the stock market. Different financial broker-age firms target different types of traders or investors. The following are different groups of traders/investors:

1. Long-term investors – investors who "buy and hold" and keep their stock portfolio for months or years.

2. Swing traders – traders who do not keep stocks for more than a week. They take advantage of the upswing and downswing of stock prices over the course of a few days.

3. Pattern Day traders – traders who buy and sell stocks during the same day. They sell stocks at the end of the day, whether they make money or not.

4. Micro-day traders – a growing number of traders who only buy and sell within a few minutes or seconds. They do not even hold stocks for an hour. Their objective is to take advantage of small fluctuations in the market and make a small profit spread with these fluctuations.

5. Penny stock and small cap traders – traders who trade only micro-caps or small caps stocks. Micro-cap stocks are often referred to as penny stocks because they can be traded for less than a dollar. Small caps stocks are also cheap and usually below $5.

6. Large cap and middle cap traders – a group of traders who believe that they should only buy stocks above $10 or $20. They believe that micro-cap and small cap stocks are cheap for

171

a reason; they are risky and trading for what they are worth.

7. Institutional traders – these are large institutions that invest their capital in stocks, like banks, insurance, and mutual fund companies.

Securities and Exchange Commission (SEC) Rules and Regulations

SEC has a number of trading rules that brokers must follow or force its clients to follow. For example, SEC has already limited day trading activities. Pattern daytraders need to have at least $25,000 in their account to meet SEC requirements. This took effect in 2001. Cadway (2001) summarize these new rulings:

As some of you might be aware, the NASD has come out with some new margin rules for day-trading accounts effective September 28th, 2001. Among these rules is the requirement for all pattern daytrading accounts to have a minimum equity of $25,000.

Stock traders have two general paths in trading stocks. One path is to buy low and sell high, while another path is to sell high and buy low (short selling). Selling high and buying low is the processing of shorting a stock. Technically, the trader just borrowing stocks from his broker when he/she short sells a stock that he/she does not own. Sooner or later, the trader must buy stocks to repay or return or cover what he/she borrowed from his/her broker (This is known as "buy to cover"). For a trader to borrow stocks from a broker, the broker must have an inventory of that stock. If the broker does not have an inventory of a particular stock and still lets the individual trader borrow it on paper, then the broker is violating SEC rules by practicing "naked shorting." While naked shorting is illegal, e-brokers are known to

violate it all the time. Data show that brokers still allow traders to do naked shorting.

How responsive are online trading systems to SEC rules and regulations? Could users of these systems be allowed to break SEC rules and regulations or does the system stop them from breaking the rules or doing anything illegal? The question is: how are online trading systems keeping up with these SEC rules? Does the trading system inform you if you are violating SEC rules or not?

Systems Reliability

The speed cycle of the trading process is assumingly faster today than it was in the late 1990s with the significant jump of retail traders joining the online trading scenario. The sheer volume of trading may be taxing the trading system of different brokers and also the systems used by different ECNs. The research initiative intends to find out how reliable the systems are.

Dogsofthedow.com posts certain feedback from users of online systems. Some of the feedbacks citing technical problems with online brokers are as follows:

After 2 months of technical issues I have closed my account today. I have lost several thousands of dollars in one day because the price of a particular stock that I shorted...was not at current prices but the day before.... I have filed a fraud complaint on April 20, 2004 with the SEC."

I've had an account with [xxx] since Oct 2002 and have seen a steady decrease in online reliability. Emailed complaints are answered with form letter responses and after hours trading seem to be farther and farther over the horizon. The problems seem to stem from poor technology implementation and overwhelming the systems with new subscribers before adequately architecting for the heavier load.

From firsthand experience, the research intends to discover how frequent the systems go down and how fast the brokers can bring their systems back running again.

CASE DESCRIPTION

Case One: E-Broker One

E-Broker One (*real name of company withheld*) was launched in 1996 as a discount online brokerage firm, and it quickly gained popularity with its guaranteed one minute execution in 1999. E-Broker One has survived the tight competition among deep discount online brokers. E-Broker One has incorporated new changes into their systems from 2002–2006 which allowed it to offer a system unique to other systems. Over the years, the E-Broker One's system has evolved from a simple transaction processing system to a system that includes several new capabilities.

Order Process Flow

The E-Broker One's system offers three choice of routing orders: (1) INET system, (2) Supermontage, one of NASDAQ's stock market trading systems, and (3) Market Maker, the order gets redirected to a Market Maker handling the particular stock being traded (see Figure 2).

For traders, INET and NASDAQ's Supermontage provide more transparent order routing flows. INET and NASDAQ have their own Web-based system for reflecting orders in real time. So, traders can immediately validate that their orders are posted. Figure 3 shows streaming quotes from INET. The Market Maker route is less transparent because, as most traders know, market makers have notoriety for manipulating trades.

In the E-Broker One trading system, once you choose to place your order in INET e-trading system (an ECN), the INET system has a program,

Figure 2. Three order routing for E-Broker One

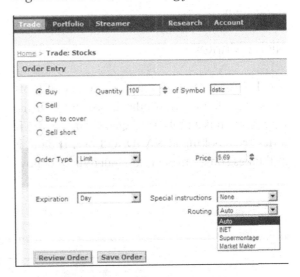

Figure 3. Java Applet showing real-time buy/sell orders

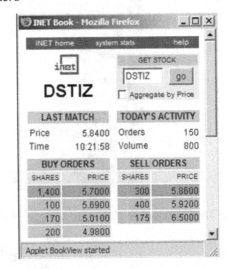

both Java and HTML-based, that will immediately reflect your buy or sell order (see Figure 3).

For traders, it is an instantaneously gratifying experience on their part to see that the order they placed via an online broker's system is reflected immediately in ECNs like INET. The order flow then becomes very transparent and credible.

The transparency of the order flow insures that there is no arbitrage by e-brokers, and that orders are executed directly by the ECNs trading system.

Niche Market

The E-Broker One system has a couple of tools that are not found in any other e-brokerage firms. One of them is a tool called Quotescope. Even if a trader is looking at NASDAQ Level II data, it still takes some time to figure out dynamic mov-

ing order volume on the buyer and seller sides. Quotescope provides a more graphic representation of both price and volume. Figure 4A shows how Quotescope depicts the buying forces on the left side of the pie and the selling forces on the right side of the pie. And traders can also see the prices where most buyers and sellers are putting their trades.

Quotescope is a tool that extracts real-time trading data and converts that data into a real-

Figure 4a. E-Broker One's Quotescope: a visual representation of volume

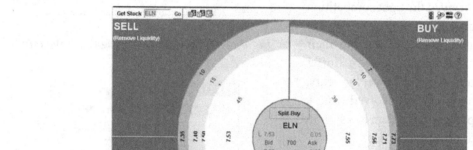

Figure 4B. Quotescope depicting a bigger left side of the pie due to buying pressure

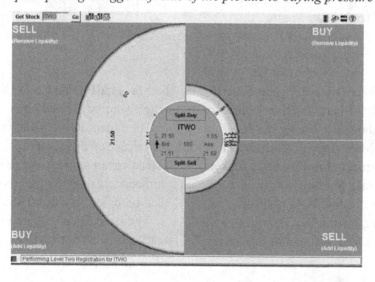

time graphic representation of the trading volume and price every few seconds. Quotescope is represented by a dynamic pie chart that has two sides. The left side represents the total buyer's volume, while the right side represents the total seller's volume. The volume at each price level is also represented in different colors. It allows traders to make a quick decision to either buy or sell stocks. In Figure 4A, the buying and selling pressures are seen as almost equal forces with the left and right sides of the pie almost even. However in Figure 4B, the buying force (the left side of the pie) is seen as more powerful than the sell side (the right side of the pie).

Monitoring the buying and selling volume at different price levels in Quotescope is much more simplified with the fast changing graphic format than watching NASDAQ's level II. However, NASDAQ Level II, which E-Broker One also provides, gives traders a sort of microscopic tool to determine the market makers' buying and selling activities. E-Broker One's NASDAQ Level II interface is shown on Figure 5.

For traders, NASDAQ Level II information is important because it lists different market makers who may be scalping for stocks at cheaper prices and selling them a few cents higher. NASDAQ Level II also gives some hint if certain market makers are manipulating prices by dumping a huge amount of share at higher prices, only to buy them back at lower prices. After all, playing the stock market is like a poker game and the more information that is transparent, the better for traders.

Trade Trigger is a feature that E-Broker One introduced in 2004 (Figure 6). This is one of the more advanced automatic programs made available for retail traders. Programmed trading is not new for the professional trader; however E-Broker One has brought it to the mainstream.

E-Broker One's trade trigger can be programmed to buy and sell stocks based on stock or major index movements. For example, if the Dow Jones index loses 50 points, a trader can

Figure 5. E-Broker One's NASDAQ Level II interface

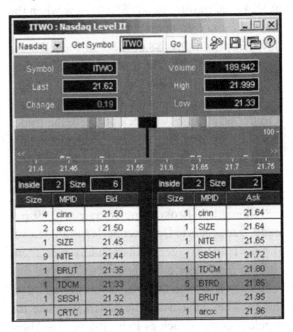

automatically sell stocks. Or if the NASDAQ falls below the 2000 level, then a sell trigger can be activated. Figure 6 shows the Trade Triggers interface of E-Broker One. Not only can a trader set trades based on index movements, but a trader can set trailing stops. Trailing stops are important when a trader wants to trigger a buy or sell order that trails price movements dynamically.

For example, if a trader bought a stock at $7.00 and it is now $7.85. The trader may decide that his target is to sell it at $8.00. However, he is thinking that it may still go up to $8.50. With other online trading systems that only give an option to buy/sell at market or limit price, the trader has no recourse but to set his sell order at $8.00. With trailing stops, the trader can set a trigger to sell at $8.00 or even higher. For example, the stock hits $8.00 but continues to go up to $8.10, $8.20, $8.30, or $8.60. The trader can set a $0.10 trailing stop, so when the stock keeps on going up, the stop sell order also follows it going up. If the stock suddenly goes up from $8.00 to $8.60, the trailing stop follows it $0.10 behind. If the price is at $8.60, the trailing stop should be at $8.50, while at $8.40 the trailing stop is $8.30. Now when the stock does not go up anymore and starts to fall down from its high of $8.60 to $8.50, the sell order is executed at $8.50. The trailing stop halts when the price movement does not go higher.

Trailing stops also work for buying stocks. If a trader wants to buy a stock at $7.50, the trader can set a trailing stop so that if the stock falls down to $7.00, he could buy it at a lower price. Trailing stops are useful if a trader cannot monitor the trading screen all day.

Although E-Broker One charges $10.99 per trade, free access to Quotescope, NASDAQ Level II, and Trade Triggers tools actually puts them cheaper than other e-brokers.

Lastly, E-Broker One also caters to traders on the go. They have a WAP-enabled Web site for wireless devices such as Palm Pilots, Blackberries, and mobile phones that have Internet access. The simplified interface for mobile devices is seen in Figure 7.

To summarize the usefulness of these tools:

- Quotescope and NASDAQ Level II are excellent tools for daytrading and swing trading because traders can make better decisions with how information is presented to them in real time, thereby enabling them to make quick decisions to sell, hold, or buy.
- Trade triggers are good tools for all non-day-traders because it allows investors and traders to automate the trading for them in ways that other online systems do not offer.
- E-Broker One seems to have a well-balanced system as it provides diverse tools that cater to the needs of different types of investors and traders.

SEC Ruling

E-Broker One has one of the more comprehensive help information for SEC rules (Figure 8). While its system does not automatically stop traders from violating SEC rules, their information is extensive and well organized regarding the rules.

For new traders who feel that it is too cumbersome to read through voluminous amounts of information in the Help Center, this is still not the best solution for SEC violation avoidance.

Figure 6. Trade triggers

Figure 7. Trading on the go

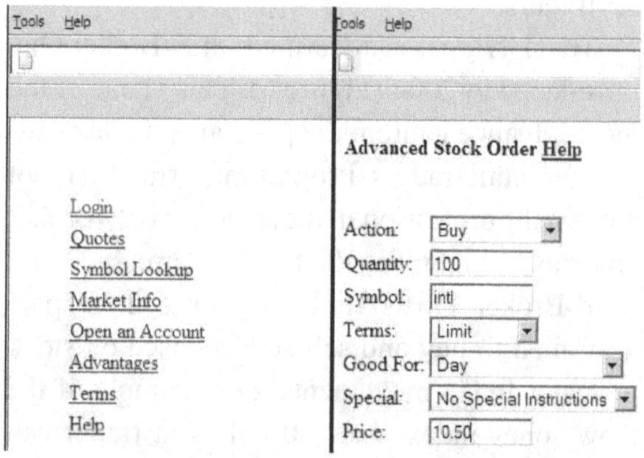

Figure 8. E-Broker One's comprehensive help center

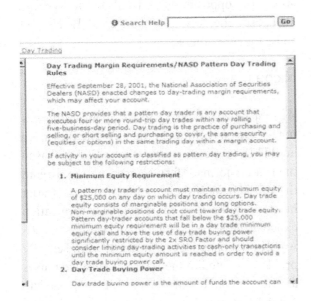

There are several new traders who fail to study these help files.

A problem with the daytrading rule is that you cannot do more than three roundtrip buy/sell trading in five consecutive moving days. This is the difficult part—tracking five consecutive moving days. So, if you daytraded twice on Thursday and daytraded once on Friday, you cannot daytrade the following Monday, Tuesday, and Wednesday. But suppose that following Monday and Tuesday are holidays, then you cannot daytrade on Wednesday, Thursday, and Friday instead. But how can traders be expected to keep tabs of all the holidays? If the system is not able to track those five consecutive days for you, you can easily forget the holidays in your counting and unintentionally violate SEC rules.

Systems Security and Stability

The streamer of E-Broker One which is Java-based can have difficulties popping up as a separate window in several instances. E-Broker One offers two interfaces for trading. One is in simple HTML format and the other is Java-based. The HTML-based interface is much easier to access and use than the Java applet. Sometimes the Java-based interface takes 15 minutes to open even with a cable modem. However, over the course of three months, E-Broker One has improved the speed of starting the Java applet. Over time, the E-Broker One system was pretty stable.

The Yahoo message boards talked about problems with E-Trade and Scottrade's system but we have not heard about E-Broker One. This confirms our experience that their system was pretty stable at the time we gathered the data.

Technology Bundling

E-Broker One had sophisticated bundling when it came to different software functions and tools. The intelligent trade triggers allowed traders to program their trading based on the movement of the general market like the Dow or NASDAQ. Quotescope provided real time charting of market supply and demand. NASDAQ Level II quote system was also available. These were software functions that other e-brokers did not have. These tools provided good information about the market in real-time. The information goods for investment/trading research were just as about as good as other e-brokers. E-Broker One did not have a fully diversified electronic market network if compared to an interactive broker. It connected to three electronic financial market systems: ARCA-Ex, INET, and Supermontage. E-Broker One could have bundled more market networks, so that traders could get the best execution of buy and sell orders.

Case Two: Interactive Brokers

Interactive Brokers is ranked the 16th largest security firm or among the institutional investor in terms of capital position (2005, Institutional Investor Inc., www.institutionalinvestor.com).

Interactive Brokers' consolidated capital of $1.9 billion puts them above other big securities firms such as Jefferies Group, ABN Amro, E-Broker One Holdings, E-Trade Holdings, and Barclays Capital.

Interactive broker claims to have 28 years of experience in creating "direct access trading technology" for professional traders. Interactive Brokers has one of the cheapest commissions at $1 per 100 shares traded or $0.50 per 100 shares if buying more than 500 shares. Interactive Brokers engages not only in stocks and options but also in forex and bonds trading in more than 50 global markets. In 2005, Barron ranked it as "the No. 1 software-based broker."

Order Process Flow

Interactive Brokers can route orders to five different ECNs: ARCA, BRUT, BTRADE, ISLAND, and SUPERSOES. In 2007, they route orders to more ECNs compared to the time data was gathered for this research in 2004–2006. Both BRUT and SUPERSOES are basically NASDAQ systems. The routing also allows you to set the default routing to "SMART." When a trader sets the routing destination to SMART, it means that Interactive Brokers' system will try to find the best price for the buy or sell orders. For example, if the seller wants to sell his/her share at a market price, and ARCA has a buyer at 9.98, ISLAND has another buyer at $9.95, and BRUT has a buyer at $10.00, then the system will route the order to

BRUT. That way the seller gets the best price for his/her order. If you are a buyer, then SMART works the opposite way; it will try to find the cheapest seller across the different ECNs and route the order there.

Niche Market

At first glance, their software application does not appear to be for beginners. While they have an HTML version for trading, their HTML-based interface is not made for advanced trading. To gain the full benefit of their trading system, a trader has to install a Java-based software application called Trader Workstation. The Java-based software is stable and well-protected from security problems related to the Internet, because it uses a different connecting port to pull and push data to the Internet.

Interactive Brokers provides traders a choice of using a single spreadsheet interface that allows traders to place/cancel orders while watching real-time streaming quotes and some accounting highlights (unrealized gains/loss) all at one glance (Figure 10). The other brokers do not have a one-shop type interface. This is advantageous to traders who need speed, because orders can be executed very fast while monitoring their gains and losses.

For day traders or microsecond traders, Interactive Brokers has an even faster way to executing trades. And that is through a tool called Book Traders (Figure 16). The Book Traders is a tool

Figure 9. Routing orders to five different ECNs

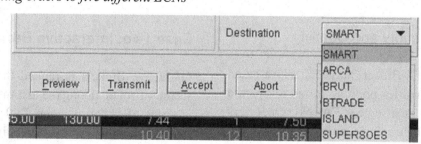

Figure 10. Single spreadsheet interface

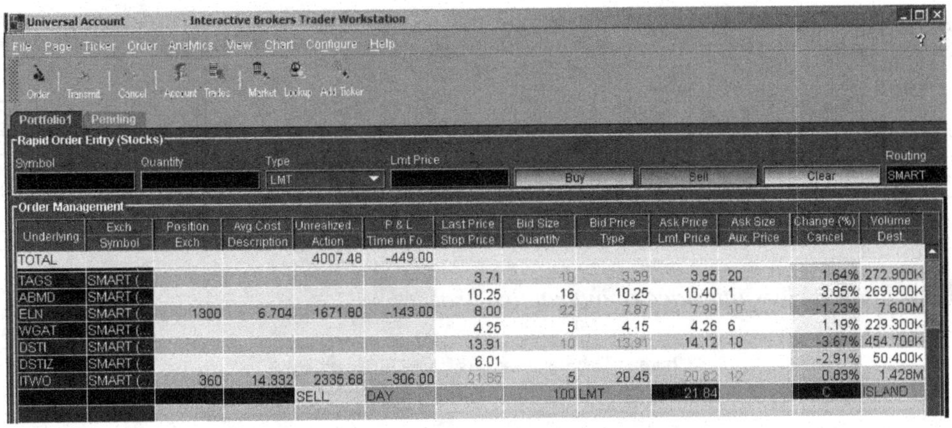

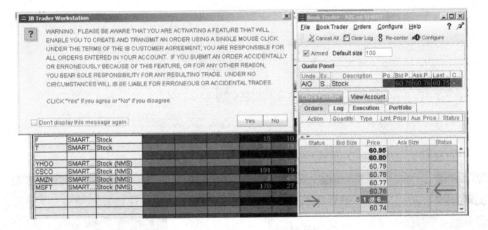

Figure 11. One-click trading

that could be set to "arm" and the trader is given an array of prices. In Figure 11, the stock AIG is being displayed with different prices from $60.74 to $60.95. The one-click feature allows traders to click either the buy side or the sell side boxes (see marked arrows in Figure 11) and the order goes through with just a single mouse click. Traders need to be really careful with this feature because it is easy to send orders accidentally in one click.

There are advantages of having to be able to access five ECNs all at the same time. In rare occasions, traders can see that the buy (bid) is actually higher than the sell (ask). In one occa-

sion, the researchers saw this discrepancy. To experiment on this, the researchers bought 300 shares of ITWO at $13.20 from the BRUT ECN and then two seconds later sold the 300 for $13.25 at the ISLAND ECN (see Figure 12). The gain was only $15, but it was to prove that some form of pure arbitrage and scalping could be realized if a system can access more ECNs. Many traders only have access to one or two ECNs while Interactive Brokers' can trade across five ECNs. This shows that electronic market fragmentation has some inefficiency that can be exploited by a system that can network more systems together. It

Figure 12. Arbitrage and scalping between two ECNs

Action	Quantity	Underlying	Comb.	Description	Price	Currency	Exch.
BOT	100	ITWO	☐	Stock	13.03	USD	ISLAND
BOT	100	ITWO	☐	Stock	12.76	USD	SUPERSOES
SLD	100	DSTIZ	☐	Stock	6.29	USD	ISLAND
SLD	100	DSTIZ	☐	Stock	6.24	USD	SUPERSOES
SLD	100	DSTIZ	☐	Stock	6.11	USD	SUPERSOES
BOT	300	ITWO	☐	Stock ITWO (NMS)	13.20	USD	BRUT
SLD	300	ITWO	☐	Stock ITWO (NMS)	13.25	USD	ISLAND

Figure 13. Mobile/wireless interface of interactive brokers

Figure 14. Interactive brokers' system stops naked shorting

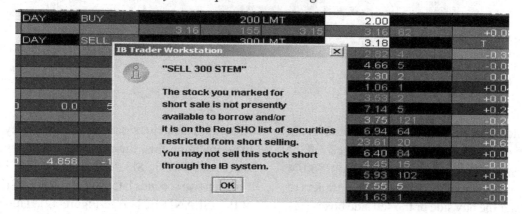

used to be done only by professional traders, but now it could be done by any retail traders.

Like E-Broker One, traders can also access the Interactive Brokers' trading system using their mobile phone or palm pilots (Figure 13).

SEC Ruling

Interactive Brokers has an excellent system that prevents traders from violating SEC regulations. By far, this is one of the best online systems that can warn traders beforehand of possible SEC

Figure 15. Interactive brokers' system tracks day-trading activity

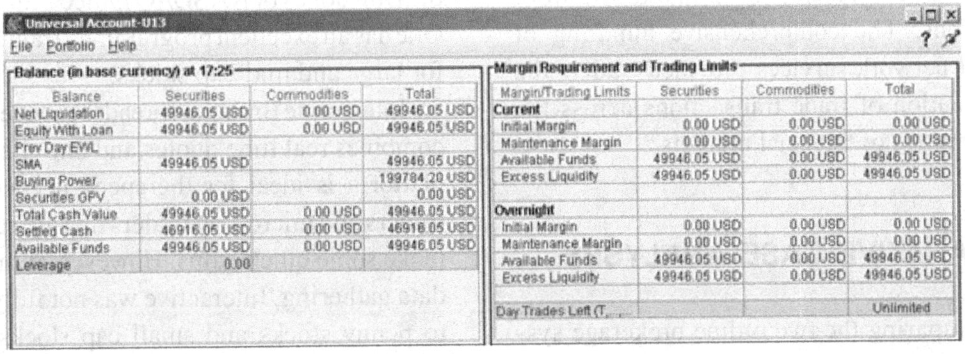

violations. In Figure 14, the researchers tried to short some STEM stocks. However, because this particular stock was being shorted naked at that time and therefore on the Reg SHO list, it could not be sold short then.

In Figure 15, Interactive Brokers has an accounting window that shows how many trading days you have left on the lower right side. As mentioned earlier, if you have more than $25,000 in your account, daytrading activities are unlimited. However, if you have less than $25,000 in your account, you are only allowed to perform three daytrades within five consecutive days. What is convenient about the Interactive Brokers' system is that if a trader/investor has used up all of his/her daytrading privileges, the system will not allow any more trading to occur. In short, the system actually stops you from breaking SEC rules. No other trading system has this capability.

Systems Security and Stability

After using Interactive Brokers for a year, there were about five days that the system lost real-time data feed, but not the ability to trade. However, in these instances, they usually rectify the lost data feed within 10 minutes.

There have been instances where data feeds were lost but they informed the traders immediately that it is not their system but data feed

coming from the ECNs (or the financial electronic markets). So, Interactive Brokers will actually classify two types of downtime: their own system's downtime and third-party downtime. Their feedback was actually quite informative.

While traders can access the online trading system of E-Broker One on Saturdays and Sunday morning, Interactive Brokers intentionally turns off their system on Saturdays and Sunday morning. They do this because they want a full maintenance check on all their systems during the weekend. This is a good practice because no one trades on Saturdays and Sunday mornings. Having it available on Sunday afternoon makes sense because some traders prefer to plan and place their trades before the Monday opening.

Technology Bundling

While Interactive Brokers did not have Quotescope and NASDAQ Level II features bundled like E-Broker One, what was bundled with Interactive Broker was more important. The critical SEC rules and regulations for trading were bundled into their system to make sure that traders/investors do not do something illegal or even become tempted to break SEC rules. For serious matured traders, the way SEC information has been tightly integrated into the system was more important than fancy charts and stock information that can be sourced elsewhere. Interactive Brokers system also had the most extensive electronic market network connections. The comprehensive bundling of e-market network services provided traders the best execution of trade transactions across the broadest range of financial markets.

COMPARATIVE CASE ANALYSES

After comparing the two online brokerage systems, the observation shows that the different systems cater to very different user and trading needs. In terms of order routing, Interactive Brokers has a better system simply because it covers more ECNs than E-Broker One. This means that traders have a better chance of selling and buying at a better price with more ECNs connected to the Interactive Brokers system. Interactive Brokers also has a smart system that can redirect orders to get the best price for the trader. Once the order is redirected, the order is immediately displayed in the particular ECN the order was sent to, and the Interactive Brokers' system also displays what ECN the order was sent to. E-Broker One also allows traders three choices for routing orders. E-Broker One has an "auto" route that is similar to the "smart" routing; however, once it is set to "auto" routing, traders are left in the dark as to where the order is redirected. Interactive has a more transparent system. Other e-brokers have no routing choice and no transparency at all. The spreadsheet interface of Interactive's system coupled with the various ECN choices also makes it ideal for scalping and daytrading stocks.

In terms of catering to different types of traders, E-Broker One had the best tools for swing traders. The trade triggers are ideal for swing trader because they can help guard traders from short-term losses while maximizing short term gains. The trade triggers can be used to ride the ups and downs of major indices (Dow, NASDAQ, S&P 500, and Russell 2000) and therefore good for swing trading securities that follow the indices

movements. Since most of the big cap stocks follow the Dow Jones or NASDAQ indices, the E-Broker One has an excellent programmed trading system for large and mid-cap stocks.

Interactive Brokers' spreadsheet interface that combines real time quotes and one click trading platform is ideal for the speed needed by day traders and micro-day traders that are scalping to make some quick gains. However, at the time of data gathering, Interactive was not fully attuned to penny stocks and small cap stocks that are sold over-the-counter (OTC) or with a pink slip (PK) status. Interactive Brokers did not have full real-time trades for some OTC and PK stocks. Neither is the system useful for trading bankrupt companies that are being restructured (their stock symbol ends with the letter Q).

Interactive Brokers has taken lengths to set up its system for institutional and professional trading. It is only with Interactive Brokers that advisor accounts are available. Advisor accounts are tailor-made for professional traders who manage separate clients' accounts. The clients can electronically transfer money to their accounts but may not do any trading. It is the professional financial advisor that does the trading for clients.

It appears that Interactive Brokers has a system that has broken grounds in areas that other brokers have not. An example of their excellent system is the feature that helps prevent traders from violating SEC regulation. Interactive Brokers' system automatically does not allow traders to daytrade three times in five consecutive days. The system just would not allow a user to buy long or sell short or take any new position once the daytrading requirement hits its limits. Of the two brokerage firms compared here, Interactive Brokers is the one that adheres strictly to the naked shorting rule. As long as a stock is listed on the SHO List (a list that confirms a stock is being naked shorted), Interactive Brokers will not allow that stock to be shorted. Other trading systems did not appear to stop the shorting of a stock on the SHO list. In this particular instance, DSTI (a publicly

Table 1. Analytical comparison of online brokers' systems capability

	E-BROKER ONE	INTER. BROKER
ROUTING ORDERS		
Routing Choices	- INET - ARCA - SuperMontage	- INET - ARCA - SuperSoes - BRUT - BTRADE
Automatic Routing For best price	Yes	Yes
Transparency of Order Flow	No	Yes
Routing for Scalping/Daytrading	Good	Best
ADDRESSING NICHE MARKETS		
The Buy and Hold Investors	GOOD	GOOD
Swing Traders	BEST	GOOD
Daytraders	GOOD	BEST
Large & Middle Cap Investors	BEST	GOOD
Small Cap & Penny Traders	GOOD	AVERAGE
Micro-Day Traders	GOOD	BEST
Institutional Traders	AVERAGE	BEST
FOLLOWING SEC REGULATIONS		
Good Warnings on SEC Violation	Average	Very Good
System Force Stops Traders from Violating Daytrader Rule	No	Yes
System Tracks Daytrading Activity Before SEC Violation Occurs	No	Yes
System Stops Traders from Naked Shorting	No	Yes (when stock appears on SHO list)
SYSTEMS STABILITY		
System Down (Cannot Trade)	No	No
Systems Down (Tools and Data Down)	Yes, Java-based tools	Yes, data feed
Internet Intrusion	SSL-Enabled (SAFE)	Non-browser Based (SAFER)

Figure 16. List of stocks shorted naked, including DSTI

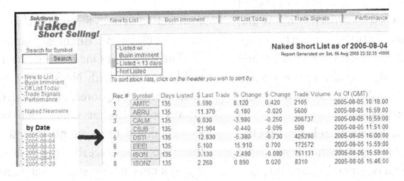

Figure 17. Naked shorting allowed by an online trading system

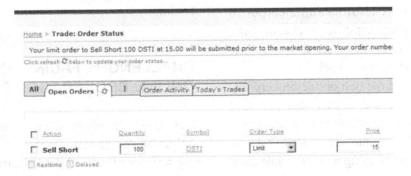

traded stock) has been heavily shorted naked for almost half a year (see Figure 16). E-Broker One's system tested in this study allowed an order to sell DSTI short without prohibition during that instance (see Figure 17). Very possibly, E-Broker One had their own inventory of DSTI stocks and allowed their inventory to be legally borrowed for short selling. Interactive Brokers' system did not allow short orders to be transmitted if it is listed as a naked short on the SHO list. The reason why naked shorting exists is that brokers and e-trading systems may allow such transaction depending on their rules and situation. As of this writing, there is still a big debate about how SEC needs to tighten controls for naked shorting, because it is common knowledge that brokerage companies allow it based on their own rules and based on their willingness to pay SEC fines.

E-Broker One and Interactive Brokers had some occasional problem with their real-time feed, but on the positive side their system still had basic trading functions that allowed buying and selling of stocks. Other e-trading systems (not covered in this chapter) had worst systems downtime and had lost trading functionalities. During the times when E-Broker One and Interactive Brokers had no real-time data feeds, the alternative was to go directly to INET or ARCA's websites to get real-time buy/sell order data.

The Web-based applications of E-Broker One use the socket layer (SSL), which is what most online banks use. So it is generally safe. Interactive Brokers' software is not dependent on a Web browser so it is least susceptible to browser attacks. The researchers noticed that Trade Workstation, Interactive's software, also uses a different port to connect to the Internet, or a different channel from what is used by Internet browsers. It is, therefore, less likely to be attacked or hacked.

After looking at the two online brokers, Interactive Brokers and E-Broker One provided excellent bundling of software and information goods (see Table 2). Interactive Broker came out on top in terms of being able to bundle their

Table 2. Rating the value of e-services by the information and capabilities being bundled into different online trading systems

Bundling of E-Services	E-Broker One	Interactive Broker
Software Functions Bundled	*Excellent* (Very Advance Trade Triggers, Quotescope, Streaming Quotes Interface, NASDAQ level II Interface, Charting)	*Excellent* (Some Intelligent Trade Triggers, Charting, Very Fast Streaming Quote Spreadsheet Interface, One-Click Trading Interface; Options Analysis Tools)
Information Goods Bundled	*Excellent* (NASDAQ Level II data, Financial data, Real-time Streaming News, Company Research)	*Excellent* (Multiple-Source Financial Data, SEC Policies Embedded in System, Real-Time Accounting)
E-Market Network Services Bundled	Good INET ARCA SuperMontage	*Excellent* INET ARCA SuperSoes BRUT BTRADE

transaction system for multiple access to a broad range of electronic financial markets.

The E-Broker One trading interface was very richly bundled with NASDAQ Level II access, Trade Triggers, Quotescope, and streaming news. However, E-Broker One's rich interface also slowed down the system. Interactive Brokers' interface was noticeably much faster than all of the systems under study. Interactive Brokers' interface was bundled with different features for options trading, real-time accounting, keeping track of SEC regulations, charting, and one-click trading.

CHALLENGES FACING THE ONLINE BROKERAGE SECTOR

One of the challenges that plague the entire online brokerage sector is the service of delivering real-time financial data electronically. Even though e-trading systems are working properly for buy/sell transactions, the glitch is that various financial electronic market systems occasionally have difficulties transmitting real-time financial data (such as real-time stock price quotes) to various e-trading systems run by different online brokers. During those occasions, clients of online brokers will not get real-time data service, and they will perceive their broker's system as "unstable" and "unreliable" without access to real-time data. Investors and traders find it difficult making decisions on whether they should buy or sell stocks without real-time data. This bundled e-service is normally not within the control of e-brokers, because e-brokers also subscribe to real-time data from the data service providers managing the financial e-markets. If real-time data is not transmitted or available, a good customer service that e-brokers can do for their clients is to honestly inform them in a timely manner that they are not getting real-time data feeds from financial e-market(s). At times, there may be compatibility problems between the e-broker's system and the data providers' system used by financial e-markets. In such cases, e-brokers must resolve any incompatibility problems that prohibit their systems from accepting data feeds from electronic markets. Technological compatibility problems need to be resolved quickly. E-brokers who are able to act fast in resolving these issues will be more successful in satisfying the needs of their clients.

While it seems that each of the online brokerage firm covered in this comparative case study have addressed the diverse needs of online traders through their innovations, the rules and regulations of the financial market can change very quickly. Challenges in the financial market sector continue to push online brokerage firms to upgrade and refine their systems. The Securities and Exchange Commission can drastically change the rules and regulations as the governing regulatory body of the U.S. financial markets, and the U.S. financial market heavily affects the global financial markets. Different markets around the world also have their own rules and regulations, which are not covered in this chapter. Any changes in the rules and regulations of different countries will have an immediate impact on global financial markets. The financial markets in China, for example, are starting to have extensive impact on global financial markets. So if China decides to make regulatory changes to their financial markets, it can have a substantial impact on other financial markets.

The way different financial electronic markets network themselves can continually alter the way stocks, options, and bonds are being bought and sold (the order process flow). As users of different online trading system advance their trading knowledge and skills, they also demand more information, better user-interface, and more intelligence in the trading system. The only way for online brokerage firms to address these challenges is for them to have a rapid application development plan and change processes that will allow them to constantly add new features or subtract outdated ones in their trading systems and bundled e-services. They must continue to look for ways to make their trading system more intelligent in handing trading rules and regulations, forwarding, and receiving orders from different financial electronic markets, and also in giving traders the analytical tools and interface to help them make better trades. The online brokers that can best address these constant changes will be the ones that will survive in this highly competitive e-service sector.

REFERENCES

Associated Press (2006). SEC approves NYSE, Archipelago Merger. *USA Today.*

Retrieved June 5, 2008, from www.usatoday.com/money/markets/us/2006-02-28-nyse-archipelago-ap_x.htm

Bakos, Y. (1991). A strategic analysis of electronic marketplaces. *MIS Quarterly, 15*(3), 295–310.

Bakos, Y. (1998). The emerging role of electronic marketplaces on the Internet. *Communications of the ACM, 41*(8), 35–42.

Bakos, Y., & Brynjolfsson, E. (2000). Aggregation and disaggregation of information goods: Implications for bundling, site licensing, and micropayment systems. In D. Hurley, B. Kahin, & H. Varian (Ed.), *Proceedings of Internet Publishing and Beyond: The Economics of Digital Information and Intellectual Property*. Cambridge, MA: MIT Press.

Barber, B.M., & Odean, T. (2002). Online investors: Do the slow die first? [Special Issue: Conference on Market Frictions and Behavioral Finance]. *Review of Financial Studies, 15*(2), 455–487.

Barber, B.M., & Odean, T. (2001). The Internet and the investor. *Journal of Economic Perspectives, 15*(1), 41–54.

Battalio, R., Greene. J., Hatch, B., & Jennings, R. (2002). Does the limit order routing decision matter? *Review of Financial Studies, 15*(1), 159–194.

Battalio, R., Greene, J., & Jennings, R. (1997). Do competing specialists and preferencing dealers affect market quality? *Review of Financial Studies, 10*(4), 969–993.

Borrus, A., McNamee, G., Carter, B., & Adrienne, M. (2005, November 24). Invasion of the stock hackers. *Business Week,* p. 38.

Cadway, R.P. (2001). *New daytrading rules.* Retrieved June 5, 2008, from

http://www.princetondaytrading.com/newsletter-princeton/NL-9-31-2001.html

Carey, T.W. (2006, July 3). Tears at Waterhouse. *Barron's,* p. 32.

Ceron, G.F. (2006, August 28). Moving the market: Big board sets expansion in electronic trading: "Hybrid market" to remove volume limits, posing risk for specialists and brokers. *Wall Street Journal,* p. C3.

Ciborra, C. (1993). *Teams, markets and systems.* Cambridge, England: Cambridge University Press.

Craig, S., & Kelly, K. (2001, November 30). Deals & deal makers: Investors can obtain report card on the execution of stock trades. *Wall Street Journal,* p. C12.

Finance and economics: Moving markets; technology and exchanges. (2006, February 4). *The Economist,* p. 73.

Globerman, S., Roehl, T.W., & Standifird, S. (2001). Globalization and electronic commerce: Inferences from retail brokerage. *Journal of International Business Studies, 32*(4), 749–768.

Hansen, J.V., & Hill, N.C. (1989). Control and audit of electronic data interchange. *MIS Quarterly, 13*(4), 403–413.

Island ECN surpasses American Stock Exchange to become largest marketplace in QQQs. (2001, October 22). *Business Wire.*

Kandel, E., & Marx, L.M. (1999). Payments for order flow on Nasdaq. *Journal of Finance, 54*(1), 35–66.

Kim, J.J. (2006, July 11). Online stock trades get even cheaper; Heightened competition among brokerage, banks drives fees as low as $1 per transaction. *Wall Street Journal,* p. D1.

Kim, J.J. (2006, July 19). Trading tools to get a boost. *Wall Street Journal,* p. D2.

Macey, J., & O'Hara, M. (1997). The law and economics of best execution. *Journal of Financial Intermediation, 6,* 188–223.

Malone, T.W., Yates, J., & Benjamin, R.I. (1987). Electronic markets and electronic hierarchies. *Communications of the ACM, 30*, 484–497.

Moregenson, G. (1999, November 23). Regulators see need for rules of the road for online trading firms. *New York Times,* p. C1.

Roberts, Pittman, & Reeds (2000). Retrieved June 5, 2008, from www.realcorporatelawyers.com

Ryan, J. (2005). *NASDAQ to Acquire Instinet.* Retrieved June 5, 2008, from www.nasdaq.com/newsroom/news/pr2005/ne_section05_044.stm

Stoll, H.R. (2006). Electronic trading in stock markets. *Journal of Economic Perspectives, 20*(1), 153–174.

Tabb, L. (2004). Perspective: Time for brokers, investors, and regulators to align. *Wall Street and Technology.* InformationWeek Media Network.

Venkataraman, K. (2001). Automated verses floor trading: An analysis of execution costs on the Paris and New York Exchanges. *Journal of Finance, 56*(4), 1445–1485. New Orleans, LA: Papers and Proceedings of the 61st Annual Meeting of the American Finance Association.

Yap, A., & Lin, X. (2001). Entering the arena of Wall Street wizards, euro-brokers, and cyber-trading samurais: A strategic imperative for online stock trading. *Electronics Market Journal, 11*(3).

RELATED WEBSITES

http://www.buyins.net/

http://www.dogsofthedow.com

http://www.tdameritrade.com

http://www.interactivebrokers.com

Section IV
Cases on E-Government

Chapter XIII
The Case of Roskilde University E–Services

Simon Heilesen
Roskilde University, Denmark

ABSTRACT

Examining electronic services both as products and as organization, this chapter discusses the development and management of e-services at Roskilde University, Denmark. The services in question can be distinguished according to purpose into products meant for administration, communication, education, and integration. The chapter discusses several examples of e-services from the point of view of adoption of technological innovation. Further, it is argued that participatory design and voluntary adoption are factors favourable to, but also challenging to the adoption of e-services. The technical and organizational integration of e-services are also touched upon, as is the importance of maintaining a creative environment for developing the services. The chapter concludes by outlining some challenges to the continued diffusion of e-services in the organization.

INTRODUCTION

This chapter reviews the development of e-services at an institution of higher learning, one that is characterized by a fairly high degree of departmental and individual autonomy. It is argued that participatory design and voluntary adoption are factors that further, but also chal- lenge the adoption of e-services. The technical and organizational integration of e-services are both touched upon; and the importance of hav- ing a creative environment for developing the services is emphasized. Before turning to the case, however, some observations on the use of the term *e-service* will be in order.

BACKGROUND

E-Service, Innovation, and Scope

In this chapter the word "service" is understood in three different meanings as (1) *facility supplying some public demand*, (2) the *process of producing an intangible commodity*, and (3) an *administrative division in an organization*. The case thus discusses the planning, implementation, organizational integration, and wider perspectives of a number of information and communication technologies (ICT) designed for facilitating work processes. These work processes may be distinguished according to purpose into: *administration*, *communication*, *education*, and *integration*.

The prefixed "e" specifies that a service is mediated in a particular way (electronically). The fact that "new media" are involved implicitly suggests that the service represents something new in terms of quality and maybe even in nature. "e"-ing a service means introducing technological innovations. An innovation may either remediate existing practice or enable an entirely new activity. Either way, the innovation—e-service, in the present context—is not guaranteed to "supply a demand" *both* from the point of view of management *and* from that of the employees.

A notable aspect of the Roskilde University case, however, is that by and large adoption of e-services has been voluntary. Thus, in this instance, one may expect a close correlation between the adoption of an e-service and its perceived usefulness. Therefore, the case would seem suitable for considering not just *how*, but also *why* innovations are adopted. To help bring out this aspect, the discussion of the various examples on the following pages will draw on the so-called *perceived attributes of innovations*. These five qualities have been identified as the key characteristics when it comes to explaining the rate of adoption of innovations (Rogers, 2003). Rephrasing Rogers slightly, to be adopted an innovation has to represent a *relative advantage* (be perceived to

be an improvement), has to be *compatible* with the experience, values, and needs of the users, has to decrease rather than increase *complexity*, has to be clearly *visible* (offer "observability," in Roger's terminology) and to be *available* for trying out (afford trialability).

Faculty, students, administrators, government, suppliers, and the general public all are target groups for university e-services. Some of these groups use the same e-services, maybe in different roles. Other services are specific to just one group. In the present context we will focus on intramural e-services, excluding, for example, electronic invoicing and general information Web sites. We will also exclude from our discussion general management tools such as finance and human resource systems that are operated only by specialists in the central university administration, and where the service consists only in automation of routines (e.g., payment of salaries) or easier access to information (e.g. statistics on sick-days, or number of holidays spent).

The Organization

Roskilde University, Denmark, was founded in 1972. It has about 1200 employees (faculty and administrative staff) and a student population of some 10,000 undergraduate, graduate, and postgraduate students distributed over six departments offering a total of 28 programs. In 2006, the total budget for the university amounted to about 78 million euros.

"Try something different" is the slogan used in marketing Roskilde University's academic programmes. What makes it "different" is a special pedagogical approach based on problem oriented project work performed by students working collaboratively in groups. When first introduced, this approach to learning was quite radical, but over the years it has been adopted by other institutions so that at least in Northern Europe it is no longer exceptional. Still, nonconformity looms large in the self-understanding of the Roskilde

University population, one effect of which has been a pronounced wariness of authority. This has been reflected in the corporate culture which right up to the 2005–2006 implementation of the Danish university reforms has favoured local autonomy in many areas, including that of ICT development.

SETTING THE STAGE

Autonomy indeed characterized e-services at Roskilde University in the 1990s. Like most other Danish universities, Roskilde University decisively entered the age of e-services by accepting the *VUE* administrative systems (*Videregående Uddannelsers EDB system*; in English: Higher Education Computing system, consisting of a finance system and an academic administrative system) that were developed under the auspices of the Ministry of Education over a decade starting in 1989. These systems, when eventually they were made to work, were targeted at a very small group of specialist end users in the central university administration. So they remain, with the exception of the academic administrative system to which has been added a self-service for students.

In the various university departments, office tools and several locally developed systems were in use, and the lack of coordination across departments was striking. Most departments ran their own servers and services. Thus, in the mid-1990s, 13 different e-mail systems were in use, and they were in no way coordinated. Therefore, when a student transferred from one department to another (which all students do at least twice) they would have to change e-mail addresses and start getting used to a different system.

This rather intolerable situation stimulated the first initiative to develop campus-wide e-service solutions. In 1996, The Computer Science Department's *IT service* unit set out to develop an e-mail service, and a consultant was hired to manage an e-mail secretariat and establish a help desk. This decision turned out to be crucial for the later development of e-services, partly because it resulted in the construction of the *Roskilde Name Database* (discussed below), upon which all later e-services have been constructed, and partly because it gave the Computer Science IT service a role as a primo inter pares in the patchwork of departmental ICT units.

Being a unit in a department which was again part of the then *Institute VII* (now the Department for Communication, Business, and Information Technologies), the IT-service occupied a humble position in the Roskilde University IT universe, and it had no authority over any of the other IT service units, let alone the departments to which these belonged. Therefore, the new e-mail service was promoted as an offer that others were free to join, if they so desired. This policy of voluntary adoption has been practiced ever since as the Computer Science IT service grew in size, importance, and range of services, and even today most nonstatutory e-services are adopted voluntarily. Hence, not all of them are universal. Large departments and large programs in some cases have their own systems that work well in their particular circumstances, and as long as they are financed and supported locally no one objects.

Demands for E-Services

Except for successes with the e-mail system, dial-in, and ftp (all run by the Computer Science IT service), management of ICT at Roskilde University was unsatisfactory. In 2001, a survey revealed that the human resources allocated to ICT-related tasks were more than double the official appropriation, that computer hardware and software accounted for at least half of all spending on equipment, and that the various local ICT units all had individual strategies that were similar in many ways. In consequence, a task force was formed to define campuswide initiatives meant to be of strategic importance for

Roskilde University as a university of the future. The task force consisted of faculty, students, and administrators. No one from any of the existing ICT services were involved, and thus the formation of the task force can be seen rather as an end user vote of no confidence.

The task force report drew a glum picture of the state of affairs (Wille, Kluth, Christensen, Jørgensen, Frederiksen, Konradsen, et al., 2002). It pointed out how for years ICT development had been left to local initiatives, resulting in a balkanization of technical solutions and total lack of coordination as to platforms and office and administrative systems. Each unit managed its own end user support, and, being insufficiently staffed, had trouble keeping up both with the "width" and the "depth" of the rapidly expanding field of ICT services.

The report recommended that ICT services should be developed within the framework of three portals (one for students, one for employees, and one for external relations) and that service and support should be optimized. The report was diplomatic to the point of being bland on this last issue involving autonomy, and it gave only a very general outline of the portal services. In August 2002, the report was approved in principle by the university management, and a second task force was formed to draw up more concrete plans. At about the same time, the university rector sponsored an interdisciplinary research project aimed at sampling existing practises and outlining some visions for how to define and achieve good practices in the use of ICT in education at Roskilde University (Cheesman, Heilesen, Josephsen, & Kristensen 2002). This project also provided an inspiration for the second task force.

The new task force, consisting of representatives for end users as well as the existing local IT services produced a report listing 27 recommendations for various features to be included in the portal: administrative tools, services related to teaching, general services, and the development of software to connect and integrate the various

systems. Additionally, the report discussed the uses to be made of a learning management system (Jensen, Jensen, Skovgaard, Heilesen, Mac, Fabricius, et al., 2003). The original concept of creating three portals was revised, because the Roskilde University official website was quite able to provide the features required for an information portal, and because technically the employee and student portal would differ not in basic design, but only in "view," that is, in the selection of services included.

The Portal Project

Upon the approval of the second task force report, a project group and a steering committee were formed, and in Spring 2003 the *Portal Project* was launched as a two year project with a funding of about 130,000 euros a year.

The Portal Project consisted of a project group, a steering group, and a reference group. The project group was composed of programmers, consultants, and systems specialists from the Computer Science IT service unit, supplemented with two new temporary positions, and occasionally by some external consultants. The project manager, referred to the head of IT service, and also physically the project was integrated into the IT service unit that was now reinforcing its position as the leading developer and host of campuswide e-services.

The reference group consisted of some 40 members, including heads of studies, secretaries to the study boards, and student representatives. Only four plenum meetings were held, but numerous informal sessions took place between the project group and reference group representatives as well as other end users in order to discuss needs and proposed solutions. Importantly, the Portal Project was an exercise in participatory design, quite in line with the prevailing local Computer Science view of systems design, manifested in the so-called MUST method (Bødker, Kensing, & Simonsen, 2004). Subsequent modifications of and additions to the services developed in the Portal Project also largely have been driven by the expressed needs of the end users. Not surprisingly, participatory design encourages a positive view of the perceived attributes of innovations.

The steering group, chaired by the university finance director, consisted of nine representatives for faculty, academic staff, students, the university library, and the Computer Science IT service. The group met 18 times during the project. These meetings, that actually determined the course of the project were quite informal, turning more or less into a forum where plans and ideas were presented by project team members and discussed in a collegial, constructive, and rather lengthy manner, whereas the supervising and controlling functions were somewhat toned down with no detriment, however, to budget and work plan.

The informality of the project, encouraging creative thinking, together with the quite pronounced sense of mutual obligation among all involved both seem to have contributed to some extent to its success. While the general goal of producing a portal of e-services remained unchanged, the order of priorities was negotiated on a regular basis, allowing for some expedient shifts of focus and the introduction of new tasks.

The Portal Project convincingly demonstrated to the Roskilde University population the advantage of planned and coordinated development of ICT services, and when the project came to an end, a campuswide ICT-committee was formed as an advisory board to the university rector so that the joint planning and supervision of e-services could continue. Members were recruited from faculty, academic staff, students, and the various ICT units. Also subcommittees on e-learning and security were formed drawing on specialists in these particular areas.

At the end of the portal project, the two temporary systems developer positions were made permanent, and the Computer Science IT service emerged as the de facto campuswide IT service provider. In Spring 2006, the university finally created a joint ICT service, *Campus-IT*, by reallocating most of the Computer Science IT service staff to the new organization and extending its responsibilities to include also all IT systems run by the university administration. Campus-IT is now a branch in the central administration, headed by a director. But physically, this new office remains on the premises of the old IT service, living next door to the Computer Science Department. This close physical and professional contact with the teaching and research environment is considered essential by Campus-IT for preserving a creative environment in close contact with the end users.

CASE DESCRIPTION

Turning next to e-services viewed as facilities, we will focus on three types of services: (1) those that support academic activities (teaching and learning), (2) those that serve an administrative purpose, and (3) the *middleware* that is essential for integrating and synchronizing the first two types of services. Below, we will discuss the three categories in reverse order. The communication services need not be considered in this chapter, as e-mail, mailing lists, and ftp are long established and universally accepted, and as later additions such as H.323-protocol based video conferencing and desktop video conferencing have been supplied by the Danish Research Network (Forskningsnettet), so that all the local institution has to do is to set up the software and plug in.

The Alpha and Omega of e-services is, or ought to be, that they should make life easier for the end user, or at least should offer some obvious relative advantage. Ideally, e-services should instill into the users a sense empowerment in terms of being able to carry out tasks and solve problems by themselves. Such disintermediation is a very strong incentive for adopting technological innovations. There is a *technical* aspect to realizing this, in that networks, hardware, software, and support have to be constantly available, updated, and running in a stable manner. There is also an *ergonomic* aspect in that the systems should be user friendly, that is, effective, efficient, and pleasant to work with within a given context. And there is also a *functional* aspect in that all forms of communication and information retrieval have to be directly and easily available independently of time and place.

Below, we will first touch briefly on the technical aspect and secondly deal with the functional aspect, offering some examples of e-services (drawn from the 50 or so e-services currently available at Roskilde University) that illustrate some relevant points in developing and managing e-services. Ergonomics and the detailed analysis of Human Computer Interaction (HCI), however, is outside the scope of this chapter. But, as already noted above, HCI concerns loom large in the development of e-service applications at Roskilde University. All systems development invariably is based on participatory design principles, and all products are tested by end users before being released.

Middleware Matters

Middleware is software that connects applications and systems. It serves as what the Germans call *Unterbau*, that is, the unseen, indispensable foundation on top of which roads, railways, and houses are constructed. The e-services at Roskilde University all draw on middleware in the form of the Roskilde Name Database dating back to the 1990s and two systems added at the time of the Portal Project, *single sign-on* and the *group-role database*. Together these systems facilitate and simplify the creation, integration, and management of e-services. Since they are essential to managing the university e-services, and since they represent some highly original systems design thinking, a short account of them is on order, even if it tends to be a bit on the technical side.

The Roskilde Name Database

As mentioned above, the Roskilde Name Database (RND) was developed in the mid-1990s to solve the specific problem of creating a uniform e-mail service. RND contains registry information on all students, faculty, administrative staff, and registered visitors, providing an unambiguous identification of each individual. A simple concept as such, its importance for the creation of e-services is owed partly to the fact that every individual associated with the university can be identified by searching just one registry database, and partly to the fact that it was implemented so early that all later e-service systems as a matter of course were constructed to draw on it. RND has proven to be an eminently useful basis for developing services requiring authentication, for example, server access, print management, *single sign-on, group-role database,* and all applications authenticating by means of LDAP (Lightweight Directory Access). It has greatly facilitated planned and coordinated development of e-services, and it has made it a relatively uncomplicated matter to integrate new e-services. The RND success is testified to by the considerable interest in the solution that has been shown by other universities developing customizable shared e-services.

Single Sign-On

Unlike RND, the *single sign-on* system is extremely visible to the end users in an unobtrusive way. Log-ins and passwords are the scourges of the information age. Not only having to memorize a variety of log-in names and passwords, but also performing the log-in ritual several times a day at best is a bother and at worst is a barrier to the adoption of e-services. Single sign-on reduces the complexity of using e-services and makes them more readily available.

A cornerstone in the Portal Project was the creation of a single sign-on system (SSO) based on the Yale Central Authentication Service (CAS), an SSO system that in principle works with any application that authenticates by means of LDAP (Petersen, 2004). In nontechnical terms, the user has to log in only *once* in order to access all the university e-services at his or her disposal. As soon as the user enters the Portalino (see below), all relevant services are available in the form of a menu, and no service is more than one click away. Depending on setup, the user can access multiple services in different browser windows at the same time, but there can be only one active SSO-session at a time; that is, the session is terminated if the user starts a new session from a different computer. Single sign-on of course works also outside the Portalino, so that once the user has logged into one particular Roskilde University e-service, all other e-services available to the user can be accessed without having to enter log-in and password.

The one considerable drawback in the single sign-on solution is that if one user leaves the computer with a browser window open, the next user will have unlimited access to the first user's e-services. Permitting only one active session at a time provides only a minimum of security. The solution therefore has been to urge users to close the browser and preferably to log off when leaving the computer. This too is not much of a security measure, even in a friendly academic environment, but as yet no major mishaps have been reported.

Group-Role Database

The group-role database (GRO) tailors university e-services to the individual user in a simple and effective way. Being associated with the university, the individual is a member of a *group* (e.g., University/), and this group can be broken down hierarchically into for example departments, disciplines, and courses (e.g., University/CBIT/ Communication_studies/netmedia/Fall_2008). In most cases, however, individuals belong to

more than one group. For instance, they can be enrolled in two or more courses, or they can be members of a project group within the discipline, or members of a committee within the department or the university. In short, the multiple hierarchies are overlapping, and it is possible to have groups of groups, for example, "all courses in Journalism" or "all study board members at CBIT." The hierarchies in fact do not even have to be in accord with existing organizational hierarchies. GRO will handle any hierarchy that one chooses to define.

Roles define the particular function of a group member. For instance, in a course, students and teachers have different roles. At a department, regular faculty, administrative staff, part-time teachers, and student counselors all perform different tasks and have different needs for services and information.

The combination of groups and roles provides a tool for identifying every individual in every conceivable context of university life. The granularity is entirely flexible, ranging from "all students," "all faculty" to "student in a particular class," "supervisor of a particular project." Thus it is possible in a learning management system to assign students and teachers to a course and provide them with a suite of tools corresponding exactly to their needs. Or it is possible in the Portalino (see below) to create a view of the e-services available to any student with a particular combination of major and minor subjects, or create a view of all the e-services available to a particular CBIT faculty member; no more, no less.

Tying Things Together

Easy, direct, and immediate access to e-services to some extent conditions adoption. If the services are either perceived as being difficult to find or complex to handle, users are less likely to make use of them. Single sign-on is a big step in the right direction. Other important factors include physical access, that is, the hardware and the way the e-services are presented to the user.

Plug'n Study and Print.ruc.dk

Mobility is a key characteristic of modern university life. Laptops more or less have replaced desktop computers as students and teachers carry their "electronic office" with them at home, in the classroom, in the lab, in the library, in the cafeteria, in the teacher's office, and indeed everywhere. To meet the requirements of these new work patterns, it is necessary to provide easy access to the computer networks and hence to the university e-services at just about every location on campus where teachers and students are likely to work. The *Plug'n Study* service provides wireless access to the Portalino in every single building on campus for everyone with a Roskilde University log-in. Setting up the laptop requires only a few clicks in the PC *Networks* menu, and connection is established by opening a browser and typing log-in and password. Plug'n Study has been an unqualified success, the number of unique users per months increasing over the first three years from 1300 to over 3000 in 2006.

Eduroam (http://www.eduroam.org/) which provides users network access at any member institution by means of the log-in and password of their home institution has been implemented in most classrooms primarily as a service to visitors. But it has not been generally implemented, because its setup is rather more complicated than Plug'n Study (it requires a client application). Hence, it would not only create an unnecessary barrier to accessing local e-services, but also most likely require user support on a scale which cannot be met at present.

Ubiquitous network access naturally creates a demand for printer access at the location where the user happens to work. Printers, however, are mostly locally owned, and (as yet) no campuswide hardware standards whatsoever have been imposed. *Print.ruc.dk* has been developed to handle extreme technological diversity. To use the service, the user has to define a virtual printer once and for all, order the print job, and then access his or her personal print.ruc.dk page in order to select a physical printer (Randrup, 2005). Technically, it is an elegant solution: The document is sent as postscript to a server where it is distilled into pdf format and added to a database. By choosing a printer, the user directs the pdf file and an appropriate printer driver to a print server where it is converted into the proper printer specific postscript format and where the user's printer account is updated in accordance with local charges (Mikkelsen & Petersen, 2006).

The Portalino

The presentation of e-services to the end users is handled by the Portalino. It offers a one-click access to an individualized list of available e-services, making them visible and easy to access. The diminutive, "Portalino," was chosen so as to indicate that technically speaking the product is not a proper portal. The average user would be hard put to tell the difference, but one unexpected advantage of this rather purist approach to terminology is that *Portalino* has become a brand name for the Roskilde University e-services.

A proper Web portal provides single point access to information that is linked from various data collections on the Internet. Omnibus portals were the craze of the late 1990s when large corporations vied with one another in providing a single point access to the entire World Wide Web. More useful and of more lasting importance, however, are specialized portals bringing together all relevant information on, for example, health services, municipal services, or in our case, services provided by an organization. The "big leap" in the development of Roskilde University e-services, the Portal Project was so named because initially all attention was on the development of a set of portals. As the project evolved, however, it became obvious that content and not framework was decisive, and that one simple and flexible portal-like interface would be quite adequate.

Strictly speaking, the Portalino e-services interface is just a customized collection of links, most of them links to internal Web sites, applications, and databases. In its original form the Portalino was a Web directory rather than an intranet, but some intranet functionality has been added later by means of links to virtual spaces for each department, created in the *eCampus* learning management system (introduced below).

In the Portalino, each user has his or her personalized view of the university e-services as well as various additional information, customized according to the group-role database information about affiliation. To be more specific, the user has access to some *general* information and services (e.g., university directory, newsletter, university library services, e-mail, two learning management systems, Campus-IT technical services, e-election, train schedule, this week's menu at the cafeteria, and more), some information and services tailored to the user's *status* (e.g., courses and course application form, exam registration, student guidance, the student grants office, student card renewal, etc., for the students, staff training, annual work reporting, vacation spent, absence due to illness, business card service, and so on for faculty and administrative staff), and some information and services customized to the user's *place of work* (e.g., intranet for a department). In addition to the automatically assigned and permanent "Roskilde University links" the user is free to create as many bookmarks as he or she desires to any kind of useful information and service inside or outside the university, thus making the Portalino a rather attractive option as browser home page.

Transforming Administrative Tasks

Systems development has journeyed from automation of routines in the 1960s to the information ecologies of today. Characteristic of the early period was the industrialization of isolated work routines by means of a fairly straightforward "translation," or remediation, from conventional forms into the computer medium. It gave rise to apprehension and aversion then, just as it will now if the introduction of ICT neither seems to offer a relative advantage to the user nor is compatible to his or her work practice. The first two examples below are slightly unfortunate illustrations of that. Developing e-services that transform existing practices for the sake of efficiency still is an act of balance where disintermediation in itself is no guarantee for acceptance. Success depends on proving that there is some added value in doing things in a different way. This could consist in the perceived empowerment of the individual user, or in reducing the workload considerably, or in the seamless integration of one or more e-services into the organization. This is illustrated by the second and third set of examples below.

Course Catalogue System and Course Application System

Traditionally, each academic programme at Roskilde University has published its own course catalogue, making it quite difficult for present and prospective students to get an overview of the full range of courses offered. Several different media are in use: some departments publish in print and supplement with Web pages, pdf files, or proprietary IT solutions; others have completed the leap into electronic publishing. The joint course catalogue offers all academic programmes a user friendly option to enter course data in a standardized format and to have it made easily available electronically to students, faculty, and administrative staff. The course catalogue system also automatically creates a course workspace in the eCampus learning management system and, drawing on the group role database, assigns teachers and students to the course.

Quite a lot of effort has gone into developing a system able to accommodate the many and varied needs of all the different programmes. Yet, so far the course catalogue has not been an unqualified success, at least from the point of view of faculty and administrative staff. Some large academic programmes have developed their own systems for generating a course catalogue and see no point in giving them up and introducing new administrative routines just for the sake of having a joint catalogue. Others complain that contributing to the catalogue is complicated and in some cases a double burden. The synchronization with eCampus, which does indeed offer a notable advantage by facilitating net based course administration, is not universally appreciated, because this particular learning management system is not yet widely used.

As yet the course application system does not synchronize with the course catalogue system. But when it eventually will, academic staff will have a powerful tool for administrating all courses, and adoption of the two systems will probably spread. At the time of writing, however, the application system is merely a means for entering data that will later have to be processed by an administrator using a different view of the system. It should also be noted that the technical and administrative problems involved in developing this system have been considerable, because of the complexity and heterogeneity of Roskilde University course administration. A student signing up for a semester's teaching is in fact applying for a package of courses that has to be correlated with several contextual factors, such as study program, level of study, number of applicants, and prioritization. The system, to be at all compatible to user needs, therefore has been made highly customizable in that within an application shell each programme administrator is able to tailor the system to local needs by means of a configuration file.

Student Card Renewal, Registering for Exams, and E-Election

Renewing the student card and registering for exams are e-services for students. Electronic election is a service for both students and employees. In all three cases, automating the processes, going from paper forms to electronic format saves a considerable amount of administrative resources and makes life easier for the users. All students are required to renew their student card once a year, most students register for exams twice a year, and elections to study boards, the academic council, the board of directors, the safety committee, etc. are held annually or every few years. The e-election in particular is a resource saver because the entire electoral register for a particular election can by drawn directly from the RND database whereas earlier it had to be checked manually.

Students (and faculty) clearly prefer filling in electronic forms to fetching paper forms, filling them in by hand, and returning them to a particular location during office hours. Thus, at present more than 80% of the students choose to renew their student card electronically, and the adoption of electronic exam registration is practically universal.

All three services are provided with a *forced application*, meaning that a reminder is shown at log-in when it is time to register or vote. Once the user has registered or voted, the reminder window is deactivated, but it is also possible to deselect it manually. Forced application is used conservatively, four or five times a year, so as not to annoy the users. But it does have a considerable effect. In the first electronic elections in the Fall of 2006 the election turnout for two elections were 25% and 20% respectively, up from an average of 9–10% in conventional on-campus elections (Preisler, 2006).

Business Card System

Little things sometimes appear more immediately appealing to end users than do large and intricate systems. The business card service may be insignificant in the administrative whole, but it is a neat example of empowerment and disintermediation. The e-service simply adds user information drawn from the RND database to a business card template and forwards a file to the Roskilde University printing office which returns a neatly packaged set of printed business cards to the user by Internal mail. It is a 24-hour service that replaces numerous, laborious, and often less than professional local practices involving a secretary, photocopies on special paper, ruler, pencil, and a pair of scissors. The user interface is simplicity itself: One only has to choose language and decide whether or not to include an image.

The relative advantage, compatibility, and simplicity are so obvious that users adopt the service without hesitation, once they learn about it. And this is what makes a service of this kind more important than it logically appears. Being accessible in a customized version only through the Portalino, most faculty members eventually are brought into contact with the Portalino even if they are not particularly interested in or relatively ignorant about the existence of the Portalino. Once there, they are able to see the full lists of e-services available, and this just might persuade them to start using the Portalino and explore more of the e-services listed.

Managing Learning

Roskilde University has been using various learning management systems since the mid-1990s. Up until the start of the Portal Project, they were used mainly in Open University blended learning settings and in a few regular programmes, Computer Science in particular. One of the aims of the Portal Project was to introduce a single learning management system (BSCW, Basic Support for Cooperative Work) across all Roskilde University departments and programmes. BSCW was then already in use at Roskilde University. It was known to support project work well, it scaled well, and it was free of charge for academic use. A simple bottom-up strategy was devised in that initially all first year and second year students were given an introductory course to the system, followed in subsequent years by introductions to BSCW in short courses for first year students and by the distribution of folders. The idea was to spread usage gradually throughout Roskilde University as the students would move on from their two years of basic studies and into the various specialized programmes. An implicit assumption was that the teachers gradually would follow suit in order to keep up with their students who would be using the learning management system to support their project work. Faculty members, therefore, were not offered formal training in the use of BSCW, nor was it strongly advertised as an e-service worth considering. On hindsight, providing some good examples of uses (i.e., providing observability) may well have made a difference.

In terms of total use, the campuswide introduction of BSCW has been a remarkable success. A little less than four years after the implementation of the strategy (January 2007) there were 10,407 unique users (slightly more than the present total university population), 82% of whom had carried out more than 100 transactions (clicks) in the system. Half of all unique users had carried out more than 1000 transactions and can be said to be regular users. The only problem is that while the students have adopted the system wholeheartedly, their teachers have not. Usage among faculty members remains very low, and consequently BSCW is not much used in courses and in communication between students and their project supervisors.

Except for the obvious fact that the strategy of letting the students persuade their teachers has failed, it would seem that BSCW did not answer the needs of the teachers. BSCW (http://www.

bscw.de) is eminently suited for cooperative and collaborative project work, but it is not really a course management system, and experiences with using it for teaching are mixed (Sikkel, Gommer, & Veen, 2001). The interface metaphor is that of a simple file archive, and all structuring of virtual space into a course interface has to be done manually. At the time it was believed that this obstacle could be overcome, because it is not that difficult to define a few course folders and upload material to them. But the system obviously proved too complex and too incompatible with existing teaching routines to catch on, and already in the later stages of the Portal Project it became clear, that BSCW would have to be supplemented if faculty were eventually to adopt a learning management system.

As a supplementary system and potential replacement for BSCW was chosen the Sakai system (http://sakaiproject.org), which is being developed by nearly a hundred partner universities all over the world. Sakai, that at Roskilde University has been introduced as *eCampus*, is an Open Source system, providing pretty much the same functionality as most standard learning management systems. However, the source code being freely available it can easily be extended, tailored to local needs, and integrated with other systems, as is the case with the course catalogue system. eCampus targets faculty, providing an easy to use framework for managing courses. However, it still has to make a breakthrough, and its existence, like that of BSCW, probably has to be advertised more insistently. Recent figures (January 2007) show a total of 1546 unique users and, on the average, a very moderate use.

CURRENT CHALLENGES FACING THE ORGANIZATION

The history of the development and management of e-services at Roskilde University may not read like a text book example of strategic planning.

Yet the road followed has not been significantly more tortuous than that of many other institutions of higher education. Quite often in the academic world the response to the challenges of ICT happens to be reactive rather than proactive. In a few respects, however, e-services management at Roskilde University has been rather exemplary. As has been argued in the preceding sections, four factors have contributed to a successful development of the university's e-services:

An all-inclusive foundation. The Roskilde Name Database, and later the group-role database, have served as bases upon which e-services could be constructed and integrated rather like Lego bricks. The simplicity and effectiveness of these systems and the philosophy of considering the university to be a single unit clearly have encouraged and facilitated the joint development of e-services.

Voluntariness. A consequence of the pronounced autonomy that has characterized Roskilde University management right up to the 2006 reform has been that, barring statutory requirements, the adoption of e-services has been optional. Each department has had the chance to observe and to try inventions, and adoption consequently has been based on a genuine sense of compatibility and relative advantage. Voluntariness, however, is Janus-faced, as we shall discuss below.

Participatory design. User involvement has been the red thread in the development of e-services at Roskilde University. In the actual detailed design of systems, user needs and requirements have been uncovered in interviews and meetings. In the broad outline, end user participation has been ensured by committees and steering groups where end user representatives have exerted considerable influence on the selection and prioritization of projects to be undertaken.

Proximity to the academic environment. It is conventional wisdom that everyone loves to hate the IT office. Often there is a real or perceived gap in worldview as well as actual contact between the programmers and systems developers who tend to think in terms of rational technical solutions and end users whose needs may not be met immediately, who are wary of regimentation, and who will blame anything that goes wrong on the IT office. Even if discontent with the IT services offered grew quite pronounced in the late1990s and sometimes still runs high locally, IT support and development at Roskilde University has never been isolated from the academic environment. In fact, it is particularly strong in the IT unit that has emerged as the fittest and eventually has been transformed into the joint Campus-IT office. It is likely that a factor contributing to its success has been the very close ties with the research and teaching environment of the Computer Science Department.

Even if the e-services that have evolved are well-functioning and contribute to the smooth running of the university, a couple of major challenges remain. As already suggested, the entirely voluntary adoption of services is one of them; the diffusion of educational e-services is another.

Over the last few years, Danish universities have been turned into independent institutions run by managers appointed by a board of directors. They are not yet actual companies, but financial considerations loom ever larger. Just as few companies are likely to succeed with each division running its own ICT solutions and using joint services arbitrarily, so the entirely voluntary adoption of e-services is becoming untenable. The original strategy of persuasion has had some positive effects in that the e-services offered and eventually adopted have had to prove specifically to represent an advantage. A major drawback is that uncontrolled diversity is wasteful. Therefore, a "stick and carrot" strategy has been adopted in that joint services are funded and supported by the university community whereas proprietary e-services will have to be supported by the individual department or programme. Indeed, there is little new in this, but the effect is becoming more pronounced in a university setting with tight

budgets and ever stricter control over spending. Holding on to a proprietary e-service solution now has to be justified by special needs, and not by habit, convenience, or local ambitions.

The combination of voluntary adoption and a too liberal approach to user driven innovation also involve risks that can be summed up by the cynical saying "give people what they want, and they will never realize what they are missing." The early diffusion of new technology is always dependent on a few innovators (Rogers, 2003), who in a university setting may be identified as the technical experts or the odd fiery soul. Most ordinary users are likely to follow suit over a period of time, depending on their needs. But they cannot be expected to envisage how present and future opportunities and demands can be met by existing or emerging technologies. The practise at Roskilde University of using committees and project steering groups as communication channels between end users and the technologists has worked quite well in uncovering and evaluating potential uses of ICT for services. And the consistent use of participatory design in systems development has been essential for creating compatible and observable solutions. However, in the wake of the university reform that has centralized management considerably and that favours a businesslike approach, holding on to the established ways of evaluating technological potential has become more of a challenge.

The second major challenge is the diffusion of educational e-services that until now have been rather successful as far as the students are concerned, and less so in the case of faculty. For years, there has been general talk about the competitive edge provided by good educational e-services that may attract students and funding. Quite recently it has also become a matter of institutional credibility and long-term survival, as the government has launched a national strategy for e-learning, explicitly demanding more use and better use of ICT in higher education (Vidensk-absministeriet, 2007). Strategies for facilitating adoption of e-learning are being developed at Roskilde University, but at the time of writing have yet to be implemented (Heilesen, Jónsson, & Randrup, 2007). They draw on the experience that little is gained by introducing new systems, sending everybody on courses, and then waiting for things to change. What is required is partly a change of attitude in the conception of ICT-supported teaching both among managers and faculty, and partly a more general recognition of the significance of teaching, an activity that strangely has never been held in the highest esteem in Danish university life (Heilesen & Jensen, 2006). Managing a more successful dissemination of the educational e-services may well require some kind of administrative unit parallel to Campus-IT and more focused on purely academic purposes.

Both challenges discussed above involve the concept of compatibility, that is, consistency with existing experience, values, and needs. What we have to address is not only *that* barriers exist, but also *how* they can be overcome. The "how" can be approached from a managerial point of view by means of regulations, requirements, and training, or it can be approached from the point of view of the individual. The latter may well prove to be the more effective, even if it is an educational process taking place over time.

Enlarging on the concept of compatibility by viewing it from the point of view of *sense making* (Dervin, Foreman-Wernet, & Lauterbach, 2003), we may explain *incompatibility* in terms of *breakdown situations* characterized by frustration and even rejection. Breakdown situations are caused by *gaps* in understanding that occur when there is a discrepancy between a given situation and the acquired competencies and worldview (cultural codes, ethics, and norms) of the individual. Gaps can be bridged by developing strategies for dealing with the unfamiliar, in uses of new technology. When successfully handled, the user will eventually appropriate the technology (or e-service) and even develop the skills to modify it to his or her particular needs. In other words,

compatibility is by no means invariable, but it is unlikely to be changed successfully by force. The challenge, as suggested above, is to stimulate the development over time of skills, experiences, practices, and indeed a "corporate culture" that will make the individual feel comfortable with the technological innovations.

To sum up, the "build it, and they will come" strategy practiced widely so far works very well up to the point of seriously affecting the user's basic understanding of how to plan and carry out his or her work. To go one step further, supplementary strategies have to be devised. They will entail organizational adjustments that will favour the adoption of new technologies and services, as well as encouragement and recognition of those who appropriate them, and also showcasing and promoting exemplary usages.

ACKNOWLEDGMENT

A warm note of thanks to Torben Bruun, Tom Helmer Hansen, Gissur Jónsson, Kim Mikkelsen, Mads Freek Petersen, and Birthe Randrup for providing information on the e-service systems and for commenting on drafts of this manuscript.

REFERENCES

Bødker, K., Kensing, F., & Simonsen, J. (2004). *Participatory IT design: Designing for business and workplace realities.* Cambridge, MA: MIT Press.

Cheesman, R., Heilesen, S.B., Josephsen, J., & Kristensen, A.K. (2002). Scenarier i computermedieret og netbaseret undervisning. *Centre for Netbased Collaboration and Learning Occasional Papers, 1*(1). Retrieved June 5, 2008, from http://rudar.ruc.dk/handle/1800/151

Dervin, B., Foreman-Wernet, L., & Lauterbach, E. (2003). *Sense-making methodology reader: selected writings of Brenda Dervin*. Cresskill, NJ: Hampton Press.

Heilesen, S.B., & Jensen, S.S. (2006). Making sense of technologically enhanced learning in context: A research agenda. In E. Korsgaard Sorensen & D.Ó. Murchú (Eds.), *Enhancing learning through technology* (pp. 269–291). Information Science Publishing.

Heilesen, S.B., Jónsson, G., & Randrup, B. (2007). *IKT-kompetenceudvikling inden for undervisning og formidling på RUC*. Roskilde: Roskilde Universitetscenter. Retrieved June 5, 2008, from http://rudar.ruc.dk/handle/1800/2691

Jensen, B.V., Jensen, I.R., Skovgaard, O., Heilesen, S., Mac, A., Fabricius, A., et al. (2003). *Studenterportalen på RUC* (unpublished report). Roskilde: Roskilde University.

Mikkelsen, K., & Petersen, M.F. (2006, October 9–12). *Ten thousand printers can't be wrong: One driver fits all*. Paper presented at the Educause Conference, Dallas, TX. Retrieved June 5, 2008, from www.educause.edu/ir/library/powerpoint/EDU06295A.pps

Petersen, M.F. (2004). *Roskilde University CAS mods: ZESLA (zero effort sso for ldap apps)*. Retrieved June 5, 2008, from http://tp.its.yale.edu/pipermail/cas/2004-May/000462.html

Preisler, H. (2006). *Succes med e-valg på RUC*. Retrieved June 5, 2008, from http://ruc.dk/ruc/omruc/nyheder/30112006b/

Randrup, B. (2006). *How to set up your own virtual printer*. Retrieved June 5, 2008, from http://www.mail.ruc.dk/pdf/winxp.htm

Rogers, E.M. (2003). *Diffusion of innovations* (5th ed.). Free Press.

Sikkel, K., Gommer, L., & Veen, J.v.d. (2001). A cross-case comparison of BSCW in different educational settings. In P. Dillenbourg, A. Eurelings, & K. Hakkarainen (Eds.), *First European Conference on Computer-Supported Collaborative Learning* (pp. 553560). Maastricht. Retrieved June 5, 2008, from www.home.cs.utwente.nl/~sikkel/papers/ps/e-cscl-01.pdf

Videnskabsministeriet (2007). *National strategi for IKT-støttet læring. Indsats for at fremme anvendelsen af IKT-støttet læring*. København: Videnskabsministeriet. Retrieved June 5, 2008, from http://itst.dk/static/National_strategi_for_IKT-stoettet_laering/index.htm

Wille, N.E., Kluth, M., Christensen, T., Jørgensen, A., Frederiksen, L.B., Konradsen, L., et al. (2002). *Afrapportering fra IT-taskforce* (internal memorandum, unpublished). Roskilde: Roskilde Universitetscenter.

FURTHER READING

Bødker, K., Kensing, F., & Simonsen, J. (2004). *Participatory IT design: Designing for business and workplace realities*. Cambridge, MA: MIT Press.

OECD. (2005). *E-learning in tertiary education: Where do we stand?* Paris: OECD Publications.

Randrup, B. (2006). *IT systems at RU*. Roskilde: Campus-IT, Roskilde University. Retrieved June 5, 2008, from https://www.mail.ruc.dk/pdf/IT-systemer_UK.pdf

Rogers, E.M. (2003). *Diffusion of innovations* (5th ed.). Free Press.

Chapter XIV
E–Services in Danish Research Libraries:
Issues and Challenges at Roskilde University Library

Ada Scupola
Roskilde University, Denmark

ABSTRACT

This chapter reports the findings of a case study of e-services adoption at research libraries. The case under consideration is Roskilde University Library (RUB), a research library supporting learning activities at Roskilde University. The research focuses on the main issues that RUB had to deal with in the process of adopting e-services and the future challenges that e-services provide for RUB. The chapter also presents the consequences of e-services adoption for Roskilde University library's organization, its business model and the relationships with customers, publishers (providers of knowledge), and other research libraries in Denmark. The main results can be summarized as follows: (1) adoption of e-services has forced RUB to innovate rapidly. Innovation is driven, among other factors, by ICT developments (technology push), but innovation is also user-driven and pervasive throughout the organization; (2) e-services have changed RUB's organizational structure and division of labour by moving more and more towards IT-based jobs and competences; (3) e-services have changed the relationships between users and publishers; (4) e-services have changed and continue to change the business model of the library; and (5) RUB is becoming a combination of a virtual and a physical library, moving more and more towards a virtual library with electronic resources and online communities, but still keeping the traditional function of a "knowledge space."

E-SERVICES AND THEIR CHARACTERISTICS

The networked ICT technologies (such as the Internet) are having a dramatic effect on how services and especially knowledge services are innovated, designed, produced, and distributed. In addition, ICT networks such as the Internet have created the basis for the development of new types of services. These networks may also change the way customers or users experience service functions.

E-services are defined here as services that are produced, provided, and/or consumed through the use of ICT networks such as Internet-based systems and mobile solutions. E-services can be used by both consumers and businesses, and can be accessed via a wide range of information appliances (Hoffman, 2003, p. 53). E-services also include the selling of physical goods on the Internet as for instance an airline ticket that is purchased online, but delivered by surface mail to the buyers or government services offered on the Internet or e-government. There are three main characteristics of e-services:

- The service is accessible across the Internet or other electronic networks
- The service is consumed by a person across the Internet or other electronic networks
- There might be a fee that the consumer pays the provider for using the e-service, but that might not always be the case as for example in some e-services offered by the government

Normally the production, provision, or consumption of a service requires the interaction between the service provider and the user of the service. Traditionally, this has been based on personal interactions, most often face-to-face interactions. In e-services, the production, consumption, and/or provision of services takes place through the intermediation of an ICT network such as Internet-based systems or mobile solutions. Examples of e-services are e-banking, e-library services, e-publishing, airline tickets, e-government, information, and location services. However, e-services also include, for example, the online selling of real estate property or the purchasing of physical goods that are then delivered by other means. The advent of e-commerce and e-services has raised a number of challenges for knowledge intensive service organizations such as consulting companies, libraries, and publishers as well as for companies selling physical goods. For example, companies have to innovate, have to develop strategies and new business models for the production and provision of e-services, and acquire or develop new competences.

The purpose of this study is to investigate the challenges that e-services are posing and will pose for research or academic libraries. The research library is chosen here because it is a particular type of knowledge intensive service organization: it has the role of acquiring and providing research and learning related knowledge as well as storing and preserving such knowledge. More specifically, the study shows how the advent of e-services has revolutionized the whole concept of the library and forced the libraries to innovate at an extremely fast rate. In fact libraries have been using information and communication technologies (ICTs) for more than 20 years, but while the first wave of ICTs and technological change had resulted in automation with consequent rationalization and decreased costs, the advent of e-services is moving the library from automation to digitalization, causing a shift of paradigm in libraries. The study has focused on the issues that RUB has had to deal with as a result of e-services adoption as well as the future challenges that e-services provide for RUB. In addition, the investigation has also focused on the consequences of e-services for Roskilde University Library's organization, its business model, and relationships with customers, publishers (providers of information), and other research libraries in Denmark.

The case is based on a number of interviews with RUB management, other secondary material provided by Roskilde University Library and information provided on the Web page.

THE ROLE AND CONCEPT OF ACADEMIC LIBRARIES

In order to understand how digitalization and e-services are changing the library and its activities, it is important to understand what a library is, and what its major roles in learning are. Libraries have historically had a central role in learning, since the first library was created 2,000 years ago in Alexandria. Libraries can be defined as "an organized set of resources, which includes human services as well as the entire spectrum of media (e.g., text, video, hypermedia). Libraries have physical components, such as space, equipment, and storage media; intellectual components such as collection policies that determine what materials will be included and organizational schemes that determine how the collection is accessed; and people, who manage the physical and intellectual components and interact with users to solve information problems" (Marchionini & Maurer, 1995, p. 68). Marchionini and Maurer (1995) distinguish three major roles that academic and research libraries serve in learning. The first role is sharing expensive resources. These resources are physical resources such as books, periodicals, media, and human resources such as the librarians that provide a number of responsive and proactive services. Responsive services include maintaining reserve materials, answering reference questions, providing bibliographic instructions, developing media packages, teaching users how to use the material. Proactive services include selectively disseminating information to the faculty and students, collaborating with instructors to plan teaching. The second role that libraries serve is a cultural role in preserving and organizing artifacts and ideas. Libraries have historically had the role

of preserving material to make it accessible to future learners in addition to ensuring access to materials through indexes, catalogues, and other aids that allow users to find what they need. The third role of the library is that of serving as a physical knowledge space, where people meet to study and read and often to exchange ideas.

DANISH LIBRARY LANDSCAPE

The Danish Library Concept

The Danish library system is based on the concept of the citizen's fundamental right to knowledge and information. Basically the library service is free of charge, but libraries can demand payment for special services (Danish National Library Authority, www.bs.dk/publikationer/english/statistics/). The Danish library system is characterized by extensive and well-functioning cooperation, both within the individual library sector and between the different library types. In Denmark there is an agency that is responsible for all matters that are related to libraries: The Danish National Library Authority. The Danish National Library Authority is an agency under the Ministry of Culture. The Authority is responsible for advising the government on the organization, coordination, and strategy for the Danish Library Service and gives professional advice to ministers and public authorities, as well as local authorities, libraries, and information services. In addition, the Authority has an active role in international collaboration within the field of libraries, documentation, and information. The major duties of the Authority consist of the administration of the Act regarding library services and a number of statutory government grants for library purposes. The Authority is also responsible for collecting and providing statistical information about Danish libraries. The Authority furthermore acts as the administrative base (secretariat) for Denmark's Electronic Research Library. This is a major initiative for the development of e-services in Denmark and the libraries digitalization process.

There are two types of libraries in Denmark: public libraries and research libraries. The purpose of public libraries is to promote information, education, and cultural activity by placing books and other media at the disposal of the public. Libraries therefore offer books, serials, talking books, recorded music, and electronic information resources (including the Internet) to the citizens. All the public libraries are connected to the Internet. In 2004 there were 224 main public libraries, 428 branch libraries, and 44 mobile libraries.

Danish research libraries are government institutions and serve mainly higher education and research, but most of them are also open to the public at large. In Denmark there are 20 major research libraries connected to universities and other institutions of higher-level education. There are also a large number of smaller research libraries that are connected to educational institutions. The Royal Library located in Copenhagen and the State and University Library in the city of Århus have specific national library functions. The Royal Library functions both as Denmark's national library—including being a legal deposit library—and as the library of the University of Copenhagen. The State and University Library in Århus is similarly a legal deposit library. It houses the national media collection and has the overall responsibility for the Danish Central Library for Immigrant Literature and the Danish Repository Library for Public Libraries. The library acts as the national superstructure for the public libraries. Appendix 1 provides detailed data about Danish research library statistics such as number of staff, stock, expenditures, salaries, interlibrary loans, and so forth (http://www.bs.dk/publikationer/english/statistics/2004/index.htm).

The Important Role of DEFF in the Digitalization of the Danish Research Library System

In the 1990s, the Danish government had made a policy plan focusing on the "IT society" or "IT for all." This vision of IT for all included the digitalization of the libraries to provide all the citizens with access to electronic resources. As a result the Ministry of Culture, the Ministry of Education and the Ministry of Science established an IT working group in May 1996 with the objective of investigating how to transform a number of research libraries into electronic research libraries. This idea laid the foundation for the establishment of the "Denmark's Electronic Research Library," via a network of cooperating electronic research libraries (http://www.bs.dk). In 1997, the "DEF report" was published with a view to creating a basis for a joint effort for the research libraries' IT development. The report described a model of reference for Denmark's Electronic Research Library (DEF), including the essential electronic functions and services to be delivered by such libraries. Consequently, a budget was allocated by the three ministers involved, a board of directors (steering committee) was appointed, and a vision and a strategy for the project were developed. In 2003, DEF became a permanent activity with the objective of improving the use of IT in supporting research and education. This is done through six programme areas:

- E-learning
- E-publishing
- Licenses
- Portals
- System architecture
- User facilities

Today, Denmark's Electronic Research Library (DEFF) is an organizational and technological partnership between research libraries cofinanced by the Ministry of Science, Technology and Innovation, the Ministry of Culture and the Ministry of Education and based at The Danish National Library Authority. Its purpose is to advance the development of a network of electronic research libraries that make available their electronic and other information resources in a coherent and simple way. This is obtained partly through government funding and partly by joint purchase of licenses (www.deff.dk). According to DEFF's Web page, the strategy of DEFF is "to improve the end user's access to information through cooperation between the Danish special and research libraries. The cooperation includes joint development in cases where cooperation will result in a greater advantage than the sum of local initiatives, including a better and total utilization of the libraries' resources; further development of the joint network of information resources; collective dissemination of the research libraries' information resources to the public" (www.deff.dk).

ORGANIZATION BACKGROUND: ROSKILDE UNIVERSITY LIBRARY

Roskilde University Library (RUB) is a research library serving the students and staff at Roskilde University. Roskilde University is a smaller university located in Roskilde, a city about 35 km from Copenhagen, the capital City of Denmark. The university counts circa 10,000 students. According to Roskilde University Statute (www.ruc.dk/library), Roskilde University Library has the following purposes:

1. To give teachers and students at Roskilde University access to information and materials containing information necessary for research and teaching, as well as to ensure information on and access to the university teachers' and students' research.
2. As a public research library to make available its collection to external users, among which

are regional research and teaching institutions, business, and citizens.
3. To participate in the national and international library collaboration.
4. To conduct research and development within the library subjects and functions, but also the surrounding community and businesses as well as anybody who would like to use the library being this a public library.

Today the library counts approximately 45 employees, and the number of employees has decreased due to the digitalization process and e-services adoption. The following table summarizes some basic information about the library.

The library counts today a number of paper books, paper journals, the entire spectrum of media as for example videos, and a number of e-journals and e-books. The library still acquires 8,000–9,000 books in paper format per year. The cataloguing of these books and paper journals is still done by people employed at the library. However they expect this number to go down, while the number of e-books goes up, especially as the quality of e-books improves. In addition, RUB counts today circa 18,000 e-journals, while the number of paper journals has gone down from circa 5,000 to 2,000. The purchase of the e-journals is based on the gateway model (Scupola, 2002). This model implies that the library buys the license to the e-journals that are stored in a central repository located at the publishing house. Information and communication technologies (ICTs) have made their way into library systems over more

Table 1. Roskilde University Library employees divided by position

Function/Position	Number of Employees
Research Librarian	9.6
Librarian	12.9
Office Functions	14.5
IT	6.5
Other	1.5

than 20 years, and today, in Denmark, libraries are the heaviest users of ICTs among the public sector institutions. At the beginning of the library digitalization process, ICTs contributed to a transformation from a card catalogue to an electronic catalogue. The advent of the World Wide Web roughly 10 years ago has completely revolutionized the way RUB operates and has made possible a number of e-services and self-services. The adoption and implementation of e-services and self-services has resulted in a number of organizational changes, changes in the organizational structure, the competencies of the librarians and relationships between the library and the publishers and the library and the users. In addition, the business model is also changing as RUB is trying to sell the services to private businesses. RUB is moving towards a combination of a physical and virtual library, as many services are getting transformed into e-services and self-services. The advent of e-commerce has raised the question of disintermediation of some actors of the value chain (e.g., Scupola, 2002; Sarkar, Butler, & Steinfield, 1995). Accordingly some speculations have been made about the disintermediation of the research library. However RUB's management believes that the library will still exist due to the value that it adds to the electronic resources provided by the publishers, the need to collect and store the knowledge produced on campus by teachers and students, and the need for a knowledge space where students meet with friends and go to study. Therefore Internet and e-services might change many aspects of the library and its relationships with users and publishers. However, RUB might preserve its historical role of knowledge space, even though after the implementation of library's online communities, such knowledge space can also become a virtual knowledge space.

E-Services Adoption at RUB

Over the last few years RUB has adopted a number of e-services and self-services that are changing many aspects of the way the library operates. Many of the services provided by RUB have been transformed into e-services after the advent of the World Wide Web. The main e-services offered at RUB are as follows:

1. Access to electronic journals
2. Access to electronic books
3. Digital repository of all the students projects
4. Chat with a librarian

Examples of self-services include:

1. Rucforsk: a self-service system for the online registration of research and other activities of the teachers
2. Online reference search, online reservation of material not available in the library, and so on

The library is also working on developing a digital repository of the compendia used in the courses. These e-services and self-services are developed on the base of open source software, although the IT department at RUB modifies it to make the software fit to their needs. However they try to use the original open source software as much as possible since it is very expensive to modify it.

ISSUES AND CHALLENGES IN THE ADOPTION OF E-SERVICES

This section presents the main issues that RUB has encountered in e-services' adoption, the organizational transformations RUB had to go through as a consequence, and the challenges that RUB is presently facing and expecting to face in the future.

Back Office

Back office processes have been completely automated as a result of e-service adoption, and they have changed from being manual to being electronic. All library work is today done with the use of ICTs. Even when they get the paper journal, they insert it into an integrated library system. Everyone working in the library is using ICTs to do their job.

Innovation

Innovation is very important at RUB. The whole e-services and self-services business model is based on it, especially IT-driven innovation. E-services related innovations at RUB are both user-driven and employee-driven. The sources of innovation are very different. A lot of projects are based on ideas coming from people employed at RUB such as librarians, management, the director, and the IT department. Also the librarians provide courses to newly enrolled students and faculty about how to use the e-services, and a lot of ideas come from these teaching sessions. In addition they have a customer-complaint box and library users may send e-mails to the library. These e-mails get screened and RUB may use such suggestions for incremental innovations. DEFF (see above) is also an important source of innovation, especially regarding the technology aspect of e-services implementation. Through DEFF, RUB can get ideas from and share experiences with other libraries. For example, each library might be in charge of testing an IT solution, then they share experiences and finally they decide to choose and adopt a system. DEFF is also important in financing new ideas or innovation projects, as RUB might lack the financial resources to start all the projects they believe are worth pursuing.

The main driving forces of e-services adoption have been the government vision and policy for an "IT society for all," the technological development of the Internet, World Wide Web and related IT solutions mainly in a technology push fashion, the pressure from cutting costs in the public sector coming either from the government or local university authorities, an IT innovation culture that has always existed in the Danish libraries (as the director of reader services says "you want to be a little bit better then your neighbour library"), competition among the different libraries' top management and, even though to a less extent, the customer wishes.

Organizational Change

The digitalization process has changed the structure of RUB's organization in several ways. First of all a new organizational level, a management level, has been introduced that can make the organization look more hierarchical than before, but it cannot really be compared with a classical hierarchical structure. In addition this management level mainly deals with library development and with political issues. Most importantly the division of labour has changed. In particular, the number of IT-related jobs has grown a lot. For example, 13 years ago, RUB had one employee dealing with IT, while today they employee six to seven people in the IT department. The IT department is expected to grow in the future in special fields. In addition almost everybody in the library has to be an IT literate and librarians have to grow together with IT as the trends change rapidly. Each employee is participating in several projects, mostly dealing with e-services and e-services development. When Roskilde University started, RUB employed circa 70 people and was servicing about one third of the number of students and faculties it has today. Nowadays, RUB employees 45 people and serves a number of students and faculties which is three times as large as the one that was servicing when the university was founded. There is a shift from the librarians to the users in the production-consumption of e-services. The use of e-services and self-services is increasing. Circa 80–85% of the users of the library are using e-services and self-services. As a result, while earlier they needed two to three librarians at the reference desk, one is now enough. As in all the organizational changes, this is causing resistance among the employees and users of e-services. As a matter of fact, even though most of RUB users (about 80–85%) are very satisfied with the digitalization trend and the introduction of e-services, there is still a small group that is missing the old library and is unsatisfied with e-services.

RUB Business Model

RUB's business model is changing as a result of e-services and self-service adoption and is going in different directions. Within Roskilde University, RUB is getting more involved with Campus IT, which is presently developed by the IT Department at Roskilde University. However, collaboration is sometimes difficult due to different priorities. RUB believes that they will play a central role in future e-learning projects at Roskilde University. In addition they are trying to collaborate with the teachers and instructors on how to best use the library for teaching and research, including a number of courses on how to use the e-services and self-services that the library offers. Outside Roskilde University, RUB is looking at the possibility of offering consulting in the field of e-services for other libraries, including business libraries. They are also trying to open their market not only to the campus' students and faculties, but also to companies, especially small and medium enterprises. Participation in the DEFF project can influence the future of RUB's business model as well. For example, they presently provide an e-service called "Chat with a Librarian", which they are running not only for RUB, but for all the other research libraries in Denmark as well.

Relationships with Customers/Users

Since the introduction of e-services and self-services, the relationships with the users of the libraries have changed a lot. The number of users coming to the physical reference desk is decreasing quickly, while the number of inquiries at the virtual desk is increasing. The total number of inquiries is decreasing. In addition user behaviour is also changing. For example while paper books are still important for the readers, the total number of library loans is decreasing and the number of downloads of e-books is increasing. This trend is also observed for the journals. While RUB still has a substantial number of paper journals, more and more downloads of e-journal articles are taking place. They expect that the loans of physical books and journals will not be important in five years and that most of the material will be provided in electronic form. The users that have a log-in to the library can access the e-services 24 hours per day, seven days per week no matter where they are. So they will have everything they need on the computer. Some things are printed; others are not. The relationships with the users are expected to change even more in the future as a result of implementation of library blogs. In fact, RUB is looking at blogs and how to use them or integrate them with e-services such as electronic journals or e-books. Blogs would have the objective of creating online communities around specific topics, specific books, or journal articles. In addition, RUB is negotiating with Google to have all its collection retrievable through Google search engines. Therefore, e-services are leading to a digitalization of knowledge that was already codified in printed form. E-services are making it easier and quicker for users to find, store, and analyze such knowledge. In addition, e-services are making it easier for more users to get access to the same piece of knowledge or information. In fact if only one user at a time could get access to a specific journal in print form, in electronic form many users can get access to the same journal, article, or book chapter simultaneously. Furthermore, e-services are pushing customer relationships towards a virtual form. This is the case both regarding the relationship between the user and librarian and the relationship among the library's users which, after the implementation of blogs, is expected both to become more virtualized and to increase in number due to the formation of online communities.

Relationships with Publishers (or Providers)

This relationship has also changed as a result of e-services. Many of the traditional transactions such as ordering, cataloguing, and so forth, of journals have almost disappeared. The total number of transactions with the publishers has decreased. The e-journals are kept at the publishers' repository and RUB only buys the access or license to them. Initially the publishers offered a huge number of e-journals at extra cost. As a result, RUB cut the number of paper journals from approximately 5,000 to around 2,000 and instead has acquired access to circa 18,000 e-journals. However the publishers are now increasing prices on e-journals, therefore the total costs might increase as a result in the future. This kind of license agreement has contributed to the formation of a Danish library consortium whose purpose is to get better prices for electronic journals and e-books from the publishers.

Relationships with Other Research Libraries

The trend towards the adoption of e-services by the Danish libraries has changed the relationship between RUB and other research libraries in Denmark by increasing collaboration and partnerships among them. While earlier they were competing on services, number, and type of journals and books offered, after the adoption of e-services there is much more collaboration among Danish research libraries. Two key examples of this collaboration and partnerships which RUB is part of are Denmark Licensing Consortium and the DEFF initiative. Denmark Licensing Consortium

is a consortium of libraries getting common licenses to publishers' e-journals and e-books. The major purpose is to put pressure on the publishers and decrease costs for the individual library. Therefore, the adoption of e-services is causing a convergence and standardization of the (e-)services offered by the different Danish libraries. Libraries were differentiating from each other much more before the adoption of e-services. Now all the research libraries members of the license consortium offer the same types of e-journals and e-books, and more or less the same type of e-services. Those few that are ahead get caught up within a six-month period.

DEFF is, as described above, a major initiative undertaken by the Danish government with the purpose of developing a network of electronic research libraries that make available their electronic and other information resources in a coherent and simple way. This is obtained partly through government funding and partly by joint license purchase (www.deff.dk). By participating in DEFF, the libraries can achieve economies of scope and scale in the development of e-services.

FUTURE CHALLENGES

There are many challenges laying ahead for RUB. RUB will continue to exist and keep the role of library as an information centre, but the way the information and knowledge is provided will change. RUB will still face several organizational and technological challenges in the future.

From a technology point of view, the ICTs platforms used in delivering e-services become obsolete quite periodically and new e-services solutions have to be found. For example with the development of Web 2.0, they will have to make new types of systems. Integration of RUB e-services into one simple system is also an important technical future challenge. Presently the e-services located on the Web page are connected to six or seven different systems, and a future challenge is to integrate all these different systems. Standardization is another technological challenge. Customers want a rapid response and RUB is working on this by looking at standardization issues and they have to keep doing so in the future. Standards are very important for library's e-services. Finally, ensuring getting the best and same results for the same search is also a future technical challenge.

Copyrights and licenses are another important obstacle and challenge for the development of RUB's e-services. For example, they are running a project to convert the library's videos into files to be kept on the local servers. The problem is though that whenever a student wants to see a video, instead of seeing the file on the computer screen, they have to save the file on the tape, since the material that they loan out has to be in analogue form due to copyrights restrictions. So copyrights of what can be digitized are a big barrier to further e-services development and especially use by the customers. Licenses on the other hand limit the use of the e-services for remote users not connected to the university and therefore do not have a log in to the library system. This implies that these users still have to walk into the library to be able to use the e-services, thus limiting to some extent their functionality.

Another future challenge comes from the library users. The users are becoming much more advanced and sophisticated in their online searches; young people have a lot of ideas about how to do things better. Here the challenge is to understand their needs and implement user-driven innovations in e-services. Budget problems are another challenge for RUB. In the last few years the budgets allocated to research libraries have been decreasing. This trend has been worsened by decentralizing the budgets concerning the research libraries from the government to the university the libraries are connected to. This creates the possibility for management at Roskilde University to cut the library's budget in favour of other activities.

Organizational challenges are also lying ahead. As the number of physical loans will decrease and the number of electronic downloads keeps increasing, there is going to be less need for the reference desk and the number of positions in the library might decrease. The way of working in the library is changing, therefore the type of competences needed might change moving more towards IT specialists and going away from the classical librarians skills. Disagreement on e-services' future development between the different groups in the library is also a major organizational and human resource challenge, even though most RUB's employees like e-services. This requires RUB to explore new functions and new directions to change their business model.

CONCLUSION

This chapter has contributed to understand e-services development by investigating a particular type of e-services: research library e-services. Specifically the study has investigated the implication of the advent of Internet and e-services for Roskilde University library as well as the future challenges that e-services provide for RUB. The study has also investigated the consequences of e-services for Roskilde University library organization, its business model, and relationships with customers, publishers (providers of information), and other research libraries. The picture that emerges is one of rapid innovation, big transformations, and change at organizational and business model level, as well as in the relationships with customers, publishers, and other research libraries. In addition there are a number of challenges that RUB has to face in the future in response to e-services. Some are IT-related; others have to deal with copyrights, licenses, standardization, and user-driven innovation. The general trend is that RUB is becoming a combination of a virtual and physical library, moving more and more towards a virtual library by providing resources and knowledge mainly in digital form and by offering blogs and possibilities of online communities to discuss books and articles. On the other hand RUB is still keeping the traditional library function of a physical knowledge space. What will RUB look like in 10 years? The only certain answer according to RUB management is that it will still exist.

REFERENCES

Hoffman, K.D. (2003). Marketing+MIS=E-Service. *Communications of the ACM, 46*(6), 53–55.

Marchionini, G., & Maurer, H. (1995). The roles of digital libraries in teaching and learning. *Communications of the ACM, 38*(4), 67–75.

Sarkar, M.B., Butler, B., & Steinfield, C. (1995). Intermediaries and cybermediaries: A continuing role for mediating players in the electronic marketplace. *Journal of Computer Mediated Communication, 1*(3).

Scupola, A. (2002). The impact of electronic commerce on industry structure: The case of scientific, technical and medical publishing. *Journal of Information Science, 28*(3).

ENDNOTE

[1] Including the metropolitan municipalities of Copenhagen and Frederiksberg

APPENDIX 1: THE DANISH RESEARCH LIBRARY STATISTICS 2004[1]

Table 1. General figures about Denmark

Area	43,094 km²
Local authorities	271
Counties[1]	**16**

Table 2. Denmarks' population per 1.1. 2005

Adults	4,459,978
Children (0-13)	951,329
Total	**5,411,307**

Table 3. Number of research libraries in 2004

National library	2
Libraries of institutions of higher education	100
Special libraries	78
Total	180

Table 4. Staff in 2004

National library	563
Libraries of institutions of higher education	788
Special libraries	219
Total	**1,570**

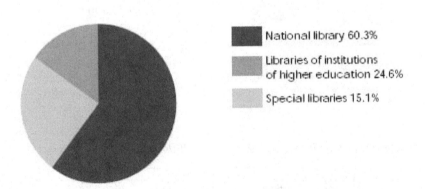

National library 60.3%

Libraries of institutions of higher education 24.6%

Special libraries 15.1%

Table 5. Research libraries stock in 2004

National library	26,573,386
Libraries of institutions of higher education	10,834,470
Special libraries	6,633,201
Total	**44,041,057**

Table 6. Serials subscriptions

National library	61,270
Libraries of institutions of higher education	32,388
Special libraries	14,021
Total	107,679

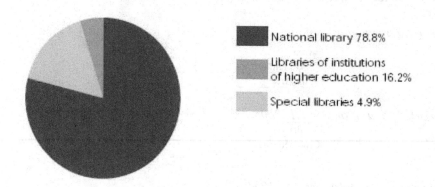

Table 7. Research libraries additions in 2004

National library	1,221,707
Libraries of institutions of higher education	251,679
Special libraries	76,085
Total	**1,549,471**

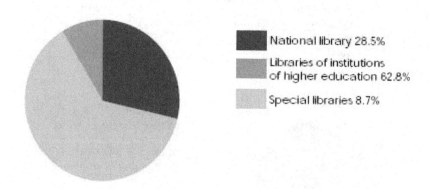

Table 8. Research libraries loans including renewals in 2004

National library	2,759,796
Libraries of institutions of higher education	6,088,009
Special libraries	844,535
Total	**9,692,340**

Table 9. Interlibrary loans supplied

by National library	513,604
by libraries of institutions of higher education	507,662
by special libraries	41,423
Total Interlibrary loans supplied	**1,062,689**

Table 10. Interlibrary loans received

by National library	61,256
by libraries of institutions of higher education	151,862
by special libraries	25,444
Total Interlibrary loans received	238,562

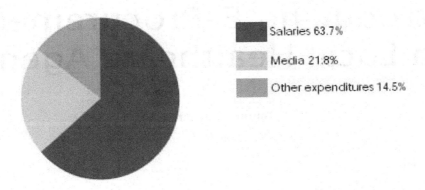

- Salaries 63.7%
- Media 21.8%
- Other expenditures 14.5%

Table 11. Research libraries operating expenditure in 2004

	1,000 DKK
Salaries	537,372
Media	183,687
Other expenditure	122,501
Total	**843,559**

Table 12. Research libraries operating expenditure in 2004

	1,000 DKK	%
National library	295,588	35.0%
Libraries of institutions of higher education	436,042	51.7%
Special libraries	111,929	13.3%
Total	843,559	100.0%

ENDNOTE

[1] These statistics are adapted from the Danish Library Authority Statistics (http://www.bs.dk/publikationer/english/statistics/2004/index.htm). The figures apply to the 180 Danish research libraries which are funded by the government, open to the public and employ professional librarian(s) on a permanent basis. There are a further 583 smaller research libraries which do not meet these requirements, including 122 institute (departmental) libraries at universities and institutions of higher education.

Chapter XV
Introducing E-Procurement in a Local Healthcare Agency

Tommaso Federici
University of Tuscia, Italy

ABSTRACT

This chapter deals with the introduction of electronic procurement in the public healthcare domain. After a brief discussion on the healthcare spending characteristics and on the suitability of e-procurement tools in the public sector, the long-lasting experience of e-procurement implementation promoted by an Italian Local Healthcare Public Agency is described. This initiative included some pilot projects and applied many different solutions, always involving both a new ICT tool and a thorough process redesign. The development of the innovation introductions is discussed, together with their organizational and managerial background, the description of the new processes, and the analysis of the most relevant results. The chapter provides a fairly comprehensive illustration of available solutions, opportunities, and challenges in this still neglected topic.

BACKGROUND

The spending for goods and services on public healthcare, significant for many years, is still growing at a fast rate, both in absolute terms and in percent of total spending, worrying many European governments that are engaged in identifying rationalization initiatives. In parallel, e-procurement solutions widened their range of application from business-to-business (B2B) transactions among companies to business-to-government (B2G) ones, introducing innovative processes in public administrations (PAs), based on information and communication technologies (ICTs). According to the i2010 eGovernment Action Plan, two recent European directives (2004/18/EC and 2004/17/EC) committed member states to give the *capability* of carrying out 100% of procurement electronically to all their PAs with the *obligation* of managing electronically at least 50% of spending.

E-procurement should enable significant efficiency improvements in the public healthcare sector, with the reduction of purchasing and administrative costs. Until now, however, most e-procurement initiatives at the country, regional, and local levels met difficulties and did not fully deliver the expected benefits. This is mainly due to the healthcare procurement complexity in terms of variety of goods and number of suppliers and to the resistances of public institutions to technology-based process innovation. Moreover, a different approach to the e-procurement opportunities is required in healthcare to take into account the specific characteristics and peculiar needs of particular supplies.

Following the initial statements, and according to many scholars (Berardi, Calvanese, De Giacomo, Lenzerini, & Mecella, 2003; De Meo, Quattrone, Terracina, & Ursino, 2006) and definitions (e.g., listen to the voice on A.dict.it, 2007) e-procurement should be included in the e-services domain, since:

- it is entirely based on the use of computers and electronic information exchanges (Internet/extranet);
- it involves the cooperation of various organizations, which integrate their services (functionalities) through these means.

It must be noticed, however, that the semantics of many "e" terms is still not universally shared and their meaning is continuously shifting and often incoherent; for instance, the term "e-service" is also applied to the public sector in the narrower sense of a service provided on the Web by an administration to their citizens.

E-procurement-related innovations in technology and organization have been considered mostly for private operators (Kim & Shunk, 2004), particularly marketplaces (Rossignoli, 2004). Fewer works deal with the public sector (Anderson, Juul, & Pedersen, 2003; Devadoss, Pan, & Huang, 2002; Zulfiqar, Pan, Lee, & Huang,

2001); they mainly discuss policies and behaviour of central PAs and central procurement authorities (Hardy & Williams, 2005; Panayioutou, Gayialis, & Tatsiopoulos, 2004; Somasundaram & Damsgaard, 2005). Even fewer are the studies on the public healthcare sector, particularly at the local operating level, where e-procurement solutions must be actually implemented, giving rise to changes on structures and knowledge already acting within each organization, thereby requesting different approaches.

Here, a case is presented that deals with an experience of e-procurement implementation promoted by the Italian Local Healthcare Public Agency (LHA) of Viterbo. This case is particularly interesting for the comprehensive design of the e-procurement system, the differentiation of the adopted tools, the long-lasting experimentations (since 2000), and the multiple solutions implemented or in progress. The decision to examine this case is also due to the following facts: the use of e-procurement tools is seen just as one aspect of a deep reorganization of the entire supply process; most performed initiatives were followed by a detailed assessment of their outcomes.

The history and key features of this experience will be examined in detail up to the ongoing project aimed at a wide e-procurement implementation. A framework of healthcare spending characteristics is also introduced in the beginning, together with a taxonomy of e-procurement tools in public healthcare sector.

HEALTH CARE SPENDING AND E-PROCUREMENT

Health Care Spending

About 27% of the public healthcare spending in Italy is for the "purchasing of goods and services," frequently named "intermediate healthcare consumptions" (Regional Healthcare Services Agency, 2005). When referring to the whole Italian *National Healthcare System,* this component reaches a huge absolute dimension—23.8 €b in the year 2005—with an increasing trend both in absolute terms (it more than doubled from 1997 to 2005) and in percent on the total spending (in 1997 spending for goods and services was lower than 10 €b and it weighted a little more than 20% of the total).

This part of spending varies largely among the Italian regions and the market is further influenced by some complexity factors: the presence of about 350 diverse healthcare structures and about 500,000 highly differentiated suppliers (multinationals, mid-size national companies, and local SMEs).

The main issue, however, is the composite structure of the spending in healthcare, which includes standard supplies for the whole PA, together with highly specific purchases. The spending for goods and services in such sector is highly differentiated and, according to the former aggregations used by the Italian Economic Ministry (very useful to single out the most suitable e-procurement tools), can be classified into three sections:

- *common spending* for the whole PA (about 25% of total healthcare spending for goods and services); the nature of this spending (e.g., phone services, office materials) is the same for all the buying administrations;
- *common-but-differentiated spending* (25% of total); it exists for all the administrations, but it is highly differentiated through the buying sector (e.g., in healthcare: maintenance and cleaning of hospital buildings);
- *healthcare-specific spending* (more than 50% of total), composed by medical devices, drugs, and materials used in case of injury, disease, handicap, physiological application, or surgical operation.

A fundamental concern is that, while healthcare *specific* goods require high quality level of each item, together with rapid and controlled logistics, the same aspects—although important—are clearly less critical for *common* goods. Furthermore, healthcare *specific* goods and healthcare *common-but-differentiated* spending often have peculiar characteristics, with limited offering standardization. This diversity must be taken into account when devising innovative ways to manage procurement before choosing the most appropriate solutions, in order to improve quality and efficiency of supplies, while rationalizing and reducing spending.

E-Procurement and E-Procurement Tools

The term "procurement" is often used in a narrow sense, associated with the sole purchasing phase, as can be seen in Panayioutou et al. (2004) or in Kim and Shunk (2004). Consequently, the term "e-procurement" is used to indicate just a class of electronic tools to link buyers and suppliers on the same network to make a deal.

Differently and according to other studies (MacManus, 2002; Somasundaram, 2004), in this work, the term "procurement" will indicate a broader process within the operations of a healthcare agency that starts with a need for a good or service and ends with its use and the payment for its supply. The procurement process then includes (see Figure 1): analysis of the needs coming from central warehouse or departments, purchase programming, sourcing choice (where and how to buy), purchasing act (through a tender or a direct order), handling of incoming material and central warehouse logistics, department warehouse replenishment, inventory control, and invoice processing and payment.

An e-procurement system then involves the whole procurement process and not just its purchasing phase. Consistently, the term "e-procurement" indicates here the organizational solutions supported by ICT-based tools that allow electronic forms of procurement, potentially more effective

Figure 1. Procurement taxonomy in the health care sector

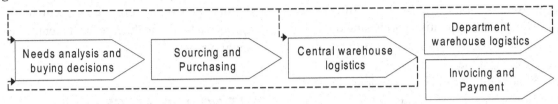

and efficient than traditional ones, where a more or less wide-reaching and thorough process re-design is required, taking into account the whole life-time of a product or service.

The tools included in e-procurement solutions can be grouped in two main areas, which should be considered in a complementary way to streamline the whole procurement process:

- *e-purchasing*, that includes very different tools which allows the purchasing phase to be entirely managed, from finding a product to invoicing and payment, through online tenders (*e-tendering*), or *marketplaces* and *electronic catalogues* (*e-requisitioning*), electronic invoice exchange and processing (*e-invoice*), and liquidation activity (*e-payment*);
- *e-logistics*, which aims at optimizing the management of inventories (in healthcare structures: pharmacy and the supply office) and internal goods flows, based on intranet/extranet technologies, integrating supply chain management (SCM) solutions, linking both internal and external players.

Correlation Between Spending Items and Tools

It must be taken into consideration that healthcare structures produce highly critical and specialized services vs. the rest of PAs. More than in other sectors, quality standards for many purchased goods and services (for their impact on the service quality) quality standards for many purchased goods and services (for their impact on the service quality), together with economy and timeliness of purchases, transparency of activities, and conformance to principles of competition among companies. This diversity, together with the large differences among the three spending for goods and services categories indicated above and the availability of diverse electronic tools require a careful analysis—and a segmented approach—to define (see Figure 2) which solution mostly suits each type of good/service (Federici, 2006). Then, a clear definition of the nature of the need (e.g., operating room specific devices) and a consistent purchase plan, capable of supporting both healthcare performance and economy of procurement, are necessary steps to be taken.

Figure 2. Correlation between spending items and e-procurement tools

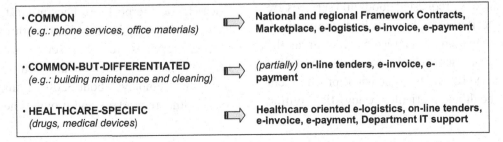

Goods and services within the *common* spending category, characterized by large utilization, wide offering, and repetitive purchasing quantities, can be standardized for all PAs. They are perfectly compatible with *e-requisitioning* tools, like the marketplaces and the e-catalogues based on framework contracts negotiated by a single body (at national, regional, or local level), that aggregate fractions of public demand, knock-down large standard supply contracts, perform unified tender procedures for a number of "client" entities (CONSIP, 2003) and, eventually, lower both the supply price and the administrative costs. The best opportunity for a local agency—in terms of reduction of purchase price, administrative costs, and delivery time—is therefore to turn to one of these tools; last but not least, e-logistics, e-invoice, and e-payment can improve supply management and further reduce its administrative costs.

The *common-but-differentiated* spending category consists of supplies which must absolutely guarantee the fulfillment of specific needs to the healthcare buyer. It requires the presentation and evaluation of even complex projects, for which it is difficult to define criteria for automatic score attribution. The traditional procedure can be substituted by a tender partially performed online, moving the call, presentation, intermediate, and final communications phases onto the Web (with clear benefits in terms of reduction of administrative time and costs), while keeping the offers evaluation phase off-line e-invoice and e-payment can provide further efficiency improvements.

To adequately manage the *healthcare-specific* spending, a wider e-procurement approach must be used: just looking for the lowest purchasing price might be counterproductive (Borgonovi, 2004) since the requested goods and services are highly specific and high quality levels are required. Benefits can then be obtained by redesigning the internal processes, merging several organizational changes and ICT tools on the whole procurement cycle—healthcare oriented e-logistics, online tenders, evolved forms of marketplace, e-invoice and e-payment—and providing adequate ICT supports to each healthcare cost centre (e.g., hospital wards).

SETTING THE STAGE

E-Procurement Introduction at the LHA of Viterbo: A Long Journey

The LHA of Viterbo, aiming at gaining efficiency and reducing the expenditure for the procurement of goods and services, started in the 2000, a long journey that can be divided in four main phases (see Figure 3):

- Phase 0 (before 2000): the time before the e-procurement introduction, with traditional paper-based and highly segmented procurement procedures;
- Phase 1 (2000-2004): a period of e-procurement pilot initiatives based on different solutions, with the first e-procurement tests promoted in partnership with public and private organizations;
- Phase 2 (since 2005): a period of progressively wider implementation of diverse e-procurement solutions, that is still ongoing;
- Phase 3 (in the next future): a time of full e-procurement implementation, when the entire procurement process will be innovated and ICT-based.

The Health Care Structure and Organization

The LHA of Viterbo, like other similar structures (Cicchetti, 2004), is organized in three areas: hospital services, territory services (first aid facilities, laboratories, etc.), and administration services. It employs about 3200 administrative and healthcare workers and provides healthcare

Figure 3. E-procurement introduction in LHA of Viterbo

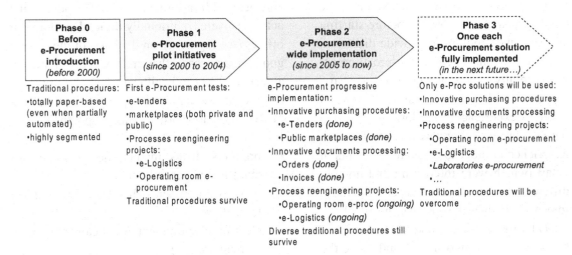

to an Italian province (859 hospital beds) with a production value of about 350 million of euros, determined according to the individual spending allocated for each citizen of the province (a total of about 300,000 people).

As regards the procurement process, the following structures were involved, although at different levels of commitment and with diverse e-procurement solutions:

- the Procurement and Logistics (P&L) Department (in charge of tenders, purchases, and management of internal flows);
- nine different warehouses: two central (one for common goods and one for medical devices and drugs), and seven local;
- hospital wards and laboratories, which store little stocks of goods and are both applicants and recipients of new supplies.

It must be noticed that most of the structures and the procedures already operating before e-procurement introduction are still working because the innovative solutions did not substitute the former ones yet, even when fully implemented.

Methodological Assumptions

The above indicated assumptions about healthcare spending and its correlation with e-procurement tools—diversity in healthcare spending; broadness of the procurement process; and need to match each type of spending with the most appropriate e-procurement solution—constitute the starting concepts on which the experiences managed by the LHA of Viterbo were based.

The e-procurement project of the LHA was characterized by a diversified and systematic approach, which relied heavily on:

- the specialized competences of individual hospital wards (core structures of a healthcare agency, which actually deliver the healthcare service and are the main final users of the new tools); because of this, they were involved in the definition of the new procurement processes and took on a direct and decisive role;
- the technology and management know-how of external companies (from technology and logistics sectors); their partnership was very important in the first experimentations;

- the willingness to test diverse e-procurement solutions on pilot contexts, along the whole procurement process, before starting an extensive program for a wide diffusion; it must be considered that e-procurement was a totally new approach in those years, especially in healthcare, and there were no previous experiences to follow;
- the setting up of a review activity for each experience in order to evaluate its results in detail (which were interesting and notably different in nature and dimension from those foreseen), analyze the obstacles met (technological, organizational, and normative, as it happens for any innovation), and make the best decision about the intended wide adoption of e-procurement.

The redesign of the procurement cycle started from a detailed analysis of the need for goods and services. Specific purchase characteristics were made explicit; spending was mapped in detail, divided among *common, common-but-differentiated, healthcare-specific;* and an organic plan to link procurement needs and e-procurement solutions according to theory was prepared.

Phase 0: The Preliminary Context

Prior to starting the e-procurement introduction process, the internal situation about climate, culture, technology availability, and utilization was just similar to other analogous Italian structures and local public administrations. The purchasing activities were traditionally divided among four offices (see Figure 4), on the basis of the type of goods or services, as they are highly differentiated and specialized in healthcare, thereby implying diverse procedures and suppliers. The subject matter of the four offices was, respectively:

- products (drugs, medical devices, consumables like paper, ink, etc.);
- general equipment (furniture, cars, elevators, etc.);
- electronic equipment (medical appliances, computers, etc.);
- services.

This division has been maintained, as this specialization is considered useful. Therefore, the distinctive characteristics and activities of such offices, described below, are still the same existing at that period.

The activity of such offices is characterized by a knowledge oriented to correctly apply the rigid external laws (settled by the national or regional government, or by UE) and procedures (determined by the same LHA) that regulate purchases in a public administration. Another important piece of knowledge concerns information about the distinguishing characteristics of the managed type of products. To properly work in this area, the main issue is then to accumulate more and

Figure 4. Structure of the purchasing and logistic department before the e-procurement introduction (Phase 0, before 2000)

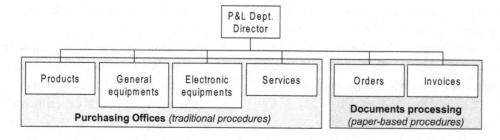

more experience in the field, while the education acquired previously to be applied in the position has little or no relevance (actually, none of the office supervisors has a degree, even less in law, as it could be expected).

The four traditional offices, which operate separately, have an average staff of four persons (generally, a supervisor and three clerks). Each of them is based on a precise division of the highly standardized tasks to be performed, that typically are sourcing of information about the product to buy (price, characteristics, suppliers), writing and revising of the tender, issuing of the same, support to the evaluation process, and award notification. Despite that knowledge is rather shared among the personnel of the same office, interchangeability is pretty difficult due to the long-lasting practice of everyone in his/her specific task. The traditional purchasing offices have then the typical form of bureaucracy. Because of their culture and organizational form, they are not flexible and not disposed to change. Moreover, even if they are effective in managing their duties, their activity is not efficient at all, as largely demonstrated by the results of the researches quoted below.

Additionally, computers are used only in the administrative offices (not in warehouses or hospital wards), and the role of IT systems is limited to automating the traditional procedures with office automation tool (word processing and occasionally spreadsheet) or legacy systems (accounting system, to check funds availability and to reserve them). Consequently, personnel are not required to have a high IT literacy.

At the beginning of the e-procurement experience, the internal climate was, and still is, highly influenced by factors like elevated level of bureaucracy, limited possibilities of career advancement, low level of responsibility, and long lasting habits to operate always in the same way (overall and particularly in areas like administration and warehouse).

These discouraging conditions to promote change were further reinforced by three other factors:

- the low cultural level outside the health departments, with only few graduated managers;
- the limited availability of different competences in staff areas: workers with a degree or a high-school qualification came all from law or accounting studies;
- the sharing of these circumstances by both employees and managers, at least middle-level ones.

Actually, the drive to introduce e-procurement in the LHA came just from two persons, both recruited after a previous career in the private sector: the former general manager and the manager of the P&L Department.

CASE DESCRIPTION

Phase 1: The Pilot Initiatives

Organizational Interventions

In order to manage the preliminary experimental phase to introduce e-procurement tools and solutions, while taking into account the obsolete culture and the poor IT education of the workers in the P&L Department, the two mentioned top managers made a strategic decision. They involved in these trials only some young people, freshly graduated in economics. At the first stage, they were two; later, two more were added. These graduates were asked to spend their postdegree training period at the LHA. As the entire staff in charge of the e-procurement experimentation, they were engaged full-time in it (see Figure 5).

Even though the educational level of the involved persons was quite high, this was directly used only in some part of the work (e.g., analysis

Figure 5. Structure of the purchasing and logistic department during the e-procurement pilot initiatives (Phase 1, 2000-2004)

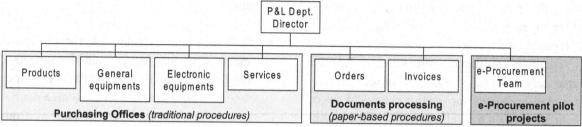

of the outcomes, auditing on costs). Actually, they were selected also because of their higher IT education (although they were not IT experts) and their greater willing to innovate, compared to the workers of traditional offices. This was a successful decision, also because it isolated the persons involved in e-procurement from those still engaged in traditional procedures. Acting in this way, it was possible to adopt a trial-and-error approach in the tests, while at the same time the supplying cycle, crucial in a healthcare structure, could proceed without any inconvenience.

Many diverse ICT systems (office automation, marketplaces, platform for e-tenders, e-logistics extranet solutions, etc.) were tested by using them in real operations for a planned period, as they form the constitutive platform for e-procurement. The aim of each test was to model a new organizational solution, in order to define streamlined and more effective process and to employ human resources in more value-added tasks.

To improve the procurement and internal management of the *healthcare-specific* and *common* goods, from ward requests up to the purchasing channels (see Figure 1), the LHA designed a fully ICT-supported process, with procurement flows designed along two distinct routes, according to goods type:

- a procurement flow for nonspecific medical devices (MDs), normally used in hospital wards for routine healthcare activities (e.g., gauzes, disinfectants, etc.), and for *common*

spending, involving online tenders, market-places, e-invoice, and e-logistics;
- another procurement flow for the specific medical devices (SMDs), used for surgical interventions in the operating rooms and for laboratory tests, with new online procurement processes aimed at optimizing the replenishment time and reducing the ward and inventory stock levels.

In the new process model, the wards, in their healthcare duty, assume a driving role, but not the responsibility to decide how to purchase specific goods.

The Trials Managed on the E-Procurement Solutions

According to the above mentioned methodological assumptions, in Phase 1 (see Figure 3) the LHA of Viterbo tested diverse e-procurement solutions before adopting them widely, in order to single out the most suitable one for each different need existing in such a complex structure. Summarizing, the experiences made in the test phase followed this path:

- in the year 2000, the first initiative was a trial of a marketplace promoted by a private merchant; despite some positive results, this experience ended quite early, when the marketplace platform failed because of the low volume of transactions;

- in 2002, even though these tools were still under construction and not yet addressed to the healthcare sector, the LHA started to use the *Public Electronic Catalogue* of the goods and services which could be purchased at predefined conditions through the *Framework Contracts* ("Convenzioni Quadro") negotiated by the Italian Central Procurement Agency (CONSIP) and the *Marketplace for the Public Administration* ("Mercato Elettronico per la Pubblica Amministrazione," MEPA), also created and managed by CONSIP (the LHA was one of the first 20 Italian PAs that took active part in the MEPA implementation);
- in 2003, a first platform for e-tenders was tested, which was later dismissed because of its lack of functionalities; it has been recently replaced by a new one, that allows to manage a tender, both partially (leaving offers evaluation off-line) or fully electronically,

but does not yet support competitive online prices reductions (*e-auction*);
- the LHA also carried out two different projects on e-logistics, both promoted by private companies and based on wide outsourcing solutions supported by extranet platforms. One of them involved the central and the departments' warehouse logistics for common goods and nonspecific devices used in hospital wards for routine healthcare (e.g., gauzes, disinfectants, etc.). The other project coupled the supply of the specific medical devices used in the operating rooms with their overall logistics management, adopting an innovative "intervention-based" concept that links procurement to the surgical operations performed (according to surgical protocols defined ad hoc, which indicate the types and quantities of medical devices needed for each type of operation), instead of the traditional

Figure 6. Replenishment request internal flow with e-logistics solution

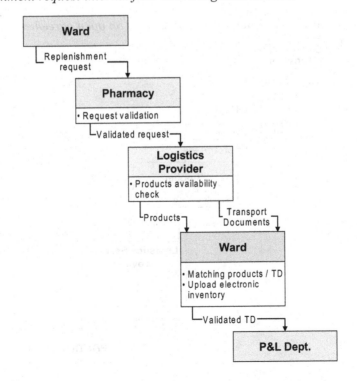

"stock-based" approach, which just manages the inventory levels.

The most significant experiences of those indicated above, due to their innovation rate and process broadness, were *e-logistics* (for common goods and nonspecific devices) and *operating room e-procurement*. They will be then described in more detail in the following paragraphs (see also Federici, 2005).

E-Logistics Solution

The LHA of Viterbo managed in 2002–2003 a pilot experiment about centralization and outsourcing of the warehouse function. The e-logistics program outsourced replenishment and inventory management for hospitals and offices to an external logistics service provider, with significant reduction of the operating and economic burden on the LHA. The results of such initiative reinforced the statement that savings in healthcare should be pursued by supporting the procurement

processes of the structures with ICT tools and by thoroughly reviewing and integrating the logistics management (Bianchini, 2002b). With the technical support of CONSIP, a pattern was later drawn to extend this solution to other LHAs.

After making the ICT support available to all the recipient structures involved in the trial, they were provided with an easy accessible product inventory, divided by categories, and a daily loading/unloading procedure with indication of actual stock levels.

The process was activated by a need, for example (see Figure 6), born in a ward. Every day, in its healthcare duty, the hospital ward unloaded the consumed goods from its inventory and issued a replenishment request when they went beyond their minimum stock levels. The replenishment request of medical devices or supply office goods, through a software application linked to the hospital management information system, was sent to the logistics service provider periodically (once or twice a week) by the ward sister, after validation by the hospital pharmacy (in case of

Figure 7. Supply order flow with e-logistics solution in case of an open agreement

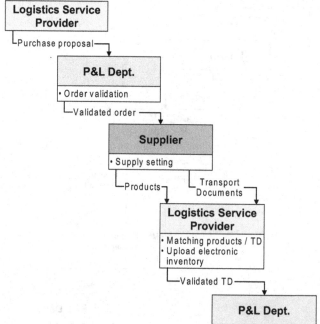

nonspecific medical devices). The logistics service provider, if the good was available, replenished the requesting ward inventory from its warehouse by sending the good together with electronic and paper transport documents (TD). The ward sister checked the conformity of the received good in quality and quantity with the transport document and loaded its electronic inventory. In this way, the P&L Department was informed centrally in real time about the stock levels of both the logistics service provider and of the individual wards.

The logistics service provider was the sole procurement intermediary, but it could not make any decision for new supplies, on behalf of the LHA, when a good was not available in its warehouse. The LHA outsourced the management of central inventory and delegated the unloading of ward inventories, but did not externalize the purchasing function, which remained exclusively in its hands. In case of stock-outs, the logistics service provider sent a purchase order proposal to the LHA:

- when the goods were part of a still open supply agreement, after the validation by the P&L Department, the order was mailed to the awarded supplier (see Figure 7), which sent the goods and related transport document to the logistics service provider, that then loaded its electronic inventory;

- when the supply agreement was closed, or for new goods, the P&L Department could decide to open a new tender (in a traditional way, or online), at the end of which the illustrated route between the awarded supplier and the logistics service provider was activated.

Operating Room E-Procurement

The traditional planning of operating room provisioning is performed by the hospital responsible and the pharmacist, who manage the hospital inventories by periodically sending types and quantity estimates of goods to be provided to the respective purchasing office, according to past consumption and future consumption forecast. This approach, based on estimates, generates problems in purchase planning when the hospital wards are not provided with adequate ICT supports: the pharmacist unloads the goods allocated to a ward from the inventory, as if it were consumed at once; the good might remain instead unused in the ward for an unpredictable period of time, with no indication to the pharmacist and, least of all, to the purchasing office.

The pilot experience of "operating room e-procurement" was carried out at the hospital of Civita Castellana since 2001 (it was chosen, because it is a little hospital and its ward personnel is willing to pursue innovation). The operating and technical staff of the General Surgery Department was

Figure 8. Flow diagram of operating room e-procurement process (at the end of each shift)

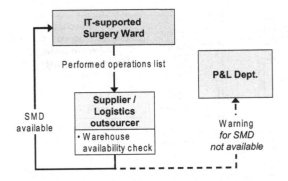

Figure 9. Flow diagram of operating room e-procurement process (monthly)

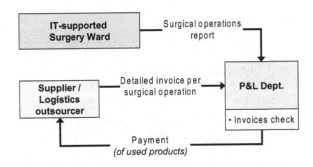

directly involved in rethinking and redesigning the specific medical devices procurement process from scratch. The model conceived is based on:

- a novel approach to provide the specific medical devices to the operating room, based on the type of surgical operation performed (information immediately available) and no longer on the specific medical devices stock level (information that requires a large administrative work);
- the definition of surgical protocols which indicate the type and quantity of the medical devices consumed by each type of operation and allow to determine the right quantities to be reordered;
- the contractual allocation of the products supply and management to a single player, with innovative paying terms.

The new procurement process was supported by a shared application platform based on an extranet. At the end of each shift (see Figure 8), the ward sister sent the list of the operations performed to the supplier. The supplier, according to the product quantities indicated by the corresponding surgical protocols, knew product consumptions in real time and could thus replenish them. The goods were delivered directly to the ward which had requested them and thus covered actual needs

with no intermediate steps, cost/time increase or stock-out risks.

The process ended monthly (see Figure 9) when:

- the surgery ward sent to the P&L Department the report of the surgical operations performed;
- the supplier issued a detailed invoice per surgical operation;
- the P&L Department activated the payment of the actually used products, after a brief cross-check.

At the same time, a so detailed invoice provided data to the P&L Department for an effective periodical comparative analysis of ward needs. The objective of the experimentation was to verify the operating-economic impact that a specific supply system, based on online methodologies and provisioning *per surgical operation*, would provide vis-à-vis the traditional procedure (Bianchini, 2002a). The analysis performed at the end of the first semester of experimentation indicated that, to reduce spending, it is necessary to consider the whole supply cost and not only the purchase price, on which the procedure was focused before, in order to negotiate the lowest one.

Actually, the economic advantages were mostly concentrated in the administrative costs,

Figure 10. Structure of the purchasing and logistic department during the e-procurement wide implementation (Phase 2, since 2005).

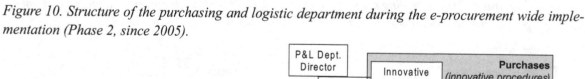
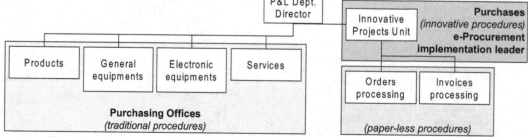

which decreased from about 100 €k per semester to only 20. On the contrary, the purchase price of the operating room devices slightly increased (by 4%, due to their increase in market price); this witnesses that the project was aimed at not sacrificing the quality of supply at all. With savings on the total final cost of the specific medical devices supply of more than 73 €k per semester (30% less than the traditional approach), the experimentation of the LHA of Viterbo suggested that the e-procurement per surgical operation can provide substantial cost savings, not to be pursued by reducing the purchase costs (in order not to dangerously penalize the supply quality), but by redesigning the procurement process and thus reducing the administrative costs.

It may be interesting to examine the breakdown of savings among the various cost items:

- 42% of savings came from reducing the fixed and financial inventory costs (management cost per squared meter of inventory premises, financial costs of the capital locked into stocks, and cost of obsolete products), by outsourcing logistics and shifting the payment terms after consumption;
- 26% of savings came from reducing personnel costs (of hospital pharmacy and operating room), for the fraction linked to the inventory management activities outsourced to the logistics provider (book-keeping, product replenishment, incoming goods inspection, order/delivery expediting);
- 24% of savings came from reducing the administrative cost for purchasing and supply monitoring, by unifying sets of diverse medical devices into surgical protocol kits, instead of using a separate procedure for each type of device, and by being provided with detailed information directly from the invoices per surgical operations;
- 8% of savings came from reduced order management and invoicing costs.

Phase 2: The Progressive Implementation

Since 2005, after these pilot experiences limited in size and time although performed in real operations, the LHA of Viterbo launched an extensive program (Phase 2, see Figure 3) with the purpose of innovating the end-to-end procurement process (as seen in Figure 1), through the adoption of diverse solutions, coherently linked to the different specific requirements. The first completed steps were the implementation of multiple e-procurement solutions in two segments of the broad procurement process: purchasing and invoice processing. The changes introduced in these first steps were analyzed in detail, as summarized below. After overcoming the resistances expressed by suppliers, the full deployment of operating room e-procurement is now ending, while the implementation of e-logistics outsourcing model for common goods and nonspecific devices is still ongoing.

New Organizational Interventions

At the end of the testing phase, when it was decided to promote the widespread adoption of e-procurement, two more graduates were selected, and the former informal project team became a unit devoted to the all e-procurement processing (named Innovative Projects, or IP).

This unit (see Figure 10) was integrated with two other offices (already moved to a totally paperless activity), in charge of orders and invoices processing, in the staff coordinated by the Director of the P&L Department. Even though innovative e-purchasing solutions are fully implemented and frequently used already, this unit is still separate from the other offices, which keep running the purchasing activity in the traditional ways.

In addition, while the traditional offices manage the sole purchasing phase, this unit not only operates as a buyer (through online tenders or

Table 1. Matching between the equivalent procedures considered (Legend: T: Traditional, I: Innovative)

COMPARISON	VERSION	PROCEDURE	DESCRIPTION	ICT TOOLS
1	T	Tender over threshold	Public tender for purchases of goods and services for amounts higher than the threshold set by the European Union (EU). Totally paper-based procedure	Office automation (word processing, spreadsheet, etc.)
	I	Online tender over threshold	Public tender for purchases of goods and services for amounts higher than the threshold set by the EU. Web-based procedure from initial notification, receipt of bids, intermediate communications, up to award notification. Evaluation of the bids can be performed off-line. Call must be published as for off-line tender	Platform for e-tendering Office automation
2	T	Tender over threshold	*see above*	
	I	Direct Order on e-catalogue	Purchase (also for amounts higher than the EU threshold) fully performed on the e-catalogue for PAs managed by CONSIP, which includes goods and services already negotiated through Framework Contracts. A limited choice of items is available.	Web-based catalogue
3	T	Negotiated procedure	Restricted tender procedure with few invited participants (faster then normal tender). To be adopted only in specific cases and under EU threshold. Totally paper-based procedure	Office automation (word processing, spreadsheet...)
	I	Request for Quotation (RfQ) on MEPA	Restricted tender procedure fully performed on CONSIP Marketplace for PAs with few participants selected by LHA (among the suppliers admitted by CONSIP), that can be asked for (and can submit) a technical tender To be adopted under EU threshold.	e-Marketplace (with special functions for tender asking and submitting)
4	T	Small direct purchase	Purchase directly performed with a single supplier. To be adopted for very small buying (under the threshold of € 5000) and only in specific cases. Totally paper-based procedure	Office automation (word processing, spreadsheet...)
	I	Direct Order on MEPA	Purchase directly performed on CONSIP Marketplace with a supplier already admitted by CONSIP, and only of goods or services allowed. To be adopted under EU threshold	e-Marketplace platform (with cart function)
5	T	Invoice processing	Paper-based procedure of: invoice acquisition, checks (on the accounting system and with orders and transport documents) and submitting of verified invoices to the persons in charge of payment	Office automation (word processing, spreadsheet...) Accounting system
	I	LIQUIWEB	After keying in the incoming invoice data, totally paper-less checks (on the accounting system and with orders and transport documents) and submission of verified invoices	Intranet application for invoice processing Accounting system

direct purchases on MEPA), but also supervises the entire procurement process (including supply chain and logistics), being directly linked to external providers, warehouses (for common goods and for medical devices and drugs), and internal departments recipient of the supplied goods. Furthermore, the IP unit manages supplies regardless to the type of goods.

After being set up, the IP unit led the full implementation projects of the new purchasing solutions and of operating room e-procurement. At present, it is leading the e-logistics project introduction, managing online purchases, and supervising the go-live phase of the operating room e-procurement.

Research Findings on the Completed Implementations

After the full implementation of e-procurement solutions in purchasing and invoice processing, a detailed research was performed (Federici, 2006) in order to assess the actual organizational changes introduced and the performance benefits obtained. Five new procedures were examined: four located in the purchasing phase (two related to e-tendering, #1 and #3, and two to e-requisitioning, #2 and #4) and one in invoice processing (#5).

The analysis compared five workflow pairs representing homologous segments of the end-to-end procurement cycle (see Table 1), each related to a traditional paper-based procedure (T) and to an innovative one (I). Although very different, the compared procedure pairs receive the same input at the same stage of the procurement cycle and produce the same output in the same overall context (normative, good or service to be purchased, value of the purchase, etc.).

In order to point out the changes introduced when implementing e-procurement solutions, the following quantitative comparisons were performed between the workflows of equivalent procedures:

- three on organizational dimensions: number of the performed tasks, number of the offices, and number of the different roles involved;
- two on performance indicators: total elapsed time (in calendar days) and total effort (in minutes), calculating for each of them the standard value, and the range between maximum and minimum values.

In short, the research revealed several changes brought in by the e-procurement solutions already implemented:

- the number of tasks is almost always lower in the innovative (I), generally simpler, pa-

perless workflows (in three cases by more than 30%);
- the number of offices involved is equal in the two versions of the workflows, except in comparisons #2 and #3 where all the evaluation or a large part of it is performed on the innovative procedures introduced by CONSIP for all PAs;
- the number of roles involved is slightly lower in the innovative (I) workflows; tenders over threshold are an exception, since the online process asks for a new activity—the technical preclassification of tenders submitted, performed by an expert in the field of the purchased goods—that is not present in the traditional (T) workflow;
- the length of the workflows (in terms of total elapsed time) is largely reduced with e-procurement in both standard value and min–max range (the reduction sometime is greater than 80%): this means that the supply contracts can be closed in a shorter and more predictable time, which is very important for critical services, like in healthcare;
- the total effort requested to achieve the same target is always lower for e-procurement workflows (I), often significantly (from 15% up to more than 90%). In three cases out of five, the reduction is greater for range than for standard value: this suggests that, besides the efficiency improvement, the use of resources could be better programmed.

The significant results measured originated anyway more from cleaning-up the workflows and using faster communication tools than from performing a deeper redesign, as suggested by the involvement of the same offices and roles, and by the similarity in the number of tasks, in each workflow pair (it must also be observed that the examined workflows refer to procedures heavily conditioned by laws and rules that limit the depth of the redesign action).

Figure 11. Structure of the purchasing and logistic department with fully implemented e-procurement (Phase 3: in the next future)

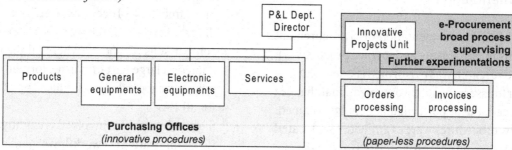

The largest differences and the best results were found in those comparisons—#2, where a tender paper-based procedure is replaced by an e-requisitioning solution, and partially #3—in which the new solutions (up to now used only for common spending) lack some activities for the buyer LHA—sourcing, evaluating, and admitting suppliers; classifying goods and services—performed in advance by an external subject (CONSIP).

Phase 3: Towards a Totally Electronic Procurement Process

The described scenario for the development of e-procurement is the outcome of a series of managerial decisions based on the assumption that the characteristics of the traditional and innovative sides are quite different in terms of: required knowledge, operating ways, and personnel profiles. The P&L Department Director's goal is now to completely substitute the traditional purchasing procedures with the innovative ones become usual for the agency, at least in the IP unit. Then he wants to reassign to the four traditional purchasing offices the use of the e-purchasing tools in all of their operations. To reach this target, the know-how related to the new solutions must be transferred to them, and he thinks to assign this task to the IP unit, to be performed with

short courses and an extended period of support on the job.

At the end of this process (see Figure 11), the IP unit will lose its buyer role and will be in charge of controlling and auditing the broad e-procurement process and of carrying out tests on other possible innovative solutions along it. The LHA of Viterbo is now planning other innovative solutions in the procurement domain, first of all, the adaptation to the laboratory tests of the "intervention-based" concept, already introduced in operating room e-procurement. This innovation involves highly specialized goods and until now encountered the resistances of the suppliers, which are very hard to be overcome because of their limited number.

CURRENT CHALLENGES

Various challenges are still open for the LHA in question, in order to achieve the full substitution of the traditional procurement procedures with brand new ICT-based solutions all along the end-to-end procurement process. These challenges are related to external factors and/or agents, or originate in the internal environment:

- some law restrictions and/or catalogue limitations (indicated in Table 1), which today prevent a wider utilization of the most favorable purchasing solutions for a Local Agency (like direct orders on e-catalogue and on MEPA); these restrictions/limitations should be removed by the Central Procurement Authority in order to increase the attainable improvements;

- limited suppliers' readiness to manage their sales with the innovative tools: most of them (even the biggest ones) often showed not to be prepared to (or not interested in) the most innovative solutions, which join supplies with other services and fully allocate their management on electronic platforms. This problem caused long delays in issuing the tenders both for operating room e-procurement and e-logistics, and still prevents other planned innovations.

- while the sanitary staff in the hospital wards showed a positive will to accept the new solutions, the personnel employed in the administrative areas, in the warehouses and in the laboratories, accustomed since long to work in traditional ways, appeared (and appear) culturally inadequate and resisted/resist to change. Therefore, it will be a hard task to spread innovation in all the environments involved in procurement activities;

- the adoption of new procurement solutions can ask to eliminate some structures (e.g., the centralization of inventory management in the e-logistics project will cause the closure of local warehouses), thereby originating strong resistances by the involved personnel, that should be transferred to other structures and/or change their duty.

Despite these significant obstacles, as stated above, the LHA of Viterbo is already planning other innovative solutions in the procurement domain, first of all the adaptation of the "intervention-based" concept in the procurement for laboratory tests.

CONCLUSION

Procurement in the healthcare sector is quite different from the rest of PA because of a much wider number of goods and sellers, technical characteristics and peculiarities of goods and services, impact on the delivery of critical and specialized services requiring high quality standards, and timeliness of purchases.

Also recalling the previously cited works (Federici, 2005; Federici, 2006), it can be suggested that:

- healthcare spending is highly varied and can be segmented in three categories: *common*, *common-but-differentiated*, and *healthcare-specific*;

- procurement is a process much broader than pure purchasing, which asks for carefully diversified ICT-based solutions as well as thorough process rethinking/redesign;

- to properly respond to the variety of needs and contexts in healthcare, it is advisable to appropriately segment the organizational solutions and adopt coherent e-procurement approaches.

The case of the LHA of Viterbo constitutes a long and articulated experience with positive results, as the adoption of e-procurement solutions led to greater effectiveness and significant efficiency improvements (although of largely different dimensions). These outcomes could be used to eventually materialize administrative cost reductions and/or service enhancements, while respecting organizational or normative restrictions and policies not dealt with in this work.

Some hints can be singled out from the experience, in order to assess its transferability:

- e-procurement can provide improvements also in those contexts, like the purchasing phase, where a deep process redesign is presently inhibited by law constraints;

- improvements are much larger when several tools are brought together to model brand-new organizational solutions, capable to link the supply of goods with their logistics and the processing of the related documents, along the entire procurement process;
- involvement of new resources, with higher education, IT literacy, and will to innovate, in the e-procurement initiatives;
- adoption of a progressive approach, with experimentations and succeeding implementations projects;
- temporary parallel presence of traditional and innovative procedures, until the latter are fixed, in order to secure the supply operations, crucial in a healthcare structure.

REFERENCES

A.dict.it (2007). Electronic service (eService). Voice in K. Lipinski (Ed.), *A dictionary of IT.* Retrieved June 7, 2008, from http://a.dict.it/definition/lexikon//eservice_electronic%20service.html

Anderson, K.V., Juul, N.C., & Pedersen, J.K. (2003, June). *Fractional institutional endeavours and eprocurement in local government.* Paper presented at the 16th Bled Electronic Commerce Conference, Bled, Slovenia.

Berardi, D., Calvanese, D., De Giacomo, G., Lenzerini, M., &. Mecella, M. (2003). *A foundational framework for e-services* (Tech. Rep. No. 10). Rome, Italy: University "La Sapienza," Dipartimento di Informatica e Sistemistica.

Bianchini, A. (2002a, May 8). *La sperimentazione dell'e-procurement negli approvvigionamenti di Sala Operatoria.* Paper presented at the Acquisti Ed E-procurement in Sanità at FORUM PA Conference, Rome. Retrieved June 7, 2008, from www.forumpa.it/forumpa2002/convegni/archivio/S.7/1363-andrea_bianchini.pdf

Bianchini, A. (2002b, November 5). I vantaggi conseguibili attraverso l'esternalizzazione della Logistica di un'azienda sanitaria, proceedings, Milano.

Borgonovi, E. (2004). E-procurement in Sanità: dalla logica di modello alla logica di processo. *Mecosan, 41,* 2–5.

Cicchetti, A. (2004). *La progettazione organizzativa.* Milan, Italy: FrancoAngeli.

CONSIP (2003). *Il Programma di razionalizzazione della spesa per beni e servizi della Pubblica Amministrazione.* CONSIP Annual Report (*house journal*), Rome, Italy.

De Meo, P., Quattrone, G., Terracina, G., & Ursino, D. (2005). Agent-based mining of user profiles for e-services. In J. Wang (Ed.), *Encyclopedia of data warehousing and mining* (pp. 23–27). Hershey, PA, USA: Idea Group Publishing.

Devadoss, P.R., Pan, S.L., & Huang, J.C. (2002). Structurational analysis of e-government initiatives: A case study of SCO. *Decision Support System, I*(34), 253–269.

Federici, T. (2005). An integrated approach in healthcare e-procurement: The case-study of the ASL of Viterbo. In M. Böhlen et al. (Eds.), *E-government: Towards electronic democracy, TCGOV 2005* (LNAI 3416, pp. 298–309). Berlin: Springer.

Federici, T. (2006). Public healthcare: Changes introduced when implementing e-procurement. In *Proceedings of the 2006 Mediterranean Conference on Information Systems.* Venice, Italy: University of Trento.

Hardy, C., & Williams, S.P. (2005). Public eprocurement in action: Policies, practice and technologies. In M. Böhlen et al. (Eds.), *E-government: Towards electronic democracy, TCGOV 2005* (LNAI 3416, pp. 286–297). Berlin: Springer.

Kim, J., & Shunk, D.L. (2004). Matching indirect procurement process with different B2B e-procurement systems. *Computers in Industry, I*(53), 153–164.

MacManus, S.A. (2002). Understanding the incremental nature of e-procurement: Implementation at the state and local levels. *Journal Public Procurement, I*(2), 5–28.

Panayiotou, N.A., Gayialis, S.P., & Tatsiopoulos, I.P. (2004). An e-procurement system for governmental purchasing. *International Journal of Production Economics, I*(90), 79102.

Rossignoli, C. (2004). Nuove forme organizzative e il ruolo delle tecnologie di coordinamento a livello intra-organizzativo e inter-organizzativo. In A. D'Atri (Ed.), *Innovazione organizzativa e tecnologie innovative* (pp. 5768). Milan, Italy: Etas.

Somasundaram, R. (2004). Diffusion of eprocurement in the public sector: Revisiting centralization versus decentralization debates as a twist in the tale. In T. Leino et al. (Eds.), *Proceedings of the 12th European Conference on Information Systems* (pp. 1546–1556). Turku, Finland: School of Economics and Business Administration.

Somasundaram, R., & Damsgaard, J. (2005). Policy recommendations for electronic public procurement. *The Electronic Journal of e-Government, 3*, 147–156.

Zulfiqar, K.A., Pan, S.L., Lee, J., & Huang, J.C. (2001). E-government: An exploratory study of on-line electronic procurement systems. In S. Smithson et al. (Eds.), *Proceedings of the 9th European Conference on Information Systems* (pp. 1010–1024). Bled, Slovenia: Moderna organizacjia.

Chapter XVI
Providing Telemental Health Services after Disasters:
A Case Based on the Post-Tsunami Experience

Shashi Bhushan Gogia
S.A.T.H.I, AMLA MEDIQUIP and Indian Association for Medical Informatics, India

ABSTRACT

The role of information technology (IT) in managing disasters is increasingly being recognized. The Healing Touch project was started after the tsunami disaster in Tamilnadu to address the healthcare needs of the survivors through IT. Specifically, it provided mental health support to the victims near their place of residence. This project has been different from other telemedicine projects because:

- *It was sponsored and managed entirely by NGOs.*
- *The local community and local NGOs were directly trained to manage there own health problems after the natural disaster.*
- *Success was linked to the intensive pre and post execution work done.*

We believe that preparation and involvement of people is the key to success in most IT projects. Some problems we faced were related to a general lack of awareness and nonpenetration of IT in the community we served. If people are using IT in their day to day work, adoption of telemedicine and other e-services will be far simpler after a disaster.

BACKGROUND

"E-Health will completely change health care," says Kendall Ho, who heads the U21 committee (http://www.innovations-report.com/html/reports/medicine_health/report-50033.html) for e-health. "It is one of the fastest-growing fields of health care today, giving undreamt-of opportunities for us to spread our medical knowledge to the whole world."

SATHI is a nongovernment organization (NGO) based in New Delhi and consists of experts from the fields of health, IT, and telecommunications. They provide consultancy services in the fields of telemedicine and healthcare informatics. Their members (see Acknowledgments for a list of the key persons) contribute to the projects on a voluntary basis, whereby SATHI tries to reimburse the actual costs incurred in managing the project. The idea of such varied professionals joining together was mooted in the realization that, at least in India, current practices and efforts in promoting telehealth and related services had not been very successful. SATHI felt that such technology showed great promise, but was providing less than desired outcomes. Important related aspects to this technology such as change management and capacity building and so forth were lacking. Probably a different approach was required.

SATHI was registered in 2004. The current report pertains to the very first project assignment of SATHI. It was named Healing Touch (Gogia & Surwade, 2006)

The Technology

The dictionary definition of *telemedicine* is the use of telecommunications technology to provide, enhance, or expedite healthcare services, as by accessing off-site databases, linking clinics or physicians' offices to central hospitals, or transmitting x-rays or other diagnostic images for examination at another site. *E-health*, however is a much more encompassing term. This has been defined by World Health Organization (WHO) as:

The delivery of healthcare services, where distance is a critical factor, by all healthcare professionals using information and communication technologies for the exchange of valid information for diagnosis, treatment and prevention of disease and injuries, research and evaluation, and for the continuing education of healthcare providers, all in the interests of advancing the health of individuals and their communities.

Telemedicine was initially conceived to provide healthcare to space travelers, thereafter to extending healthcare facilities for the geographically hard-to-reach and the underserved, literally providing a virtual doctor to places where a physical presence is a problem. With time, telemedicine is becoming more widespread, less costly, and new applications are emerging. The technology has moved from expensive room-sized systems to the desktop personal computer, and now further to the Internet, as well as mobile phones and palm tops.

Healthcare in India

India, with its large population (1029 million in 2001), has vastly varied terrains. The range consists of deserts, coastal regions, tropical jungles, islands, and mountains (CIA, 2001). Roads and physical reach are a problem in many areas. 72.2% of India's population is rural (United Nations Economic and Social Commission for Asia and the Pacific, 2000), and this population is supplied by less than 30% of medical professionals. The ratio for specialized medical care is worse with less than 4% of specialists serving in rural areas.

Even while healthcare in India is free and the responsibility of the state, over 70% of the population prefers to pay for treatment as the actual availability of the facilities leaves much to be desired. To service this demand, rural areas are filled with healthcare workers without adequate training as most doctors having better qualification are unwilling to work in such places. There is a lack of adequate facilities for them to satisfactorily practice to the level of training imparted to them. Good schools for their children as well as social and entertainment facilities matching the standards of living which they are used to are also lacking.

While actual healthcare expenditure in India constitutes 5.2% of GDP (gross development product), as compared with 2.7% in China (WHO World Health Report, 2000), it is widely believed that it can go up to 15% of the budget of most families. In rural areas, much of the expenditure is wasted on the transportation to the nearest healthcare facility. Bringing down transportation costs, including the time wasted for travel, is the real boon which telemedicine can provide. Traditionally, in India any sick person is accompanied by three or four persons when he goes to a hospital. Thus, the time off work for them is an additional hidden cost.

Though not widely publicized, we have come to know that China has been doing teleconsultations for a long time mostly through telephone as well as other means using experts in the cities and a wide network of less qualified barefoot doctors present in the community (Dr. B.S. Bedi, personal communication, 2006). Telemedicine as a concept was designed to take care of health problems of space travelers (Garshnek, 1991) and first applied in a disaster situation after the Mexico earthquake (Garshnek & Burkle, 1999).

Setting the Stage

Telemedicine is a generic term but comes in various streams:

- **Between patient and doctor** which generally means a direct virtual consultation by the patient or his relative through e-mail or telephone.

- **Between a general practitioner** or any healthcare provider which could be an untrained village health practitioner or nurse (as the setting in this case) *and an expert/specialist* who happens to know more about a particular problem (see below).
- **Between specialists**. These are online discussion forums and user groups. The Association of Plastic Surgeons of India (APSI) runs an active discussion group (plastic_surgery@yahoogroup.com) where difficult and interesting cases are presented and the ensuing discussion helps the members to manage the patients with similar problems better.
- **Through e-learning programs**. Training and skill upgrading of healthcare workers can be provided online. Joshi (in press) cites that his organization provides education and training to parents on how to take care of spastic as well as disabled children.
- **Through home telemedicine**. Many gadgets are available which can monitor the elderly and infirm for problems and provide timely reminders for taking medicines.
- **By telerobotic surgery**, and so on,

The stream with the most relevance to developing countries is through improving the skills of any local healthcare practitioner with the expert. The average individual goes to her nearest medicine man whenever unwell. Generally, in India, for persons in rural areas and other far-flung places, the healthcare provider would be untrained and practicing medicine as per the family occupation or after working as an apprentice with a doctor for some time in a town.

80–90% of diseases are known to be self limiting or treatable by simple measures. However, since one would have taken advice, credit is provided to the health provider from whom the advice was taken, irrespective of whether the improvement was a result of, or in spite of, the advice. Thus, over time, faith, respect, and fame of varying degrees is achieved by any healthcare service provider whatever the qualification. Ensuring a licensing regime for such untrained persons is difficult to achieve due to the lack of suitable alternatives. However, in such a scenario, persons who have a genuine problem will suffer due to a delay in treatment and, occasionally, inappropriate treatment. A consultancy with the trained persons can help the local practitioner decide on what is to be done: Is local treatment possible?, its specifics, and if not, where and how to shift (Gogia, 2002). Each teleconsultation becomes an opportunity to interact with the specialist to learn more about the problem at hand and upgrading one's knowledge.

The Tsunami Disaster

The worldwide response to the tsunami disaster on December 26, 2004 resulted in a massive outpouring of personnel, materials, and funds. Healthcare was felt as a primary need for the survivors.

Management of disasters is broadly categorized into four phases: preparedness, mitigation, response, and recovery (Warfield, 2007). The phase immediate after the disaster is the response phase which can be further subclassified (see Box 1).

After any natural or man-made disaster, supplies, food, and so forth can be moved to the affected area, but disease and healthcare needs require specialized care which in most cases mean a reverse transfer.

Box 1. Phases of healthcare response after disasters; Use of IT can improve the outcome in all three.

Acute *(0-72 hours)* – Evacuation and care of the injured, taking care of dead bodies, emergency supplies of food and medicines
Intermediate *(3–21 days)* – Sanitation, providing shelter, continuing water supply to prevent epidemics
Late *(after 3 weeks)* – Rehabilitation and care of the late health problems like PTSD

Citing his experience after the Kashmir Earthquake of 2005, Patoli (2006) found telemedicine to be an effective method of helping the healthcare aspects of disasters. It can provide the specialists virtually to the affected area(s), overcoming time and geographical barriers. However, most studies in telemedicine in general and specifically in disasters have concentrated on the technology rather than the implementation. Shifting from a normal physical healthcare provision to a virtual availability is a significant change. This requires following change management principles and the key to SATHI's approach to this project.

Box 2. Telemedicine processes

There are two main forms of teleconsultations, the most common called **Store and Forward** technology.

In this, all medical records are stored electronically in a local database. On need for opinion, patients' records with all images and reports are transmitted normally during the night or hours of low telecommunication demand, although with current available technology of high speeds, such a restriction may be superfluous.

The other type is **Real Time** where dynamic active video conferencing or live data transfer takes place.

In a normal teleconsultation, a combination is used per need. Data are transferred beforehand and appointment set for a live session. In this, speech and eye contact for the patient provided online and reports are reviewed. Some questions are asked for clarification or even a possible online clinical examination may be done. Examples would be skin lesions sent through a digital or the VC camera, listening to heart sounds by using a digital stethoscope, asking the patient to walk, and so forth.

Thereafter, the patient may be asked to do some tasks as explained by the specialist or further tests may be requested. After that, the patient maybe provided a prescription online.

A referring doctor or the patient is then informed on what to do. Telecounseling, especially for psychiatric cases, is possible through VC.

Sometimes the patient may be asked to come to the expert center for a procedure. An appointment is given and problems and means of transfer explained. In emergency situations, preparations are made for receiving the patient.

Schiesser (2002) defines Change Management as "a process to control and coordinate all changes to an IT production environment."

According to Wikipedia (2007), change management is responsible for managing change process involving:

- Hardware
- Communications equipment and software
- System software

Box 3. List of activities performed by SATHI (further details in full text)

- **Preliminary planning** and design of project.

- Preliminary visit to the project area consisting of a **needs assessment survey**. This helped to identify the health problems faced by the survivors. An evaluation of the existing health system was also done for adequacy and possible areas of reinforcement.

A personal visit and interview of the identified NGOs who were potential partners, both in periphery as well as expert end, was done alongside with discussions with government functionaries.

These interviews were accompanied with **concept marketing and orientation** of the persons interviewed. A look into connectivity needs and how they could be fulfilled. Based on the visit report, the project was redesigned and a formal order the systems (hardware and software) was placed.

- **Create MOUs**. These were between the various identified partners of the project meaning OXFAM, SCARF, and other local NGOs.

- **Install the systems** in the identified locations. **Training** of the local persons who will manage the sessions, on how identifying the problem cases, running the systems, conducting the sessions, troubleshooting, and so on. Test sessions were held before a formal launch under SATHI's supervision as well as an engineering representative from the vendor.

- **Streamlining** of the project included setting and fine tuning protocols for identified problems and setting up the time table for the consultations, which was called TCS (telemedicine consultation session) time table.

- **Feedback** was obtained on a regular basis with reporting mechanisms in place.

- Outcome analysis, done by an outside agency, was planned at the outset as this was to be a pilot.

- All documentation and procedures associated with the running, support, and maintenance of live systems.

As will be shown later, this was the route SATHI followed and some of the problems faced were due to lack of maintenance support, failing hardware and software as well absent communication links—factors which were beyond our control or not managed well due to our inexperience in properly dealing with vendors, and so on.

Telemedicine is yet to be regarded as a primary tool in the management of disasters. However, many e-health experts (e.g., Mathew, 2004) have emphasized that IT will and can help disaster management, but much preparatory work is required.

While worldwide telemedicine programs have increased in number in hospitals, academic departments, managed care organizations, homes, schools, prisons, and so on, in India most efforts were limited to government organizations, the most prominent being ISRO (Indian Space Research Organization). Most of these efforts were to provide teleconsultations to persons in far-flung places However, the rural community, the one desperately in need of quality care, has so far been unable to reap the benefits. A perusal of the above Web site has shown that most linkages are between district hospitals with referral hospitals. The tsunami had affected areas largely at the village and block level where any health services let alone technology was simply unavailable.

The tsunami disaster spurred SATHI, like many other organizations, to reach out to help those affected. With a basic guiding principle that "More people die of after-effects of natural disaster than the disaster itself," SATHI felt that telemedicine can and should provide a solution to control the "disaster after the disaster" through efficiency and greater reach of the health services on offer. SATHI offered its services to various organizations, stating that SATHI could provide data collection services as well as help in improving the health status in a sustainable manner. It received support from OXFAM Trust India, the Indian branch of OXFAM International wherein the SATHI would be providing consultancy to manage healthcare in the relief centres run by OXFAM and its sister organizations. OXFAM was also concerned with the mental affects of disasters having experienced during their rehabilitation efforts in previous disasters (Sharma, 2002).

SATHI was fortunate to get funding for the project with a relatively free hand. The project was to be treated as pilot which could show sustainability of telemedicine along with providing some immediate gains to the tsunami victims, an attempt to showcase the use of IT in healthcare after disasters.

CASE DESCRIPTION

A summary of the procedures that follows is listed in Box 4.

Once the MOU was signed, a detailed plan to execute the project was drawn out. Preliminary discussions were done between OXFAM as well as the possible vendors of the hardware and software. BSNL (Bharat Sanchar Nigam Limited), the local telephone service provider in the area of concern, was identified as the resource for connectivity.

The **needs assessment** was done through a personal field visit to the affected areas in the second half of January 2005. This consisted of a survey of the affected areas where we analyzed the location-specific health needs and available health services provisions directly by the government or

camps run by other NGOs. Our emphasis was to look for and thereon fill the gaps, if any.

Simultaneously, meetings were held with local NGOs to assess their willingness as well as capabilities to do the tasks required. Availability of connectivity was to be at a level which could ensure video conferencing (VC).

The needs assessment survey showed that as far as healthcare was concerned, the first and second phases of the disaster were well managed by the government and supporting NGOs in the areas visited (parts of Pondicherry and Nagapattinam district of Tamilnadu). Epidemiology and disease surveillance had already been activated in the entire district. This was part of an Integrated Disease Surveillance Program (IDSP) run by National Institute of Communicable Diseases (NICD), a central government organization.

However, a need for mental health support was found due to a high incidence of a sense of loss and bewilderment among the survivors who continued to be gripped with fear and a sense of shock. They were anxious, depressed, displaced from their homes, and had lost their family members and loved ones. Most were too frightened to rejoin their regular occupation of fishing.

Illustration 1. Map of areas affected by the Tsunami. Chennai was our main centre

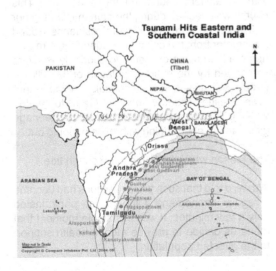

Box 4. IDSP program

The IDSP program is a World Bank funded project where the local health care workers collect door to door data pertaining to disease incidence and health status and then upload to a central server via a satellite link from the district centre. Nagapattinam district, after the tsunami, was the very first place to launch this program.

Alcoholism was rampant as well as mass panic reactions; we experienced one ourselves where we found the entire populace, vehicles, and even animals running away form the coast at a time of a particular high tide (see Box 5).

The people were ignorant about the tsunami: What was it? Will it strike again? How will we be prepared? How will we cope with its after effects?

The occurrence of this problem was articulated by WHO (The Hindu, 2005). Steps taken by the government for upgrading of mental health of the victims were found to be inadequate as well as wrongly directed. There was a mismatch between needs and services with an inadequate number of mental health specialists. A high incidence of stress and fatigue among relief workers with no community participation was also found.

As per the WHO reports, following disasters, 80–90% of the population have a lowered mental health status, a situation which would improve in most. However, 4–5% would be serious cases requiring specialist help. PTSD (post-traumatic stress disorder) and other serious mental problems

Text 5. Panic reaction in Vellangani

The village of Vellangani is a religious tourist spot with an ancient church on the sea coast. This church was flooded during the tsunami. During our visit there, we were at a villagers' residence around a kilometer from the coast. At around 5:00 p.m., we heard a loud noise outside and suddenly we were confronted by the entire population of the village, people, vehicles, and even animals running further inland yelling "*Thaneer Thaneer*" (Tamil for "water, water"). The most vivid image was of two teenage girls panting and running with eyes popping out.

The reason was later found to be a high tide.

We were told that such panic reactions had become a regular phenomena. Although the panic lasted only a few minutes, it was this single moment that made us decide to provide mental health support to the affected population.

manifest a few weeks after the disaster and the effects can last for up to 1–2 years in some cases.

The problem was in identifying the exact victims who would require specialized medical help. This meant a virtual door-to-door search on a repeated basis. Telemedicine was thought to be the right solution to these problems since it would allow the specialist to train the health workers, who being in the community could organize such searches better and on a continual basis to identify this 4–5%. This would ensure access to specialists' services for the real victims and would also ensure quality. Since health workers might themselves be affected, one could not rely on them alone without external specialist help.

The Healing Touch was conceptualized after the above assessment. Possible solutions were analyzed and specifics of the telemedicine network planned. Various possible additional partners and stakeholders were identified and an advocacy and orientation plan rolled out. This included concept marketing and social mobilization of additional NGOs and those who could contribute specialized mental health support.

Once the partnering NGOs were identified and found agreeable, Memoriam of Understandings (MOUs) between the various stakeholders, between OXFAM and local NGO, as well as between various NGOs themselves, were drafted and presented for formal signature.

During preliminary discussions, SATHI had planned for and thereby placed an initial order for complete telemedicine systems, with peripherals like scanners and the like. On reassessment, mental health support was found to be the sole healthcare requirement with all other healthcare needs of the tsunami victims already being well provisioned for by the government and other agencies. Disease surveillance was well in progress through IDSP. Thereby, the planned epidemiology module was found unnecessary. With funding becoming a problem, orders for the entire set of add-on peripherals like an ECG machine and scanner and other equipment were also shelved. A limited scope meant a more focused approach with a decreased need for orientation and capacity building. Thus, finally VC and basic data collection through an EMR (electronic medical record) module were selected as the components to be used.

The following were provided at each location:

1. Pentium II PC with Windows 2000 as OS and standard hardware prevalent at that time:
   - 256 MB RAM
   - 40 GB hard disk
   - External modem
   - Printer
2. Video-conferencing equipment was provided by the systems vendor which consisted of:
   - Add on VC card to the above PC
   - PC based VC camera
   - Multimedia speakers
   - PC microphone
   - Telephone type handset
3. EMR software was provided as part of the system. The entire system was a stand-alone self sufficient plug and play type, the vendor also sent its own engineer to train the community workers for usage.
4. USB (universal serial bus) and other relevant ports were provided for connectivity through external devices, modem, and ethernet card.
5. Regular power was a problem so a UPS (Un-interrrupted Power Supply) was provided. Option of a generator was left to the local NGO managing the system.

Connectivity add-ons were to be provided as per local availability. Possibilities were:

- **Satellite,** which could provide mobile connectivity and could reach all possible areas.

Free satellite connectivity daily for one hour was promised for a month or so along with the relevant hardware (INMARSAT) through the equipment vendor who happened to have a relevant tie up with European Space Agency for the same. However, it did not happen as trials by them regarding VC had not been very successful with the INMARSAT equipment in a separate project in Sri Lanka. The only local provider of satellite connectivity was ISRO. After disappointment with INMARSATs, we petitioned ISRO, but could not get the requisite linkages. The quoted cost of satellite connectivity (Rs 60/approximately US $1.33 per minute as per 2005 currency rates) was a limiting factor. Connectivity costs were to be managed by the local NGO.

- **ISDN** (integrated switching data network) was found to be the low cost option wherein the average per minute cost was one local phone call (less than one U.S. cent per minute for every 64 Kbps connectivity). 128 Kbps was felt to be adequate for video conferencing. ISDN connectivity, although promised by the local telephone company at all possible locations, was found to have limitations and could not be used wherever we desired. There were some limitations: The regional telephone exchange had to be electronic and capable of providing ISDN services, and the final location should require less than 2.5 Kms of wiring from the regional exchange. At some places, the exchange itself had been flooded. Therefore, provision of any land line service was expected to take time.
- **Dial-up networking,** though possible at all places, was found to provide inadequate bandwidth as video conferencing was an essential component.
- **Mobile** connectivity was again found to provide inadequate bandwidth.
- **Broadband** Internet through ADSL (asynchronous digital subscriber link) was not yet prevalent in the affected areas, except in Chennai.

- **WiMax** similarly has still not become prevalent widely.

Finally, ISDN was decided to be the connectivity option of choice as it was the cheapest, could support video conferencing, and was available albeit at select locations. An application was placed with BSNL, the company providing telephone and ISDN services locally. Though connectivity on demand had been promised in view of the scale and emergent nature of the problem, actual delivery was delayed by a few months.

SATHI ascribed the delay to a poor initial understanding of the above requirements. In one place, considered ideal for provision of telemedicine services (Tharangammbadi), the equipment could not be utilized and had to be shifted elsewhere as ISDN connectivity was not possible. Associated training of personnel and preparation of the site got wasted (see Table 1).

The network provided counseling (through video conferencing for the victim) in the presence of the health worker. Individual and group sessions were possible. No traveling was required by the victims. The local volunteers were responsible for identifying the possible members of the community who required support after a short training course by a personal visit of the expert team to the field. A time and date for the counseling sessions was set and the volunteers held responsible for providing continuous learning and supervision on the job as well as on the spot.

Box 6. Health systems in India

In India the health system is structured according to the Bhore Committee report (1948) wherein the basic health services are provisioned at the primary, or community, level through PHCs (primary health centres) and their subcentres who refer, if required, to the secondary level (district and Taluk hospitals) and thereafter for specialty services to the tertiary level (medical colleges and tertiary care hospitals in select locations).

A teleconference based training module was developed by SATHI. This was used for the orientation of the community health workers and experts. Hard copies were also made available for review. These were based on WHO recommendations with some separate guidelines for relief workers themselves affected directly or indirectly by the disaster.

Experts from SCARF, on their own, had arranged to travel to the affected areas before the start of the project to familiarize themselves with the persons whom they would be meeting through VC. The local volunteers were trained to identify mental health problems in the community and how to bring the more affected to the telecentre for direct teleconsultations with the experts. Initial sessions were managed in the presence of our representative or the engineer installing the systems. Later, on the job and continuous training using an innovative interactive and participatory training methodology supported through audiovisuals was made possible through VC.

Since SATHI is based in New Delhi, far from the affected area, the experts traveled to the affected area for planning and implementation spending over 40 days for the project planning and implementation. Many activities and online discussions took place later through VC from its office with the project partners at the peripheral as well as expert locations.

Since SATHI could only offer occasional and limited help after the initial orientation and installation, it can be said that the project has been conceptualized and managed by the community itself. Being operable at the village level, it integrated well with the present health system in India (see Box 6) both vertically (i.e., across the primary, secondary, and tertiary care providers) as well as horizontally (i.e., among the networked units). It turned out to be an empowering exercise for the community and an exemplary partnership between the government, NGOs, as well as community and development support agencies.

Telemedicine enabled the affected people

and community to reach out and to articulate their needs. The affected persons participated in interactive sessions with experts and enabled healthcare service provider to be need specific. It strengthened the healthcare delivery system and increased the efficiency of service provider by allowing wider coverage.

The Project Cycle

The tsunami disaster occurred on December 26, 2004. The project was conceptualized in January 2005. All initial processes, identification of stakeholders, operators, locations, and so forth were ready by mid-February 6–7 units were planned in the periphery and one in the centre. SCARF (Schizophrenia Research Foundation), a psychiatric care centre in Chennai, was identified as the expert or central unit, which would provide mental health support.

This selection was based on the aspects of willingness to do voluntary work, familiarity with the local (Tamil) language, as well as proximity to the affected areas. SATHI tried to ensure that in case of need, actual transfer for the more serious cases and continued care through the same facility would be possible.

Units in the periphery were to be located in various places depending on:

- The percentage of the population affected by the tsunami.
- Motivation level and capability of the local NGOs. In this, their motivation and initiative was assessed along with the ability to run the system. They had to have access to or in possession of a room at least 10 feet by 10 feet with relevant furniture for housing the telemedicine facility. Access to government channels if using government facilities IT skilled personnel capable of running and troubleshooting the equipment were required. Adequate financial capability with a willing-

ness to pay the day to day running costs of the staff and connectivity was essential.
- Proximity of the proposed location to the exchange (to allow ISDN connectivity).

The units were to be located in the Primary Health Centre or a government hospital in the tsunami affected area and run by the health workers with supervision and support by local NGOs. Funding support for the machines as well as for maintenance and connectivity for the first 6 months was assured by the funding organization. Alternatively, as stated above, if the NGO had enough funds and their own doctors, they were invited to run it fully themselves.

A review of the decided locations and there eventual outcome is hereby listed in Table 1.

Thus, in summary, the project could not start until middle of May 2005 due to the reasons outlined above and summarized below:

- **Funding** was slow. It was never fully released.
- **New type of technology**, so there were doubts about the project. Some senior functionaries in the funding organization were not in favor. SATHI being a recently registered organization, its capabilities were felt to be suspect by some. Delays meant that continues retraining of volunteers was required. With delayed funding which was cut short, the expansion plan was delayed and had to be shelved ultimately. By the time it was actually released (October 2005), many earmarked places had already lost interest and some of the need for mental health support had decreased.
- **Connectivity** took too long. In Chennai connectivity was provided in a day in early February 2005. In the periphery, the regional office was around 100 Kms from the coast. Though orders were placed for ISDN lines in February, the lines were not made available until May. Reasons for nonrelease of the con-

Table 1. Implementation details of various locations for the Healing Touch Project

Location	Reasons	Outcome and Remarks
Tharangammbadi	Largest rehabilitation colony in affected area with over 1000 families Local Taluk hospital in midst of rehabilitation colony Support from local NGO available (PEDA) Willing staff and doctors in the hospital	The first peripheral location where the equipment was installed. Local staff and doctors both from the Taluk (community) hospital as well as PEDA were trained. Later connectivity by ISDN was not found possible as the local exchange was too old. Attempts for reaching though satellite were also unsuccessful for reasons cited above. Finally the equipment was shifted out.
SCARF Chennai (Expert service provider)	Reputed mental health facility Voluntary organization already working in providing support to the Tsunami victims Willing and ample support from the director (Dr. R. Thara) and staff IT aware and knowledgeable staff No language problems	Equipment and staff were trained within a day of installation. This was in late February 2005. ISDN connectivity was provided on demand. SCARF sent its doctors and staff for its initial orientation and training to all peripheral locations. They have been a major contributor to the success of the program.
Dharmakulam	Support from local NGO (ISED) Part of affected area Connectivity possible	It was initially planned to install in the local government health facility (Thiruvengadu) but that was too far from the affected area. Thereafter a room was taken on rent near the affected area in Dharamkulam village near Poompuhar a noted tourism centre of Tamilnadu. ISDN connectivity took a long time and finally was made available only in May 2005. This centre has been successfully working since then. The mental needs are over after 79 teleconsultation sessions and 249 patients seen over 6 months. Two possible suicides have reportedly been prevented.
Kariakal	Support from local NGO (PEDA) Good connectivity options	Equipment promised for Tharangambaddi was eventually shifted here with management by the same local NGO. However, the decision to shift was taken late, as there had been hope of getting satellite connectivity through INMARSATs or ISRO in the previous location. Equipment and connectivity became available only by February 2006. This centre has been successfully working since then (see enclosed case report).
Seradure Village	Deeply affected area Supporting staff and orientation provided in the government health centre	Could not find a suitable local NGO to manage the project.
Kalpakkam, Akaripettai and many others	Affected area Exchange has ISDN capability	Late decision and funding limited though local NGOs were identified for some of these locations.
Sundaram Medical Foundation (SMF) (Expert Service Provider)	Super specialty medical facility in Chennai Works in close alliance with SCARF No language problems	Decision to limit the project as a pilot Consultations for nonmental health needs could be done by the doctors traveling to the SCARF centre nearby in the absence of their own telemedicine unit.
Various places in Nagapattinam	These were possible partners of the project for the expansion which did not take place.	Planned for mobile connectivity wherein a van hired or owned by the NGO would travel to the location at a fixed time and provide consultancy. Lack of satellite linkages shelved this approach.

Box 7. Case report from our project. Courtesy of OXFAM.

Towards a better childhood

There were many children who were traumatized due to the aftermath of the tsunami, as they were either sole survivors or those who have escaped the clutches of death in a fraction of second due to their presence of mind. Arul, aged 14 years who belongs to the fishermen village of Karaikalmedu, is one such lucky victim. He has two younger sisters. Arul's mother was helpless even though she knew that her son showed abnormal symptoms and reported the same to her neighbors. Barefoot counselors who visited the village did provide some counseling help to the family and tried to verbally motivate Arul. However Arul's condition had been the same for the past 1 year with more irritating symptoms and conditions unmanageable.

His mother was not able to even take him to the district hospital, as he was not cooperative and used to disappear from the neighborhood when insisted. PEDAs initial community training that was imparted with the help of SCARF, Chennai to the Self-Help Group Leaders was the stepping-stone in bringing back the lost childhood for Arul. Maivizhi, the SHG leader who attended the training on identifying people with psychological symptoms noticed the child and confirmed the same with the community health worker from PEDA during her field visit. She was very instrumental in bringing the child to the telemedicine centre by motivating her parents. Arul's family did have the opportunity to speak to the psychiatrist about his condition and his treatment plan was put in place.

The community health worker and the SHG group leader today are regular in following his improvement. Today Arul is back to normalcy after 4 months of treatment, he was also the first among the few who were referred to the telemedicine centre. He has shown remarkable improvement in his mental health condition that has been very beneficial for the PEDA staff to reach out to more number of people. Maivizhi has become an ardent supporter of the system and the technology. She advocates to many who chat with her about such symptoms and provides voluntary service and referrals to the telemedicine centre on a weekly basis as she puts it right by saying "I have seen the progress of Arul and many others back to normal like us and that is the reason why I am very much involved in raising awareness about the issue of mental illness as it is one area which our community believed to be as witchcraft."

A happy and reformed Arul posing with his sister.

Box 8. Quotations from evaluation report. Courtesy of OXFAM.

"Telemental Health is economically viable"

"This project has indeed provided a working model to provide quality mental health care to the rural population. Further use of Telemedicine as a tool to cater to the health needs of the communities has improved availability, reduced cost and improves health outcomes at large"

"Community empowered to seek the mental health care using telemedicine network providing access to specialists"

"Significant local capacity built ensuring sustainability of service delivery system. Community Mental Health volunteers trained, Local facilitating NGO's capacity built"

"In general, acceptance of Telemedicine by the public and patients is far higher than the physicians"

---

nectivity (see above) were understood only following a personal visit from a SATHI representative to the regional office during mid-April 2005 in what was its fourth visit. Thereafter, the location plans were changed but it still took a month more for starting the sessions.

Currently, there are three systems, two in the periphery and one in the centre (SCARF). At all these places, connectivity has been established and the system are up and running. Initially, there used to be thrice weekly sessions wherein patients—those felt to be most affected—were asked to come to the local telemedicine centre by the specially trained community health workers. These patients were seen online by doctors from SCARF and counseling was done; medicines prescribed by the doctors online were provided to the patients by the attending volunteers; a separate stock of medicines used was kept locally as no chemists were available in the periphery.

The patients in Dharmakulam and surrounding areas requiring mental health support have been largely treated. Volunteers from here are now asking for online treatment for other specialties like general medicine, cardiology, and so on.

An evaluation has been done independently by OXFAM. This was by Mr. Saharaj Louis and submitted in May 2006. The summary of his findings have been listed in Box 8.

Current Status and Outcomes

A model telemedicine network has been developed. The design of this model is specific to the needs and integrates the service providers with field level facilitators.

The capacity of the field level NGOs has been built in terms of the operation of the telemedicine network and skills to conduct counseling sessions at the community level.

A unified approach to respond to the disaster situation with application of the communication technology and network of health and other professionals has been developed. This would enable reducing the response time to future disasters. Professionals as well as a service providers' network will be available in future.

The project has contributed to defining the modalities for disaster response.

A parallel attempt of using IT to improve disaster preparedness has been recommended. This includes making available IT facilities in many areas so that trained persons are readily available as well as a national database of the population, NGOs, healthcare facilities, and so forth, which can quickly set up a response team.

FUTURE CHALLENGES

Funding has been a problem for most healthcare IT projects as the outcomes of previous ventures had been disappointing.

Excessive promotional efforts by vendors used to result in far higher allocation for the technology itself rather than its implementation. Technology however, contributes only 20% to the success of any new technology project; 75% depends on proper implementation (i.e., change management) and 5% on luck (Karthikeyan, personal communication, 2006).

The role of IT in managing healthcare has been recognized but implementation has been a problem. A proper response requires a cultural change and availability of software and hardware at all and especially the disaster prone ones who are running the systems as part of daily routine. Once they are trained, getting such systems to work in emergencies will not require the massive orientation and marketing exercise that SATHI had to do.

ACKNOWLEDGMENT

- **Members of SATHI (**http://www.sathi.org**)** The actual work and field trips were done by Dr. S.B. Gogia (the current author) and Dr. M.R. Surwade.
  Dr. Vidya Surwade, Ms. Arun Rekha, Mr. Ramesh Verma, Dr. Sanjay Bedi, Dr. Lazar Mathew, Dr. R.S. Tyagi and Prof. Sneh Bhargava helped in the background work, administrative assistance, and assessments.
- **The OXFAM Team (**http://www.oxfamint.org.in**)** Ms. Gurinder Kaur, then Executive Director
  Ms. Meetha Parti
  Ms. Madhushree Bannerjee
  Mr. Manishi Chandra
  Ms. Shubhangi Sharma
  Others
- **SCARF (**http://www.scarfonline.org**)** Schizophrenia Research Foundation, Anna Nagar Chennai, the *expert* service provider
- **PEDA (**Peoples Education Development Association, Karaikal, Pondicherry), the NGO working in Kariakal
- **ISED (**Institute for Social Education and Development, Chennai and Thiruvengadu), the NGO working in Dharmakulam
- **Other NGOs** were involved in the discussions
- **Tamilnadu Government**
  Dr. R. Damodharan (then Deputy Directory of Health Services, Nagapattinam District)
  Dr. Supriya Sahu (then Joint Secretary of Health, Tamilnadu state)
- **Vendors of the Equipment**
  Ms Online Infocomm, Ahmedabad, India
  Ms I-Diagnosis, Ahmedabad, India
- **Mr. Saharaj Louis** for photographs and quotations (Box 8) as well as the submitted case report (Box 7)

REFERENCES

CIA. (2001). *The world factbook 2001*. Washington, DC: Office of Public Affairs.

DECU (a unit of ISRO) describing ISRO Telemedicine Projects. Retrieved June 7, 2008, from http://www.isro.org/decu/projects/indextele.htm

Free Dictionary, The. Retrieved June 7, 2008, from http://www.thefreedictionary.com/telemedicine

Garshnek, V. (1991). Applications of space communications technology to critical human needs: Rescue, disaster relief, and remote medical assistance. *Space Communication. 8*, 311–317.

Garshnek. V., & Burkle, F.M. (1999). Applications of telemedicine and telecommunications to disaster medicine: Historical and future perspectives. *Journal American Medical Information Association, 6*(1), 26–37.

Gogia, S.B. (2002). *Towards a national telemedicine network*. Paper presented at the 1st National Conference of Telemedicine Society of India at SGPGI, Lucknow, India.

Gogia, S.B., & Surwade, M.R. (2006). *Healthcare technology aspects of disaster management*. Paper presented at the 2nd Global E Health Conference,

New Delhi. Retrieved June 7, 2008, http://openmed.nic.in/1774/01/telmedtsunami.pdf

Hindu, The (Chennai ed.). (2005, January 21). p. 5.

Joshi, G.A. (in press). Role of ICT in disability rehabilitation in rural environment. In *IT and Indian rural healthcare.* Macmillan India.

Louis, S. (2006). *Project Healing Touch: Telemedicine healthcare for tsunami survivors in TamilNadu evaluation report.* (Private publication commissioned by OXFAM Trust, excerpted with permission)

Mathew, D. (2004). Information technology and public health management of disasters: A model for South Asian countries. *Prehospital and Disaster Medicine, 20*(1), 54–60.

Patoli, A.Q. (2006). Role of telemedicine in disaster management. *E Health International Journal, 2*(2), 34.

Schiesser, R. (2002). *IT systems management.* Prentice Hall. ISBN 0-13-087678-X.

Sharma, R. (2002, February 2). Gujarat earthquake causes major mental health problems. *BMJ, 324*(7332), 259.

U21 and the World Health Organization. *E-health is a global revolution for the poor populations of the world.* Retrieved June 7, 2008, from http://www.innovations-report.com/html/reports/medicine_health/report-50033.html

United Nations Economic and Social Commission for Asia and the Pacific (ESCAP) (2000). *Asia and the Pacific in figures 2000.* UN Statistics Division.

Warfield, C. *The disaster management cycle.* Retrieved June 7, 2008, from http://www.gdrc.org/uem/disasters/1-dm_cycle.html

WHO World Health Report. (2000). *Health systems: Improving performance.* WHO.

Wikipedia. (2007). Change Management. Retrieved June 7, 2008, from http://en.wikipedia.org/wiki/Change_Management_(ITIL)

Chapter XVII
vGOV:
Remote Video Access to Government Services

Robert F. Rubeck
University of North Dakota, USA

Glenn A. Miller
University of North Dakota, USA

ABSTRACT

The need of rural and reservation residents to receive better government services has been long-standing. In spite of the best efforts of the Social Security Administration, a vast number of Native Americans living in rural and remote areas have had their access to program information and social benefits limited by distance, economic, and cultural challenges. A project at the University of North Dakota has found a way to transform the delivery of government services to these citizens. As an off-shoot of work in telemedicine and rural outreach, staff members of the Center for Rural Service Delivery collaborated with the Social Security Administration and the Indian Health Service to create the first video link connecting a hospital to a Social Security Office. The IHS hospital, in Belcourt, ND was connected to the SSA office in Minot, ND, some 120 miles away. The video link went live in October of 2003. The social benefits of remote video access to SSA services have been measured by the number of citizens who use video access to seek answers to questions and to make application for benefits each year. Since it went live, the link has resulted in more than 300 completed applications for disability benefits or income supplements. That total is more than 50 times the number produced through conventional service delivery. The economic impact to VSD has been measured as the cumulative value of monthly Supplemental Security Income and Disability payments to individual citizens and the total of annual Medicare and Medicaid reimbursement payments made to local healthcare facilities. The service impact includes increased application completion rates, accelerated claims processing, and increased third party assistance in the application process.

BACKGROUND

Citizens who choose to live in rural and remote communities have long been disadvantaged in their access to healthcare and government services. This inequity is most pronounced among those who are most isolated, the rural elderly, and Native Americans.

Native Americans have long had disproportionate need for government services. Culture, isolation, and scarcity have also helped set the stage for their social disparity and economic dependence. Various, well-intended, federal policies to take care of Indian people have been implemented over the years. However, the very federal agencies charged with 'taking care of' Indian people have routinely been underfunded (Indian Health Service, 2007). Lack of funding then translates into fewer programs and personnel to administer them.

Approximately 55% of American Indians and Alaska Natives living in the United States rely on the Indian Health Service to provide access to health care services in 49 hospitals and nearly 600 other facilities operated by the IHS, Tribes,

and Alaska Native corporations.... The American Indian and Alaska Native people have long experienced lower health status when compared with other Americans. (Indian Health Service, 2006)

The lack of resources to meet the health needs of Native Americans has had dramatic consequences.

- Infant mortality rate is 150% greater for Indians than that of Caucasian infants
- Life expectancy for Indians is nearly 6 years less than the rest of the U.S. population
- Suicide for Indians is 2.5 times higher than the national average
- There are proportionately fewer mental health professionals available to treat Indians than the rest of the U.S. population
- Healthcare expenditures for Indians are less than half of what America spends for federal prisoners (National Indian American Health Board, 2007)

"These are broad quality of life issues rooted in economic adversity and poor social conditions" (IHS, 2006). The poverty rate for American Indi-

Figure 1. Turtle Mountain, North Dakota

ans in North Dakota is more than three times the rate for the North Dakota All Races population: 38% compared to 11% (Indian Health Service, 2007).

Turtle Mountain

The Turtle Mountain Band of Chippewa is 28,000 strong, with 8,000 living on the 6-mile by 12-mile reservation in north central North Dakota near the Canadian border. Social challenges on the reservation include poverty and unemployment. Thirty-six percent of the tribe lives below the poverty level. The average individual income is $8,855. Unemployment on the Turtle Mountain Indian Reservation stands at 70% (Northwest Area Foundation, 2006).

University of North Dakota

The University of North Dakota (UND) "is the state's most comprehensive intensive research university and the primary center for professional education and training. UND enrolls 12,834 students (fall 2006), with its largest minority being American Indians." The University is located in Grand Forks, a college town of 50,000 on the Red River of the North separating North Dakota and Minnesota (University of North Dakota, 2007).

Figure 2. Entrance to Indian Health Service Hospital in Belcourt, North Dakota

UND School of Medicine & Health Sciences prepares nearly 1,000 students for careers as physicians, occupational therapists, physical therapists, clinical laboratory scientists, and physician assistants. It has trained nearly half of the physicians in North Dakota and 20% of the American Indian physicians in the nation (University of North Dakota, 2007). The School of Medicine has a very active program of grants and contracts including many from the federal government.

In 2002, the school received a $1-million grant from the U.S. Congress through their program for using digital technology to reduce the penalty of distance that is paid by rural Americans as they try to obtain healthcare and related services. Funding was used to develop the Health Information Technology initiative, intended to advance telehealth through demonstrations of telehealth technologies, and studies of the impact of telehealth capabilities for overcoming the impact of distance for Native Americans, Alaskan Natives, the rural elderly, and others living in remote areas.

Indian Health Service

The Indian Health Service (IHS) is the agency within the U.S. Department of Health and Human Services responsible for providing federal health services to American Indians and Alaska Natives. The provision of health services to members of federally-recognized tribes grew out of the special government-to-government relationship between the federal government and sovereign Indian tribes. Most IHS funds are appropriated for American Indians who live on or near reservations (Indian Health Service, 2007). Funding for IHS healthcare has long been limited. "The current funding level for the Indian Health Service system is only 52 to 60 percent of the need. There are just too many stories of too many people who don't get proper care because of that limitation," said Baucus. "We've got to find a way to get that solved as quickly as we can. It bothers me no end. It's totally unconscionable, in my judgment" (Baucus, 2007).

Social Security Administration

The mission of the SSA is:

To advance the economic security of the nation's people through compassionate and vigilant leadership in shaping and managing America's Social Security programs.... We pay retirement, disability and survivors benefits to workers and their families and administer the Supplemental Security Income program. We also issue Social Security numbers. (Social Security Administration, 2007) SSA continually strives to meet customer service expectations through its network of field offices and contact stations. Contact stations are an integral part of SSA's service delivery network. Managed through SSA's field offices, contact stations are usually located in remote areas to provide service to individuals who lack transportation or telephone access. (Social Security Administration, 2000)

The University of North Dakota School of Medicine & Health Sciences, The Social Security Administration, and the Indian Health Service each have their own business, organizational culture, and economic climate but joined forces in an attempt to meet these needs.

Setting the Stage

Each of the Social Security Administration's programs of benefits for the unemployed, the underemployed, the disabled, and the elderly require qualification through an application and approval process. The application process has historically required acquiring, completing, and mailing of an extensive paper packet, participation in a lengthy telephone interview, or an in-person visit to a SSA office.

Each avenue of service presents associated benefits and challenges. Mail-based services require the applicant to have the understanding, organization, patience, and discipline to independently complete a lengthy and complex paper application. For individuals who do not possess these qualities, mail-based services are of limited utility. Telephone-based services require that an applicant have reliable, economical, and extended access to telephone service, in a private and quiet location. If the applicant's home does not provide a good setting for telephone-based services, they are not a viable option. Visits to SSA offices require reliable transportation, money for travel, time for travel, and possibly care for other family members. The neediest citizen often lack some or all of these resources, thus removing office visits as viable options for receiving SSA services (Social Security Administration, 2007).

The effectiveness of SSA service options varies within different population segments. The Turtle Mountain Band of Chippewa Indians has experienced barriers associated with each of the conventional avenues of government service. Few have all of the skills necessary and the personal inertia to see a paper application through to completion. Most members do not have easy access to a telephone. Many tend to distrust communication that is not face to face, particularly communication involving non-Indians. The nearest SSA office is 121 miles from the reservation. And the drive, during winter months, can challenge even the most seasoned traveler.

These barriers have resulted in a lack of access to beneficial government programs. Most members of this tribal community would qualify for SSA benefits. Yet the number of completed applications for income supplementation, disability payments, and health coverage was averaging one to three per year prior to the Video Service Delivery effort (Staff members, Social Security Administration, personal communication, 2004).

North Dakota's 600,000 people are spread over more than 68,000 square miles. The state has regularly been challenged in the delivery of services to rural and remote areas. Correspondingly, it has had a significant history of using telecommunications technology to bridge vast distances. The North Dakota Interactive Video Network was established in 1990 to offer degree programs to rural North Dakotans and is now "responsible for managing North Dakota's education and government videoconferencing," and manages more than 400 IP video conferencing end-points, approximately one for every 1500 citizens in the State of North Dakota (North Dakota Interactive Video Network, 2007).

A growing demand for telecommunications services drove the creation of new capabilities. In 1996, Dakota Carrier Network, LLC, was established by 15 independent rural telecommunications companies representing 85% of all the telephone exchanges in North Dakota and over 90% of the state's total surface area. Dakota Carrier Network provides economical broadband, ATM/frame relay, and high speed Internet services over a statewide fiber optic SONET network to 164,000 customers in 244 communities (Dakota Carrier Network, 2007). The North Dakota Legislature soon used the new capability to create STAGEnet, "broadband connectivity, Internet access, video conferencing and other network-

ing services for state entities. All state agencies, colleges and universities, local government, and K–12 are required to participate in STAGEnet" (North Dakota STAGEnet, 2006).

In 2002, the Health Information Technology Initiative was launched at UND. It was funded to extend and enhance healthcare services by applying telecommunications' technologies.

The notion of using telecommunications in the healthcare industry goes back to the early 1900s. There had been experiments using radio telecardiology (from the 1910s), telephone-mediated telestethoscopy (from the 1920s), and radiology image transfer and videophone experiments (from the early 1950s). The first generation of face-to-face telemedicine, using video conferencing, began in the late 1950s with Dr. Cecil Wittson's microwave-mediated rural telepsychiatry program in Omaha, Nebraska and with Dr. Albert Jutras' cable-mediated teleradiology program in Montreal. Telemedicine's second generation was based on the use of digital compression and transmission technologies in the late 1980s, allowing point-to-point interactive videoconferencing to and from anywhere that had access to T-1, Fractional T-1, or ISDN lines. (California Telemedicine & eHealth Center, 2006)

Figure 3. Telemedicine planning meeting at Turtle Mountain

The confluence of North Dakota's telecommunication capabilities combined with telemedicine's technology traditions and flexible funding provided for the Health Information Technology initiative provided a fertile setting for using technology to address barriers to the delivery of government services in the state's rural and reservation areas.

CASE DESCRIPTION

The Health Information Technology Initiative began its field work on the Turtle Mountain Reservation in Belcourt, ND, just a few miles from the Canadian border. The host site for the emerging telemedicine projects was Quentin N. Burdick Memorial Medical Center, an IHS Hospital and principal provider of reservation healthcare services. Turtle Mountain, like many Indian Reservations, had seen a stream of non-Indians with government money seeking to "help." In early meetings to plan telemedicine projects, many invitees were silent and some seemed skeptical. Each meeting attracted a different group of potential telemedicine project participants. Representatives of the hospital administration were a constant at the meetings. After more that half a dozen meetings and repeated reassurance that the Health Information Technology team was there solely to meet local needs with agendas that were neither self-serving nor hidden, hospital staff members began to share some of their deeper concerns and most urgent needs. Over the ensuing months, a number of telemedicine applications were put in place and provided telecommunication of digital radiology, dental imaging, medical photography, and digital retinal imaging.

During one of the later meetings in the series of telemedicine needs assessment meetings, administrators and medical staff were asked to identify their greatest remaining organizational need. They said, "Money...Funding for care." When asked from where funding might come,

they said, "Third party payers...Private and government medical insurance coverage." They further indicated that a very small portion of their patients have any supplemental or third-party medical coverage (Staff Members, Turtle Mountain Comprehensive Healthcare Center, personal communication, Fall 2002).

Enrolling American Indians in insurance plans has historically been challenging. All Indians are covered by an IHS funded program of medical care. Most therefore see little need for outside coverage. Conventional approaches to service delivery created further barriers to enrollment. Still, additional coverage for tribal members is financially crucial. IHS services are limited by annual funding from HHS and cover only a portion of a native community's medical needs.

Providing improved access to sources of medical coverage for qualifying tribal members offers the potential for influencing more to apply. An increase in completed applications translates into more tribal members being approved for coverage. The additional coverage provides funding for needy and disabled individuals and to reduce financial pressures felt by the local IHS hospital. Financial relief for the hospital in turn allows healthcare services to be spread over more individuals or months of the year.

With the social need apparent, a technology capable context present, and flexible funding available, the Belcourt IHS Hospital seemed an ideal setting to begin exploring the use of telecommunications technologies to facilitate the process of applying for Social Security benefits. Stakeholders were approached about a potential project. A decision was made to make HIT project resources available to explore the use telecommunications technologies to facilitate the process of applying for Social Security benefits. Given continuing trends in IHS hospital funding, this exploration could not have come at a better time.

A close relationship has long existed between the Hospital's Benefits Coordinator and the Service Representative from the nearest SSA's office. Both immediately expressed willingness to play a part in the emerging project. The SSA was approached through their Director of Electronic Service Delivery. The Commissioner of the Denver Region was quick to sign them on. Approval came from the hospital Chief Executive Officer after a project briefing during a regular telemedicine planning meeting.

The decision was then made to implement pilot use of video conferencing technology to connect the IHS Hospital, in Belcourt, with a SSA Office in Minot, ND, some 120 miles away for the purpose of taking applications for benefits, remotely. From the beginning, it was anticipated that this installation might serve as a model for

more widespread future installations. A successful first implementation was important. Criteria defining success were established. The video link had to be a very reliable, always-on connection providing the capability for on-demand. The image and sound needed to be of high quality to present a professional image and to provide a natural communication experience. In addition, the link had to offer secure connectivity to protect the privacy of clients and their information.

An inventory of technology assets for the project showed that the IHS facility had a video end-point for the sole use of the IHS administration. And that the IHS video, voice, and data communications networks, secured nationally

Figure 4. Inauguration of Video Service Delivery between Belcourt, North Dakota and Minot, North

Figure 5. SSA's Denver Regional Comissioner visits Video Service Delivery Site in Belcourt, North Dakota

by firewalls, were unavailable to the project. The SSA office in Minot had no video end-point and all of its communications networks were behind national firewalls and unavailable for project use. From this assessment it was clear that the project would have to provide all of the video and communications technology required.

At the time of the project, Tandberg offered the only video conferencing end-points with on-board encryption. For the hospital, a Tandberg T-1000 was selected. It offered compact size, and an unintimidating design. The T-1000 has a 12.1-inch color LCD screen, is capable of point-to-point conferencing at speeds of 768kbps, and produces very natural images at 30 frames per second with CD-quality sound. The footprint is 2.6in/6.6cm by 11.8in/30.0cm. The camera, microphone, and speaker are integrated. For the SSA Office end-point, a Tandberg T-1500 was selected. The "1500" has a 19-inch screen and is capable of multipoint calling (joining up to four sites) at speeds up to 2Mbps. Both end-points are capable of telecommunications encryption, both AES and DES.

The video telecommunications installation also needed to respect and protect the integrity of both institution's communications and data systems. The resulting overall design needed to provide point to point video communication over a dedicated line to a high speed network. With one end of the connection was in a very rural area, few telecommunications options were available. No community-wide broadband services were available. The only available choice for secure, dedicated service was a T-1 line capable of 1.5 Mbps transmission. The line was installed using commercial Cisco switching and routing equipment. Service was initiated at 1 Mbps with quality of service protection for the Internet protocol video conferencing transmission. A connection to the Internet was also installed, for future use including project communications.

In October of 2003, at the Upper Great Plains Technology Show and Exposition in Fargo, North Dakota, the Health Information Technology project team and the Social Security Administration inaugurated the delivery of Social Security services, via video telecommunications, to Indian Health Service Hospital in Belcourt, ND from the SSA Office in Minot, ND, more than 120 miles away. U.S. Senator Byron Dorgan and U.S. Representative Earl Pomeroy witnessed the first transmissions. The Denver Regional Commissioner of SSA named the new video connection Video Claims Taking. It was later renamed Video Service Delivery.

It was not long before the question was asked, "How good is Video Service Delivery as an approach to government service delivery?" Answers to the question would determine whether the Belcourt to Minot video link stayed up and whether additional rural service delivery video links might become available. An evaluation plan was developed to answer those and other pertinent questions. The plan was based upon classic telemedicine evaluation studies which compare "the costs and other consequences of delivering specific services through telemedicine vs. alternative means" (Doze, Simpson, Hailey, & Jacobs, 1999; McIntosh & Cairns, 1997; Sisk & Sanders, 1998). It compared the process of applying for benefits done through convention means to the process done using Video Service Delivery. Measurements were planned for each of the stakeholders, the telemedicine project, the tribal community, and the social security administration. Details of the plan are presented here.

VIDEO SERVICE DELIVERY EVALUATION PLAN

Impact on Project
   VSD Costs
    Equipment
    Technical consultation
    Labor
     Chargeable

In-kind
Line Installation
Line charges
VSD Benefits
Meeting needs
for improved service to Turtle mountain
applicants
of SSA to increase services to reservation
of hospital for increased coverage for IHS
population
Historic use of telemedicine

Impact on Tribal Community
Change in:
wait time for interview
scheduling of interview appointments
quality of application interview
Confidence in SSA representative
Confidence in own ability to communicate
effectively
duration of application interview
duration of application process
Preference:
In-person interview
Belcourt IHS
Belcourt Tribal office
Minot SSA
Telephone interview
Video medical interview

Impact on Social Security Service Delivery
Change in:
number of applications processed
appointments made
application begun
application finished
application signed
completion rate
scheduling of interview appointments
drop-in rate
scheduled appt rate
availability of staff to interview
quality of application interview

vs in-person
vs telephone
duration of application interview
vs in-person
vs telephone

It became immediately apparent, once Video Service Delivery began, that this early evaluation plan was inadequate. Clients took to video communications so easily and were so comfortable with it that the evaluation challenges changed dramatically. Remote video access provided applicants for benefits with a direct audio and visual communication with distant government representatives. The video communications channel allowed both client and representative to remain in their own most familiar, comfortable, and productive settings. The video link offered natural communication and enhances interpersonal trust. A claimant interview was now void of the most of the weaknesses associated with previous service outreach methods.

A revised plan was included assessment of the remaining social impact of Video Service Delivery was needed. Measurements included the number of applicants, the number of allowed (approved) applications, the value of benefits to applicants, and the value of associated hospital reimbursements. Implementing the revised evaluation plan required the participation of a three stakeholders. The Social Security Administration confidentially reported on the number of applications made, the number of allowances made, the processing time for each application, and the amount of the benefit associated with each allowed claim. The hospital then confidentially matched SSA data to report on health care expenses associated with each tribal patient. Expenses for in-hospital care and for contracted specialty care, available outside the hospital. The telemedicine project next served data aggregation, analysis, and reporting functions. The revised evaluation methodology provided the stakeholders with the information

Figure 6. Numerical results of the video link between the IHS Hospital in Belcourt, ND and the SSA Office in Minot, ND as of June 1, 2007

Figure 7. The benefits coordinator at the IHS Hospital in Belcourt, ND

they required to assess the effort and advocate for its expansion.

Performance metrics were presented in graphic form. The presentation tallied applications and allowances for personal Supplemental Security Income, applications and allowances for personal disability, reimbursement for hospital services, and reimbursement for contracted health services. Figure 6 shows the numerical results of the video link between the IHS Hospital in Belcourt, ND and the SSA Office in Minot, ND as of June 1, 2007. In summary, the number of applicants for benefits using the video channel exceeded 12 per month or 250 for the period. More than 18% of the applicants were allowed more than 45 individuals were approved for benefits.

Economic results followed from application and allowance tallies. Disability and Supplement benefits to individual tribal members ranged from $400–$650 per month. Reimbursement to the hospital ranged from $17,500–$34,000 per qualifying patient. Annual benefits to the hospital exceed $750,000 and to the community members they exceed $600,000 annually. The total financial impact of VSD, over 44 months, has been $2,250,000 directly to individuals and $2,000,000 in reimbursement to the hospital for a total economic impact to community of $4,293,591.

In addition to the preceding numerical results, observations were collected from those closest to the project in the Indian Health Service and the Social Security Administration. Video interviews were conducted to determine the impact of the video link on the IHS and the SSA. The benefits coordinator, at the Belcourt Hospital, reported that video had gotten a better response from the public than had conventional methods. She indicated the diffusion of this innovation was by word of mouth. She found that video communication matched a cultural preference for visual communication (Rubeck, 2004). A SSA claims representative in the Minot office reported that more applications were completed and fewer abandoned than by previous means. She also indicated that clients and representatives both like the method. She indicated that the application process goes faster via video link (Rubeck, 2004). The hospital benefits coordinator also indicated that the presence of a video channel prompted the hospital to form a benefits committee to guide the identification of candidates for third party coverage and to encourage applications.

Additional observations, information, and opinions were collected from stakeholders by documenting comments made during meetings, visits, and calls. A summary of these results is presented here.

SSA Service Delivery Enhancements

Video Service Delivery produces several enhancements to the way SSA delivery services to rural Americans.

Service Enhancement for Clients:

- Increases number of applications from previously underserved rural and reservation communities.
- Increases appeal rates
  - More applicants accessing appeal process
  - More successful appeals
- Accelerates claims processing,
  - Reduces time spent by service representatives
- Improves access to service,
  - Provides greater access to benefits by reducing distance barriers
  - Serves more citizens
  - Increases comfort and trust for those served via video communications over other methods
  - Increases hours of service for small and single person offices

- Reduces travel for citizens
  - Reduces travel expense including mileage, wear and tear, and sometimes lodging and meals
  - Reduces rural travel risk, particularly in bad weather
  - Reduces travel inconvenience including the need for child care or adult care while absent traveling

Service Enhancement for Operations:

- Increases third party assistance in the application process,
  - Reduces the amount of time SSA reps need to spend on each associated claims
- Increases staffing flexibility,
  - Offices with video connectivity and staff capacity can handle clients from understaffed offices
- Allows remote assistance for rural workloads.
  - Removes threats to service instability in remote offices with very small staff by allowing relief for deserving employees, covering staffing shortages with remote services, and helping to transition new employees by off-loading the early and complex work through video channels
- Increases application completion rates,
  - Reduces incomplete applications that need to be followed, accounted for, and reported
- Reduces missed appointment rates
  - Saves service representatives processing time in preparing for appointments that may not happen
- Reduces staff travel
  - Saves dollars spend to travel
  - Increases morale by reducing a frequently onerous activity

- Reduces rural travel risk, particularly in bad weather
- Economies in office operation,
  - Recovers staff time lost to productivity during actual travel (SSA, 2007; IHS, 2007)

Perhaps the most significant result of the first Video Service Delivery link between Belcourt, ND and Minot, ND has been expansion of Video Service Delivery to new sites. Over the three years since the inauguration of the Belcourt site, 31 additional sites including 12 reservation sites have been established in five states.

CURRENT CHALLENGES

Communication

The VSD connection was new to each organization and their staff and reflected a change in operations for the benefits office. This presented an early challenge. Communication between the benefits coordinator and hospital administrators was normally sparse. The advent of the VSD link created organizational change that generated the need for supplementary communication. During frequent visits to the hospital the HIT Director provided the needed additional communication.

Evaluation

Performing an evaluation of Video Service Delivery that reflected the complexities of the IHS Hospital accounting and SSA systems for record keeping created the next challenge for the project team. Detailed records of SSA clients from individual sites were not readily available from automated systems and had to be hand entered in spreadsheets. Similarly, individual patient records had not been correlated with SSA application/allowance data previously and had to be aggregated by hand. No model existed for the meaningful representation of cross institutional data of this type. A business intelligence software program was modified to provide the needed "data views."

The following project milestones illustrate the expansiveness and innovativeness that has characterized the project since the fall of 2003.

VIDEO SERVICE DELIVERY SUCCESSES MILESTONES

- Video Service Delivery (VSD) is operational in five of six states in the Denver SSA Region: Montana (6 sites), North Dakota (8 sites), South Dakota (15 sites), Utah (2 sites), and Wyoming (2 sites).
- 24 rural communities have Video Service Delivery sites, including 10 Indian reservation sites.
- 10 selected Social Security Offices respond to community VSD clients.
- Trials are underway in North Dakota to interconnect a Disability Determination Services Office, a SSA Office in Minot, ND, and an IHS Hospital on a single video call, to cut total claims processing time.
- The SSA VSD site at Ft. Washakie, WY, assisted citizens with the Drug Card and Medicare Part D process.
- To provide assistance to veterans in underserved areas, SSA used Video, for the first time ever, as part of an annual VA "Stand Down" in Ft. Yates, ND, where a mobile VA office was set up to provide assistance and help Veterans apply for program benefits. Veterans were able to video conference with Social Security staff to answer questions and apply for benefits on-the-spot.
- Services to Pine Ridge are offered as scheduled appointments and "on-demand" by the SSA Office in Rapid City, SD.
- A video link to the SSA Office in Huron, SD provides a "virtual service window" to the Pierre, SD, from a community video site in the Capital University Center.
- Three Montana VSD sites are interlinked to provide rural and reservation citizens with services from each agency at all three locations. The sites include MT Job Services, Human Development Service Center, and the Public Health Services Hospital.
- A Video Service Center has been set up at the SSA office in Fergus Falls, MN, to take video claims applications at-a-distance from smaller SSA offices in Montana and North Dakota.
- Unlimited capabilities for interconnected video services sites among various agencies and their constituencies; for example, an IHS Clinic Director at Ft Totten, ND has expressed his willingness to use an IHS provided video unit to connect with a regional SSA Office.
- The first video site on the Turtle Mountain Reservation in Belcourt, ND has produced more than 300 completed applications for SSI and Disability. This translates into more than $3 million in benefits into the community in the form of individual benefits and local hospital medical payments.
- In only 20 months, three video sites on the Pine Ridge Reservation in South Dakota have produced more than 700 completed applications for a total cumulative financial return for the Pine Ridge Community of $6.5 million.
- The video site in a St. Joseph's hospital in Dickinson, ND has resulted in benefits to that rural community and hospital of more than $700,000 in its first 18 months of operation.

Expansion

With an operational first installation and documentation of its success, needs of tribal members for healthcare insurance coverage and supplemental income were being met for the first time. Calls for additional sites were not far behind, creating the next challenge—expansion. A staffing challenge brought a request for the second VSD site. Once operational, this nonreservation site, showed the added potential of VSD for non-Indian, rural populations and created the call for additional sites in neighboring states. The challenge created by this new call for expansion was met by a more formal approach to project management. Steps in the Video Service Delivery selection and installation process were identified, organized, and verified. A summary of key steps is included in here.

Summary of Video Service Delivery Installation Process

1. Plan for new SSA/Community VSD connections:
   - Identify possible Community sites
   - Conduct initial conversations about Community
   - Collect local "intelligence"
   - Confirm the selection of the Community site
2. Implement VSD at SSA Location:
   - Identify Local SSA Participants
   - Identify Key Project team members
   - Identify SSA Key Influentials to Receive Progress Reports
   - Conduct Initial SSA/ VSD Telephone Cluster Conference
   - Conduct Initial Community Visit
   - Establish Communications
   - Set timeline for video service
   - Implement Video Conferencing
   - Implement Evaluation
     a. RSD Impact
     b. Community Impact
2. Economic Modeling:
   - SSA Impact
     a. Community Impact
3. Implement VSD at Community Location:
   - Identify Community/VSD Local Influentials

- Conduct Initial Local Community/VSD Meeting
- Establish Needed Communications Services
- Install Video Technology
  a. Identify Conferencing Possibilities
  b. Determine Connectivity Requirements
  c. Determine Video Conferencing
  d. Install Video Conferencing
  e. Conferencing Test Date
  f. Conferencing Ready Date
- Document Community/SSA Progress

Funding

Funding for a second site was found in the budget the Government Rural Outreach Initiative in the UND College of Business and Public Administration. Three rounds of funding from SSA provided support for expansion to additional sites and additional service innovations, including installations in a number of nonreservation hospital sites, several nonhospital community video sites, one video site (Pierre, SD) with on-demand SSA information via video to a university center, and a video site (Fergus Falls, MN) that serves as a video service center for a number of remote single person or small offices.

The remaining challenge is continuation. With 31 sites live, continuation is essential. With only five of the 50 states included continuation is desirable. With much in the way of research and innovation to be done continuation is sought. Changes in the government spending and priorities have dried up the sources of funding used thus far. An effort is underway to include funding for Video Service Delivery in the Social Security Administration budget for FY 2008. Word on that initiative is expected in the fall of 2007.

ACKNOWLEDGMENT

The authors would like to acknowledge the contributions made by Rick Schremp to this project. Without his vision and assistance, this important innovation in government service would not have been possible. Mr. Schremp is Director of Electronic Service Delivery and CIO, Denver Region, U. S. Social Security Administration.

REFERENCES

Baucus, M. (2007). *Baucus calls for funding, improvements, on Indian health and child welfare.* Retrieved June 7, 2008, from http://www.senate.gov/~finance/press/Bpress/2007press/prb032207c.pdf

California Telemedicine & eHealth Center (2007). *The history of telemedicine.* Retrieved July 16, 2007, from http://www.cteconline.org/telemedicine_history.html

Dakota Carrier Network (2007). *About DCN.* Retrieved June 7, 2008, from http://dakotacarrier.com/about/

Doze, S., Simpson, J., Hailey, D., & Jacobs, P. (1999). Evaluation of a telepsychiatry pilot project. *Journal of Telemedicine Telecare, 5*, 38–46.

General Accounting Office (1991). *Indian Health Service.* Retrieved June 7, 2008, from http://stinet.dtic.mil/oai/oai?&verb=getRecord&metadataPrefix=html&identifier=ADA270312

Indian Health Service (2006). *Indian Health Service facts on Indian health disparities.* Retrieved June 7, 2008, from http://info.ihs.gov/Files/DisparitiesFacts-Jan2006.pdf

Indian Health Service (2007). *Indian Health Service introduction.* Retrieved June 7, 2008, from http://www.ihs.gov/PublicInfo/PublicAffairs/Welcome_Info/IHSintro.asp

Indian Health Service. (2007). *Turtle Mountain Comprehensive Healthcare Center.* Retrieved June 7, 2008, from http://www.ihs.gov/FacilitiesServices/AreaOffices/Aberdeen/turtlemountain/

McIntosh, E., & Cairns, J. A framework for the economic evaluation of telemedicine. *Journal of Telemedicine Telecare, 3*, 132–139.

National Indian American Health Board (2007). *Reauthorization of the Indian Health Care Improvement Act.* Retrieved June 7, 2008, from http://www.nihb.org/docs/ihcia_fact_sheet_2007_feb.pdf

North Dakota Interactive Video Network (2007). Retrieved June 7, 2008, from http://www.ndivn.nodak.edu/web/User_groups/Higher_Ed/Degree.htm

North Dakota Interactive Video Network (2007). Retrieved June 7, 2008, from http://www.ndivn.nodak.edu/web/About_IVN/mission.asp

North Dakota STAGEnet (2006). *STAGEnet.* Retrieved June 7, 2008, from www.stagenet.nd.gov/

Northwest Area Foundation (2006). *Turtle Mountain Band of Chippewa.* Retrieved June 7, 2008, from http://www.nwaf.org/ProgramsNoHdrImage.aspx?pg=Programs/ventures_turtle_mountain.htm

Rubeck, R. (2004, August). *Delivering government services to the beat of a different drum!* Keynote presentation at the 2004 Western CIO Forum, Santa Fe, NM.

Sisk, J.E., & Sanders, J.H. (1998). A proposed framework for economic evaluation of telemedicine. *Telemed Journal, 4*, 31–37.

Social Security Administration (2000). *Management Advisory Report: Contact stations.* Retrieved June 7, 2008, from www.ssa.gov/oig/ADOBEPDF/Final%2099-01001.pdf

Social Security Administration (2006). *Social Security is important to American Indians and Alaska Natives*. Retrieved June 7, 2008, from http://www.ssa.gov/pressoffice/factsheets/amerindian.htm

Social Security Administration (2007). *Information about the Social Security Administration*. Retrieved June 7, 2008, from http://www.ssa.gov/aboutus/

Underrepresented Nations and Peoples Organization (2004). *Lakota: The forgotten people of Pine Ridge*. Retrieved June 7, 2008, from http://www.unpo.org/article.php?id=518

University of North Dakota (2007). *About the University*. Retrieved June 7, 2008, from http://www.und.edu/aboutund/

Compilation of References

A.dict.it (2007). Electronic service (eService). Voice in K. Lipinski (Ed.), *A dictionary of IT*. Retrieved June 7, 2008, from http://a.dict.it/definition/lexikon//eservice_electronic%20service.html

Aalberts, B., & Van der Hof, S. (1999). *Digital signature blindness: Analysis of legislative approaches toward electronic authentication*. Tilburg, The Netherlands: Tilburg University. Retrieved June 1, 2008, from http://www.buscalegis.ufsc.br/busca.php?acao=abrir&id=15433

Aberer, K., & Despotovic, Z. (2001, November 5–10). Managing trust in a peer-2-peer information system. *Proceedings of the 10th International Conference on Information and Knowledge Management (CIKM01)* (pp. 310–317). New York: ACM Press.

Accounting Act (AA) 1336/30.12.1997.

Accounting Board (2000, May 22). *Yleisohje Koneellisessa Kirjanpidossa Käytettävistä Menetelmistä.*

Adobe. (2007). Adobe Shockwave Player. Adobe Systems Incorporated. Retrieved June 5, 2008, from http://www.adobe.com/products/shockwaveplayer/

Ahonen, A. (2007). *From complex to simple: Designing a customer-friendly electronic insurance service environment*. Dissertation, Tampere University.

Ahonen, A., & Salonen, J. (2005). *eInsurance: Kohti asiakaslähtöisempää sähköistä vakuutuspalvelua* [eInsurance: Towards a more customer-oriented electronic insurance service]. Tampere, Finland: VTT Industrial Systems.

Ahonen, A., & Windischhofer, R. (2005). The Web performance of different types of online insurance providers: A wake up call to traditional insurance providers. In

Zhao, Xiande, Liu, & Baoding (Eds.), *Proceedings of the Fifth International Conference on Electronic Business (ICEB2005)* (pp. 245–252). Hong Kong: The Chinese University of Hong Kong.

Ahonen, A., Salonen, J., Kivistö-Rahnasto, J., Järvinen, R., & Silius, K. (2007, April 26–28). *eInsurance: Novel services in the electronic environment*. Paper presented at the Innovation in Services Conference, Berkeley, CA. UC Berkeley Tekes.

Alba, J., Lynch, J., Weitz, B., Janiszewski, O., Lutz, R., Sawyer, A., & Wood, S. (1997). Interactive home shopping: Consumer, retailer and manufacturer incentives to participate in electronic marketplaces. *Journal of Marketing, 61*, 38–53.

Alles, M., Kogan, A., & Vasarhelyi, M.A. (2000). Accounting in 2015. *The CPA Journal, 70*(11), 14–20.

Anderson, K.V., Juul, N.C., & Pedersen, J.K. (2003, June). *Fractional institutional endeavours and eprocurement in local government*. Paper presented at the 16th Bled Electronic Commerce Conference, Bled, Slovenia.

Armstrong, C.P., & Sambamurthy, V. (1999). Information technology assimilation in firms: The influence of senior leadership and IT infrastructures. *Information Systems Research, 10*(4), 304–327.

Asociación Española de Comercio Electrónico (AECE) (2005). Retrieved June 2, 2008, from www.aece.org

Asociación para la Investigación de Medios de Comunicación (AIMC) (2006). Retrieved June 2, 2008, from www.aimc.es

Associated Press (2006). SEC approves NYSE, Archipelago Merger. *USA Today.*

Association of Finnish Accounting Firms (2006). Data retrieved July 2007 from http://www.taloushallintoliitto.fi/

Bakos, Y. (1991). A strategic analysis of electronic marketplaces. *MIS Quarterly, 15*(3), 295–310.

Bakos, Y. (1998). The emerging role of electronic marketplaces on the Internet. *Communications of the ACM, 41*(8), 35–42.

Bakos, Y., & Brynjolfsson, E. (2000). Aggregation and disaggregation of information goods: Implications for bundling, site licensing, and micropayment systems. In D. Hurley, B. Kahin, & H. Varian (Ed.), *Proceedings of Internet Publishing and Beyond: The Economics of Digital Information and Intellectual Property*. Cambridge, MA: MIT Press.

Baldrige National Quality Program (2006). *Criteria for performance excellence*. Retrieved June 8, 2008, from http://www.quality.nist.gov/

Barber, B.M., & Odean, T. (2001). The Internet and the investor. *Journal of Economic Perspectives, 15*(1), 41–54.

Barber, B.M., & Odean, T. (2002). Online investors: Do the slow die first? [Special Issue: Conference on Market Frictions and Behavioral Finance]. *Review of Financial Studies, 15*(2), 455–487.

Barczac, G., Ellen, P.S., & Pilling, B.K. (1997). Developing typologies of consumer motives for use of technologically based banking services. *Journal of Business Research, 38*(2), 131–139.

Barnes, D., Hinton, M., & Mieczkowska, S. (2004). Avoiding the fate of the dotbombs: Lessons from three surviving dotcom start-ups. Journal of Small Business and Enterprise Development, 11(3), 329–337.

Bateson, J. (1985). Self-service consumer: An exploratory study. *Journal of Retailing, 61*(3), 49–76.

Battalio, R., Greene, J., & Jennings, R. (1997). Do competing specialists and preferencing dealers affect market quality? *Review of Financial Studies, 10*(4), 969–993.

Battalio, R., Greene. J., Hatch, B., & Jennings, R. (2002). Does the limit order routing decision matter? *Review of Financial Studies, 15*(1), 159–194.

Baucus, M. (2007). *Baucus calls for funding, improvements, on Indian health and child welfare.* Retrieved June 7, 2008, from http://www.senate.gov/~finance/press/Bpress/2007press/prb032207c.pdf

Bedi, P., & Banati, H. (2006). Assessing user trust to improve Web usability. *Journal of Computer Science, 2*(3), 283–287.

Berardi, D., Calvanese, D., De Giacomo, G., Lenzerini, M., &. Mecella, M. (2003). *A foundational framework for e-services* (Tech. Rep. No. 10). Rome, Italy: University "La Sapienza," Dipartimento di Informatica e Sistemistica.

Berg, B. (2004). *Qualitative research methods for the social sciences* (5th ed.). Allyn & Bacon.

Bianchini, A. (2002a, May 8). *La sperimentazione dell'e-procurement negli approvvigionamenti di Sala Operatoria.* Paper presented at the Acquisti Ed E-procurement in Sanità at FORUM PA Conference, Rome. Retrieved June 7, 2008, from www.forumpa.it/forumpa2002/convegni/archivio/S.7/1363-andrea_bianchini.pdf

Bianchini, A. (2002b, November 5). I vantaggi conseguibili attraverso l'esternalizzazione della Logistica di un'azienda sanitaria, proceedings, Milano.

Black, N., Lockett, A., Ennew, C., Winklhofer, H., & McKechnie, S. (2002). Modelling consumer choice of distribution channels: An illustration from financial services. *International Journal of Bank Marketing, 20*(4), 161–173.

Black, N.J., Lockett, A., Wiklofer, H., & Ennew, C. (2001). The adoption of Internet financial services: A qualitative study. *International Journal of Retail & Distribution Management, 29*(8), 390–398.

Bobbitt, L.M., & Dadholkar, P.A. (2001). Integrating attitudinal theories to understand and predict use of technology-based self-service. *International Journal of Service Industry Management, 12*(5), 423–450.

Bødker, K., Kensing, F., & Simonsen, J. (2004). *Participatory IT design: Designing for business and workplace realities.* Cambridge, MA: MIT Press.

Bogart, L. (1992). *The state of the industry.* In P. Cook, D. Gomery, & W. Lichty (Eds.), The future of news (pp. 85–103). Washington, DC: The Woodrow Wilson Center Press.

Borgonovi, E. (2004). E-procurement in Sanità: dalla logica di modello alla logica di processo. *Mecosan, 41*, 2–5.

Borrus, A., McNamee, G., Carter, B., & Adrienne, M. (2005, November 24). Invasion of the stock hackers. *Business Week*, p. 38.

Bouwman, H., & Van de Wijngaert, L. (2002). Content and context: An exploration of the basic characteristic of information needs. *New Media & Society, 4*(3), 329–353.

Boyd, C., & Mathuria, A. (2003). *Protocols for key establishment and authentication.* Berlin/Heidelberg, Germany: Springer-Verlag GmbH & Co.

Boyer, K.K., Hallowell, R., & Roth, A.V. (2002). E-services: Operating strategy—a case study and a method for analyzing operational benefits. *Journal of Operations Management, 20*(2), 175–188.

Brown, M. (2000). Bringing people closer to news. *Adweek, 41*(40).

Brynjolfsson, E., & Smith, M.D. (2000). Frictionless commerce? A comparison of Internet and conventional retailers. *Management Science, 46*(4), 563–585.

Bunnell, D. (2001). *The eBay phenomenon* (1st ed.). New York: John Wiley & Sons, Inc.

Bush, V., & Gilbert, F. (2002). The Web as a medium: An exploratory comparison of Internet users versus newspapers readers. *Journal of Marketing Theory and Practice, 10*(1), 1–10.

Cadway, R.P. (2001). *New daytrading rules.* Retrieved June 5, 2008, from

CAF Resource Center (2006). *Common assessment framework.* Retrieved June 8, 2008, from http://www.eipa.nl/CAF/CAFmenu.htm

Cai, X. (2003). Is the computer a functional alternative to traditional media? *Communication Research Reports.*

California Telemedicine & eHealth Center (2007). *The history of telemedicine.* Retrieved July 16, 2007, from http://www.cteconline.org/telemedicine_history.html

Cardoso, J., Sheth, A., & Miller, J. (2002, April). Workflow quality of service. In *Proceedings of the IFIP Tc5/Wg5.12 International Conference on Enterprise Integration and Modeling Technique: Enterprise Inter- and Intra-Organizational Integration: Building International Consensus*, Valencia, Spain (pp. 303–311).

Carey, T.W. (2006, July 3). Tears at Waterhouse. *Barron's*, p. 32.

Carson, D., & Perry, C. (2001). *Qualitative marketing research.* Sage Publications.

Carson, D., Gilmore, A., Cummins, D., O'Donnell, A., & Grant, K. (1998). Price setting in SMEs: Some empirical findings. Journal of Product & Brand Management, 7(1), 74–86.

Carson, D., Gilmore, A., Perry, C., & Gronhaug, K. (2001). *Qualitative research in marketing.* London: Sage.

Cartwright, S., & Oliver, R. (2000). Untangling the value Web. *The Journal of Business Strategy, 21*(1), 22–27.

Cass, J. (2006, March 2). What culture does a company need to adopt to use cooperative marketing effectively? *Backbone Media.* Retrieved June 5, 2008, from http://blogsurvey.backbonemedia.com

CEN Workshop Agreement (2001). *CWA 14168: Secure signature-creation devices.* Brussels, Belgium: CEN (European Committee for Standardization).

CEN Workshop Agreement (2003a). *CWA 14167-1: Security requirements for trustworthy systems managing certificates for electronic signatures* (Part 1: System security requirements). Brussels, Belgium: CEN.

CEN Workshop Agreement (2003b). *CWA 14167-2: Cryptographic module for CSP signing Operations with backup: Protection profile (CMCSOB-PP).* Brussels, Belgium: CEN.

CEN Workshop Agreement (2004a). *CWA 14355: Guidelines for the implementation of secure signature-creation devices.* Brussels, Belgium: CEN.

CEN Workshop Agreement (2004b). *CWA 14169: Secure signature-creation devices "EAL 4+."* Brussels, Belgium: CEN.

CEN Workshop Agreement (2004c). *CWA 14170: Security requirements for signature creation applications.* Brussels, Belgium: CEN.

CEN Workshop Agreement (2004d). *CWA 14171: General guidelines for electronic signature verification*. Brussels, Belgium: CEN.

CEN Workshop Agreement (2004e). *CWA 14172: EESSI conformity assessment guidance. General introduction*. Brussels, Belgium: CEN.

Ceron, G.F. (2006, August 28). Moving the market: Big board sets expansion in electronic trading: "Hybrid market" to remove volume limits, posing risk for specialists and brokers. *Wall Street Journal*, p. C3.

Charron, C., Favier, J., & Li, C. (2006). *Social computing: How networks erode institutional power, and what to do about it*. Forrester Research.

Chatterjee, D., Grewal, R., & Sambamurthy, V. (2002). Shaping up for e-commerce: Institutional enablers of the organizational assimilation of Web technologies. *MIS Quarterly, 26*(2), 65–89.

Cheesman, R., Heilesen, S.B., Josephsen, J., & Kristensen, A.K. (2002). Scenarier i computer-medieret og netbaseret undervisning. *Centre for Netbased Collaboration and Learning Occasional Papers, 1*(1). Retrieved June 5, 2008, from http://rudar.ruc.dk/handle/1800/151

Chesbrough, H., & Spohrer, J. (2006). A research manifesto for services science. *Communications of the ACM, 49*(7), 35-40.

Chiou, J., & Shen, C. (2006). The effects of satisfaction, opportunism, and asset specificity on consumers' loyalty intention toward internet portal sites. International Journal of Service Industry Management, 11(1), 7–11.

Chircu, A.M., & Kauffman, R.J. (2000). Reintermediation strategies in business-to-business electronic commerce. International Journal of Electronic Commerce, 4(4), 7–42.

Chochliouros, I. P., & Spiliopoulou, A.S. (2003b). Innovative horizons for Europe: The new European telecom framework for the development of modern electronic networks and services. *The Journal of the Communications Network (TCN), 2*(4), 53–62.

Chochliouros, I.P., & Spiliopoulou, A.S. (2003a). European standardization activities: An enabling factor for the competitive development of the information society

technologies market. *The Journal of The Communications Network (TCN), 2*(1), 62–68.

Chochliouros, I.P., & Spiliopoulou, A.S. (2004). Potential and basic perspectives of the European Electronic Commerce (e-Commerce) Directive for the Effective Promotion of Modern Business Applications in the Internet (article in Greek). *Telecommunications Audit and Law of New Technologies Magazine, 1*(4), 502–535.

Chochliouros, I.P., & Spiliopoulou, A.S. (2005). Broadband access in the European Union: An enabler for technical progress, business renewal and social development. *The International Journal of Infonomics (IJI), 1*, 5–1.

Chochliouros, I.P., & Spiliopoulou, A.S. (2006, August 30–September 02). Privacy protection vs. privacy offences in the European regulatory context: The cases for interception of communications and the retention of traffic data. In Federation of telecommunications Engineers of the European Union (Ed.), *Proceedings of the 45th International Congress: "Telecom Wars—The Return of the Profit,"* Athens, Greece (pp. 197–203). Athens, Greece: FITCE.

Chochliouros, I.P., Chochliouros, S.P., Spiliopoulou, A.S., & Lambadari, E. (2007). Public key infrastructures (PKI): A means for increasing network security. In L.J. Janczewski & A.M. Colarik (Eds.), *Cyber warfare and cyber terrorism* (pp. 281–290). Hershey, PA: Information Science Reference.

Chyi, H., & Lasorsa, D. (2002). An explorative study on the market relation between online and print newspaper. *The Journal of Media Economics, 15*(2), 91–106.

CIA. (2001). *The world factbook 2001*. Washington, DC: Office of Public Affairs.

Ciborra, C. (1993). *Teams, markets and systems*. Cambridge, England: Cambridge University Press.

Cicchetti, A. (2004). *La progettazione organizzativa*. Milan, Italy: FrancoAngeli.

Claburn, T. (2006). eBay's growth strategy; Community, not acquisitions. *Information Week, 1094*, 26.

Cliffe, S.J., & Motion, J. (2005). Building contemporary brands: A sponsorship-based strategy. Journal of Business Research, 58(8), 1068–1077.

Cohen, N. (2003). Early-stage marketing for start-ups. Retrieved June 3, 2008, from http://www.clickz.com/showPage.html?page=825181

Commission of the European Communities (2003). *The role of e-government for Europe's future* (Communication from the commission to the council, the European parliament, the European economic and social committee, and the committee of the regions). Brussels.

Commission of the European Communities (2005). *Communication on i2010: A European Information Society for growth and employment* [COM(2005) 229 final, 01.06.2005]. Brussels, Belgium: Commission of the European Communities.

Commission of the European Communities (2006). *Report on the operation of Directive 1999/93/EC on a community framework for electronic signatures* [COM(2006) 120 final, 15.03.2006]. Brussels, Belgium: Commission of the European Communities.

CONSIP (2003). *Il Programma di razionalizzazione della spesa per beni e servizi della Pubblica Amministrazione*. CONSIP Annual Report (*house journal*), Rome, Italy.

Cooper, C., & Taylor, P. (2000). From Taylorism to Ms Taylor: The transformation of the accounting craft. *Accounting, Organizations and Society, 25*, 555–587.

Corradini, F., Ercoli, C., Merelli, E., & Re, B. (2004, November). An agent-based matchmaker. In *Proceedings of WOA04 Sistemi Complessi e Agenti Razionali*, Torino, Italy (pp. 150–156).

Corradini, F., Forastieri, L., Polzonetti, A., Riganelli, O., & Sergiacomi, A. (2005, February). Shared Services Center for E-Government Policy. In *Proceedings of the 1st International Conference on Interoperability of eGovernment Services (eGov-Interop'05)*, Geneva, France (pp. 140–151).

Corradini, F., Sabucedo, L.A., Polzonetti, A., Rifón, L.A., & Re, B. (2007, September). A case study of semantic solutions for citizen-centered Web portals in eGovernment: The TecUt Portal. In *Proceedings of the 6th International EGOV Conference 2007, DEXA*, Regensburg, Germany (pp. 204–215, LNCS).

Cothrel, J.P. (2000). Measuring the success of an online community. Strategy & Leadership, 28(2), 17–21.

Cowan, R., David, P.A., & Foray, D. (2000). The explicit economics of knowledge codification and tacitness. *Industrial and Corporate Change, 9*(2), 211-253.

Craig, S., & Kelly, K. (2001, November 30). Deals & deal makers: Investors can obtain report card on the execution of stock trades. *Wall Street Journal*, p. C12.

Crowe, M. (1999, May 21). eBay Inc.: Going, going, gone! *The Business Journal, 17*(4), B4.

Curran, J., & Meuter, M. (2005). Self-service technology adoption: Comparing three technologies. *Journal of Services Marketing, 19*(2), 103–113.

D'Haenens, L., Jankowski, N., & Heuvelman, A. (2004). News in online and print newspapers: Differences in reader comsumption and recall. *New Media & Society, 6*(3), 363–382.

Dabholkar, P.A. (1996). Consumer evaluations of new technology-based self-service options: An investigation of alternative models of service quality. *International Journal of Research in Marketing, 13*(1), 29–51.

Dakota Carrier Network (2007). *About DCN*. Retrieved June 7, 2008, from http://dakotacarrier.com/about/

Dans, E. (2000). Internet newspapers: Are some more equal than others? *The International Journal on Media Management, 2*(1), 4–13.

Das, T.H. (1983). Qualitative research in organisational behaviour. *Journal of Management Studies, 20*(3), 311.

Davies, A.J., & Garcia-Sierra, A.J. (1999). Implementing electronic commerce in SMEs: Three case studies. *BT Technology Journal, 17*(3), 97–111.

De Feo, J.A., & Barnard, W.W. (2005). *JURAN Institute's Six Sigma breakthrough and beyond: Quality performance breakthrough methods*. Tata McGraw-Hill Publishing Company Limited.

De Meo, P., Quattrone, G., Terracina, G., & Ursino, D. (2005). Agent-based mining of user profiles for e-services. In J. Wang (Ed.), *Encyclopedia of data warehousing and mining* (pp. 23–27). Hershey, PA, USA: Idea Group Publishing.

De Ruyter, K., & Scholl, N. (1998). Positioning qualitative market research: From theory and practice. *Qualita-*

tive Market Research: An International Journal, 1(1), 7–14.

De Vries, H.J. (2006). IT standards typology. In K. Jakobs (Ed.), *Advanced topics in information technology standards and standardization research, 1*, 1–26.

De Waal, E., Schönbach, K., & Lauf, E. (2004, May 12–15). *Online newspapers: A substitute for print newspapers and other information channels?* Paper presented at 6th World Media Economics Conference, Canada.

DECU (a unit of ISRO) describing ISRO Telemedicine Projects. Retrieved June 7, 2008, from http://www.isro.org/decu/projects/indextele.htm

Dell, M. (2000). *Direct from Dell: Strategies that revolutionized an industry.* New York: Collins.

Dempsey, J.X. (2003). Creating the legal framework for ICT development: The example of e-signature legislation in emerging market economies. Washington, DC: Center for Democracy and Technology. *Information Technologies and International Development (ITID), 1*(2), 39-52. Washington, DC: Center for Democracy and Technology. Retrieved June 1, 2008, from http://www.internetpolicy.net/e-commerce/20030900esignature.pdf

Denzin, N.K. (1989). *The research act.* Englewood Cliffs, NJ: Prentice Hall.

Dervin, B., Foreman-Wernet, L., & Lauterbach, E. (2003). *Sense-making methodology reader: selected writings of Brenda Dervin.* Cresskill, NJ: Hampton Press.

Deshmukh, A. (2006). *Digital accounting: The effects of the Internet and ERP on accounting.* Hershey, PA: Idea Group.

Devadoss, P.R., Pan, S.L., & Huang, J.C. (2002). Structurational analysis of e-government initiatives: A case study of SCO. *Decision Support System, 1*(34), 253–269.

Devore, J.L. (1995). *Probability and statistics for engineering and the sciences.* Duxbury Press.

Dimmick, J., Kline, S., & Stafford, L. (2000). The gratification niches of personal e-mail and the telephone. *Communication Research, 27,* 227–248.

Doze, S., Simpson, J., Hailey, D., & Jacobs, P. (1999). Evaluation of a telepsychiatry pilot project. *Journal of Telemedicine Telecare, 5,* 38–46.

Dozier, D., & Rice, R. (1984). Rival theories of electronic news reading. In *The new media* (pp. 103–128). London: Sage Publications.

Duffie, D., & Singleton, K.J. (2003). Credit risk: Pricing, measurement and management. Princeton University Press.

Dumortier, J., Kelm, S., Nillson, H., Skouma, G., & Van Eecke, P. (2003). *The legal and market aspects of electronic signatures: Study for the European Commission* (DG Information Society, Service Contract No. C28.400). Brussels, Belgium: The Interdisciplinary Centre for Law & Information Technology & Katholieke Universiteit Leuven. Retrieved June 1, 2008, from europa.eu.int/information_society/eeurope/2005/all_about/security/electronic_sig_report.pdf

Easingwood, C.J. (1986). New product development for service companies. *Journal of Product Innovation Management, 3*(4), 264–275.

eBay. (2005a) Annual report to shareholders. Retrieved June 5, 2008, from http://investor.ebay.com/annual.cfm

eBay. (2005b). 10K. Retrieved June 5, 2008, from http://yahoo.brand.edgar-online.com/fetchFilingFrameset.aspx?dcn=0000950134-06-003678&Type=HTML

Editor & Publisher (2004). Retrieved June 2, 2008, from www.editorandpublisher.com

Edmunds, H. (1999). *The focus group research handbook.* Chicago: NTC Business Books.

Eighmey, J., & McCord, L. (1998). Adding value in the information age: Uses and gratifications of sites on the World Wide Web. *Journal of Business Research, 41,* 187–194.

Elmagarmid, A.K., & McIver, W.J. (2001). Guest editors' introduction: The ongoing march toward digital government. *IEEE Computer, 34*(2), 32–38.

eMarketer (2002). El impacto de Internet en la prensa. In J. Cerezo & J. Zafra (Eds.), *Cuadernos sociedad de la información.* Fundación Auna.

European Commission (1997). *Communication on ensuring security and trust in electronic communication: Towards a European framework for digital signatures and encryption* [COM(97) 503 final, 01.10.1997]. Brussels, Belgium: European Commission.

European Commission (2000). *Communication on creating a safer information society by improving the security of information infrastructures and combating computer-related crime—eEurope 2002* [COM(2000) 890 final, 26.01.2001]. Brussels, Belgium: European Commission.

European Commission (2001). *Communication on network and information security: Proposal for a European policy approach* [COM(2001) 298 final, 06.06.2001]. Brussels, Belgium: European Commission.

European Commission (2002). *Communication on eEurope 2005: An information society for all* [COM(2002) 263 final, 28.05.2002]. Brussels, Belgium: European Commission.

European Commission (2003). *Communication decision 2003/511/ERC of 14 July 2003 on the publication of reference numbers of generally recognized standards for electronic signature products in accordance with Directive 1999/93/EC of the European Parliament and of the Council* [Official Journal (OJ) L175, 15.07.2003, pp. 45–46]. Brussels, Belgium: European Commission.

European Commission (2004). *Communication on the role of European standardisation in the framework of European policies and legislation* [COM(2004) 674 final, 18.10.2004]. Brussels, Belgium: European Commission.

European Commission (2005). *Communication on more research and innovation: Investing for growth and employment: A common approach* [COM(2005) 488 final, 12.10.2005]. Brussels, Belgium: European Commission.

European Commission (2006). *Communication to the Council, the European Parliament, the European Economic and Social Committee and the Committee of the Regions, on Bridging the Broadband Gap* [COM(2006) 129 final, 20.03.2006]. Brussels, Belgium: European Commission.

European Parliament & Council of the European Union (2000a). *Directive 1999/93/EC of the European Parliament and of the Council of 13 December 1999 on a community framework for electronic signatures*

[Official Journal (OJ) L13, 19.01.2000, pp. 12–20]. Brussels, Belgium: European Parliament & Council of the European Union.

European Parliament & Council of the European Union (2000b). *Directive 2000/31/EC of the European Parliament and of the Council of 8 June 2000 on certain legal aspects of information society services, in particular electronic commerce, in the internal market (Directive on Electronic Commerce)* [Official Journal (OJ) L178, 17.07.2000, pp. 1–16]. Brussels, Belgium: European Parliament & Council of the European Union.

European Telecommunications Standards Institute (2002a). *ETSI TR 102 041 V1.1.1 (2002-02): Signature Policies Report.* Sophia-Antipolis, France: ETSI.

European Telecommunications Standards Institute (2002b). *ETSI TR 102 030 V1.1.1 (2002-03): Provision of harmonized trust service provider status information.* Sophia-Antipolis, France: ETSI.

European Telecommunications Standards Institute (2002c). *ETSI TR 102 038 V1.1.1 (2002-04): TC Security - Electronic Signatures and Infrastructures (ESI); XML format for signature policies.* Sophia-Antipolis, France: ETSI.

European Telecommunications Standards Institute (2003). *ETSI TR 102 023 V1.2.1 (2003-01): Electronic signatures and infrastructures (ESI); Policy requirements for time-stamping authorities.* Sophia-Antipolis, France: ETSI.

European Telecommunications Standards Institute (2005). *ETSI TR 102 040 V1.3.1 (2005-03): Electronic signatures and infrastructures (ESI); International harmonization of policy requirements for CAs issuing certificates.* Sophia-Antipolis, France: ETSI.

European Telecommunications Standards Institute (2006a). *ETSI TS 101 862 V1.3.3 (2006-01): Qualified certificate profile.* Sophia-Antipolis, France: ETSI.

European Telecommunications Standards Institute (2006b). *ETSI TS 101 861 V1.3.1 (2006-01): Time stamping profile.* Sophia-Antipolis, France: ETSI.

European Telecommunications Standards Institute (2006c). *ETSI TS 101 903 V1.3.2 (2006-03): XML advanced electronic signatures (XAdES).* Sophia-Antipolis, France: ETSI.

European Telecommunications Standards Institute (2006d). *ETSI TS 101 456 V1.4.2 (2006-12): Electronic signatures and infrastructures (ESI); Policy requirements for certification authorities issuing qualified certificates.* Sophia-Antipolis, France: ETSI.

European Telecommunications Standards Institute (2007a). *ETSI TS 101 733 V1.7.3 (2007-01): Electronic signatures and infrastructures (ESI); CMS Advanced Electronic Signatures (CAdES).* Sophia-Antipolis, France: ETSI.

European Telecommunications Standards Institute (2007b). *ETSI TS 102 042 V1.2.4 (2007-03): Electronic Signatures and Infrastructures (ESI); Policy requirements for certification authorities issuing public key certificates.* Sophia-Antipolis, France: ETSI.

Farkas, P., & Charaf, H. (2003). Web services planning concepts. *Journal of WSCG, 11*(1).

Federici, T. (2005). An integrated approach in healthcare e-procurement: The case-study of the ASL of Viterbo. In M. Böhlen et al. (Eds.), *E-government: Towards electronic democracy, TCGOV 2005* (LNAI 3416, pp. 298–309). Berlin: Springer.

Federici, T. (2006). Public healthcare: Changes introduced when implementing e-procurement. In *Proceedings of the 2006 Mediterranean Conference on Information Systems*. Venice, Italy: University of Trento.

Feghhi, J., Williams, P., & Feghhi, J. (1998). *Digital certificates: Applied Internet security.* Addison-Wesley.

Ferguson, D.A., & Perse, E.M. (2000). The World Wide Web as a functional alternative to television. *Journal of Broadcasting & Electronic Media, 44*(2), 155–174.

Fern, E. (2001). *Advanced focus group research.* London: Sage Publications.

Finance and economics: Moving markets; technology and exchanges. (2006, February 4). *The Economist*, p. 73.

Fitzsimmons, J., & Fitzsimmons, M. (1994). *Service management for competitive advantage.* McGraw-Hill.

Fitzsimmons, J.A., & Fitzsimmons, M.J. (2006). *Service management: Operations, strategy, information technology* (5th ed.). New York: McGraw-Hill.

Flavián, C., & Gurrea, R. (2006). The choice of digital newspapers: Influence of readers goals and user experience. *Internet Research, 16*(3), 231–247.

Flavián, C., & Gurrea, R. (in press). Exploring the influence of reading motivations on perceived substitutability between digital and traditional newspapers. *International Journal of Market Research.*

Fletcher, R. (2006). The impact of culture on Web site content, design, and structure. Journal of Communication Management, 10(3), 259–273.

Ford, W., & Baum, M. (2001). *Secure electronic commerce* (2nd ed.). Upper River Saddle, NJ: Prentice Hall.

Frank, B.G., & Krake, J.M. (2005). Successful brand management in SMEs: A new theory and practical hints. Journal of Product & Brand Management, 14(4), 228–238.

Frazier, G.L. (1999). Organizing and managing channels of distribution. *Journal of the Academy of Marketing Science, 27*(2), 226–240.

Free Dictionary, The. Retrieved June 7, 2008, from http://www.thefreedictionary.com/telemedicine

Garcia, A.C., Maciel, C., & Pinto, F.B. (2005, August). A quality inspection method to evaluate e-government sites. In *Proceedings of the 4th International EGOV Conference 2005, DEXA*, Copenhagen, Denmark (pp. 198–209, LNCS).

Garcia, R., & Calantone, R. (2002). A critical look at technological innovation typology and innovativeness terminology: A literature review. *Journal of Product Innovation Management, 19*, 110–132.

Garshnek, V. (1991). Applications of space communications technology to critical human needs: Rescue, disaster relief, and remote medical assistance. *Space Communication. 8*, 311–317.

Garshnek. V., & Burkle, F.M. (1999). Applications of telemedicine and telecommunications to disaster medicine: Historical and future perspectives. *Journal American Medical Information Association, 6*(1), 26–37.

Gaskell, G. (2000). Individual and group interviewing. In M.W. Bauer & G. Gaskell (Eds.), *Qualitative researching with text, image and sound: A practical handbook.* Londres: Sage.

General Accounting Office (1991). *Indian Health Service*. Retrieved June 7, 2008, from http://stinet.dtic.mil/oai/oai?&verb=getRecord&metadataPrefix=html&identifier=ADA270312

Gerrad, P., & Cunningham, J.B. (2003). The diffusion of Internet banking among Singapore consumers. *International Journal of Bank Marketing, 21*(1), 16–28.

Gershuny, J., & Miles, I. (1983). *The new service economy: The transformation of employment in industrial societies*. New York: Praeger.

Geyskens, I., Gielens, K., & Dekimpe, M. (2000). *Establishing the Internet channel: Short term pain but long term gain?* (Working Paper). E-Business Research Center.

Gfk (2005). Number of Internet users in Croatia. Retrieved June 3, 2008, from http://www.gfk.hr/press/internet6.htm

Gfk (2006). Citizens and the Internet. Retrieved June 3, 2008, from http://www.gfk.hr/press1/internet.htm

Ghobadian, A., & Gallear, D.N. (1996). Total quality management in SMS's. *Omega, 24*(1), 83–106.

Giessler, A., & Lindemann, R. (2003, July 29). *ISIS-MTT compliance criteria* (Version 1.1). Berlin, Germany: T7 & TeleTrusT. Retrieved June 1, 2008, from teletrust.de/fileadmin/files/ag8_isis-mtt-compliancecrit-v1.1.pdf

Gilmore, J.H., & Pine., J., II. (2002). Customer experience places: The new offering frontier. Strategy & Leadership, 30(4), 4–11.

Globerman, S., Roehl, T.W., & Standifird, S. (2001). Globalization and electronic commerce: Inferences from retail brokerage. *Journal of International Business Studies, 32*(4), 749–768.

Gogia, S.B. (2002). *Towards a national telemedicine network*. Paper presented at the 1st National Conference of Telemedicine Society of India at SGPGI, Lucknow, India.

Gogia, S.B., & Surwade, M.R. (2006). *Healthcare technology aspects of disaster management*. Paper presented at the 2nd Global E Health Conference, New Delhi. Retrieved June 7, 2008, http://openmed.nic.in/1774/01/telmedtsunami.pdf

Google.com (2007). Learn about AdWords. Retrieved June 3, 2008, from http://adwords.google.com/select/Login

Görsch, D. (2002). *The impact of hybrid channel structures on the customer purchase process: A research outline* (Working Paper). E-Business Research Center.

Gottlieb, M.M. (1996). Electronic transactions: Their impact on financial reporting. *International Advances in Economic Research, 2*, 146–150.

Gournaris, S., & Dimitriadis, S. (2003). Assessing service quality on the Web: Evidence from business-to-consumer portals. *Journal of Services Marketing, 17*(5), 529–548.

Gray, J. (1981). The transaction concept: Virtues and limitations. In *Proceedings of the 7th International Conference on Very Large Data Bases*, Cannes, France (pp. 144–154).

Greer, J., & Mensing, D. (2003). *The evolution of online newspapers: A longitudinal content analysis, 1997–2003*. Paper presented at the meeting of the Association for Education in Journalism and Mass Communication, Kansas City, MO.

Griffin, T. (1994). International marketing communications. Oxford: Butterworth Heinemann.

Groucutt, J. (2006). The life, death and resuscitation of brands. Handbook of Business Strategy, 7(1), 101–106.

Gullkvist, B., & Ylinen, M. (2006). E-accounting systems use in Finnish accounting agencies. In M. Seppä, M. Hannula, A.-M. Järvelin, J. Kujala, M. Ruohonen, & T. Tiainen (Ed.), *Frontiers of E-Business Research 2005*. Tampere.

Gurstein, M. (2000). Community informatics: Enabling communities with information and communications technologies. Hershey, PA: Idea Group Publishing.

Guth, R., & Mangalindan, M. (2006, April 21). Behemoths' dance: eBay talks to Microsoft, Yahoo about a common foe: Google. *The Wall Street Journal* (eastern), A1.

Hagedorn-Rasmussen, P. (2006). Making sense of "e-knowation": Exploring the relationship between emerging strategy, innovation and entrepreneurial nets of critical capabilities and resources (Working Paper No. 8). Lyngby: E-Service Project.

Hagel, J., III, & Armstrong, A.G. (1998). Net gain: Expanding markets through virtual communities. Boston: Harvard Business School Press.

Hansen, J.V., & Hill, N.C. (1989). Control and audit of electronic data interchange. *MIS Quarterly, 13*(4), 403–413.

Hansen, M.T., Nohria, N., et al. (1999, March–April). Whats your strategy for managing knowledge? *Harvard Business Review.*

Hardy, C., & Williams, S.P. (2005). Public eprocurement in action: Policies, practice and technologies. In M. Böhlen et al. (Eds.), *E-government: Towards electronic democracy, TCGOV 2005* (LNAI 3416, pp. 286–297). Berlin: Springer.

Hart, P., & Saunders, C. (1997). Power and trust: Critical factors in the adoption and use of electronic data interchange. *Organization Science, 8*(1), 23–42.

Hayat, A., Leitold, H., Rechberger, C., & Rössler, T. (2004, August 10). *Survey on EU's electronic-ID solutions* (Version 1.0). Vienna, Austria: Secure Information Technology Center (A-SIT). Retrieved June 1, 2008, from www.a-sit.at/pdfs/A-SIT_EID_SURVEY.pdf

Heilesen, S.B., & Jensen, S.S. (2006). Making sense of technologically enhanced learning in context: A research agenda. In E. Korsgaard Sorensen & D.Ó. Murchú (Eds.), *Enhancing learning through technology* (pp. 269–291). Information Science Publishing.

Heilesen, S.B., Jónsson, G., & Randrup, B. (2007). *IKT-kompetenceudvikling inden for undervisning og formidling på RUC.* Roskilde: Roskilde Universitetscenter. Retrieved June 5, 2008, from http://rudar.ruc.dk/handle/1800/2691

Henten, A. (1994). *Impacts of information and communication technologies on trade in services.* Lyngby: Technical University of Denmark.

Henten, A. (2005, October 25–26). *Internationalisation of knowledge services: The case of engineering consultancy services – Ramboll.* Presentation at the Nordic Conference on Innovation and Value Creation in the Service Economy, Oslo, Norway.

Hewer, P., & Howcroft, B. (1999). Consumers distribution channel adoption and usage in the financial services industry: A review of existing approaches. *Journal of Financial Services Marketing, 3*(4), 344–358.

Hill, T.P. (1977). On goods and services. *Review of Income and Wealth, 23*(4), 314–339.

Hindu, The (Chennai ed.). (2005, January 21). p. 5.

Hof, R. (2005). No head-scratching at eBay about Skype's potential. *Business Week Online.* Retrieved June 5, 2008, from http://www.businessweek.com

Hoffman, D.L., & Novak, T.P. (2000). How to acquire customers on the Web. Harvard Business Review, 78(3), 179–183.

Hoffman, K.D. (2003). Marketing+MIS=E-Service. *Communications of the ACM, 46*(6), 53–55.

Holak, S.L. (1988). Determinants of innovative durable adoption: An empirical study with implications for early product screening. *Journal of Product Innovation Management, 5*(1), 50–69.

Holzer, J. (2006, May 16). Supreme court buries patent trolls. *Forbes,* pp. 67–68.

Hou, J., & Rego, C. (2007, November). A classification of online bidders in a private value auction: Evidence from eBay. *International Journal of Electronic Marketing and Retailing Issue, 1*(4), 322–338.

Hsein, C., & Lin, B. (1998). Internet commerce for small business. Industrial Management & Data Systems, 3(1), 113–119.

http://www.princetondaytrading.com/newsletter-princeton/NL-9-31-2001.html

Hunton, J.E. (2002). Blending information and communication technology with accounting research. *Accounting Horizons, 16*(1), 55–67.

i2010 High Level Group (2006, December). *The challenges of convergence* (Discussion paper). Brussels, Belgium: European Commission. Retrieved June 1, 2008, from http://ec.europa.eu/information_society/eeurope/i2010/docs/i2010_high_level_group/i2010_hlg_convergence_paper_final.pdf

IFAC (2002). *E-business and the accountant.* Retrieved June 4, 2008, from http://www.ifac.org/

Illeris, S. (1996). *The service economy: A geographical approach.* Hoboken: John Wiley and Sons.

Indian Health Service (2006). *Indian Health Service facts on Indian health disparities.* Retrieved June 7, 2008, from http://info.ihs.gov/Files/DisparitiesFacts-Jan2006.pdf

Indian Health Service (2007). *Indian Health Service introduction.* Retrieved June 7, 2008, from http://www.ihs.gov/PublicInfo/PublicAffairs/Welcome_Info/IH-Sintro.asp

Indian Health Service. (2007). *Turtle Mountain Comprehensive Healthcare Center.* Retrieved June 7, 2008, from http://www.ihs.gov/FacilitiesServices/AreaOffices/Aberdeen/turtlemountain/

International Organization for Standardization (2005). *ISO/IEC 17799: Information technology: Security techniques: Code of practice for information security management.* Geneva, Switzerland: ISO.

International Telecommunication Union (2001). *ITU-T recommendation X.509 (2000)/ISO/IEC 9594-8: Information technology: Open Systems Interconnection: The Directory: Public-key and attribute certificate frameworks.* Geneva, Switzerland: ITU.

Island ECN surpasses American Stock Exchange to become largest marketplace in QQQs. (2001, October 22). *Business Wire.*

ISO (1994). *ISO 8402: Quality management and quality assurance* (Vocabulary, 2nd ed.). Geneva: Author.

Ives, B., & Mason, R.O. (1990). Can information technology revitalize your customer service? *Academy of Management Executive, 4*(4), 52–69.

Jansen, A., & Olnes, S. (2004, June). Quality assessment and benchmarking of Norwegian public Web sites. In *Proceedings of the 4th European Conference on E-government*, Dublin.

Jansen, B.J., Brown, A., & Resnick, M. (in press). Factors relating to the decision to click on a sponsored link. Decision Support Systems.

Järvinen, R., & Heino, H. (2004). *Kuluttajien palvelukokemuksia vakuutus: ja pankkisektorilta* (Publications 3/2004) [Consumer experience from insurance and banking sectors]. Helsinki, Finland: National Consumer Research Centre (English summary).

Järvinen, R., Eriksson, P., Saastamoinen, M., & Lystimäki, M. (2001). *Vakuutukset verkossa: Vakuutusyhtiöiden tarjonta ja kuluttajien odotukset* (Research paper report no. 7) [Insurance on the Web: The offerings of the insurance companies and the expectations of consumers]. Helsinki: National Consumer Research Centre.

Järvinen, R., Lehtinen, U., & Vuorinen, I. (2003). Options of strategic decision making in services: Tech, touch and customisation in financial services. *European Journal of Marketing, 37*(5/6), 774795.

Jayanti, R.K., & Burns, A.C. (1998). The antecedents of preventative health care behavior: An empirical study. *Journal of the Academy of Marketing Science, 26*(1), 6–15.

Jenkins, H. (2006). *Convergence culture: When old and new media collide.* New York: NYU.

Jensen, B.V., Jensen, I.R., Skovgaard, O., Heilesen, S., Mac, A., Fabricius, A., et al. (2003). *Studenterportalen på RUC* (unpublished report). Roskilde: Roskilde University.

Johnson, C. (2005a, November 2). Q3 2005 online sales: Weak, but not a trend for Q4. *Forrester Research, 1.*

Johnson, C. (2005b, September 14). US eCommerce: 2005 to 2010: a five-year forecast and analysis of US online retail sales. *Forrester Research, 1.*

Joshi, G.A. (in press). Role of ICT in disability rehabilitation in rural environment. In *IT and Indian rural healthcare.* Macmillan India.

Jun, M., & Cai, S. (2001). The key determinants of Internet banking service quality: A content analysis. *International Journal of Bank Marketing, 19*(7), 276–291.

Kamal, A. (2005). *The law of cyber-space.* Geneva, Switzerland: United Nations Institute of Training and Research (UNITAR).

Kandel, E., & Marx, L.M. (1999). Payments for order flow on Nasdaq. *Journal of Finance, 54*(1), 35–66.

Kang, M., & Atkin, D. (1999). Exploring the role of media uses and gratifications in multimedia cable adoption. *Telematics and Informatics, 16*, 59–74.

Kaplan, R.S., & Norton, D.P. (1992). *The balanced scorecard: Measures that drive performance.* Harvard Business Review.

Kaufman, C. (2002). *Network security: Private communication in a public world* (2nd ed.). Prentice Hall.

Kaye, B., & Johnson, T. (2004). A Web for all reasons: Uses and gratifications of Internet components for political information. *Telematics and Informatics, 21,* 197–223.

Kennedy, A., & Coughlan, J. (2006). Online shopping portals: An option for traditional retailers? International Journal of Retail & Distribution Management, 34(7), 516–528.

Kim, J., & Shunk, D.L. (2004). Matching indirect procurement process with different B2B e-procurement systems. *Computers in Industry, I(53)*, 153–164.

Kim, J.J. (2006, July 11). Online stock trades get even cheaper; Heightened competition among brokerage, banks drives fees as low as $1 per transaction. *Wall Street Journal,* p. D1.

Kim, J.J. (2006, July 19). Trading tools to get a boost. *Wall Street Journal,* p. D2.

Kim, Jung, J., Cohen, E., & Ball-Rokeach, S. (2004). Internet connectedness before and after September 11 2001. *New Media & Society, 6*(5), 611–631.

Kim, Y. (2005). The effects of buyer and product traits with seller reputation on price premiums in e-auction. *The Journal of Computer Information Systems, 46*(1), 79–92.

Kirby, D., Najak, B., & Greene, F. (1998). *Accounting for growth: Ways accountants can add value to small businesses.* London: ICAEW.

Kivistö-Rahnasto, J., Ahonen, A., & Salonen, J. (2006). *New service concepts for selecting and evaluating insurance cover within the electronic environment.* Paper presented at the 4th International Conference on Occupational Risk Prevention (ORP), Seville, Spain.

Kotler, P. (2003). Marketing management (11th ed.). New York: Prentice Hall.

Kotler, P., Armstrong, G., Saunders, J., & Wong, V. (2002). *Introduction to marketing* (2nd ed.). London: Pearsons Education, S.A.

Kotler, P., Hayes, T., & Bloom, P. (2002). *Marketing professional services: Forward thinking strategies for boosting your business, your image and your profits* (2nd ed.). Paramius, NJ: Prentice Hall Press.

Krampf, R., & Griffith, D. (2003). Print and online catalogs: The influence of communication mode on consumer information processing. *Journal of Marketing Channels, 10*(1), 25–39.

Labay, D.G., & Kinnear, T.C. (1981). Exploring the consumer decision process in the adoption of solar energy systems. *Journal of Consumer Research, 8*(3), 271–278.

Lacity, M., & Willcocks, L. (1998). An empirical investigation of information technology sourcing practices: Lessons from experience. *MIS Quarterly, 22*(3), 363–408.

Laffey, D. (2007). Paid search: The innovation that changed the Web. Business Horizons, 50(3), 211–218.

Lalopoulos, G.K., Chochliouros, I.P., & Spiliopoulou, A.S. (2004). Challenges and perspectives for Web-based applications in organizations. In M. Pagani (Ed.), *The encyclopedia of multimedia technology and networking* (pp. 82–88). Hershey, PA: IRM Press.

Larsson, R., & Bowen, D.E. (1989). Organization and customer: Managing design and coordination of services. *Academy of Management Review, 14*(2), 213–233.

Lashinsky, A., & Roth, D. (2005, October 3). The net's new odd couple. *Fortune, 152*(7), 26.

Lee, C., & Helal, S. (2003). Context attributes: An approach to enable context-awareness for service discovery. In *Proceedings of the 2003 Symposium on Applications and the Internet, SAINT* (p. 23). IEEE Computer Society.

Lee, J., & Allaway, A. (2002). Effects of personal control on adoption of self-service technology innovations. *Journal of Services Marketing, 16*(6), 553–572.

Len Rios, M., & Bentley, C. (2001). *Use of online news site: Development of habit and automatic procedural processing.* Paper presented at the AEJMC Conference.

Lin, C. (2002). Perceived gratifications of online media service use among potential users. *Telematics and Informatics, 19*, 3–19.

Lin, S., & Wu, C. S. (2002, January). Exploring the impact of online service quality on portal site usage. In *Proceedings of the 35th Annual Hawaii International Conference on System Sciences (HICSS'02)*, Maui, Hawaii (pp. 2654–2661).

Lith, P. (2004). Tili- ja tilintarkastustoimistojen liikevaihto kasvu-uralla. *Tilisanomat, 1*, 21–25.

Liu, Y., Ngu, A.H., & Zeng, L.Z. (2004, May). QoS computation and policing in dynamic Web service selection. In *Proceedings of the 13th International World Wide Web Conference on Alternate Track Papers and Posters*, New York (pp. 66–73).

Livingston, J. (2005). How valuable is a good reputation? A sample selection model of Internet auctions. *The Review of Economics and Statistics, 87*(3), 453–465.

Lloyd-Reason, L., & Mughan, T. (2002). Strategies for internationalization within SMEs: The key role of the owner manager. Journal of Small Business and Enterprise Development, 9(2), 120–129.

Lockett, A., & Littler, D. (1997). The adoption of direct banking services. *Journal of Marketing Management, 13*, 791–811.

Loflin, M.D., & Winogrond, I.R. (1976). A culture as a set of beliefs. Current Anthropology, 17(4), 723–725.

Loudon, D.L., & Della Bitta, A.J. (1993). *Consumer behaviour: Concepts and applications* (4th ed.). New York: McGraw-Hill.

Louis, S. (2006). *Project Healing Touch: Telemedicine healthcare for tsunami survivors in TamilNadu evaluation report.* (Private publication commissioned by OX-FAM Trust, excerpted with permission)

Lucking-Reiley, D., Bryan, D., Prasad, N., & Reeves, D. (2007, June). Pennies from eBay: The determinants of price in online auctions. *Journal of Industrial Economics, 55*(2), 223–233.

Macey, J., & O'Hara, M. (1997). The law and economics of best execution. *Journal of Financial Intermediation, 6*, 188–223.

MacInnes, I., Li, Y., & Yurcik, W. (2005). Reputation and dispute in eBay transactions. *International Journal of Electronic Commerce, 10*(1), 27–54.

MacManus, S.A. (2002). Understanding the incremental nature of e-procurement: Implementation at the state and local levels. *Journal Public Procurement, I*(2), 5–28.

Majaro, S. (1983). Marketing insurance services: The main challenges. In G. Foxall (Ed.), *Marketing in the service industries* (pp. 77–91). London.

Mäkinen, L. (2000). Tilitoimistoala murroksessa. *Tilisanomat, 5*, 45–50.

Malic-Bandu, K. (2006). Electronic media as a key of competitiveness of transition countries. Informatologia, 39(4), 280–285.

Malone, T.W., Yates, J., & Benjamin, R.I. (1987). Electronic markets and electronic hierarchies. *Communications of the ACM, 30*, 484–497.

Mangalindan, M. (2005, June 24). EBay aims two new services at merchants looking elsewhere. *Wall Street Journal* (Eastern Edition), B.3.

Marath, A., Shepherd, M., & Watters, C. (2002). *Adaptive user modelling for filtering electronic news.* Paper presented at 35th Annual Hawaii International Conference on Systems Sciences (vol. 4).

Marchionini, G., & Maurer, H. (1995). The roles of digital libraries in teaching and learning. *Communications of the ACM, 38*(4), 67–75.

Marketing Science Institute (2006). Featured academic of John D. C Little. Retrieved June 5, 2008, from www.msi.org/

Marriott, N., & Marriott, P. (2000). Professional accountants and the development of a management accounting service for the small firm: Barriers and possibility. *Management Accounting Research, 11*(4), 475–492.

Mathew, D. (2004). Information technology and public health management of disasters: A model for South Asian countries. *Prehospital and Disaster Medicine, 20*(1), 54–60.

Mattila, M., Karjaluoto, H., & Pento, T. (2003). Customer channel preferences in the Finnish banking sector. *Journal of Marketing Channels, 10*(1), 41–64.

Maximilien, E.M., & Singh, M.P. (2004). A framework and ontology for dynamic Web services selection. *IEEE Computer Society, 8*(5), 84–92.

McCauley, T., & Nesbitt, M. (2003). *The newspaper experience study.* Retrieved June 2, 2008, from http://www.readership.org/consumers/data/newspaper_exp.pdf#search=%22mccauley%20y%20nesbitt%202003%22

McDermott, C. (1999). Managing radical product development in large manufacturing firms: A longitudinal study. *Journal of Operations Management, 17,* 631–644.

McIntosh, E., & Cairns, J. A framework for the economic evaluation of telemedicine. *Journal of Telemedicine Telecare, 3,* 132–139.

McQuail, D. (1987). *Mass communication theory: An introduction* (2nd ed.). Londres: Sage.

Media Contacts (2007). *Online press consumption.* Retrieved June 2, 2008, from www.mediacontacts.com

Mediabriefing (2005). Retrieved June 2, 2008, from www.mediabriefing.com

Menascé, D.A. (2003). Automatic QoS control. *IEEE Computer Society, 7*(1), 92–95.

Menascé, D.A. (2004a). Composing Web services: A QoS view. *IEEE Computer Society, 4*(6), 88–90.

Menascé, D.A. (2004b). Response-time analysis of composite Web services. *IEEE Internet Computing, 8*(1), 90–92.

Meuter, M., Ostrom, A., Roundtree, R., & Bitner, M. (2000). Self-service technologies: Understanding customer satisfaction with technology-based service encounters. *Journal of Marketing, 64*(3), 50–64.

Meuter, M.L., Bitner, M.J., Ostrom, A.L., & Brown, S.W. (2005). Choosing among alternative service delivery modes: An investigation of customer trial of self-service technologies. *Journal of Marketing, 69*(2), 61–83.

Meuter, M.L., Ostrom, A.L., Bitner, M.J., & Roundtree, R.I. (2003). The influence of technology anxiety on consumer use and experience with self-service technologies. *Journal of Business Research, 56*(11), 899–906.

Meuter, M.L., Ostrom, A.L., Roundtree, R.I, & Bitner, M.J. (2000). Self-service technologies: Understanding customer satisfaction with technology-based service encounters. *Journal of Marketing, 64*(3), 5064.

Mikkelsen, K., & Petersen, M.F. (2006, October 9–12). *Ten thousand printers can't be wrong: One driver fits all.* Paper presented at the Educause Conference, Dallas, TX. Retrieved June 5, 2008, from www.educause.edu/ir/library/powerpoint/EDU06295A.pps

Miles, M., & Huberman, A.M. (1994). *Qualitative data analysis: An expanded sourcebook* (2nd ed.). Sage Publications.

Millward, L. (1995). Focus groups. In G.M. Breakwell, S. Hammond, & C. Fife-Scha (Eds.), *Research methods in psychology* (pp. 304–324). London: Sage Publications.

Min, H., Caltagirone, J., & Serpico, A. (in press). Life after a dot-com bubble. *International Journal of Information Technology and Management (IJITM), 7*(1).

Moregenson, G. (1999, November 23). Regulators see need for rules of the road for online trading firms. *New York Times,* p. C1.

Nahrstedt, K., Xu, D., Wichadakul, D., & Li, B. (2001). QoS-aware middleware for ubiquitous and heterogeneous environments. *Communications Magazine, IEEE, 39*(11), 140–148.

National Indian American Health Board (2007). *Reauthorization of the Indian Health Care Improvement Act.* Retrieved June 7, 2008, from http://www.nihb.org/docs/ihcia_fact_sheet_2007_feb.pdf

Newspaper Association of America (2003). Retrieved June 2, 2008, from www.naa.org

Nielsen, J. (2003). Usability 101. Retrieved June 2, 2008, from www.useit.com/alertbox/20030825.html

Nielsen/Net Ratings (2007). Retrieved June 2, 2008, from www.nielsen-netratings.com/

Nilsson, H., Van Eecke, P., Medina, M., Pinkas, D., & Pope, N. (1999, July 20). *Final report of the EESSI Expert Team.* European Electronic Signature Standardization Initiative (EESSI). Retrieved June 1, 2008, from http://www.ictsb.org/EESSI_home.htm

North Dakota Interactive Video Network (2007). Retrieved June 7, 2008, from http://www.ndivn.nodak.edu/web/User_groups/Higher_Ed/Degree.htm

North Dakota Interactive Video Network (2007). Retrieved June 7, 2008, from http://www.ndivn.nodak.edu/web/About_IVN/mission.asp

North Dakota STAGEnet (2006). *STAGEnet.* Retrieved June 7, 2008, from www.stagenet.nd.gov/

Northwest Area Foundation (2006). *Turtle Mountain Band of Chippewa.* Retrieved June 7, 2008, from http://www.nwaf.org/ProgramsNoHdrImage.aspx?pg=Programs/ventures_turtle_mountain.htm

O'Connor, G., & McDermott, C. (2004). The human side of radical innovation. *Journal of Engineering and Technology Management, 21,* 1130.

O'Connor, G., & O'Keefe, B. (1997). Viewing the Web as a marketplace: The case of small companies. *Decision Support Systems, 21*(3), 171–183.

O'Reilly, T. (2007). What is Web 2.0: Design patterns and business models for the next generation of software. *Communications & Strategies, 65,* 17–37.

Oliva, R., & Kallenberg, R. (2003). Managing the transition from products to services. International Journal of Service Industry Management, 14(2), 160–172.

Olivier, H. (2000). Challenges facing the accountancy profession. *The European Accounting Review, 9*(4), 603–624.

Organization for Economic Coordination and Development (2004). *Digital delivery of business services (JT00162724).* Paris, France: OECD.

Ostlund, L.E. (1974). Perceived innovation attributes as predictors of innovativeness. *Journal of Consumer Research, 1*(2), 23–29.

Panayiotou, N.A., Gayialis, S.P., & Tatsiopoulos, I.P. (2004). An e-procurement system for governmental purchasing. *International Journal of Production Economics, 1*(90), 79102.

Papadomichelaki, X., Magoutas, B., Halaris, C., Apostolou, D., & Mentzas, G. (2006). A review of quality dimensions in e-government services. In *Proceedings of the 5th International EGOV Conference 2006, DEXA,* Krakow, Poland (pp. 128–138).

Parasuraman, A. (2000). Technology readiness index (TRI): A multiple-item scale to measure readiness to embrace new technologies. *Journal of Service Research, 2*(4), 307–320.

Parasuraman, A., Berry, L.L., & Zeithaml, V.A. (1988). Servqual: A multiple-item scales for measuring consumer perceptions of service quality. *Journal of Retailing, 64*(1), 12–40.

Parasuraman, A., Zeithaml, V.A., & Berry, L. (1998). SERVQUAL: A multiple-item scale for measuring consumer perceptions of service quality. *Journal of Retailing, 64*(1), 12–40.

Parasuraman, A., Zeithaml, V.A., & Berry, L.L. (1985). A conceptual model of service quality and its implications for future research. *Journal of Marketing, 49*(4), 41–50.

Patoli, A.Q. (2006). Role of telemedicine in disaster management. *E Health International Journal, 2*(2), 34.

Pavlou, P.A., Liang, H., & Xue, Y. (2007). Understanding and mitigating uncertainty in online exchange relationships: A principal-agent perspective. *MIS Quarterly, 31*(1), 105–136.

Penttinen, E. (2007). Transition from products to services within the manufacturing business. Doctoral dissertation, Helsinki School of Economics, Finland. Retrieved June 5, 2008, from http://hsepubl.lib.hse.fi/FI/diss/?cmd=show&dissid=343

Penttinen, E., & Palmer, J. (2007). Improving firm positioning through enhanced offerings and buyer-seller relationships. Industrial Marketing Management, 36(5), 552–564.

Penttinen, E., & Saarinen, T. (2005). Opportunities and challenges for B2B industrial manufacturing firms: Case SKF. In T. Saarinen, M. Tinnila, & A. Tseng (Eds.), Managing business in a multi-channel world: Success factors for e-business (pp. 117–127). Idea Group Publishing.

Petersen, M.F. (2004). *Roskilde University CAS mods: ZESLA (zero effort sso for ldap apps).* Retrieved June 5, 2008, from http://tp.its.yale.edu/pipermail/cas/2004-May/000462.html

Peura-Kapanen, L., & Järvinen, R. (2006). *Kuluttajien käsityksiä riskeistä, niiden hallinnasta ja sähköisestä vakuuttamisesta* (Publications 7/2006) [Consumer perceptions of risk, risk management and electronic insurance]. Helsinki, Finland: National Consumer Research Centre (English summary).

Peura-Kapanen, L., Nenonen, S., Järvinen, R., & Kivistö-Rahnasto, J. (2007). *Kuluttajien arkipäivän riskit ja turvallisuus. Riskeihin liittyvät käsitykset, turvallisuuden edistäminen ja suhtautuminen sähköiseen asiointiin turvallisuuskontekstissa* [Consumers' everyday risks and safety: Risk-related views, promotion of safety and attitude towards electronic transactions in safety context]. (Publications 8/2007). Helsinki, Finland: National Consumer Research Centre.

Pew Research Center for the People and the Press (2000). Retrieved June 2, 2008, from www.people-press.org

Piccinelli, G., & Stammers, E. (2001). *From e-processes to e-networks: An e-service-oriented approach.* Retrieved June 1, 2008, from http://www.research.ibm.com/people/b/bth/OOWS2001/piccinelli.pdf

Polanyi, M. (1958). *The tacit dimension.* New York: Doubleday.

Polatoglu, V.N., & Ekin, S. (2001). An empirical investigation of the Turkish consumers' acceptance of Internet banking services. *International Journal of Bank Marketing, 19*(4), 156–165.

Poon, S., & Matthew, J. (2000). Product characteristics and Internet commerce benefit among small businesses. Journal of Product & Brand Management, 9(1), 21–34.

Porter, M.E. (1998). Competitive advantage of nations. New York: The Free Press.

Powazek, D.M. (2002). Design for community: The art of connecting real people in virtual places. Indianapolis: New Riders.

Preisler, H. (2006). *Succes med e-valg på RUC.* Retrieved June 5, 2008, from http://ruc.dk/ruc/omruc/nyheder/30112006b/

PriceWaterhouseCoopers (2001). European Economic Crime Survey 2001. *European Report.* Retrieved June 1, 2008, from http://www.pwcglobal.com

project. *Journal of the American Society for Information Science, 49*(2), 134–150.

Quinn, J. (1992). Intelligent enterprise: A knowledge and service based paradigm for industry. New York: Free Press.

Ran, S. (2003). A model for Web services discovery with QoS. *SIGecom Exchange, 4*(1), 1–10.

Randrup, B. (2006). *How to set up your own virtual printer.* Retrieved June 5, 2008, from http://www.mail.ruc.dk/pdf/winxp.htm

Rao Subba, S., Metts, G., & Mora Monge, C.A. (2003). Electronic commerce development in small and medium sized enterprises: A stage model and its implications. Business Process Management Journal, 9(1), 11–32.

Rathmann, T. (2002). Supplement or substitution? The relationship between reading a local print newspaper and the use of its online version. *Communications, 27,* 485–498.

Raymond, L. (1985). Organizational characteristics and MIS success in the context of small business. *MIS Quarterly, 9*(1), 37–52.

Retrieved June 5, 2008, from www.usatoday.com/money/markets/us/2006-02-28-nyse-archipelago-ap_x.htm

Reyndols, F. (2003). Managing exports: Navigating the complex rules, controls, barriers, and laws. New York: Wiley.

Richard, M., & Chandra, R. (2005). A model of consumer Web navigational behavior: Conceptual development and application. *Journal of Business Research, 58,* 1019–1029.

Richards, J. (2000). The Utah Digital Signature Act as a "model" legislation: A critical analysis. *The John Marshal Journal of Computer & Information Law, XVII*(3).

Rietjens, B. (2006). Trust and reputation on eBay: Towards a legal framework for feedback intermediaries. *Information & Communications Technology Law, 15*(1), 56.

Roberts, Pittman, & Reeds (2000). Retrieved June 5, 2008, from www.realcorporatelawyers.com

Rogers, E.M. (1962). *The diffusion of innovations.* New York: The Free Press.

Rogers, E.M. (1995). *The diffusion of innovations* (4th ed.). New York: The Free Press.

Rogers, E.M. (2003). *Diffusion of innovations* (5th ed.). Free Press.

Rossignoli, C. (2004). Nuove forme organizzative e il ruolo delle tecnologie di coordinamento a livello intra-organizzativo e inter-organizzativo. In A. D'Atri (Ed.), *Innovazione organizzativa e tecnologie innovative* (pp. 5768). Milan, Italy: Etas.

Rotchanakitumnuai, S., & Speece, M. (2003). Barriers to Internet banking adoption: A qualitative stud among corporate customers in Thailand. *International Journal of Bank Marketing, 21*(6/7), 312–323.

Rubeck, R. (2004, August). *Delivering government services to the beat of a different drum!* Keynote presentation at the 2004 Western CIO Forum, Santa Fe, NM.

Rust, R.T., & Kannan, P.K. (2002). *E-service: New direction in theory and practice.* Armonk, NY: M.E. Sharpe.

Rust, R.T., & Lemon, K.L. (2001). E-service and the consumer. *International Journal of Electronic Commerce, 5*(3), 85–101.

Ryan, J. (2005). *NASDAQ to Acquire Instinet.* Retrieved June 5, 2008, from www.nasdaq.com/newsroom/news/pr2005/ne_section05_044.stm

Salonen, J., & Ahonen, A. (2007). eInsurance project Web site. Retrieved June 5, 2008, from http://www.einsurance.fi

Sandy, G., & Burgess, S. (2003). A decision chart for small business Web site content. Logistic Information Management, 16(1), 36–47.

Santos, J. (2003). E-service quality: A model of virtual service quality dimensions. *Managing Service Quality, 13*(3), 233–246.

Sarkar, M.B., Butler, B., & Steinfield, C. (1995). Intermediaries and cybermediaries: A continuing role for mediating players in the electronic marketplace. *Journal of Computer Mediated Communication, 1*(3).

Savitz, E. (2005, June 6). Time to bid on: eBay. *Barron's, 85*(23), 25–27.

Savolainen, R., & Kari, J. (2004). Placing the Internet in information source horizons. A study of information seeking by Internet users in the context of self-development. *Library & Information Science Research, 26*(4), 415–433.

Schiesser, R. (2002). *IT systems management.* Prentice Hall. ISBN 0-13-087678-X.

Schneider, B., & Bowen, D.E. (1995). *Winning the service game.* Boston: Harvard Business School Press.

Scupola, A. (2002). The impact of electronic commerce on industry structure: The case of scientific, technical and medical publishing. *Journal of Information Science, 28*(3).

Seth, N., Deshmukh, S.G., & Vrat, P. (2005). Service quality models: A review. *International Journal of Quality & Reliability Management, 22*(9), 913–949.

Sharma, R. (2002, February 2). Gujarat earthquake causes major mental health problems. *BMJ, 324*(7332), 259.

Sherif, M.H. (2006). Standards for telecommunication services. In K. Jakobs (Ed.), *Information technology standards and standardization research.* Hershey, PA: Idea Group Publishing.

Shewhart, W. (1980). *Economic control of quality of manufactured product.* American Society for Quality.

Shoniregun, C.A., Chochliouros, I.P., Laperche, B., Logvynovskiy, O., & Spiliopoulou, A.S. (2004). *Questioning the boundary issues of Internet security.* London: e-Centre for Infonomics.

Shunk, D.L., Carter, J.R., Hovis, J., & Talwar, A. (2007). Electronics industry drivers of intermediation and disintermediation. International Journal of Physical Distribution & Logistics Management, 37(3), 248–261.

Sikkel, K., Gommer, L., & Veen, J.v.d. (2001). A cross-case comparison of BSCW in different educational settings. In P. Dillenbourg, A. Eurelings, & K. Hakkarainen (Eds.), *First European Conference on Computer-Supported Collaborative Learning* (pp. 553560). Maastricht. Retrieved June 5, 2008, from www.home.cs.utwente.nl/~sikkel/papers/ps/e-cscl-01.pdf

Silverman, D. (2004). *Qualitative research: Theory, method and practice* (2nd ed.). Sage Publications.

Sinclair, J.T. (2007). *EBay the smart way: Selling, buying, and profiting on the Web's #1 auction site.* New York: Amacom.

Sisk, J.E., & Sanders, J.H. (1998). A proposed framework for economic evaluation of telemedicine. *Telemed Journal, 4*, 31–37.

Social Security Administration (2000). *Management Advisory Report: Contact stations.* Retrieved June 7, 2008, from www.ssa.gov/oig/ADOBEPDF/Final%2099-01001.pdf

Social Security Administration (2006). *Social Security is important to American Indians and Alaska Natives.* Retrieved June 7, 2008, from http://www.ssa.gov/pressoffice/factsheets/amerindian.htm

Social Security Administration (2007). *Information about the Social Security Administration.* Retrieved June 7, 2008, from http://www.ssa.gov/aboutus/

Somasundaram, R. (2004). Diffusion of eprocurement in the public sector: Revisiting centralization versus decentralization debates as a twist in the tale. In T. Leino et al. (Eds.), *Proceedings of the 12th European Conference on Information Systems* (pp. 1546–1556). Turku, Finland: School of Economics and Business Administration.

Somasundaram, R., & Damsgaard, J. (2005). Policy recommendations for electronic public procurement. *The Electronic Journal of e-Government, 3*, 147–156.

Srinivasan, S., Anderson, R., & Ponnavolu (2002). Customer loyalty in e-commerce: An exploration of its antecedents and consequences. *Journal of Retailing, 78*, 41–50.

Stafford, T.F. (2003). E-services. *Communications of the ACM, 46*(6), 26–28.

Star, S.L., & Griesemer, J.R. (1989). Institutional ecology, translations and boundary objects: Amateurs and professionals in Berkeleys Museum of Vertebrate Zoology, 1907-39. *Social Studies of Science, 19*, 387–420.

Stephenson, W. (1967). *The play theory of mass communication.* Chicago: The University of Chicago Press.

Stoll, H.R. (2006). Electronic trading in stock markets. *Journal of Economic Perspectives, 20*(1), 153–174.

Strauss, A., & Corbin, J. (1998). *Basics of qualitative research: Techniques and procedures for developing grounded theory* (2nd ed.). Sage Publications.

Sukasame, N. (2004). The development of e-service in Thai government. *BU Academic Review, 3*(1), 17–24.

Sundbo, J. (1997). Management of innovation in services. *The Service Industries Journal, 17*(3), 432–455.

Sutton, S.G. (2000). The changing face of accounting in an information technology dominated world. *International Journal of Accounting Information Systems, 1*, 1–8.

Szymanski, D., & Hise, R. (2000). E-satisfaction: An initial examination. *Journal of Retailing, 73*(3), 309–322.

Tabb, L. (2004). Perspective: Time for brokers, investors, and regulators to align. *Wall Street and Technology.* InformationWeek Media Network.

Teece, D.J. (1980). Economies of scope and the scope of the enterprise. *Journal of Economic Behavior & Organization, 1*(3), 223-247.

Templeman, J.G., & Wootton, C. (1987). *Small business: Management information needs.* London: Charter Institute of Management Accountants.

Thelwall, M. (2000). Effective Websites for small and medium-sized enterprises. Journal of Small Business and Enterprise Development, 7(2), 149–159.

Thompson, J.D. (1967). *Organizations in action.* New York: McGraw-Hill.

Tiwana, A., & Balasubramaniam, R. (2001, March). *E-services, problems, opportunities, and digital platforms.* Paper presented at the 34th Hawaii International Conference on System Sciences.

Tiwana, A., & Ramesh, B. (2001, January 3–6). e-services: Problems, opportunities, and digital platforms. In *Proceedings of the 34th Annual Hawaii International Conference on System Sciences (HICSS-34)*, Maui, Hawaii (pp. 3018). IEEE Computer Society.

Toffler, A. (1980). *The third wave.* Bentham Books.

Toivonen, M. (2004). *Expertise as business: Long-term development and future prospects of knowledge-intensive business services.* Doctoral dissertation, Helsinki University of Technology, Laboratory of Industrial Management (Series 2004/2, Espoo).

Toivonen, M. (2005). *Taloushallinnon palvelut.* Toimialaraportti ennakoi liiketoiminta-ympäristön muutoksia. KTM:n ja TE-keskuksen julkaisu.

Treasury Board of Canada Secretariat (1999). *Digital signature and confidentiality: Certificate policies for the Government of Canada public key infrastructure* (Government of Canada (GOC), PKI Certificate Policies version 3.02).

Trott, P. (2005). *Innovation management and new product development* (3rd ed.). Essex, England: Pearson Education Limited.

Tsetsekas, C., Manitias, S., Funfstuck, F., Thoma, A., & Karadimas, Y. (2001). A QoS middleware between users, applications and the network. In *Proceedings of the 8th International Conference on Advances in Communications and Control*, Crete, Greece.

Tv.com (2007). The Ultimate Fighter. Retrieved June 3, 2008, from http://www.tv.com/the-ultimate-fighter/show/31862/summary.html

Tyacke, N., & Higgins, R. (2004). Searching for trouble: Keyword advertising and trade mark infringement. Computer Law & Security Report, 20(6), 453–465.

U21 and the World Health Organization. *E-health is a global revolution for the poor populations of the world.* Retrieved June 7, 2008, from http://www.innovations-report.com/html/reports/medicine_health/report-50033.html

Ultimate Fighting Championship (2007). Fighters. Retrieved June 3, 2008, from http://www.ufc.com

Underrepresented Nations and Peoples Organization (2004). *Lakota: The forgotten people of Pine Ridge.* Retrieved June 7, 2008, from http://www.unpo.org/article.php?id=518

United Nations Economic and Social Commission for Asia and the Pacific (ESCAP) (2000). *Asia and the Pacific in figures 2000.* UN Statistics Division.

University of North Dakota (2007). *About the University.* Retrieved June 7, 2008, from http://www.und.edu/aboutund/

Upin, E.B., Beckwith, M.J., Jennings, C.L., Chen, B.Y., & Schaeffer, K.B. (2000). *B2B: Building technology bridges outside the four walls of the enterprise.* FleetBoston Robertson Stephens Inc.

Urriolagoitia, L., & Planellas, M. (2007). Sponsorship relationships as strategic alliances: A life cycle model approach. Business Horizons, 50(2), 157–166.

Vahtera, P., & Salmi, H. (1998). *Paperiton Kirjanpito.* Jyväskylä.

Valentin, F., & Hansen, P.V. (2004). *Udvikling af videnservice* [Development of knowledge service]. Copenhagen: Nyt Teknisk Forlag.

Van Eecke, P., Pinto, P., & Egyedi, T. (2007, July). *EU study on the specific policy needs for ICT standardisation* (Final Report, Ref. ENTR/05/059). Brussels, Belgium: DG Enterprise, European Commission. Retrieved June 1, 2008, from http://www.ictstandardisation.eu/

Vargo, S., & Lusch, R. (2004). Evolving to a new dominant logic for marketing. Journal of Marketing, 68(1), 1–17.

Vasarhelyi, M., & Greenstein, M. (2003). Underlying principles of the electronization of business: A research agenda. *International Journal of Accounting Information Systems, 4*, 1–25.

Venkataraman, K. (2001). Automated verses floor trading: An analysis of execution costs on the Paris and New York Exchanges. *Journal of Finance, 56*(4), 1445–1485. New Orleans, LA: Papers and Proceedings of the 61st Annual Meeting of the American Finance Association.

Videnskabsministeriet (2007). *National strategi for IKT-støttet læring. Indsats for at fremme anvendelsen af IKT-støttet læring.* København: Videnskabsministeriet. Retrieved June 5, 2008, from http://itst.dk/static/National_strategi_for_IKT-stoettet_laering/index.htm

Vroomen, B., Donkers, B., Verhoef, P.C., & Franses, P.H. (2005). Selecting profitable customers for complex services on the Internet. *Journal of Service Research, 8*(1), 37–47.

Waite, K., & Harrison, T. (2007). Internet acheaeology: Uncovering pension sector Web site evolution. Internet Research, 17(2), 180–195.

Wallman, S.M.H. (1997). Commentary: The future of accounting and financial reporting (Part IV: "Access" accounting). *Accounting Horizons, 11*(2), 103116.

Warfield, C. *The disaster management cycle.* Retrieved June 7, 2008, from http://www.gdrc.org/uem/disasters/1-dm_cycle.html

Watters, C., Shepherd, M., & Burkowski, F. (1998, February). Electronic news delivery

Webb, H.W., & Webb, L.A. (2004). SiteQual: An integrated measure of Web site quality. *Journal of Enterprise Information Management, 17*(6), 430–440.

Weber, R. (2002). *Regulatory models for the online world.* Zurich, Switzerland: Schulthess Juristische Medien.

Wen, H.J., Chen, H., & Hwang, H. (2001). E-commerce Web site design: Strategies and models. Information Management & Computer Security, 9(1), 5–12.

WHO World Health Report. (2000). *Health systems: Improving performance.* WHO.

Wikipedia. (2007). Change Management. Retrieved June 7, 2008, from http://en.wikipedia.org/wiki/Change_Management_(ITIL)

Wille, N.E., Kluth, M., Christensen, T., Jørgensen, A., Frederiksen, L.B., Konradsen, L., et al. (2002). *Afrapportering fra IT-taskforce* (internal memorandum, unpublished). Roskilde: Roskilde Universitetscenter.

Windischhofer, R., & Ahonen, A. (2004). The effect of physical distribution channels on online distribution channels in the insurance industry: An examination of electronic insurance services on the Internet. In J. Chen (Ed.), *Service systems and service management: Proceedings of ICSSSM'04, Vol. II* (pp. 753758). Beijing: International Academic Publishers/Beijing World Publishing Corporation.

Wise, R., & Baumgartner, P. (1999). Go downstream: The new profit imperative in manufacturing. Harvard Business Review, 77(5), 133–141.

World Association of Newspapers (2004). *Shaping the future of the newspaper: Analysing strategic developments and opportunities in the press industry* (Strategy report 4.1: Profiting from digital, pp. 19–23).

World Newspapers Online (2007). Retrieved June 2, 2008, from www.worldnewspapersonline.com

Yang, Z., & Jun, M. (2002). Consumer perception of e-service quality: From Internet purchaser and non-purchaser perspectives. *Journal of Business Strategies, 19*(1), 19–41.

Yang, Z., Cai, S., Zhou, Z., & Zhou, N. (2005). Development and validation of an instrument to measure user perceived service quality of information presenting Web portals. *Information Management, 42*(4), 575–589.

Yap, A., & Lin, X. (2001). Entering the arena of Wall Street wizards, euro-brokers, and cyber-trading samurais: A strategic imperative for online stock trading. *Electronics Market Journal, 11*(3).

Yin, R.K. (2003). Case study research design and methods. London: Sage Publications.

Yrjölä, E. (2003). Kilpa kovenee, kirjanpitäjä. *Talouselämä, 1,* 4446.

Zeithaml, V., Parasuraman, A., & Berry, L. (1985). Problems and strategies in services marketing. Journal of Marketing, 49(2), 33–46.

Zeithaml, V.A., Bitner, M.J., & Gremler, D.D. (2002a). *Services marketing* (3rd ed.). New York: McGraw-Hill.

Zeithaml, V.A., Parasuraman, A., & Malhotra, A. (2001). *A conceptual framework for understanding e-service quality: Implications for future research and managerial practice* (MSI Working Paper Series No. 00-115, pp. 1-49). Cambridge, MA: MSI.

Zeithaml, V.A., Parasuraman, A., & Malhotra, A. (2002b). Service quality delivery through Web sites: A critical review of extant knowledge. *Journal of the Academy of Marketing Science, 30*(4), 362–375.

Zeng, L., Benatallah, B., Dumas, M., Kalagnanam, J., & Sheng, Q.Z. (2003, May). Quality driven Web services composition. In *Proceedings of the 12th International Conference on World Wide Web,* Budapest, Hungary (pp. 411–421). ACM Press.

Zuboff, S. (1989). *In the age of the smart machine.* Oxford: The Perseus Books Group.

Zulfiqar, K.A., Pan, S.L., Lee, J., & Huang, J.C. (2001). E-government: An exploratory study of on-line electronic procurement systems. In S. Smithson et al. (Eds.), *Proceedings of the 9th European Conference on Information Systems* (pp. 1010–1024). Bled, Slovenia: Moderna organizacjia.

About the Contributors

Ada Scupola is an associate professor at the Department of Communication, Business and Information Technologies, Roskilde University, Denmark. She holds a PhD in social sciences from Roskilde University, an MBA from the University of Maryland at College Park, USA and an MSc from the University of Bari, Italy. She is the editor-in-chief of *The International Journal of E-Services and Mobile Applications*. Her main research interests are e-services, adoption and diffusion of e-commerce and e-services in SMEs, ICTs in clusters of companies, and the impact of e-commerce on industrial and organizational structures. She is collaborating and has collaborated with several national and international research projects on the above subjects. Her research has been published in several international journals, including the *Journal of Electronic Commerce in Organizations, The Journal of Information Science, The Journal of Global Information Technology Management, Scandinavian Journal of Information Systems, The Journal of Electronic Commerce in Developing Countries*, and in numerous book chapters and international conferences.

* * *

Aki Ahonen was born in 1976. He earned his master's degree in insurance science from the University of Tampere in 2002 and his doctoral degree in 2007 in management and organization from the University of Tampere. Between 2002 and 2007, he worked as a project manager by being responsible for two e-insurance research and development projects and as a researcher at the University of Tampere. Currently, he is working as development manager at OP Bank Group Central Cooperative. His main areas of expertise and research concern service management and marketing, and electronic services, especially within financial sector.

Elpida P. Chochliouros is a medical doctor (MD), graduated from the Aristotle University of Thessaloniki, Greece. During her studies, she has been involved in various medical research activities, and she has participated in several international conferences. At the present time, she works at the Paediatric Clinic of the George Gennimatas Hospital in Thessaloniki. She has also completed a postgraduate study in nuclear medicine, working in cooperation with the Aristotle University of Thessaloniki.

Ioannis P. Chochliouros is a telecommunications electrical engineer, graduated from the Polytechnic School of the Aristotle University of Thessaloniki, Greece, holding also an MSc and a PhD from the

University Pierre et Marie Curie, Paris VI, France. He worked as a research and teaching assistant at the University Paris VI, in cooperation with other European countries. His practical experience as an engineer has been mainly in telecommunications, as well as in various construction projects in Greece and the wider Balkan area. Since 1997, he has been working at the Competition Department and then as an engineer-consultant of the chief technical officer of OTE (Hellenic Telecoms S.A.) for regulatory and technical matters. He has been very strongly involved in major OTE's national and international business activities, as a specialist consultant for technical and regulatory affairs especially for the evaluation and adoption of innovative e-infrastructures and e-services. He currently works as the head of the Research Programs section of the Labs and New Technologies Division. Under his supervision, the section has received several awards from the European Commission for the successful realization of European research activities. He also works as a lecturer in the Faculty of Science and Technology in the Department of Telecommunications and Informatics Sciences in the University of Peloponnese, Greece. He has been involved in different European and international projects and activities. He is author (and/or co-author) of more than 100 distinct scientific and business works (i.e., books, book chapters, papers, articles, studies, and reports) in the international literature. He has participated in many conferences, workshops, fora, and other events, in most as an invited speaker and official OTE representative. He is also an active participant of various international and national associations, both of scientific and business nature.

Flavio Corradini is full professor of computer science at the University of Camerino. He received a master's degree in computer science from the University of Pisa and a PhD in computer engineering from the University of Rome La Sapienza. His research interests are centered around design methods, formal and semiformal specification and verification of complex systems, e-government, and information society. He is the coordinator of UEG (Unicam E-Government Research Group) and COSY (Complex Systems' Research Group). He collaborates with several companies and public administrations for the development of innovation technology, technology transfer, and scientific research.

Tilemachos D. Doukoglou holds a diploma of electrical engineering from the Aristotle University of Thessaloniki, Greece (1986), a MEng from McGill University of Montreal-Canada (1989), and a PhD in electrical and biomedical engineering from the same university (1994). He was also a visiting research engineer and postdoctoral fellow at the Massachusetts Institute of Technology, Cambridge, MA, USA (1994–1995). He is currently the head of the Labs and New Technologies Division of the Hellenic Telecommunications Organization (OTE S.A.). His interests are in the area of IP over DWDM technologies, broadband services over xDSL technologies (VoD, video-streaming, GoD, etc.), and development of platforms for modern services like telemedicine and tele-education. He has been the OTE's ADSL rollout project manager in 2004 and 2005. Since 1995, he has been involved in various European R&D programs as technical responsible and project manager. He has more than 40 publications in international magazines, conferences, and workshops.

Morten Falch is an associate professor at the Center for Information and Communication Technologies at the Technical University of Denmark. He holds a PhD from DTU, a master's degree in economics, and a bachelor's degree in math. His research interests include a wide range of issues related to information and communication technologies such as cost analysis of telecom networks, e-government, regulation of the telecom sector, ICT industry policy, the role of competition in innovation of new services, use of

ICT in knowledge services, and tele-based community centers. He has participated in many EU funded research projects and conducted a large number of consultancies for national and international organizations such as ITU, UNCTAD, the World Bank, and the National Telecom Agencies in Denmark, Norway, and Sweden.

Tommaso Federici (1960, Italy) teaches information systems organization in the Faculty of Economics at the University of Tuscia in Viterbo, Italy, and at the MBA of the LUISS-University Guido Carli in Rome. As author or co-author, he has published papers, articles, and books (a list of them is available at www.tommasofederici.it). His current research domains are e-procurement as a booster to promote change in the public sector and the ERP introduction in the SMEs segment.

Carlos Flavián holds a PhD in business administration and is professor of marketing in the Faculty of Economics and Business Studies at the University of Zaragoza (Spain). His research has been published in several academic journals, specialized in marketing (*European Journal of Marketing, Journal of Consumer Marketing, Journal of Strategic Marketing, International Journal of Market Research,* etc.) and new technologies (*Information & Management, Industrial Management and Data Systems, Internet Research,* etc.). He is a member of the editorial boards of *Industrial Marketing Management,* the *Journal of Retailing and Consumer Services,* the *International Journal of Services and Standards,* and the *Journal of Marketing Communications.*

Shashi Bhushan Gogia is a practicing surgeon who obtained his medical degrees from AIIMS (www.aiims.ac.in), arguably India's best medical training institution. He ventured into medical informatics as a hobby but later started making his own software for healthcare needs. He is running his own company, AMLA MEDIQUIP (www.amlamed.com), where this software, called Medic Aid, is downloadable. He is currently president of the Indian Association of Medical Informatics (IAMI, www.iami.org.in) and also president of SATHI (www.sathi.org). He is advisor to the Ministry of Health in India and helps it in many activities for promoting telemedicine.

Benita M. Gullkvist is a senior lecturer in accounting at Hanken, the Swedish School of Economics and Business Administration, in Vaasa, Finland. She obtained her PhD from Åbo Akademi University in 2005. Prior to joining Hanken in 2006, Gullkvist taught accounting at the undergraduate and graduate levels at the University of Applied Sciences Vaasa and spent a few years as a CFO at an international manufacturing group, handling areas including information system implementation projects. Her main research interests lie in the field of accounting and information systems with particular interest in digital technology adoption and use as well as financial, behavioral, and managerial implications of usage. She has served as an ad-hoc reviewer of several international journals and presented her research at national seminars as well as international conferences to corporate executives and academic audiences.

Călin Gurău has been associate professor of marketing at Montpellier Business School, France, since September 2004. He is a junior fellow of the World Academy of Art and Science, Minneapolis, MN, USA. He worked as marketing manager in two Romanian companies, and he has received degrees and distinctions for studies and research from the University of Triest, Italy; University of Vienna, Austria; Duke University, USA; University of Angers, France; and Oxford University and Southampton Business School and Heriot-Watt University, United Kingdom. His present research interests are focused on marketing strategies for high-technology firms and Internet marketing. He has published more than 25 papers in internationally refereed journals, such as *International Marketing Review, Journal of Consumer Marketing, Journal of Marketing Communications,* and so forth.

Raquel Gurrea holds a PhD in business administration and is assistant professor in the Faculty of Economics and Business Studies at the University of Zaragoza (Spain). Her main research lines are online consumer behavior, multichannel distribution, and the analysis of the advantages and limitations of the Internet in the development of the economic activity. Her work has been published in several journals such as *International Journal of Market Research, Information & Management, Journal of Retailing and Consumer Services, Internet Research* or *Journal of Targeting,* and *Measurement and Analysis for Marketing.*

Simon Heilesen is an associate professor of communication studies at Roskilde University, Denmark. His principle research interests are learning and collaboration in net environments, and, more broadly, designing, planning, and evaluating various forms of net based communication. Since the mid-1980s, he has been engaged in planning and implementing ICT for academic purposes, first at Copenhagen University, and since 1999 at Roskilde University. He is chairman of the Roskilde University E-learning Committee, and is also a member of various national committees for the development and dissemination of information and communication technology in higher education. His Web site at Roskilde University is http://www.ruc.dk/~simonhei.

Anders Henten is associate professor at Aalborg University in Denmark. He is a graduate in communications and international development studies from Roskilde University and holds a PhD from the Technical University of Denmark. His main areas of research are information and knowledge society developments, information and communication technology innovation, service innovation and internationalization, regulation of communications, socio-economic implications of information and communication technologies, and e-commerce and business models. Anders Henten has worked professionally in the areas of communications economy and policy for 20 years and has published nationally and internationally more than 200 academic publications in international journals, books, conference proceedings, and so on.

Jeffrey Hsu is an associate professor of information systems at the Silberman College of Business, Fairleigh Dickinson University. He is the author of numerous papers, chapters, and books, and has previous business and IT experience in the software, telecommunications, and financial industries. His research interests include human–computer interaction, e-commerce, IS education, and business intelligence. Dr. Hsu received his PhD in information systems from Rutgers University.

Raija Järvinen was born in 1956. She graduated from Helsinki School of Economics and Business Administration in 1986. Her licentiate degree (1996) and doctoral degree (1998) are from the University of Tampere. Since 2005, she has been appointed as head of research at National Consumer Research Centre in Finland and, between 2001 and 2005, as professor of insurance at the University of Tampere. Previously, she has been working altogether 12 years in the financial sector in specialist and manager positions. Her main areas of research are financial services, risk management, and retailing. Currently, she is in charge of two research projects, one concerning consumer investment activities and the other concerning safety and security in retailing.

Jouni Kivistö-Rahnasto was born in 1967. He graduated in mechanical engineering and design from Tampere University of Technology in 1993, and in 2000, he got the doctoral degree in safety engineering. Since 2003, he has been professor at Tampere University of Technology in the Center for Safety Management and Engineering. Previously, he has worked at the VTT Technical Research Centre of Finland. Jouni Kivistö-Rahnasto's major areas of research and teaching are risk management and safety engineering. His current projects focus on, for example, safety and risk management of industrial services and safety related information systems. As a consultant, he has also helped companies in safety design and global exporting projects.

Glenn Miller became the University of North Dakota's director for the Government Rural Outreach (GRO) initiative on June 1, 2002. In December 2005, Glenn was named codirector of the Center for Rural Service Delivery. Prior to joining the University of North Dakota, Glenn was an independent sales and marketing consultant. He spent 33 years at Control Data. There he held a variety of positions in sales, marketing, and program management. Glenn Miller and Robert Rubeck, PhD, codirectors of the Center for Rural Service Delivery, received the Fifth Annual 2006 Healthcare IT Innovators Award for their work helping impoverished healthcare consumers. The RSD/Social Security Administration Video Claims Taking (VCT) program has been named one of the top 50 government innovations for 2006 by The Ash Institute for Democratic Governance and Innovation at Harvard University's John F. Kennedy School of Government—in cooperation with the Council for Excellence in Government.

Hanne Westh Nicolajsen is an assistant professor in the Center for Information and Communication Technologies at the Technical University of Denmark. Her research interests include organizational implementation and use of IT, knowledge management, and computer-mediated communication. Her current research focuses on the use of information and communication technology for innovation in the service sector. Nicolajsen holds a PhD from the Technical University of Denmark.

Miran Pejic-Bach was born in Zagreb, Croatia in 1969. He graduated from the Faculty of Economics and Business–Zagreb with a major in trade, and also from the Faculty of Textile Technology–Zagreb. He worked in the market research agency Puls as field work manager. In 2003, he set up his own company specialized in international trade. He is especially interested in using Internet technologies as a competitive advantage for his firm.

Mirjana Pejic-Bach was born in Zagreb, Croatia in 1971. She graduated from the Faculty of Economics and Business–Zagreb, where she also received her PhD in business, submitting a thesis on "System Dynamics Applications in Business Modelling" in 2003. She works at the Department of Informatics at the Faculty of Economics and Business as assistant professor. She is the recipient of the 2004 Mijo Mirkovic award for the paper "Surviving in an Environment of Financial Indiscipline: A Case Study from a Transition Country," published in *System Dynamics Review*. Her research interests are decision support systems, electronic commerce, and data mining.

Esko Penttinen is a researcher in information systems science at the Helsinki School of Economics. He holds a PhD in information systems science and a MSc in economics from the Helsinki School of Economics, as well as the diploma of the Dijon Business School, France. Esko has published in *Industrial Marketing Management*, as well as in several conference proceedings and book chapters. His research interests include bundling of products and services and the transition from the product focus to the service focus, especially in the traditional manufacturing industry. Currently, he is conducting research on the fundamental organizational changes in business relations and product offerings initiated by new technologies.

Alberto Polzonetti is a professor of computer network and service oriented computing at the University of Camerino. Since 2004, he has been a member of the UEG (Unicam E-Government Research Group, and he is active in several projects for realization of service infrastructure and broadband initiatives for e-government development. He is also involved in many didactics activities for the courses Computer Networking and Foundation of Computer Science. His research activity is focused on the study and on the introduction of technological advanced, innovative, and interoperable solutions able to encourage the information and communication technology inside the information society.

Barbara Re is a PhD student in computer science and complex systems at Camerino University, Italy, where she received cum laude the bachelor's and master's degree in computer science. She is member of UEG (Unicam E-Government Research Group, coordinated by Professor Flavio Corradini at the Department of Mathematics and Computer Science. Her research interests include models and languages for e-government interoperability, quality in e-government service and methodologies, and technologies for e-government development. Her scientific activity is documented from communications in national and international conferences. She was organizing chair of the first international conference MeTTeG07 (*Methodology Technology and Tool Enabling E-Government*).

Robert Rubeck has been with the School of Medicine and Health Sciences at the University of North Dakota for 9 years. He joined the school as the associate dean for academic affairs, responsible for academic programs, information systems, and technology. He is also an associate professor with responsibility for telemedicine and the Health Information Technology initiative. In 2001, he was appointed as the school's first chief information officer. Dr. Rubeck was responsible for the advent of government services being delivered by video and jointly responsible for the development of the UND Rural Service Delivery Center, a university system center for the enhancement of government and healthcare service delivery. Dr. Rubeck's background in innovation and technology management is extensive. He has been a consultant to IBM, ICI-Pharmacia, Canada Manpower, University of Kentucky, and others. His work has been recognized by IBM, U.S. Social Security Administration, Harvard University, Battelle Columbus Laboratories, Oracle, Zenith, and Kodak.

Timo Saarinen is a professor of information systems and electronic commerce at the Department of Business Technology and a vice-rector for research at the Helsinki School of Economics. He holds a PhD in information systems from the Helsinki School of Economics. Timo has published in major journals such as *MIS Quarterly, Journal of Management Information Systems, Information & Management,* and *Journal of Strategic Information Systems*. His research interests include economics of information systems and the development of efficient market-driven services, with the focus on the multichannel environment of electronic commerce.

Jarno Salonen was born in 1975. He holds a bachelor's degree in mechanical engineering from Tampere Polytechnic University and is currently working on a master's degree at the Tampere University of Technology. He has worked as research engineer and project manager at VTT Technical Research Centre of Finland since 2002. His main areas of expertise are security and privacy, development of electronic services, and radio frequency identification (RFID). Salonen has been involved in many national and international projects related to electronic services, and currently, he is actively participating in the standardization work of RFID-based near field communication (NFC).

Pekka Sinervo is the country general manager for Lexmark Finland. He holds an eMBA in international business from the Helsinki School of Economics, the Business College Examination from the Helsinki Business College, and the Diploma in Marketing from the Finnish Institute of Marketing. He is currently responsible for the business operations of Lexmark Finland. Pekka is a sales professional with over 20 years of sales and marketing experience in Finland. During his career, he has been in different sales-related managerial positions, for example, over 12 years as a sales director at Xerox, where he was responsible for sales operations for several industries such as graphical arts, trade, bank and insurance, and the public sector.

Anastasia S. Spiliopoulou is a lawyer also holding a postgraduate diploma of the Athens University Law School. She is a member of the Athens Bar Association. She has an extended experience as a lawyer, while she has been involved in various research and business affairs. Her postgraduate diploma has been performed with specific emphasis given to the investigation of multiple regulatory aspects related to the Internet (infrastructure, services, software, and content). During the latest years, she had a major participation in matters related to telecommunications and broadcasting policy in Greece and abroad within the framework of the information society. She has been involved in current research and business activities, as a specialist for e-commerce, electronic signatures, e-contracts, e-security, and other information society applications. She is author or co-author of more than 75 recognized works in the international literature. She currently works as OTE's (Hellenic Telecommunications Organization S.A.) lawyer, for the Department of Regulatory Issues of the General Directorate for Regulatory Affairs.

Wonhi Synn is a professor of finance at the Martha and Spencer Love School of Business, Elon University, Elon, NC, where he primarily teaches corporate finance and investments. His areas of academic interest include enterprise valuation, performance evaluation, market innovations, and business education. He has recently published articles on government sponsored enterprises (GSEs), online stock trading, bankruptcy prediction, and various business curriculum and pedagogical issues. He received a bachelor's degree from Seoul National University, an MBA from University of New Orleans, and a PhD from the University at Buffalo, The State University of New York.

Zhongxian Wang is a professor in the Department of Management and Information Systems at Montclair State University, New Jersey, USA. Professor Wang teaches operations analysis, production/ operations management, decision support and expert systems, business statistics, operations research, and management sciences. He is a member of the Institute for Operations Research and the Management Sciences (INFORMS), Information Resources Management Association (IRMA), The Decision Sciences Institute (DSI), and The Production and Operations Management Society (POMS).

Ruiliang Yan is an assistant professor of marketing at the School of Business, Virginia State University. He received his PhD in marketing from the University of Wisconsin, Milwaukee; MS from Sichuan University, China; and bachelor's degree from Southwest Agricultural University, China. He specializes in e-marketing, retailing, and supply chain management.

James E. Yao is a professor in the Department of Management and Information Systems, School of Business, Montclair State University, New Jersey, USA. Professor Yao teaches management information systems, database, programming, and other MIS courses. His research interests are in the areas of IT innovation adoption, diffusion, and infusion in organizations, e-business, e-commerce, and m-commerce. Professor Yao's research papers have been published in journals on information technology and information systems.

Alexander Y. Yap is an associate professor at Elon University, North Carolina. He holds a PhD in information systems from Copenhagen Business School (Denmark), an MBA in international management from Exeter University (UK), and a master's degree in development economics from Williams College (USA). He won the prestigious ICIS Best Paper Award in Helsinki, Finland. He currently teaches e-business and Web development. His research papers have been published in the *Journal of Global Information Management*, *Journal of E-Commerce Research*, *Journal of Electronics Market*, and the *Journal of Enterprise Information Systems*, among others. He has also published in prestigious IS conferences, which include the ICIS, ECIS, and ACM.

Index